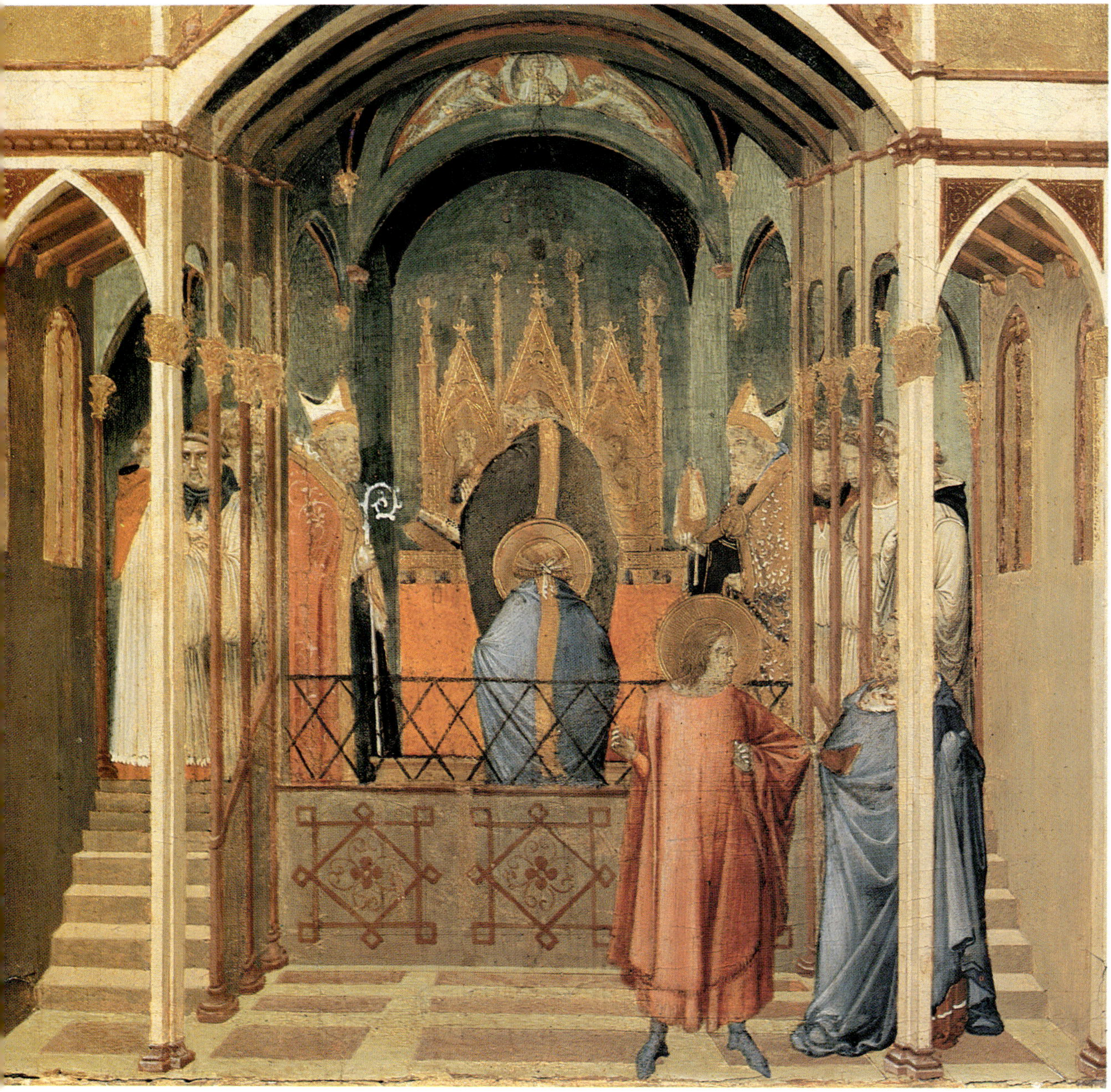

SIENESE ALTARPIECES

1215-1460

MEDIAEVALIA GRONINGANA

EDENDA CURANT
L.J. ENGELS, A.G. JONGKEES,
W. NOOMEN, N. VAN DER WAL

FASCICULUS IV

MDMLXXXVIII
EGBERT FORSTEN
GRONINGAE

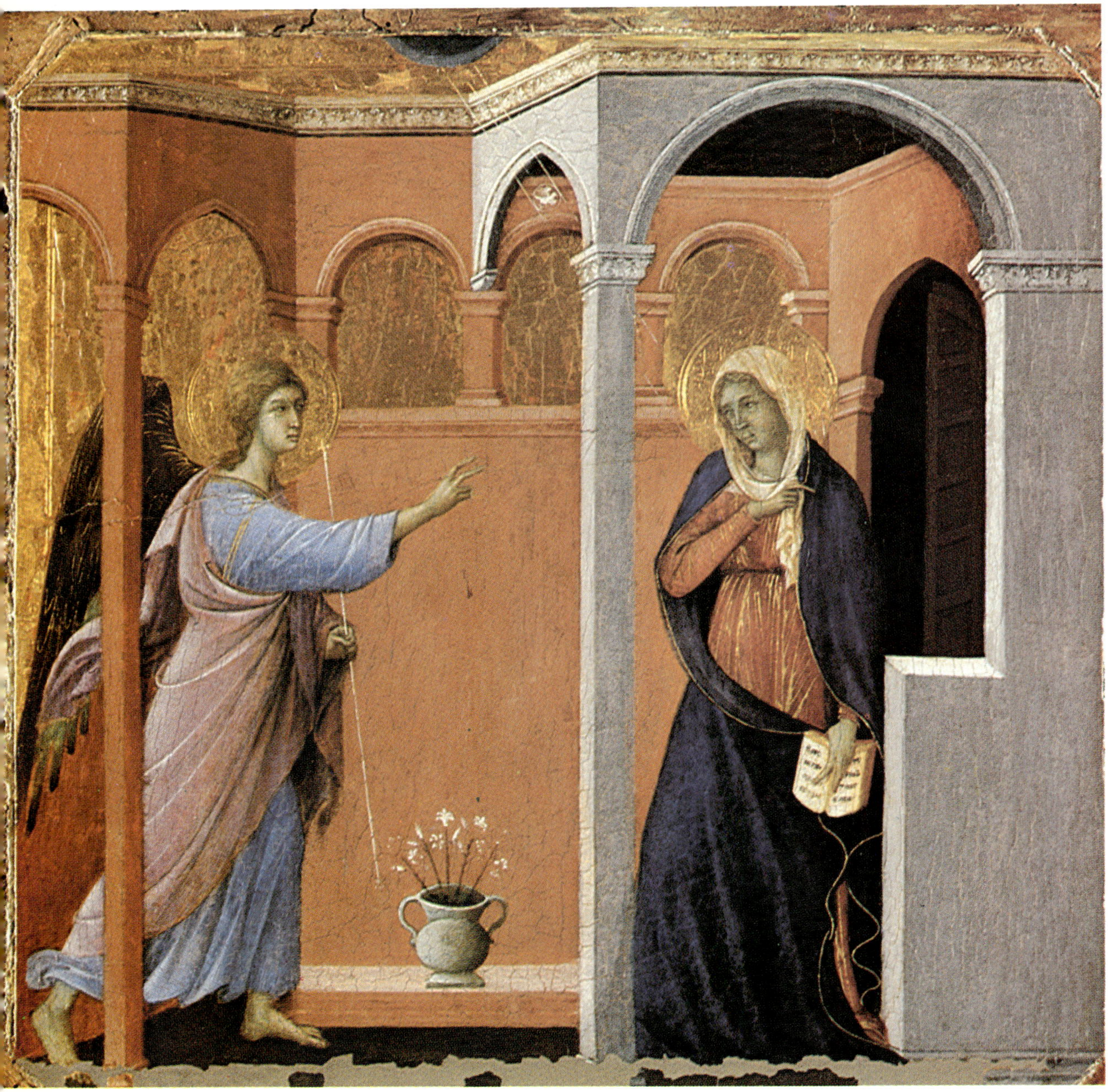

HENK VAN OS

SIENESE ALTARPIECES 1215-1460

FORM, CONTENT, FUNCTION
VOLUME I: 1215-1344

WITH A CONTRIBUTION BY KEES VAN DER PLOEG
'ON ARCHITECTURAL AND
LITURGICAL ASPECTS OF SIENA CATHEDRAL
IN THE MIDDLE AGES'

EGBERT FORSTEN
GRONINGEN 1988

ISBN 90 6980 022 5

First edition 1984
Second printing 1988

Translated into English by Michael Hoyle

This book was translated and printed with financial support
from the Netherlands Organisation
for the Advancement of Pure Research (z.w.o.)

Made and printed by
Wolters-Noordhoff Grafische Bedrijven bv, Groningen
Design by Françoise Berserik

Illustration on dust cover:
Duccio, Apparition on the road to Emmaus from the Maestà
51 x 52.9 cm
Museo dell'Opera del Duoma. Siena

CONTENTS

APPENDIX

ARCHITECTURAL AND LITURGICAL ASPECTS OF SIENA CATHEDRAL IN THE MIDDLE AGES BY KEES VAN DER PLOEG

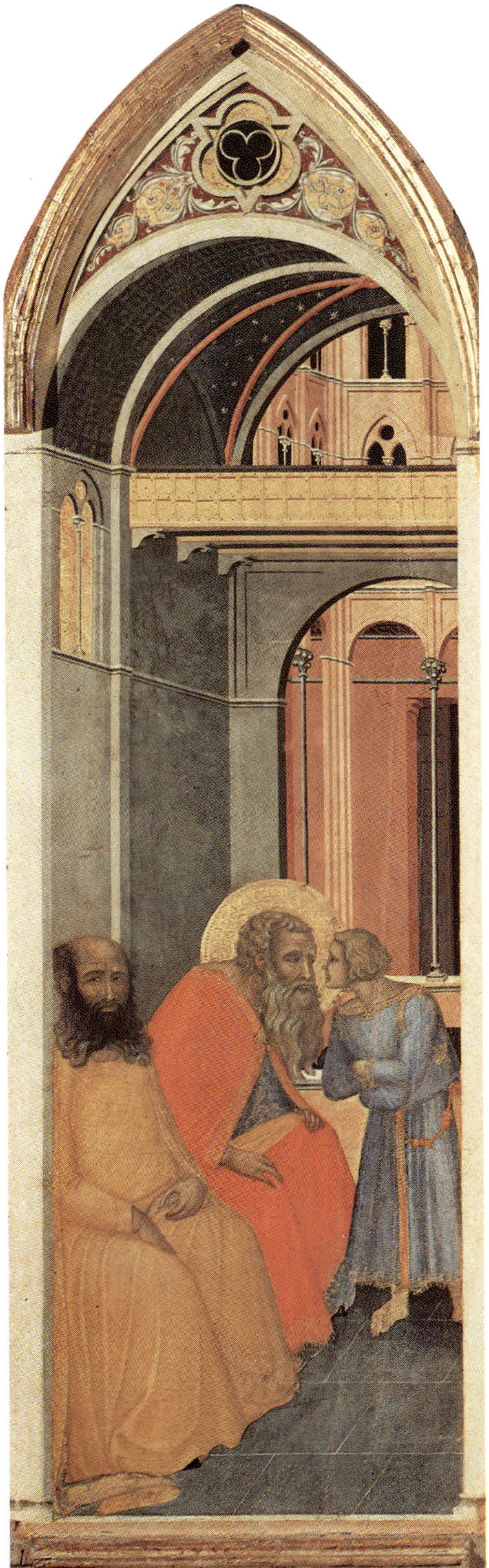

TO MY RESEARCH STUDENTS,
PAST AND PRESENT

INTRODUCTION

In the autumn of 1981, when he delivered the first Horst Gerson lecture,* Horst Janson echoed the words of Jakob Burckhardt in arguing for a 'Kunstgeschichte nach Aufgaben'. The present work is intended as a contribution to the kind of art history envisaged by Janson and Burckhardt. It examines the form and content of works of art in the light of their function, and deals with patrons and public, the physical settings in which the paintings belonged, and their particular significance in those settings. One can relate the morphological history of the altarpiece as a gradual evolution interspersed with a few major innovations. Function, though, is not amenable to this approach, certainly not when it refers to something as specific as the significance of an altarpiece in the setting for which it was designed. There one is dealing with the isolated instances which can still be reconstructed. In the following pages I have therefore tried to strike a balance between an analysis of the physical context, in which function plays a key role, and morphological description. This virtually rules out painted crucifixes and altarpieces for saints. Too few of them survive for us to trace any clear line of development, and it is hard to be specific about their original function.

Altarpieces were first and foremost liturgical accessories, and their form and content were associated with their liturgical function. However, form and content were not determined solely by function. There were other factors at play, including civic pride, the desire for pomp and splendour, the propaganda endeavours of the urban religious orders, competition between patrons, and rivalry among artists. All, in their way, contributed to the development of the altarpiece.

But why have I chosen to tell the story of Sienese altarpieces? My immediate answer is that I lost my heart to Siena 25 years ago, and since then I have found that there is nothing that gives me greater joy than researching Sienese art. Fortunately, though, there are less personal reasons for my choice. The Siena we know today gives us the most rounded picture of a large, late-medieval Italian city with a distinct tradition of painting. That is extremely alluring, not only to the art-loving romantic, but also to the art historian who wishes to analyse art in its historical context. Siena is the ideal city for reconstructing the historical setting within which art functioned. Most of its late-medieval buildings are still standing, and its archives and libraries are storehouses of information. This sometimes gives the art historian the feeling that he could almost step into a distant past. The Sienese have been aware of the special nature of their art since the fifteenth century, and this is reflected in their writings. There was an element of urban chauvinism in Sienese painting from a very early date, and for once it was perfectly justified, for Siena was one of the major centres of painting in terms of both quantity and quality.

Siena enjoyed a long period of peace and prosperity from 1287 to 1344. Throughout that period it was ruled by the 'Nine', representatives of an urban oligarchy which supported the Guelph cause. In 1260, at Montaperti, it had been a Ghibelline Siena which had repulsed the threat of a Guelph Florence. Shortly afterwards Siena too became Guelph, and political power came into the hands of those who controlled the city's economy: the plutocracy. The urban self-assurance which emerged during the rule of the Nine found expression in the creation of a beautiful city adorned with the finest art. Altars were decorated throughout the city. New and larger churches were built, and new and even more beautiful altarpieces replaced earlier works. Large workshops sprang up, and before long they were exporting altarpieces to other towns.

From the end of the thirteenth century the development of the altarpiece in Tuscany and Umbria

* H.W. Janson, *Form follows function – or does it?*, Maarssen 1982.

was dominated for several decades by artists from Siena. Sienese altarpieces are not isolated incidents; they are an integral part of the city's history and its thriving economic fortunes. This brings us to a problem of definition which Irene Hueck once drew to my attention.** What is Sienese art? More specifically, what is a Sienese altarpiece? Is it an altarpiece which was made for a church in the city or province of Siena? A reasonable assumption, one might think, but it would debar many important altarpieces made by Sienese painters and would preclude any analysis of the way in which Sienese art spread beyond Siena. Above all, though, it would obliterate the quite obvious interrelationship of a group of art works. It is therefore better to regard a Sienese altarpiece as an altarpiece painted by a Sienese artist. This has the added advantage of enabling us to say something about the socio-economic aspects of altarpiece history, even if it is couched in terms of conjecture and cautious hypothesis. Rapid changes in the balance of supply and demand, for example, were reflected in the inducements offered to artists to settle in the city and in the emigration of Sienese artists (generally the young ones) to work for patrons elsewhere.

This book owes its origins to a research project, financed by the Netherlands Organisation for the Advancement of Pure Research (ZWO), on which I have been engaged with Dolf van Asperen de Boer and Charlotte Wiethoff. Since 1979 we have been working on a new edition of a catalogue of Sienese paintings in Dutch collections, assisted by a group of seminar students. We discovered that the historical framework which would enable us to deal with the wide range of problems raised by our study was virtually non-existent. Moreover, a variety of recent monographs and articles revealed the need for a broader survey which had not yet been written. In the autumn of 1979 I gave a series of lectures on the Sienese altarpiece, and it is on those lectures that the general structure of this book is based.

A survey of this kind requires far more research than I had imagined. Hellmut Hager's pioneering work on the origins of the Italian altarpiece was an indispensable guide, and I was able to glean valuable information from new monographs on Duccio, notably that by John White, and from Hayden Maginnis's work on Pietro Lorenzetti. Recent articles by Christa Gardner-van Teuffel contained thought-provoking ideas on the morphological development of the fourteenth-century altarpiece. Areas requiring further research, however, included the interaction between iconography and the liturgy, the matching of extant paintings with altarpieces mentioned in documentary sources, and the relationship between patron and artist. The latter is a very vexed question, and here I have done no more than put forward a few suggestions. In dealing with the remaining areas I have also enlarged on the observations I made in 1969 on the iconography of the polyptych and of the altarpieces in the patronal chapels of Siena cathedral. Here I received the invaluable assistance of Kees van der Ploeg, who has made a detailed study of the relationship between structural alterations to the cathedral and the organisation of the liturgy. In many cases our collaboration enabled me to place 'my' altarpieces on 'his' altars. The value of his work is such that it has been included in this book as a contribution in its own right.

I conducted most of my research in Florence, at the Netherlands Institute for Art History, at the German Institute for Art History, and at the Harvard Center for Renaissance Studies, Villa I Tatti, Settignano. These centres have provided me with a base for my studies from the time I first went to Italy, and the warmth with which I am greeted each time I return means a great deal to me. I am greatly indebted to the staff of the Soprintendenza alle Gallerie of Siena, and especially to Alberto Cornice, for all the assistance I have received. Enzo Carli used to say jokingly that I was an 'impiegato non pagato della Soprintendenza'. It is a title which I am proud to bear.

This book would never have been written were it not for the friendship and encouragement of my colleagues at the Institute for Art History of Groningen University. I am particularly grateful to Hans Locher and Bernard Ridderbos, who were prepared to act as readers. Their criticism enabled me to improve my presentation of several important points. Anton Boschloo of Leiden University, Christian Klamt of Utrecht University, Gail Solberg of the Metropolitan Museum, New York and Bram Kempers of Amsterdam University also made valuable suggestions. Egbert Forsten's critical understanding of my work made him as much a colleague as a publisher. I am also indebted to Dora Bijleveld and Anjelien Meijers for the dedication with which they prepared the manuscript and assembled the illustrations. I have dedicated this book to my research students in gratitude for their enthusiasm, even if it does occasionally take the form of irritating questions and astonishing simplifications. With them to keep me on my toes I need have no fear of my personal nightmare – being trapped on a treadmill of academic complacency.

Groningen, 1 May 1982

** I. Hueck, 'H.W. van Os, Marias Demut und Verherrlichung in der sienesischen Malerei 1300-1450, 's-Gravenhage 1969', (review) *The Art Bulletin* 53 (1971), p. 117.

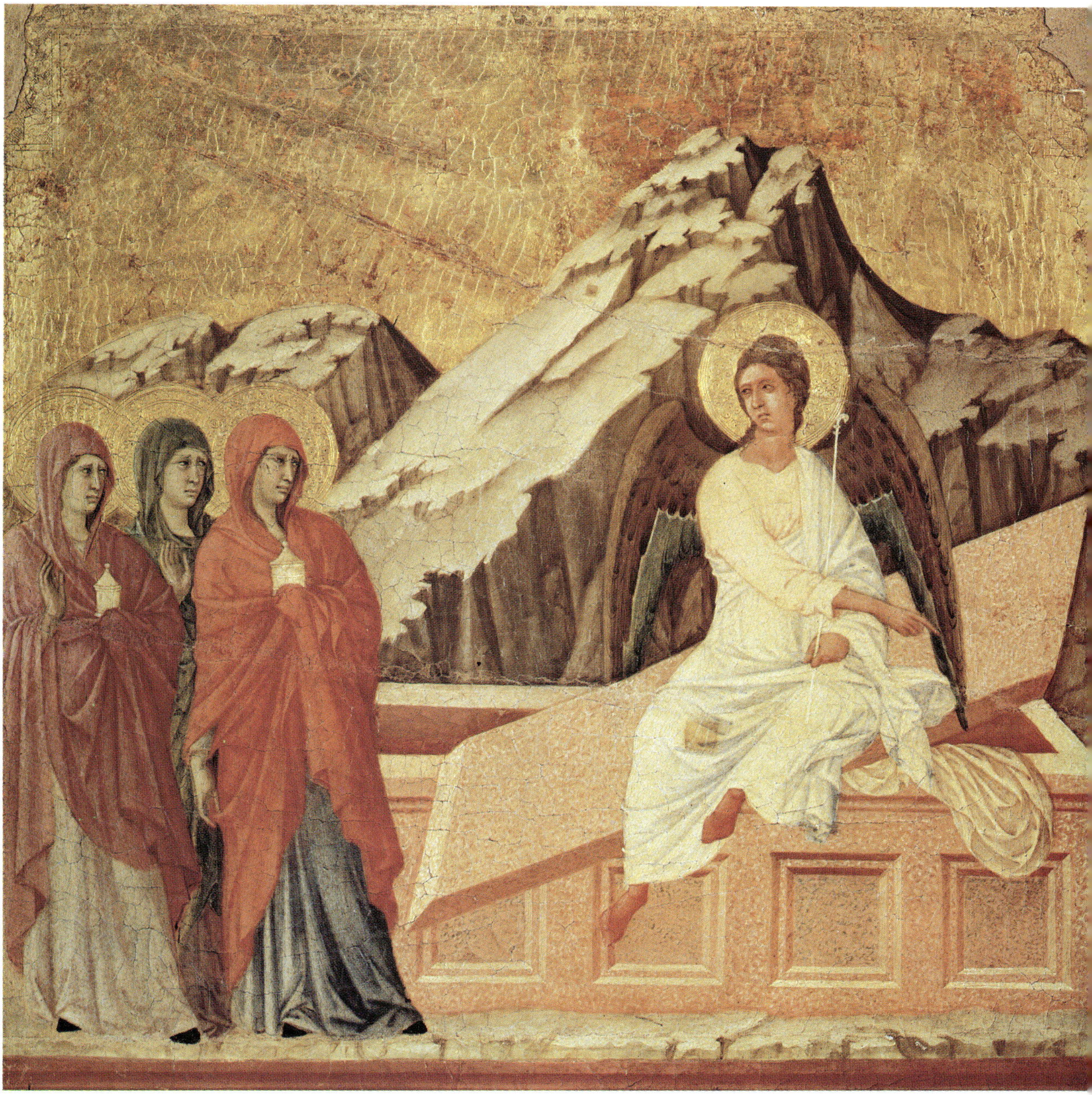

FRONTISPIECE
Ambrogio Lorenzetti, St. Nicolas consecrated Bishop
48 x 53 cm
Galleria degli Uffizi, Florence

OPP. TITLEPAGE
Duccio, Annunciation from the predella of the Maestà
43 x 44 cm
National Gallery, London

OPP. PAGE 6
Pietro Lorenzetti, The Birth of the Virgin announced to Joachim
(detail)
Museo Opera del Duomo

OPP. PAGE 8
Duccio, The three Marys at the sepulchre
51 x 52.9 cm
Museo dell'Opera del Duomo, Siena

The dimensions of the figures
are rounded to the nearest half centimetre

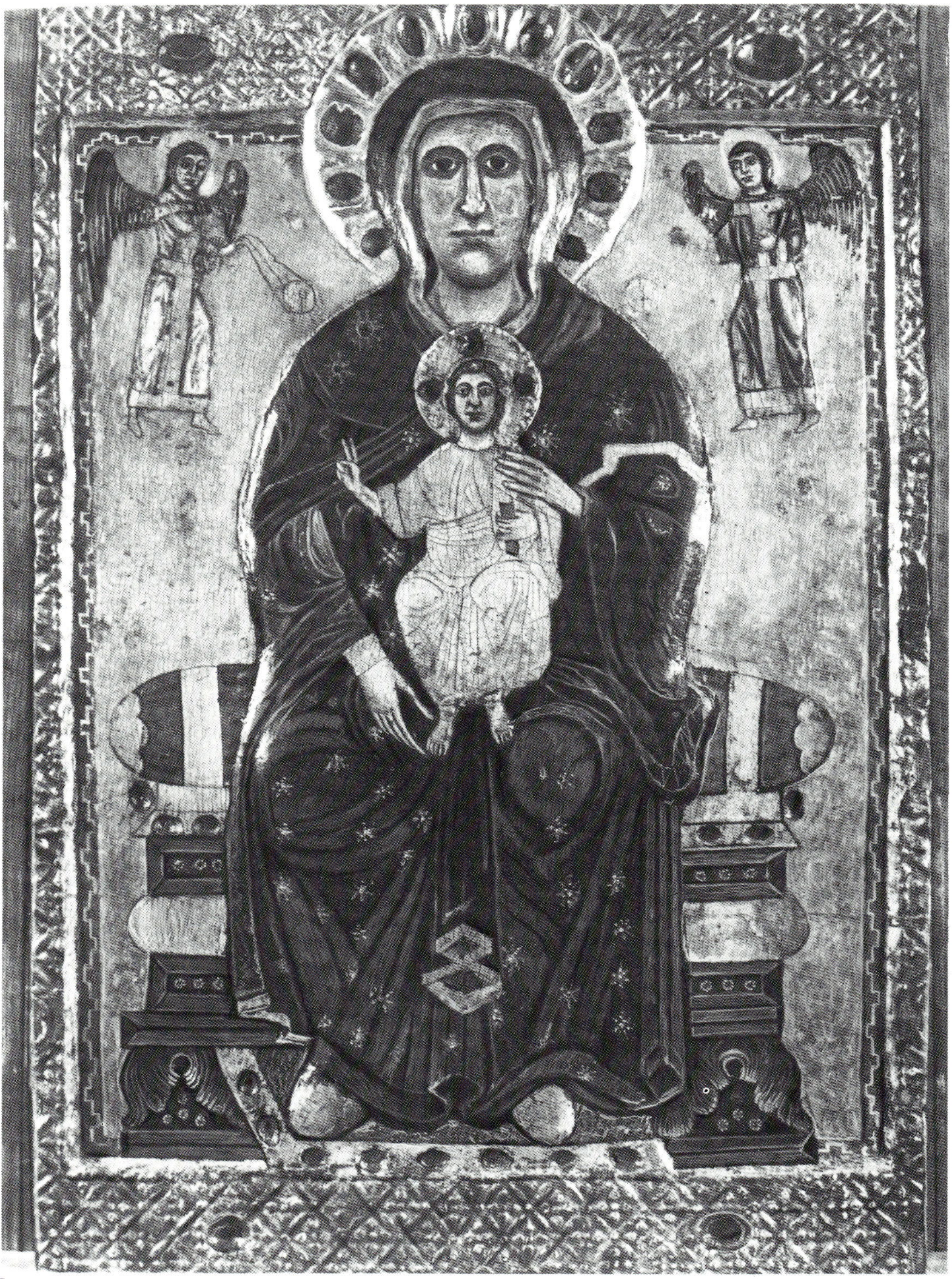

1 Sienese early 13th century, 'Madonna degli occhi grossi', 47 x 67 cm, Museo dell'Opera del Duomo, Siena.

I

THE EARLIEST ALTARPIECES IN SIENA CATHEDRAL

Fifteenth-century Sienese authors have left us a colourful story which is such a vivid illustration of the function of religious art in a thirteenth-century urban community and of the importance attached to works of art that it deserves to be quoted at length at the very outset of this book.

The time is September 1260. A strong Florentine army has massed outside the walls of Siena, and it seems that only a miracle can save the city. It is at this point that a prominent Sienese, one Buonaguida, takes matters into his own hands and puts on what we today would call a 'performance', the only difference being that his 'act' was far more effective than its modern counterpart. The following is a free and condensed rendering of the episode.

'This Buonaguida disrobed himself to his shirt. He removed his shoes and his cap. He took his belt and fashioned it into a noose, which he placed around his neck. He put himself at the head of his fellow-citizens and thus he made his way to the cathedral, with the people following behind. When the multitude arrived there the bishop walked in procession through the cathedral until he came before the high altar of Our Lady full of grace, the Virgin Mary. All the people of whom I have spoken went to the cathedral, and when they came to the door of the cathedral they began to cry out, lamenting: 'Misericordia, misericordia'. On hearing this piteous lamentation the bishop turned, and with him all the priests. He went to meet Buonaguida and when they met all knelt down, and Buonaguida made as if to prostrate himself on the ground. But the bishop raised him to his feet and gave him the sign of peace. This took place below the choir of the cathedral. The bishop and Buonaguida took each other by the hand and went up together to the altar of Mary, our Mother and Virgin. There they knelt, amidst loud lamentation. The worthy Buonaguida fell to the ground and lay prostrate. He then arose, and standing in front of Mary, our Mother and Virgin, he spoke most wisely and fittingly, thus: –

'Glorious Virgin, Queen of Heaven, I, a miserable sinner, give and dedicate to you this city of Siena and the lands around. I pray, O most tender of mothers, that you will accept her in your mercy, for our shortcomings and sins are many. Overlook the error of our ways. I beseech you to pay us heed, that you may protect the city, that you may defend and deliver her from the hands of those arrant curs of Florence, who would subdue her.'

He then called upon all those present to form a procession with the bishop and all the priests, who were gathered there. The carved crucifix of the cathedral was borne at the head of the procession. Then came the monks and friars, then the crosses with the holy relics from the cathedral, then many priests preceding a banner which was red throughout. Behind this came the bishop, with Buonaguida at his side, and they were followed by all the canons of the cathedral. And so they went in procession through the city to Santo Cristofano and the Campo, from whence they made their way back to the cathedral. Buonaguida, having made his confession, then left with a select band and returned to Santo Cristofano, together with his twenty-four companions. They then prayed to the Lord, asking Him to guide their actions. These events took place on Wednesday, the third of September, towards nightfall.'

The following day the citizens of this City of the Virgin ('Civitas Virginis') went out to do battle. They met the Florentines by Montaperti, east of Siena. For a long time the issue was undecided, but the protection of the queen of heaven is not invoked in vain. Siena finally carried the day and inflicted a crushing defeat on Florence and her allies.

Some of the more florid accounts of this episode

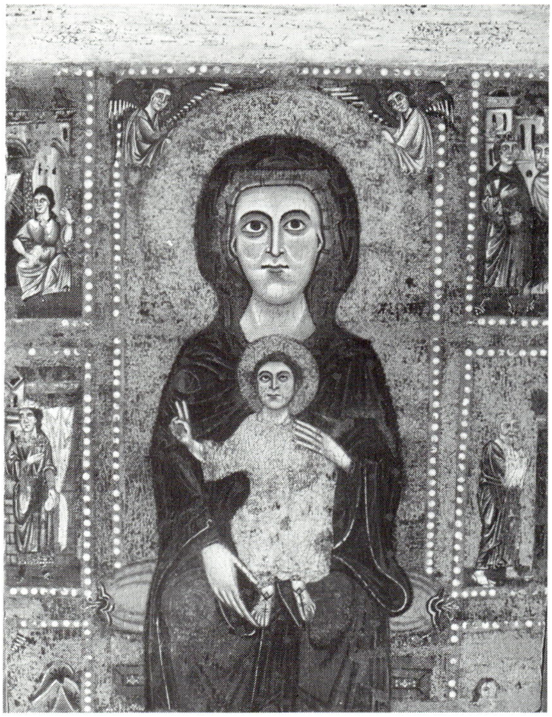

2 Sienese early 13th century, 'Tressa Madonna', 75.5 x 56.5 cm, Chiesa parrocchiale di Tressa, Siena.

show that fifteenth-century Sienese historians were not averse to bending the historical truth if they saw an opportunity of fortifying urban chauvinism.[1] But however unreliable the reports, the fact remains that Siena was dedicated to the Virgin in 1260, the Sienese really did win the battle of Montaperti, and the altarpiece of the Madonna, which Buonaguida addressed so movingly, still exists today (fig. 1).[2] It is one of the earliest altarpieces to have come down to us. It is a painted relief of the Madonna in a rigidly frontal pose. Her majesty is expressed by the ornamented throne and by the angels who are censing her. She is holding up the Christ Child in front of her, with her right hand supporting his foot. This pose, in which the Virgin presents her child to the viewer, is in the Byzantine tradition of the 'Hodegetria' (She who indicates the way). Christ, wearing a toga, is enthroned on her lap. His right hand is raised in blessing, and in his left hand he holds a scroll. It is an uncompromisingly theological presentation of the Virgin and Child, with not a trace of an emotional relationship between the two figures. This lack of warmth helps to explain the name which the Sienese later gave this Virgin: the *Madonna degli occhi grossi* (The Madonna with the bulging eyes).

Examination of the frame reveals that it has been trimmed down the sides. This was also the fate of the so-called *Madonna of Tressa* (fig. 2), which is closely related to the *Madonna degli occhi grossi* in both style and iconography. Here, though, the painting has not been cut down through the frame, but through the scenes painted at either side of the Madonna. The only example of this kind of altarpiece in Sienese art to have survived unscathed is a *Majestas Domini* with scenes from the legend of the True Cross, which is dated 1215 on the frame (fig. 3). There are such striking similarities in style and technique between this Saviour and the *Madonna degli occhi grossi* that both works must be dated to the same period.

All the evidence indicates that these three paintings were executed not as altarpieces but as antependia, covering the front of an altar. Antependia were often made of precious metal or wood, with the latter often being imitations of the more costly metal versions, as in the case of the *Madonna degli occhi grossi* and the *Majestas Domini*. Their broad frames are richly ornamented, and the painting of the Madonna is even set with semi-precious stones. The scuff marks at the base of the *Majestas Domini* panel are clear evidence that it was originally used as an antependium, for the damaged areas exactly match the points where a priest would stand when celebrating mass. There are marks down the sides showing where the painting was originally attached to the front of the altar, and there are others which indicate that it was later placed on top of the altar.[3]

Painted panels which had originally been installed as antependia were moved to the top of the altar table in the course of the thirteenth century. In other words, the first Sienese altarpieces were not designed as altarpieces at all. Although there was clearly a need for some new kind of painting, the forms specific to that new function had not yet been developed and so, as a stopgap measure, existing forms were put to a new use.

Why, though, was there this sudden need for a painting on top of the altar? The altar was a table, and on it stood a whole array of liturgical objects: caskets, ciboria, pyxes, reliquaries large and small, and eucharistic doves.[4] The most eye-catching objects, if only because of their size, were wooden statues of the Virgin and Child (fig. 6). They were used as reliquaries, were borne in procession, and played the leading roles in liturgical plays. As Forsyth says, 'they were sculptured representatives of the Virgin and Son in a most tangible way',[5] and that is exactly how Buonaguida experienced the *Madonna degli occhi grossi* – as the earthly representative of the queen of heaven. The presence of that image on their high altar brought the Sienese into direct contact with the sacred. At a later date such representations were made more responsive to the spectator's desire for emotional involvement, but initially it was purely a

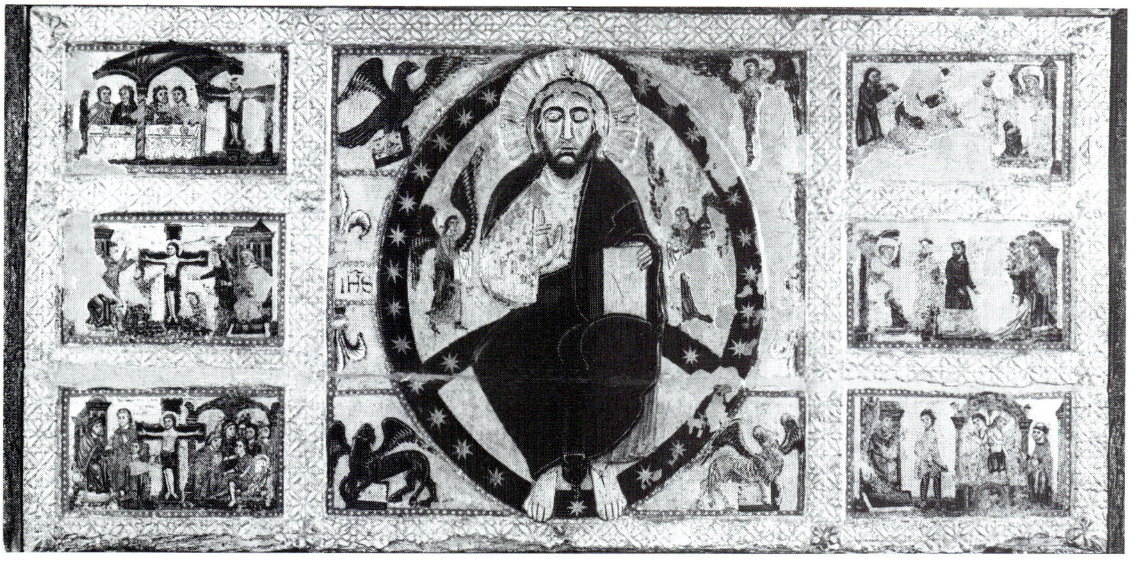

3 Sienese 1215, Majestas Domini, 98 x 198 cm, Pinacoteca Nazionale, Siena.

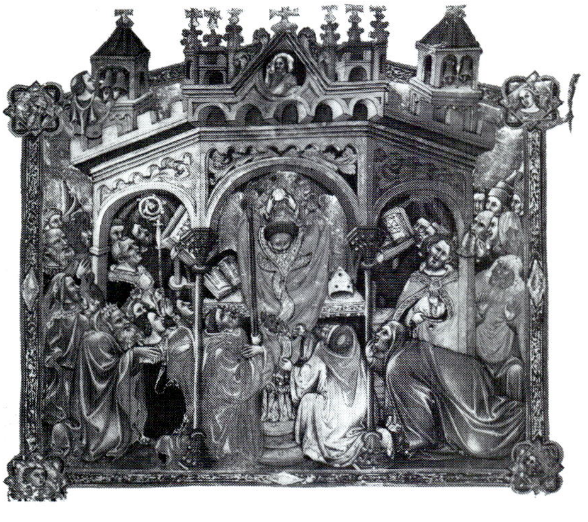

4 Niccolò da Bologna, Elevation of the host, Vat. Lat. 2534, fol 1r, Bibliotheca Apostolica Vaticana, Rome.

matter of physical proximity. Bernard of Clairvaux had foreshadowed the new development when he confessed in a sermon to his fellow-monks: 'I cannot say it without tears coming to my eyes, but I have not been permitted to see or apprehend Him as the king who sits in glory above the cherubim, on his high, exalted throne'.[6] In other words, he could only identify with representations of salvation if they were somehow made more immediate.

Buonaguida, of course, could have prayed to a statue just as well as to a painting. Why did the statues disappear, and why did paintings take their place? In order to answer that question we have to examine some of the fundamental changes which had taken place in the theory underlying the liturgy. In 1215, at the Lateran Council in Rome, it was officially decreed that Christ was physically present in the Eucharist as flesh and blood. That too was a way, albeit ritualistic, of bringing the Redeemer closer to the faithful. From now on priests were to make the person of the Redeemer immanent. This vastly increased the power of the church as an institution, as well as introducing a new liturgical framework for the sacrifice of the mass. The council decision meant that the priest now had to consummate the mystery of the ritual incarnation with his back to the congregation. After he had consecrated the host and the wine he elevated them, enabling the faithful to behold their redemption. In that act of seeing they partook in salvation (fig. 4).[7]

This visual presentation was one of the key elements in the liturgical expression of the doctrine of transubstantiation, and that in turn required a backdrop to serve as a physical framework for the ritual. The point of the elevation is that it focusses the spectator's attention, which should not be allowed to wander. The ritual, in other words, had to be demarcated from the space around the altar. None of the objects usually found on the altar were suitable for this purpose, and nor were the statues of the Virgin and Child, for they were too narrow and elongated to make an adequate backdrop for the elevation. Some altars had narrow, horizontal strips known as dossals at the back of the altar table, but they were set too low down to be of any use.

Various types of 'decor' were developed in Italy to heighten the impact of the priest's actions. Not sur-

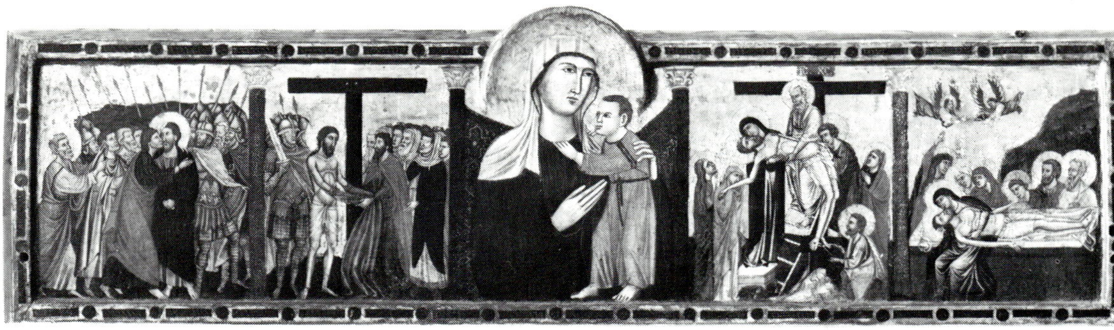

5 Maestro del Farneto, Madonna with scenes from the Passion, 60 x 215 cm, Galleria Nazionale dell'Umbria, Perugia.

prisingly, the first attempts to find a solution were based largely on the traditional objects. The wooden statues, for example, were given side-pieces illustrating Christ's life and Passion. A very early example of this type is the *Madonna of Alatri* (fig. 6), but otherwise the only surviving examples of this kind of arrangement from provincial centres are of a fairly late date. Nevertheless, it can be assumed that many of the individual wooden Madonnas which have come down to us were originally extended in this way. Another way of creating an altarpiece from existing elements was to take the wooden antependium and place it on top of the altar.

It is perfectly understandable that large wooden or painted crucifixes in a triumphal arch should be used to mark the place where the sacrifice of the mass was consummated (fig. 7), and a depiction of the Saviour on the altar was obviously an ideal visual accompaniment to the visual presentation of Christ in the consecrated bread and wine. However, the reason why Madonnas became so popular on late medieval altars requires a certain amount of explanation. The image of the Virgin and her Child suggests the theme of Christ's repeated rebirth in the Eucharist, which is why there was such an emphasis on the Incarnation in the eucharistic doctrine of the period. However, quite apart from this strictly liturgical function, the Madonna was also the focus of a devotion in which

6 Italian ca. 1250, Madonna and scenes from the New Testament, height 160 cm, Alatri, S. Maria Maggiore.

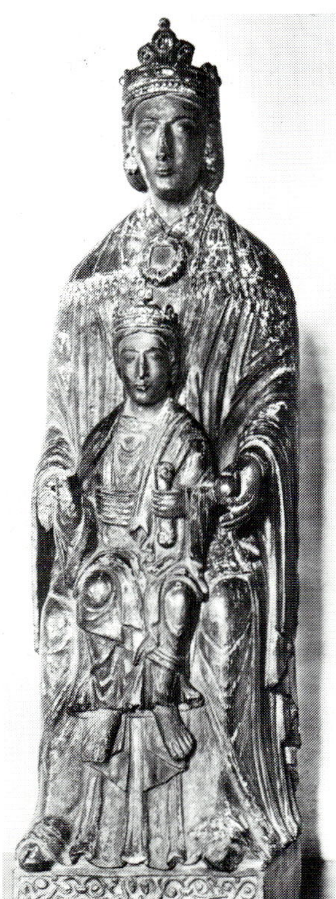

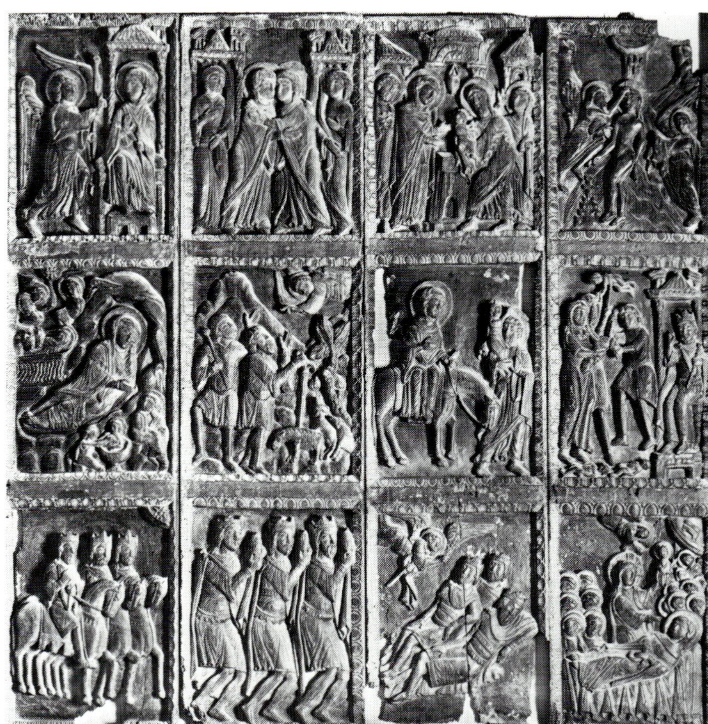

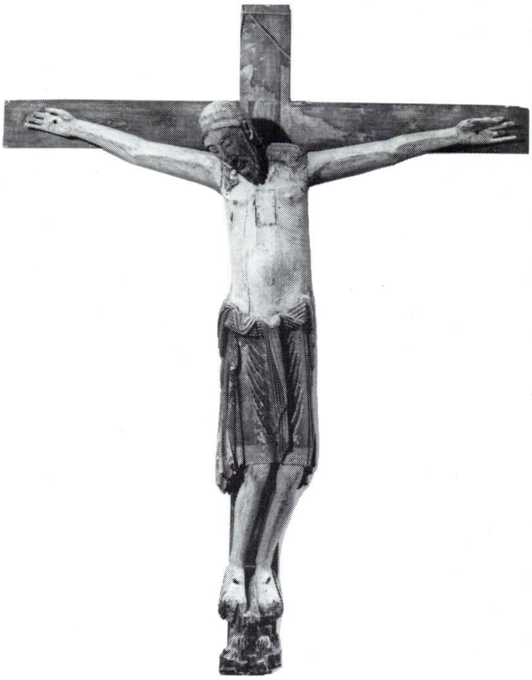

7 Second half 12th century, Crucifix, height 260 cm, Chiesa abbaziale di S. Antimo, Montalcino (Siena).

human emotions about a mother and child played a very real role. In Sienese art, in particular, the relationship between the Virgin and the Christ Child rapidly became more personal. The rigidly frontal pose was abandoned in favour of arrangements suggesting a greater intimacy. Ultimately that particular function of the Madonna on the altar was to supersede the original liturgical significance. That, in turn, explains why the Sienese removed so many Madonnas from their high altars in the second half of the fifteenth century, when attention was once again focussed on the liturgy.[8]

Let us return to Buonaguida in Siena cathedral. Although we still have the Madonna which he venerated in 1260, and although we know a great deal about this first Madonna altarpiece in Sienese art, we have not yet said anything about its physical setting on that memorable day when Siena was dedicated to the Virgin. In the first place we kwow that the church bore no resemblance to the cathedral as it is today. It was more of a Romanesque church, with an elevated choir above a crypt, like the Pieve of Arezzo. The high altar with the *Madonna degli occhi grossi* stood at the front of that elevated choir, facing the congregation below. A careful re-reading of old documents, notably the *Ordo officiorum ecclesiae Senensis*, which was written in 1215 by a canon called Odericus, tells us that there was also an altar for the canons at the back of the choir.[9] We are able to pinpoint the location of the altars from the fairly detailed instructions for the performance of the liturgy contained in the *Ordo*. The choir-stalls were ranged along the sides of the choir, flanking these two altars. There are grounds for believing that the *Majestas Domini* (fig. 3) stood on the sacrament altar, and that it was not made for the altar of the monastery church of Badia Ardenga,

8 Sienese ca. 1260, St John the Baptist and scenes from his life, 92 x 170.5 cm, Pinacoteca Nazionale, Siena.

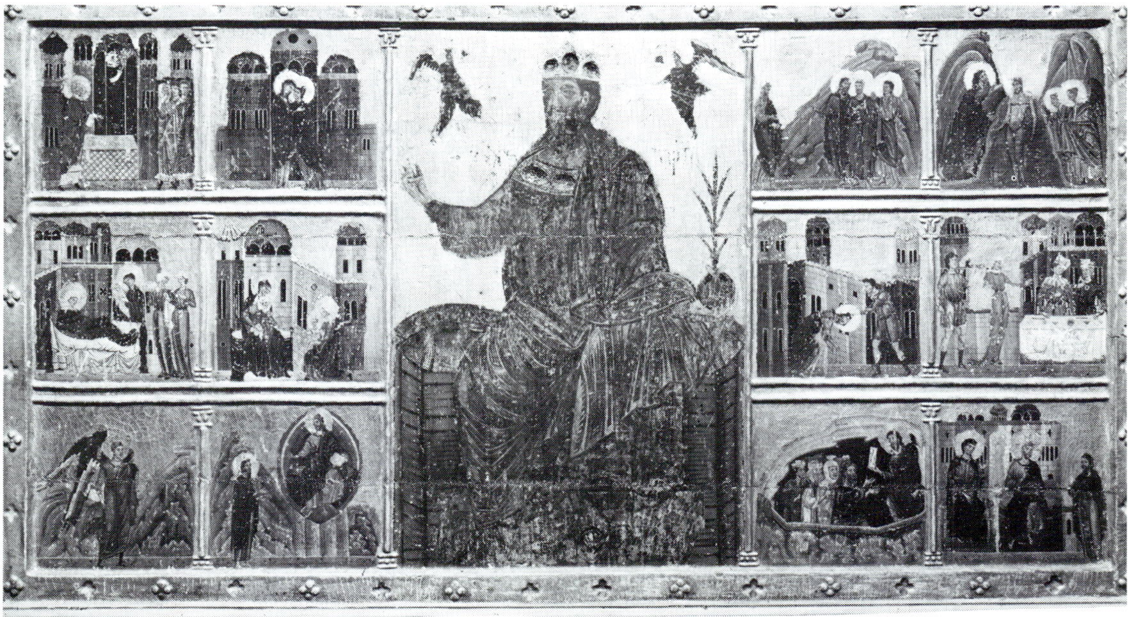

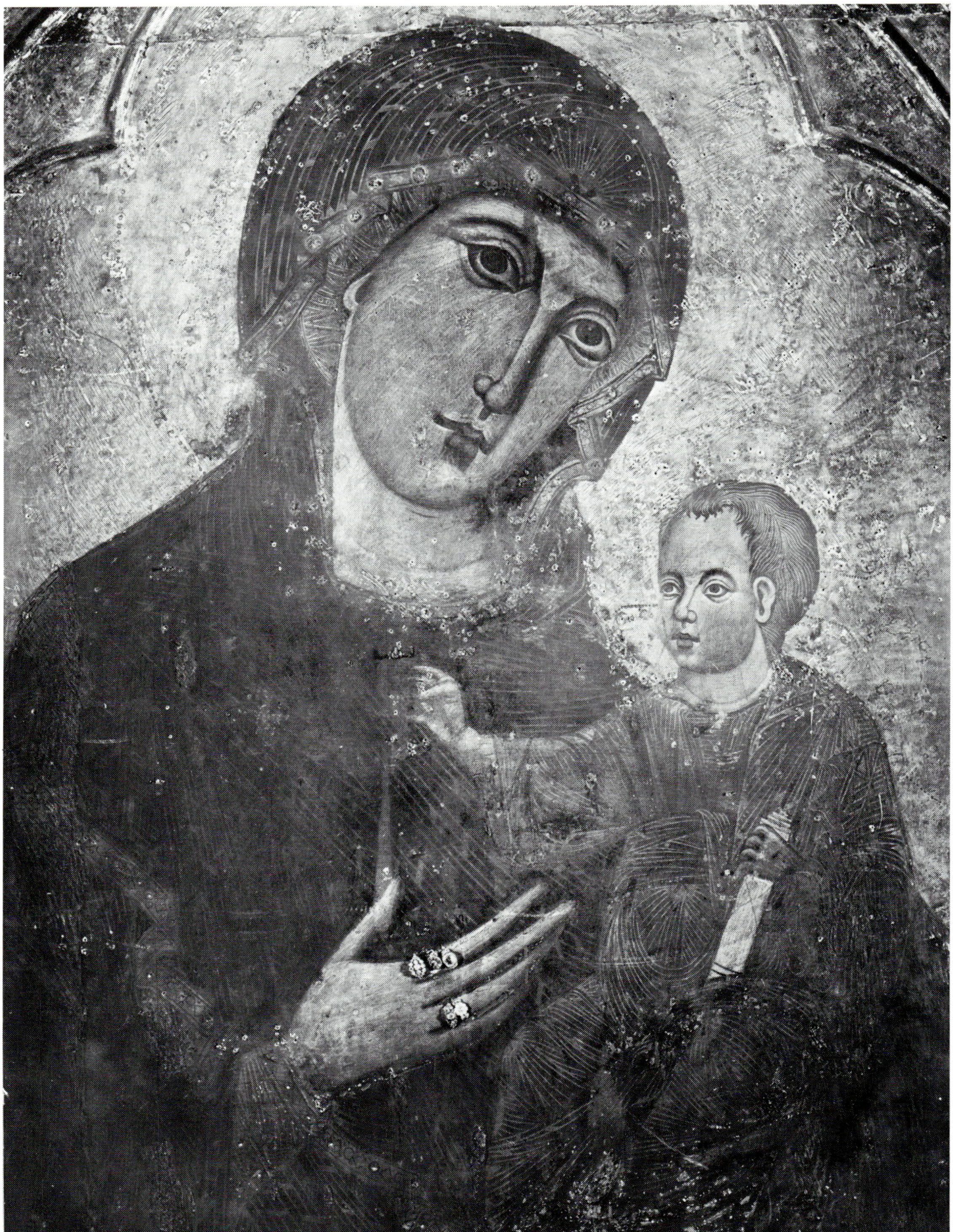

9 Guido da Siena, 'Madonna del Voto', 112 x 82 cm,
Capella del Voto, Duomo, Siena.

from which it was removed to the Pinacoteca in 1820.[10] This would also account for the remarkable similarities in style, technique and ornamentation between the two paintings. It can hardly be a coincidence that both the *Ordo* and the *Majestas Domini* date from 1215. The probable explanation is that the *Ordo* and the two antependia were by-products of the general reorganisation of the liturgy which had been set in train by the canonical reform movement.[11]

The year 1215 marked a watershed in the development of the liturgy. As we have seen, it was the year in which the doctrine of transubstantiation became dogma, so one can well imagine that it was followed by a period in which secondary choir altars were erected in churches everywhere. There is an interesting feature of the iconography of the scenes flanking the *Majestas Domini* which lends added emphasis to this relationship with the Eucharist. It has long been assumed that they depict episodes from the legend of the True Cross, although it is difficult to say precisely which episodes. The trouble arises because the three scenes on the left are not about the Cross as such, but about the crucified Christ. The scenes illustrate the Corpus Christi and the miracles it performs. One could hardly wish for a better illustration of the conception of the liturgy which led to the doctrine of transubstantiation in 1215.

Siena cathedral was in the throes of a major rebuilding programme when Buonaguida gave his moving performance in front of the *Madonna degli occhi grossi*. The new, enlarged cathedral was dedicated in 1267. The old high altar had been demolished and a new one erected on the same site, a low screen with carved decoration was built around the choir-stalls, and there was a new pulpit, sculpted by Nicola and Giovanni Pisano. It was inevitable that the *Madonna degli occhi grossi* should also be replaced, for even in 1260 it had been totally obsolete. The renewal which had been taking place in Tuscan art since 1250 could be described in very general terms as a new approach to Byzantine art. Byzantium not only possessed a far superior manner of painting but had also introduced new forms of panel painting with the iconostasis and with icons for private devotion. The Byzantine influence reached the cities of Tuscany through the schools of Pisa and Lucca, which were in the forefront of this artistic renewal, but artists and works of art were also imported directly from Byzantium itself. The so-called *St John antependium* in the Pinacoteca in Siena, with its slender, elegant figures and its flat, multi-coloured buildings (fig. 8), could hardly be the work of anyone but a Byzantine artist. That, however, is an exception, for at this period Siena was evolving a variant of Byzantine art which had a distinct character of its own.

The *Madonna* which was installed on the high altar

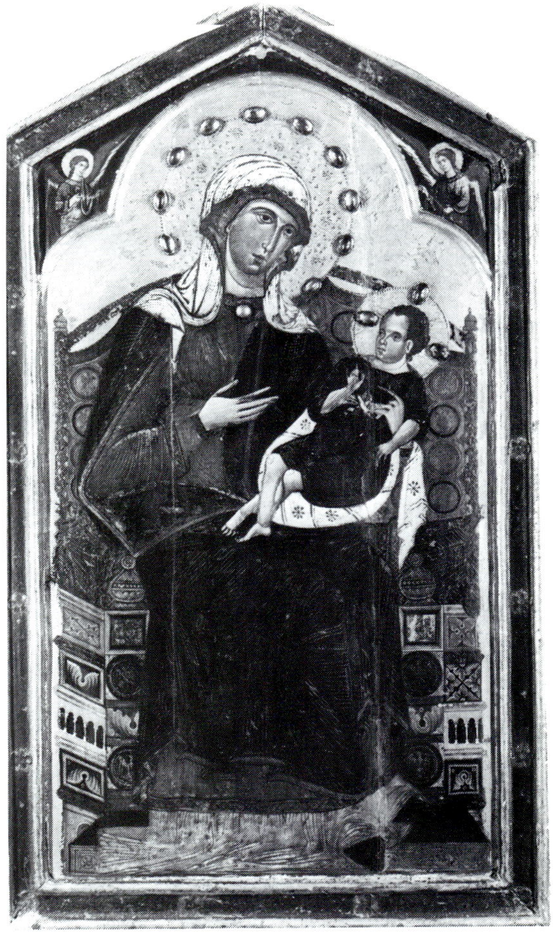

10 Guido da Siena, 'Galli-Dunn Madonna', 125 x 73 cm, Pinacoteca Nazionale, Siena.

shortly after the momentous battle at Montaperti is representative of the art which was current in Siena at the time (fig. 9). The figures follow the Byzantine model, with rather round faces and richly decorated robes. It is a style which is generally associated with Guido da Siena, although as we shall see in the next chapter Guido is little more than a name, and the attribution of specific works to his hand is fraught with uncertainty. There is a world of difference between this, the *Madonna del voto*, and the Virgin and Child which it replaced on the high altar. Quite apart from the obvious difference in style, the type of image has been transformed by the introduction of a completely new element. Although the Madonna is still a Hodegetria, holding the young Saviour with one hand and pointing to him with the other, the Christ Child has now broken through his mother's silhouette. The rigid symmetry has been abandoned, and with it the impassive frontal pose. The Virgin holds the Child on her left arm and is bending her head towards him. Christ has raised his right hand, but appears to be in two minds about whether to bless the faithful or play with his mother's robe.

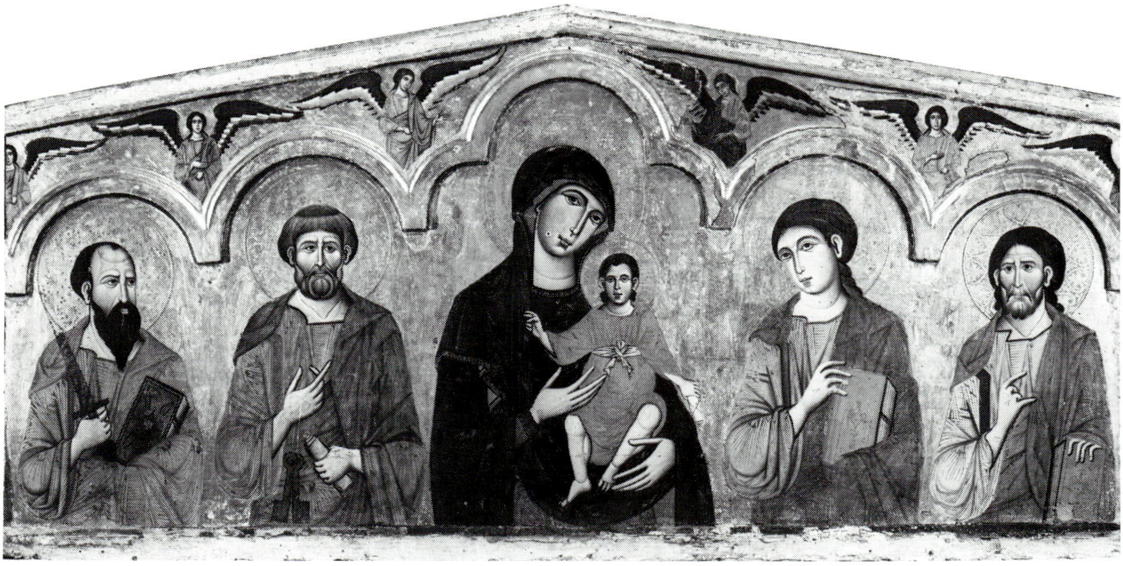

11 Guido da Siena, Madonna with Sts Paul, Peter, John the Evangelist and Andrew, 102 x 214 cm, Pinacoteca Nazionale, Siena.

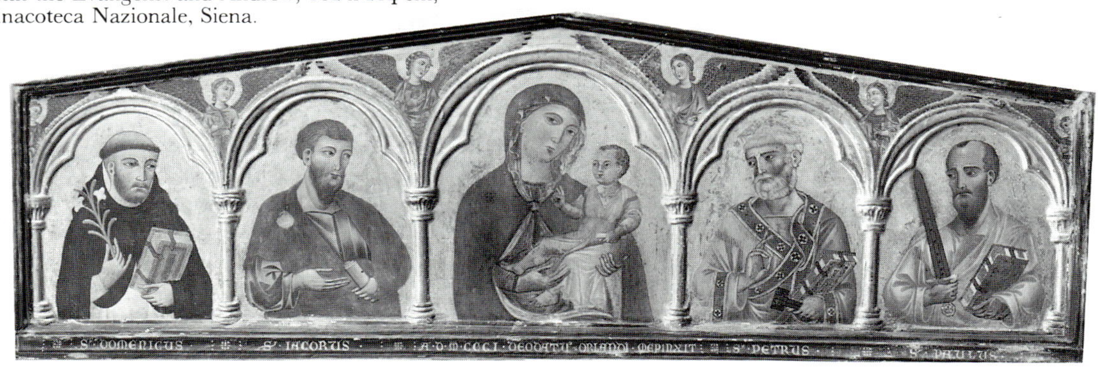

12 Deodato Orlandi, Madonna with Sts James, Peter, Paul and Dominic, 71 x 206 cm, Museo Nazionale di S. Matteo, Pisa.

Once again, though, we have been left with just a fragment of a painting. A saw has been used not only down the sides, but along the top and bottom as well. The problem is to reconstruct the original form. Some authors have suggested that it was a full-length painting of the Madonna and Child enthroned, which is a form known from other Sienese altarpieces (fig. 10).[12] However, if that were the case there would be at least some trace of the throne, which invariably had a high, ornamental back in Sienese Madonnas of this period. Another suggestion is that the *Madonna del voto* was once the central panel of a triptych, [13] but this ignores the fact that this period has given us not a single triptych of a comparable size with a half-length Madonna in the centre. Moreover, it can be seen from the top of the *Madonna del voto* that the panel is built up of horizontal planks. This suggests that the original structure was far wider than a triptych, for if the panel had been higher than it was wide the planks would have been arranged vertically. A more rewarding line of enquiry points in the direction of a large gabled dossal (fig. 11),[14] which was evidently a very common form of altarpiece in Siena at this time, judging by the relatively large number of examples to have survived. The only difficulty is that the Madonna and saints in Sienese dossals are set in a framework which is totally different from that suggested by the fragmentary mouldings on the *Madonna del voto* panel. For want of a better model, former reconstructions have been based on a Pisan dossal of 1301 by Deodato Orlandi (fig. 12). Recently, though, I discovered a previously unknown Sienese dossal with a very rustic version of the same surround (fig. 13). The painted surface is almost obliterated, but the actual framework is in good condition. There are even traces of an old inscription along the top edge.

So a dossal replaced a former antependium on top

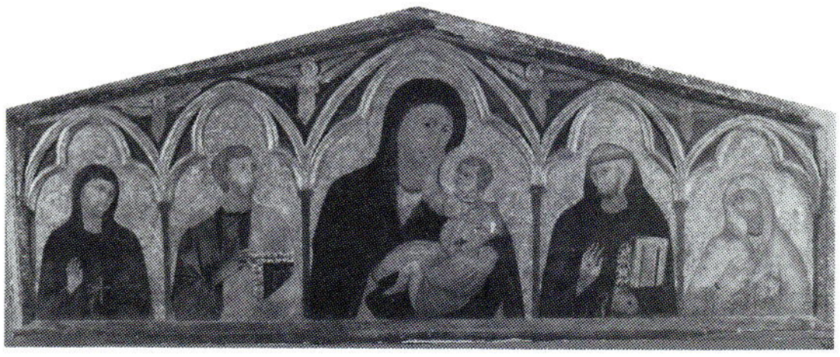

13 Sienese 13th century, Madonna with Sts Margaret, John, Francis and Mary Magdalen, Private collection, Colle di Val d'Elsa.

of the high altar in Siena cathedral. The narrow frieze closing off the back of the altar had now been extended to a reasonable height. The gabled shape also gave rise to a hierarchical arrangement, which was reflected in the scale of the figures, with the Madonna in the centre and saints on either side. The more important saints were usually placed closest to the Madonna, while those further away generally had some connection with the donor or donors. The Deodato Orlandi dossal, for example, was made for a Dominican church, so it was axiomatic that the company of saints should include St Dominic. Although the kind of dossal developed in Siena was fairly low, it still served as a useful visual framework for the liturgy, particularly when the altar stood in a large open space beneath a high vault. Another type of altarpiece which made its appearance at this time was the upright Madonna panel. Although the enthroned Madonna was ideal for focussing attention on the altar, these single panels were too narrow for the width of the altar table.

We know from the re-reading of Odericus's *Ordo* that there was another altar in the choir. What happened to this sacrament altar and, even more to the point, what happened to the *Majestas Domini* of 1215? There was not just an image of the Madonna involved, but also one of Christ in majesty. There is not a shred of evidence to show that the altar for the canons was renewed along with the high altar, so we must assume that it simply disappeared in the reorganisation of the church. However, that does not mean that there was no longer any interest in the *Majestas Domini* as a subject. Would the canons in their choir-stalls have been content to look at the plain back of a large dossal? It is far more likely that the dossal was painted on both sides, with the Madonna and the saints on the front, and scenes of the

14-15 Reconstruction of the high altarpiece of the church of S. Francesco Perugia (after Gordon).

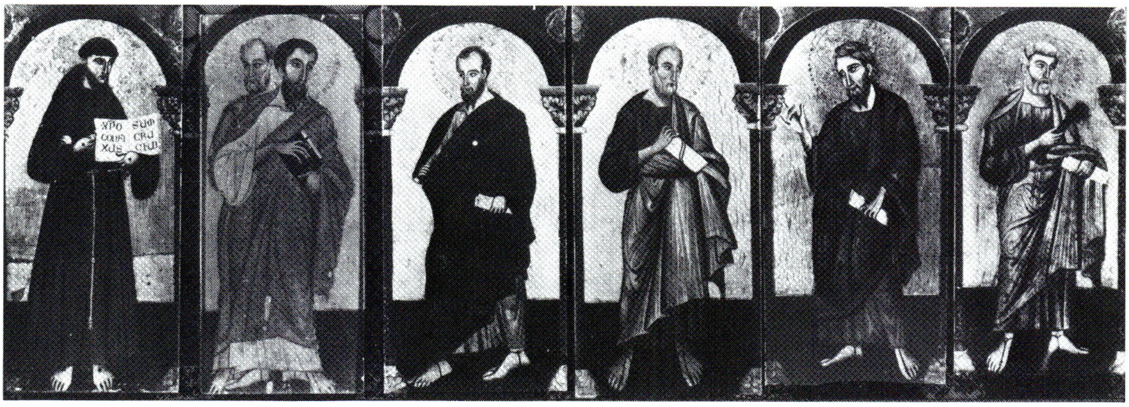

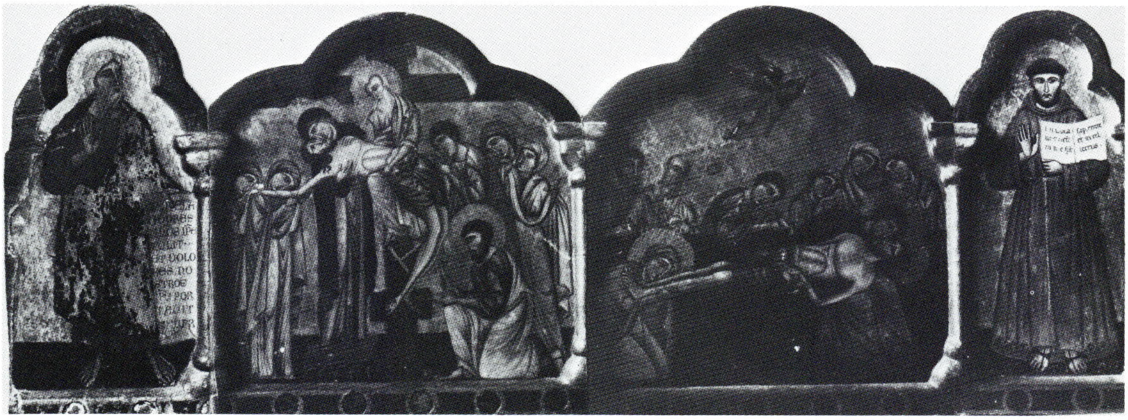

Saviour on the back. But is there any evidence for such double-sided dossals in this period? As it happens, we do know of at least one such dossal. It stood in the church of San Francesco in Perugia (figs. 14, 15), and can be dated ca. 1272.[15] Although it only survives in the form of a few fragments, painstaking reconstruction has yielded an altarpiece which probably had a Madonna and saints on the front, and scenes from the Passion and more saints on the reverse.

We know that there was a tendency in the thirteenth century to focus attention on the high altar, and there is every reason to believe that by the middle of the century both Perugia and Siena had double-sided altarpieces. Both churches had a deep choir, which would have encouraged this development. Liturgical ritual has always been the Sienese way of expressing urban chauvinism. In 1260, when the city was dedicated to the Virgin, the high altar became an ideological focus of that patriotism, and that should always be borne in mind when considering the renovation of the cathedral and its choir. It was not the same story everywhere. In Florence, for example, it was to be another fifty years before a double-sided dossal stood on the high altar, and by then the Sienese had adorned their high altar with the largest and most beautiful altarpiece imaginable: Duccio's *Maestà*.

II

THE ALTARPIECES OF THE URBAN RELIGIOUS ORDERS

Having examined the origins of the earliest forms of painted altarpieces in Siena we must turn our attention to one of the most important sources of artistic patronage in the thirteenth century – the urban religious orders.

The urban oligarchs appreciated the important contribution which monks and friars could make to life in a fast-growing city, and they went to great lengths to create the conditions which would attract them to the community. They financed the building of churches, monasteries and hospitals, became members of lay orders, and supported charitable causes. They also offered financial inducements to the Franciscans to abandon their life as hermits in the countryside around Siena and to settle in the city instead. There are numerous examples of city-dwellers encouraging monks and friars to move within the city walls, for these new orders had something to offer in return. In very general terms, beyond a favourable moral ethic, new forms of worship and the encouragement of charitable donations, the new orders supplied city people with what may justly be called an urban ideology. They spoke the language of the city-dweller. Francis, after all, had been a merchant himself. His preaching of voluntary poverty supplied the necessary spiritual counterweight to the evolving capitalism of urban society.[16]

The main orders in Siena, as elsewhere in Italy, were the Augustinians, Servites, Dominicans, Franciscans and Carmelites. They settled throughout the city, each dominating an area of its own. It has often been suggested that the spectacular rise of Mariolatry in the late middle ages was due to the activities of these new orders. Although it is true that they were largely responsible for shaping the spiritual life of the Sienese, it should not be forgotten that the city's cathedral had long been dedicated to the Virgin, or that Odericus had codified a fervent veneration of the Virgin as early as 1215 in his *Ordo officiorum*. It is quite impossible to say whether one order did more to encourage this Mariolatry than another, as some authors have tried to do. Whether it was the Servites, those 'servants of Blessed Mary', or the Carmelites, whose claim to be the earliest adherents of the Virgin derived from their origins in the Holy Land, all the new orders subscribed to her veneration in one way or another. There is also a widespread misconception that the Franciscans were especial patrons of the visual arts. Heinrich Thode, the great nineteenth-century cultural historian, postulated a specific Franciscan religiosity on the evidence of the vast programme of visual propaganda for St Francis in Assisi, and believed that the Franciscans were responsible for the blossoming of visual art in the thirteenth and fourteenth centuries. Consequently, many an art historian has suffered from a conditioned reflex when confronted with a thirteenth-century Madonna altarpiece, even when the altar in question was situated in a non-Franciscan church.[17] It is true, of course, that St Francis was a far more attractive subject for visual propaganda than St Dominic, as we can see from the many thirteenth-century altarpieces bearing his 'image' and the many fresco series of his 'vita'. However, that does not mean that the Dominicans were any less important as donors of altarpieces. It was often the Franciscans who received the largest donations, and they showed themselves to be wise investors in art, but when other orders could afford to do so they too acted as generous patrons.

The point of this background sketch is to place the Sienese situation in context, for the sad fact is that not a single thirteenth-century altarpiece has survived from the church of San Francesco. This is hardly surprising when one recalls all the disasters which have befallen this church in its long history, but what

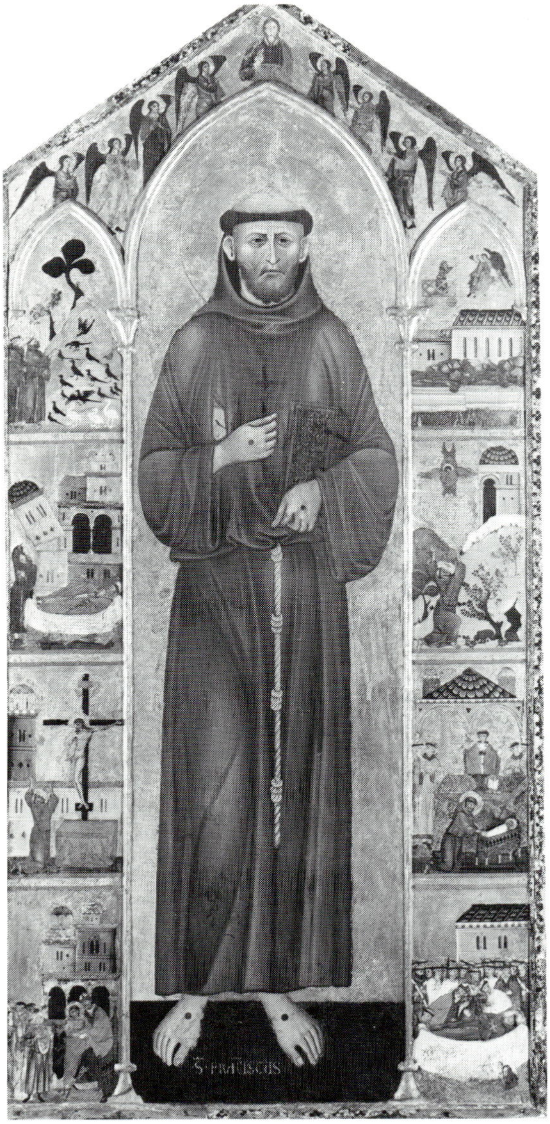

16 Guido da Siena (related to), St Francis, 237 x 113 cm, Pinacoteca Nazionale, Siena.

is more remarkable is that there is not even any documentary evidence that San Francesco ever had an altarpiece to rival Guido da Siena's *Madonna and Child enthroned* on the high altar of San Domenico (fig. 24). Nor is St Francis particularly common among the saints on dossals. We know of just one altarpiece with St Francis from the Sienese region (fig. 16), but then there is also a thirteenth-century panel of St Dominic from Siena (fig. 17), even if the saint has had three facelifts in the intervening centuries.[18]

In the fifteenth-century Servite church, which is dedicated to the Virgin, there is a Baroque chapel with a thirteenth-century Madonna above the altar (fig. 18). It was clearly executed for the original high altar, and was moved to the chapel at a later date. The inscription on the frame reads: MCCLXI. COPP' D'FLORĒNTIA MEPIX̄ ('1261. Coppo of Florence painted me.'). The painter in question is Coppo di Marcovaldo, and the reason why he is referred to as 'de Florentia' could be that he had been taken prisoner by the Sienese at the battle of Montaperti. He had enlisted in the Florentine army as a shield-bearer, like his colleague Meliore, so there were evidently some rugged specimens among the Florentine artists of the time. The Servites in Siena turned his misfortune to their advantage and commissioned him to paint this Madonna for their church. It later became known as the *Madonna del bordone* from a pilgrim's staff which had been placed near the panel, either in fulfilment of a vow or as a sign of gratitude for grace received.[19]

The *Madonna del bordone* fills the entire picture surface. The effect of breadth and monumentality is due largely to the deep, extravagant folds of the drapery. Coppo had had every opportunity to study Byzantine models when he had been working on the vault of the Baptistery in Florence, but by comparison this Madonna reflects a feeling for monumental grandeur which might even be regarded as a coarsening of more refined Byzantine models. The sensitive modelling of the faces cannot possibly date from 1261 (cf. fig. 23), and this has been confirmed by X-ray examination, which shows that they have been overpainted within the original contours. A few years later Coppo painted a *Madonna and Child enthroned* for the Servites of Orvieto (fig. 19). Unfortunately it has been discovered that this Madonna's face has also been repainted, and at a far later date. Although this renders any direct comparison invalid it nevertheless remains a fact that the two altarpieces are strikingly similar.

The overpainting of the faces in the *Madonna del bordone* is rightly assumed to date from the beginning of the fourteenth century. Modelling has softened the hard, linear schemata of 1261 in a manner characteristic of Duccio and his pupils. It is believed that this kind of overpainting (another example is the face of St Dominic in the Fogg Museum) indicates a stylistic awareness on the part of patrons around 1300, and even of an 'awareness between two stylistic eras'.[20] I think that we must tread very carefully here if we are not to fall into the simplistic trap of projecting our own stylistic categories onto the past. It was a question not so much of style but of function. If it was felt that a Madonna was no longer satisfactory as a devotional image steps were taken to bring her up to date. It was in that sense alone that 'beauty' was a criterion. Sometimes she was given a new layer of paint to adapt her to a new religious sentiment, but

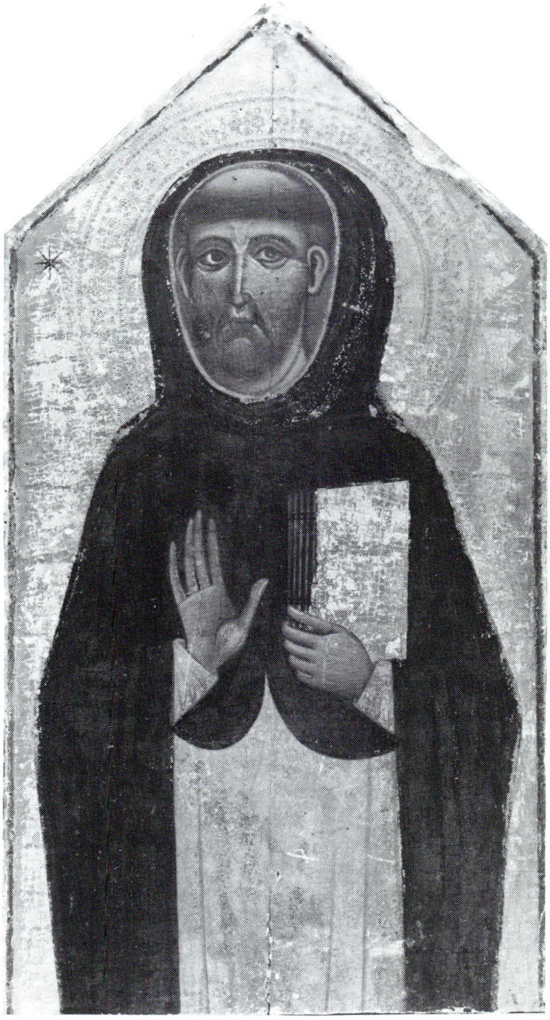

17 Sienese 13th century, St Dominic 116.5 x 62 cm, Fogg Art Museum, Cambridge (Mass.).

occasionally she was simply replaced, as on the high altar of Siena cathedral.

What, though, was the origin of this type of vertical altarpiece with the Madonna enthroned? It is tempting to think that it was a statue of the Madonna projected onto a plane surface, were it not for the fact that there are other Madonnas which are far more obviously two-dimensional representations of a three-dimensional image. In some of them the Virgin's head actually encroaches on the frame, as if she were trying to escape from her rectangular prison. There is a fascinating altarpiece by Coppo di Marcovaldo in Santa Maria Maggiore in Florence which really is a statue mounted on a panel (fig. 20). The decorative work is painted, as is the theological commentary in the scenes below the Madonna. Christ's presence as the Redeemer on his mother's lap is matched by the scene of the Virgin overshadowed by the Holy Ghost at the Annunciation. The Resurrection is represented by the customary scene of the women at the empty tomb. These scenes have the added function of raising the Madonna physically above the liturgical objects on the altar. The prophets below the throne in Cimabue's famous *Madonna* for the high altar of Santa Trinità have exactly the same dual purpose. The *Madonna del bordone* clearly does not belong to this tradition of the painted Madonna sculpture located high up in the picture surface.

Another possibility is that the visual type, but not the style, of Coppo's two Servite Madonnas was modelled directly on a Byzantine prototype. Might there be an eastern precedent for this type of altarpiece? Any attempt to answer this question is complicated by the fact that most Byzantine paintings either belonged to iconostases or were made for private devotion. The east had a different liturgical tradition, which is why there was no development of the altarpiece comparable to that which took place in Italy. As it happens, though, there are two Madonnas which are as closely related as the two by Coppo. They have convincingly been attributed to Byzantine masters working in Tuscany in the 1280s (fig. 21, 22).[21] We know virtually nothing about their provenance beyond the fact that they represent a type of altarpiece whose closest relatives are Coppo's two Madonnas in Siena and Orvieto.

It is clear from the two Servite Madonnas that donors could be quite specific about the type of painting they wanted. The commission for Orvieto evidently resulted from contact between the friars, who asked Coppo to paint a Madonna similar to the one in Siena. There is a growing belief that chapter meetings of the mendicant orders were important 'transfer points' of visual art. Just as the Servites sent Coppo from Siena to Orvieto to execute a second Madonna, so fifty years later the Dominicans brought Simone Martini from Pisa to Orvieto to paint polyptychs. It is even possible that the Servites, who travelled more extensively than artists did, actually gave the captive Coppo the model for his Sienese altarpiece.

The *Madonna del bordone* has always been regarded as having a major influence on Sienese art, particularly by those who attribute Sienese advances to Florentine artists. However, careful comparison with Sienese Madonnas of the period reveals such remarkable differences as to make one doubt whether Coppo had any influence at all. Let us compare Coppo's Madonna with one of the most important Sienese altarpieces of the period (fig. 23), which was apparently executed in 1262 for a confraternity of the Holy Virgin, according to a record of the original inscrip-

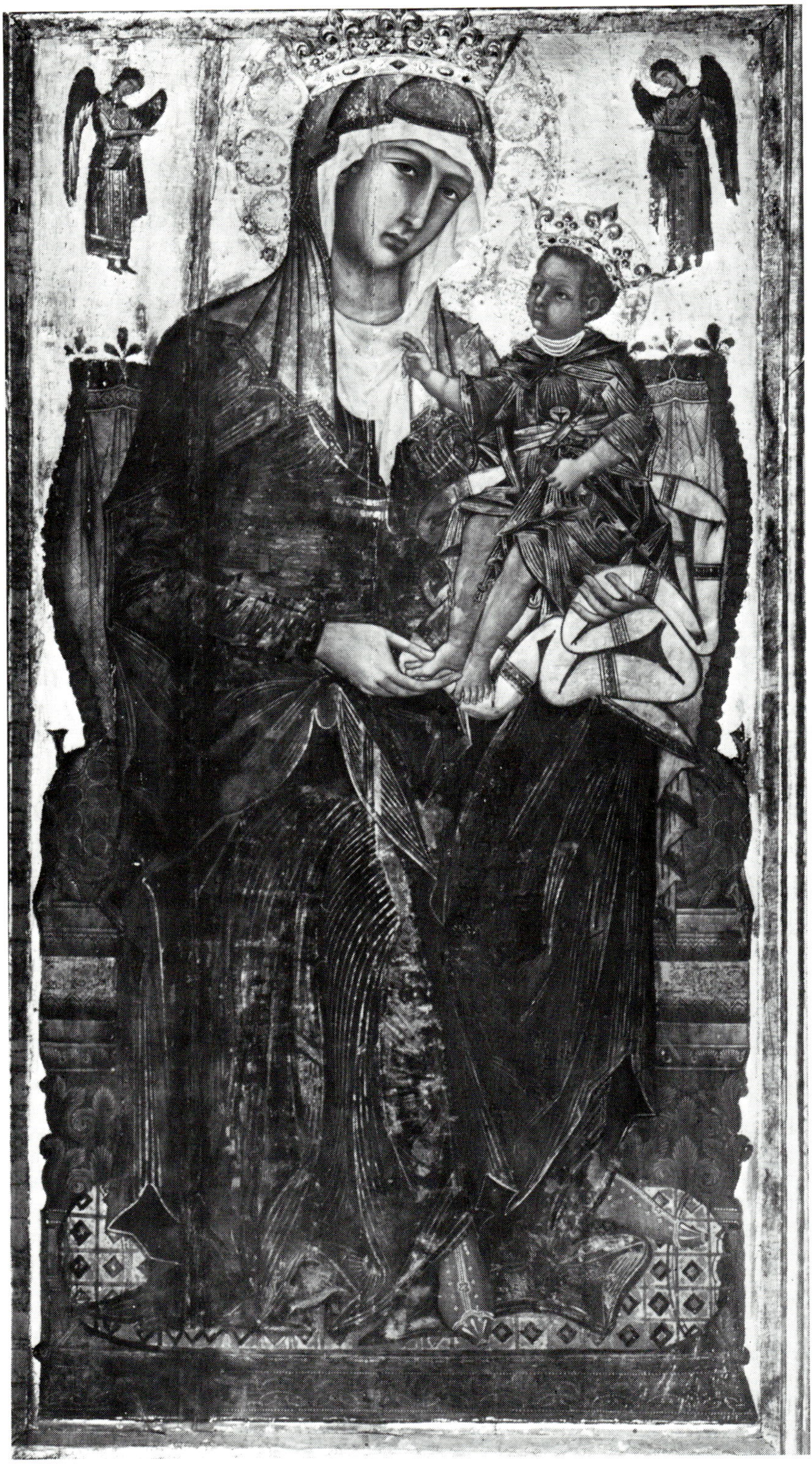

18 Coppo di Marcovaldo, 'Madonna del Bordone', 225 x 125 cm, S. Maria dei Servi, Siena.

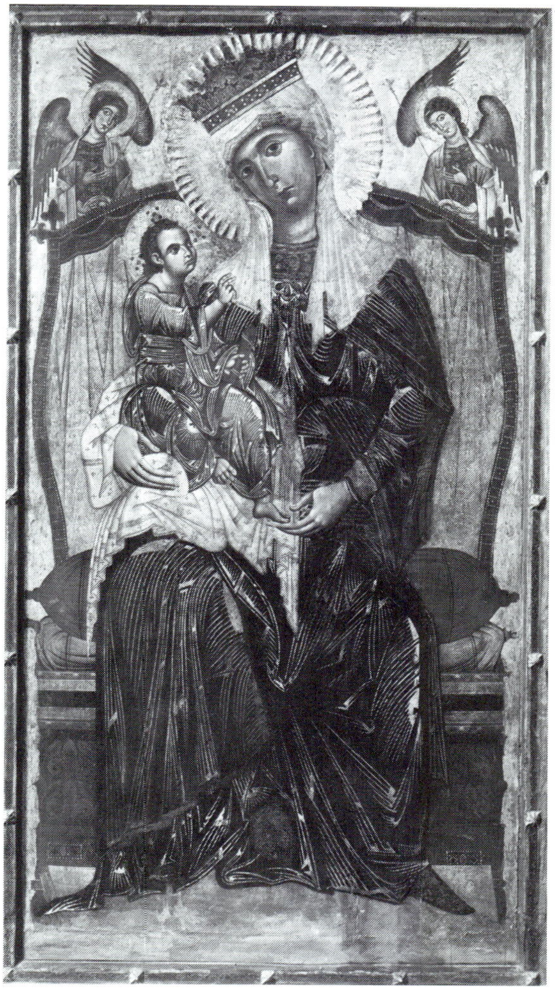

19 Coppo di Marcovaldo, Madonna, 238 x 135 cm, S. Maria dei Servi, Orvieto.

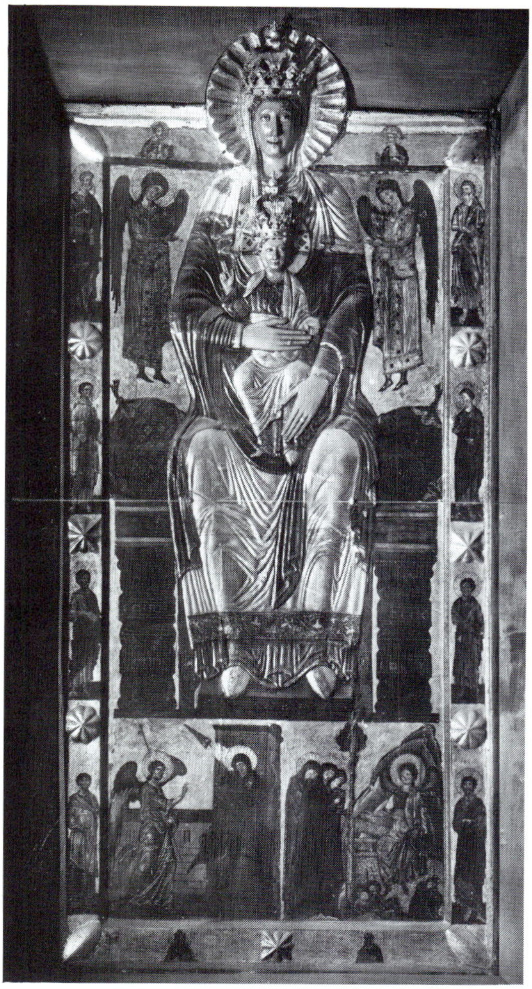

20 Coppo di Marcovaldo, Madonna, 250 x 123 cm, S. Maria Maggiore, Florence.

tion. That inscription was lost when the Madonna was severely cut down. Almost every Sienese Madonna of the period has two iconographic features which are lacking in the *Madonna del bordone*. The confraternity's Madonna is pointing at her Child (see also figs. 9-11), whereas Coppo's is holding its foot. The latter motif is not found at all in the group of Madonnas attributed to Guido. The back of the Madonna's throne is invariably rounded in Sienese paintings of this period. This is not the case in Coppo's altarpieces, with the singular exception of the Orvieto Madonna (fig. 19).

There are also major stylistic differences in the figure of the Virgin. The Sienese favoured slender Madonnas; the breadth of the figure comes from the way in which the robe falls open by the right arm, for which there was a mandatory, angular stencil. In Coppo the flaring of the garment is an integral part of the overall pattern of folds. The blanket on which the Child is seated is also totally different. In the *Madonna del bordone* it looks like a semi-inflated airbed, contrasting sharply with the more natural arrangement in the confraternity's Madonna.

Comparison shows that we are dealing with two very different approaches to Byzantine art. These differences cannot be explained by assuming that the Sienese Madonna is a schematic derivation of Coppo's Servite Madonna. Sienese art had its own sources to draw on, as we saw with the *St John antependium*, and there is really nothing to support the contention that Coppo, the Florentine prisoner-of-war, was the great innovator of Sienese art.

If we are to judge solely by the surviving works of

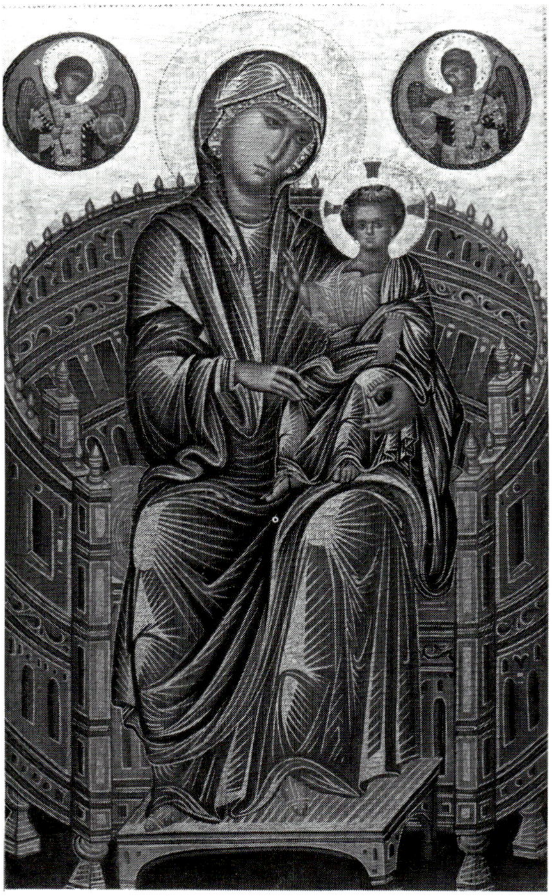

21 Byzantine school 13th century, Madonna, 81.5 x 49 cm, National Gallery, Washington (D.C.).

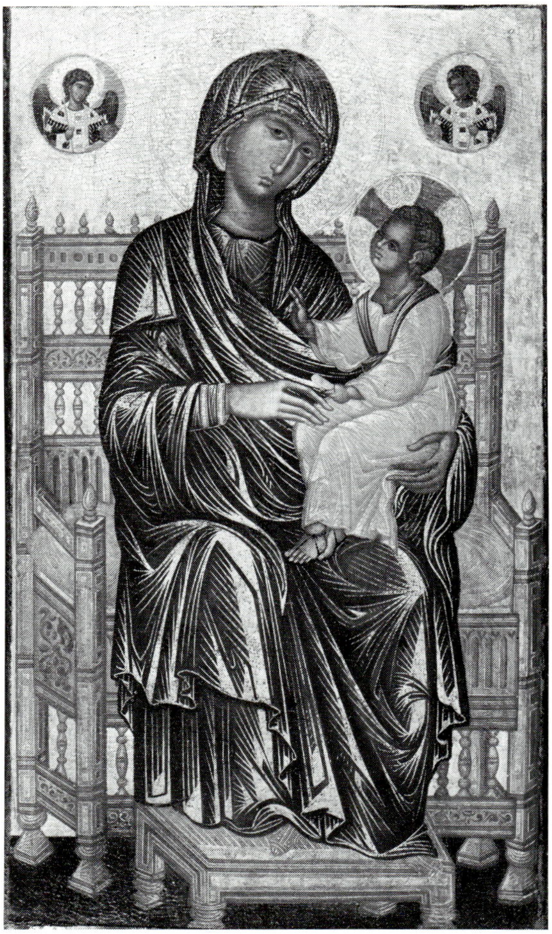

22 Byzantine school 13th century, Madonna, 131 x 77 cm, National Gallery, Washington (D.C.).

thirteenth-century Sienese art we can only conclude that the Dominicans were far and away the most important donors. One impressive example of their patronage is a *Madonna and Child enthroned* which seems to have been commissioned for the high altar of the church of San Domenico. It is now in the Palazzo Pubblico (fig. 24). Once again, the Madonna's original appearance has been obliterated in the interests of modernising a cherished image. The retouching, which was again done in Duccio's day, not only affected the faces and the Madonna's inner veil. It is now generally believed that the lower structure of the throne, the footstool and the inscription are also later modifications. The original inscription was probably on the frame, and when it was transferred to the painting it was made to fit into a field for which it was never intended. It reads: ME GUIDO DE SENIS DIEBUS DEPINXIT AMENIS: QUEM X̄R̄S̄ LENIS NULUS VELIT ĀGERE PENIS ANO. D.M.CCXXI ('Guido da Siena painted me in the delectable days; may the gentle Christ spare him all punishment, AD 1221').

The date 1221 caused great excitement, of course. If it was correct it made Siena not only the source of the Madonna altarpiece as such (a question which was of little interest to art historians until quite recently), but also the birthplace of a new form of painting which Florence only adopted several decades later. Many Florentinocentric art historians simply ignored the painting (or dismissed the date as a forgery), while the partisans of Siena jubilantly proclaimed the primacy of their city. However, this meant that they had to gloss over or even contradict known facts about the history of Sienese art. Fortunately recent research has provided a way out of this awkward problem.[22] The explanation hinges on the fact that 1221 was the year in which St Dominic died, and that naturally made it an extremely important

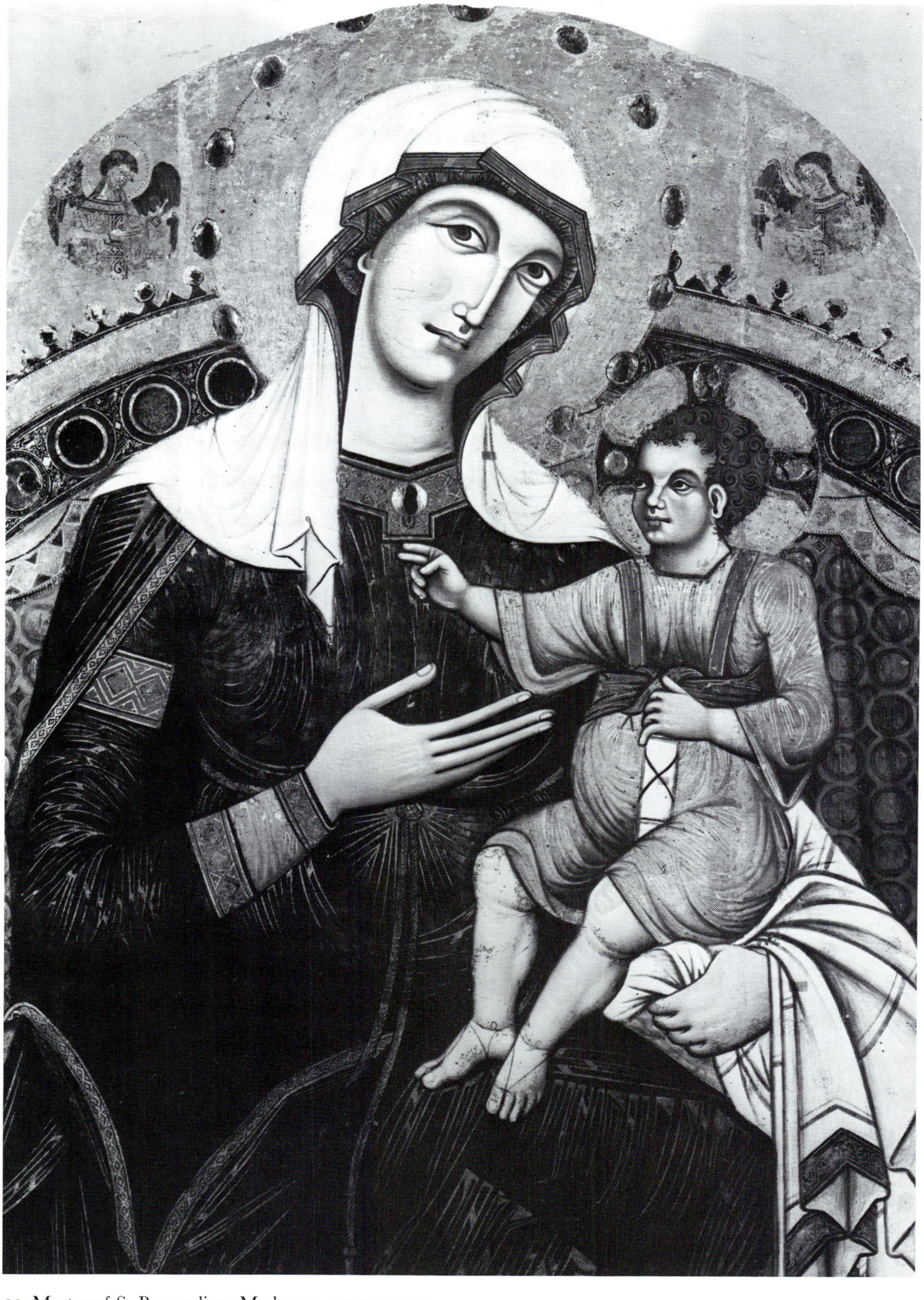

23 Master of S. Bernardino, Madonna, 142 x 100 cm, 1362, Pinacoteca Nazionale, Siena.

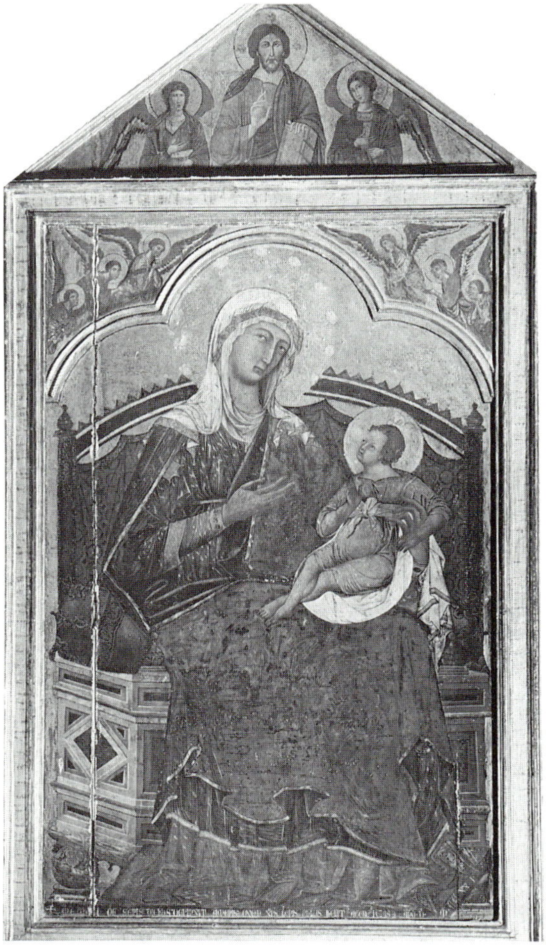

24 Guido da Siena, 'Palazzo Pubblico Madonna', 283 x 194 cm, Pinacoteca Nazionale, Siena.

date in the Dominican calendar. The inclusion of that date on the painting immediately associated the image with the origin of the order. The same date also appears in an inscription accompanying frescoes which Tommaso da Modena executed in 1352 in the Dominican chapter house at Treviso, and there too its purpose was to link these portraits of eminent Dominicans with this important event in the order's history. The Siena painting is an excellent illustration of the role which donors could play. Their pious wishes led to an antedating which would have made this painting virtually the earliest Madonna altarpiece in existence. However, it is clear from the areas which have not been retouched that the painting should properly be dated ca. 1270-80.

The date was not the only reason why Guido's Madonna became an art-historical conversation piece. Attempts to reconstruct a composite work with the Madonna as the centrepiece also aroused considerable interest. The evidence for side panels comes from a famous description written in the early sixteenth century. It was believed that some of those lateral scenes could be identified with twelve paintings which are now dispersed over various collections but which were still together in a monastery near Siena in the nineteenth century. However, that would leave another twelve scenes to be found, and there are many who believe (and rightly so) that this is a highly implausible suggestion. In their opinion the existing scenes originally belonged with a smaller Madonna which has since been lost (fig. 25). Two of the panels lack the upper left and right corner respectively, which has led to the suggestion that the full altarpiece was surmounted by an elongated triangular pediment, a specimen of which is known from Guido's workshop (fig. 26).[23]

Did Guido's Madonna ever have side panels at all? The sixteenth-century description is quite explicit on this point, but how reliable is it as a source? It has been argued that the broad frame of the *Madonna and Child enthroned* would have precluded side panels, but we known that the pediment above the Madonna, showing Christ Logos flanked by angels, has been part of the altarpiece from the very beginning. Apart from anything else, the vertical seams between the planks of the pediment exactly match those on the Madonna panel. Moreover, there are Madonnas from other parts of Italy which combine a robust frame with lateral scenes from Christ's life, Passion and glorification (fig. 27). So there may well have been panels flanking Guido's Madonna, although it may no longer be possible to identify them. A detailed technical examination of the edges of the panel might help to clarify the issue. The important point as far as the history of the Sienese altarpiece is concerned is that there is every reason to believe that enthroned Madonnas appeared in combination with scenes from the life of Christ. In other words, Sienese painting adhered to the traditional visual programme found in such sculptures as the *Madonna of Alatri* (fig. 6).

One of the most striking features of Guido's *Madonna and Child enthroned* is its size. It is far larger than Coppo's altarpiece; indeed it is a huge work for its period. The iconography follows that of the Madonna commissioned by the Marian confraternity (fig. 23). The prominent cusped arch framing the group of Mother and Child relegates the adoring angels to the spandrels, where they serve as decorative cornerpieces, with their colourful outspread wings. The pediment with Christ Logos and two angels is an interesting iconographic feature. It is a visual device formerly found on crucifixes, many of which had a cimasa at the top with the figure of a glorified Christ

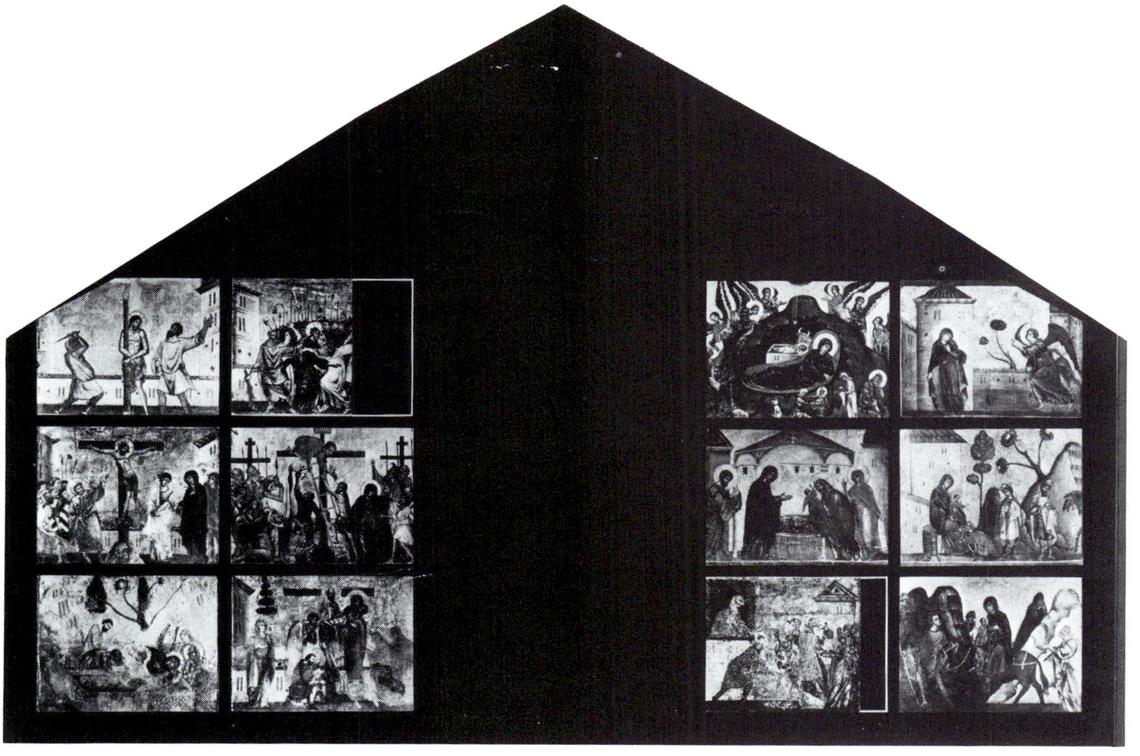

25 Guida da Siena, Scenes from the infancy and passion of Christ (reconstruction after Ressort, 1978).

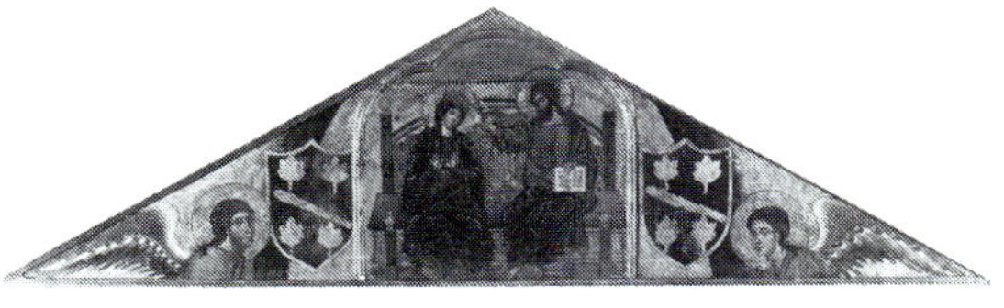

26 Guido da Siena, Coronation of the Virgin, 56 x 164 cm, Courtauld Gallery, London.

raised above earthly time (fig. 28). Below he appears in his chosen guise on earth: the Redeemer on the Cross. That visual sequence has here been applied to a Madonna altarpiece, and should be interpreted as Christ, the Word, appearing on earth as Jesus, the son of Mary. That visual coupling was fully in accord with liturgical thinking, which predicated a direct link between the Incarnation and the Eucharist.

The Augustinians of San Gimignano were evidently so impressed by Guido's altarpiece for the high altar of San Domenico that they commissioned another artist to produce a similar but smaller Madonna for their church (fig. 29). It is not known whether this second Madonna had side panels. It was extensively overpainted towards the end of the seventeenth century, and the greater part of the pediment was sawn off. The original paint layers were removed from the areas to be retouched, and when the panel was restored it was discovered that only the

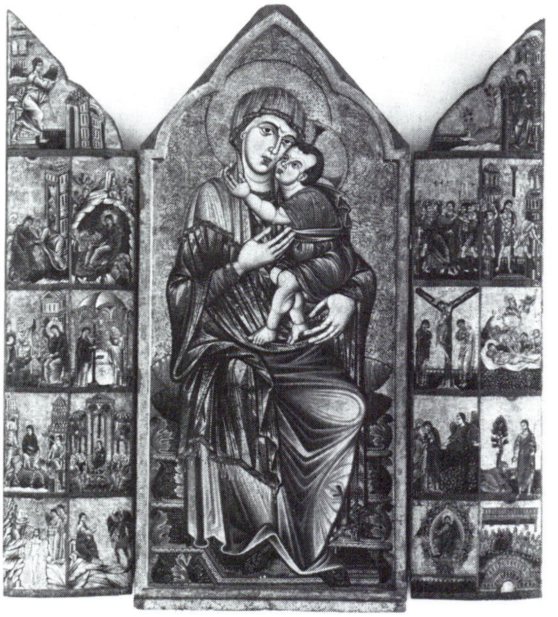

27 Umbrian school, Madonna with scenes from the infancy and passion of Christ, 215 x 95 cm, Galleria Nazionale dell'Umbria, Perugia.

flesh tones of the original faces remained. Fortunately the painting was mounted in a wide frame, so everything beneath the frame was preserved, including two figures below the throne – a bishop and an Augustinian nun with a halo. Carli has identified the

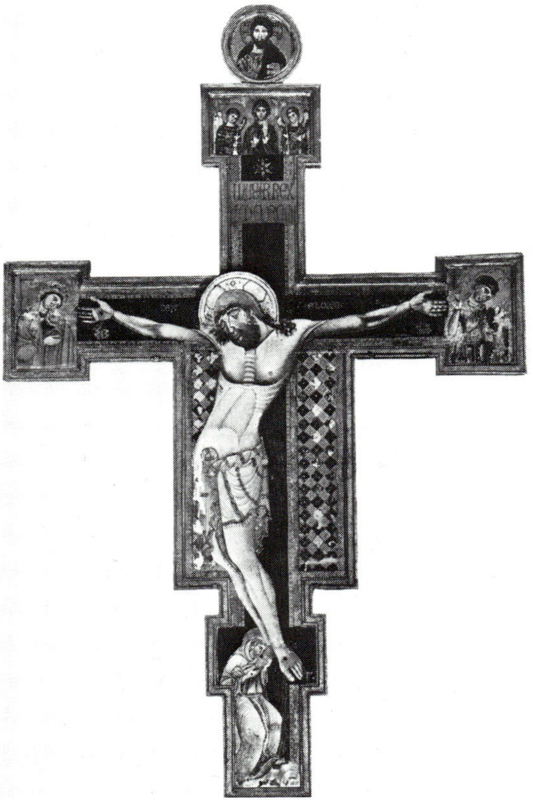

28 St Francis Master, Crucifix, 575 x 370 cm, S. Francesco, Arezzo.

nun as Giuliana da Imola.[24] They were clearly not the donors of the altarpiece, but figures venerated by the local Augustinians who could intercede on behalf of the order with Christ and his Mother. This painting is an important document in several respects. In the first place it tells us that Guido's altarpiece was regarded as a yardstick in his own day. In other words, that is not just our opinion projected backwards on the basis of only a fraction of the paintings that existed at the time. This Madonna would be inconceivable without the San Domenico altarpiece. Secondly, the areas which have been preserved are precisely those which have been lost in Guido's work. For instance, we now know the original form of the Virgin's throne. The Child is depicted far more naturalistically, with a far greater suppleness and freedom in the pose and without the tortuously entwined legs of the San Domenico altarpiece. This helps us to understand the transition from Guido's altarpiece to later Madonnas. The artist also adopted the visual device of Christ Logos above the Virgin. The frames which separate the various areas in the San Domenico Madonna have made way for painted borders, and the cusped arch is now a credible architectural element in that it springs from painted colonettes. This Madonna is an excellent illustration of a phenomenon which runs throughout Sienese painting, namely that altarpieces in the *contado* reflect the art of the city.

Another supremely important Dominican contribution to the development of the thirteenth-century Sienese altarpiece was the commission for Duccio's *Rucellai Madonna* (fig. 30), which came from a Dominican confraternity in Florence. The urban orders used confraternities of this kind to organise the religious activities of the laity. Duccio's patron on this occasion was the Laudesi confraternity, which had been founded to combat heresy and was thus closely involved in Dominican policy. Its members had various liturgical duties, including 'the performance of daily praises of Christ and the Blessed Virgin'. They acquired the name Laudesi from the singing of Lauds, and their altarpiece became known as the *Rucellai Madonna* from its later location near the chapel of the Rucellai family. Here, for the first time, we actually have a contract between the donors and the artist.

The leaders of the Society of the Holy Virgin 'assigned to Duccio di Buoninsegna, the painter of Siena, for painting with the most beautiful picture a certain large panel.' He was 'to paint the said panel and to adorn it with the image of the Blessed Virgin Mary and her omnipotent Son and other figures, in accordance with the wishes and pleasure of the said commissioners, and to gild it, and to do each and every thing which will contribute to the beauty of the said panel...'.[25] It was also agreed that Duccio would do the work for a fixed price. The first thing we learn from this document is that Duccio was expected to paint a panel which the donors would supply. We do not know whether he was consulted on the shape and dimensions of the altarpiece, but it seems more likely that the donors and their carpenter were responsible for its monumental scale and balanced proportions.

Nowadays art historians are beginning to take a very close interest in the purely physical aspects of early Italian paintings. Any study of the development of altarpieces has to take into account the form and workmanship of the panels on which they are painted. Art historians, by the very nature of their profession, are accustomed to thinking of art history as the history of innovative artists, and it is probably for this reason that they tend to assume that any innovations in the form or workmanship of the support are due to the artist's creativity. The contract between Duccio and the Laudesi should serve as a salutary warning.[26] The document also specifies the general content of the altarpiece; it was to be a

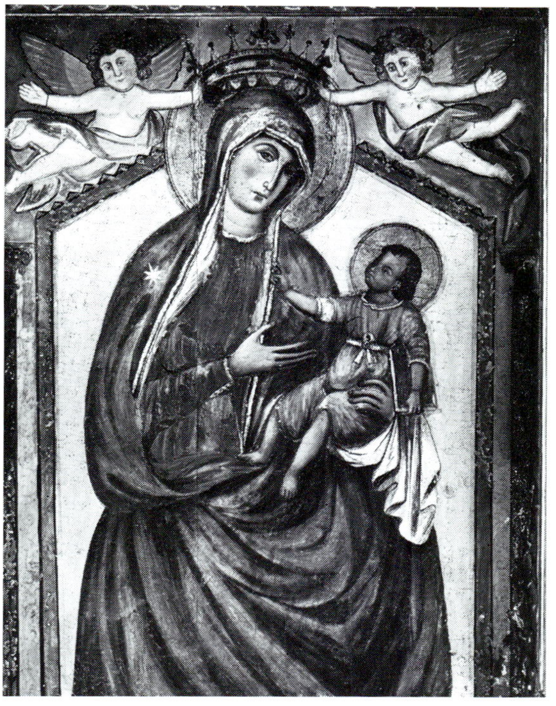
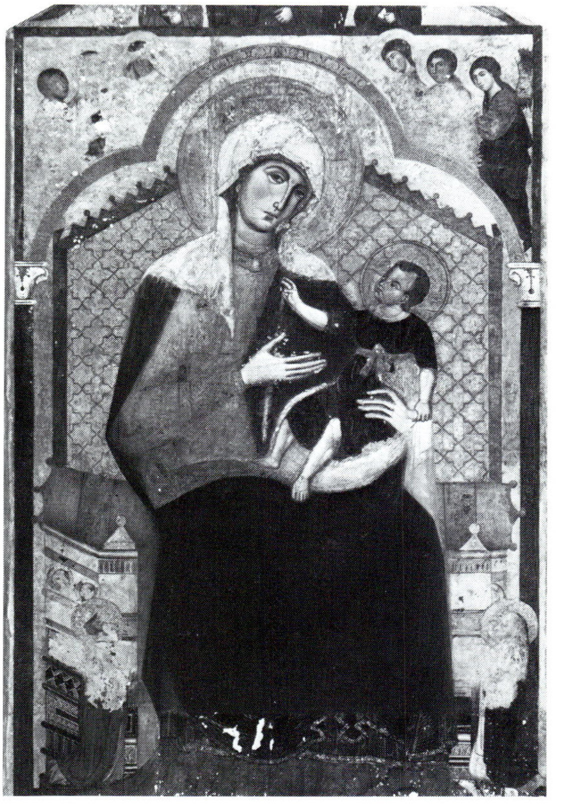

29 Guido da Siena (follower of), Madonna, 170 x 134 cm (a: before restoration, b: after restoration) Palazzo Comunale, San Gimignano.

Madonna. It also allows for further consultation between artist and donors. Gilding and beauty are mentioned in the same breath, illustrating the fact that the appreciation of beauty was directly associated with material value. The reasoning was that the costliness of a painting, its golden sheen, set the soul on the road to higher things. That is why many such contracts specify the amount and quality of the gold to be used and list certain expensive pigments, such as ultramarine.

The *Rucellai Madonna* is far larger than any of the altarpieces discussed so far. The wide, heavy frame was clearly designed to hold this large object together. One would automatically assume that a painting of this size would have stood on the high altar of Santa Maria Novella, were it not for the fact that the donors had their own chapel in the transept. Was it made for that altar? At one time it was thought that the Laudesi could not possibly have commissioned such a large altarpiece, and that as a result it was not the painting referred to in the contract and was therefore not by Duccio at all. That view has now been abandoned. There is a widespread assumption that it stood in the Laudesi chapel, and a number of convenient but rather weak arguments derived from the chapel frescoes have been advanced in support.[27] However, this is to overlook the possibility that the confraternity paid for a painting for the high altar, which is still the most likely location for a work of this size. As already mentioned, the Laudesi were a confraternity dedicated to furthering the principal aims of the Dominicans, so one should not automatically rule out the possibility that they paid for a painting to adorn the high altar. After all, there were many other paintings on high altars which had been commissioned by private individuals, such as the *Madonna in majesty* by Duccio's pupil, Segna di Bonaventura, which was made for the Collegiata of Castiglion Fiorentino (fig. 31). The pious donors not only figure in that painting, but are actually named. However, even if Duccio's monumental Madonna did adorn the high altar its radiance would not have fallen on the faithful entering Santa Maria Novella, for the nave was separated from the rest of the church by a rood screen. No matter what painting stood on the high altar, it was almost always hidden from the congregation.[28]

As we have seen, a Madonna on a single picture surface with a wide frame and a pedimental top was not unusual in Sienese art. Florence would have provided Duccio with examples of angels clustered around a throne, as in Cimabue's painting for the

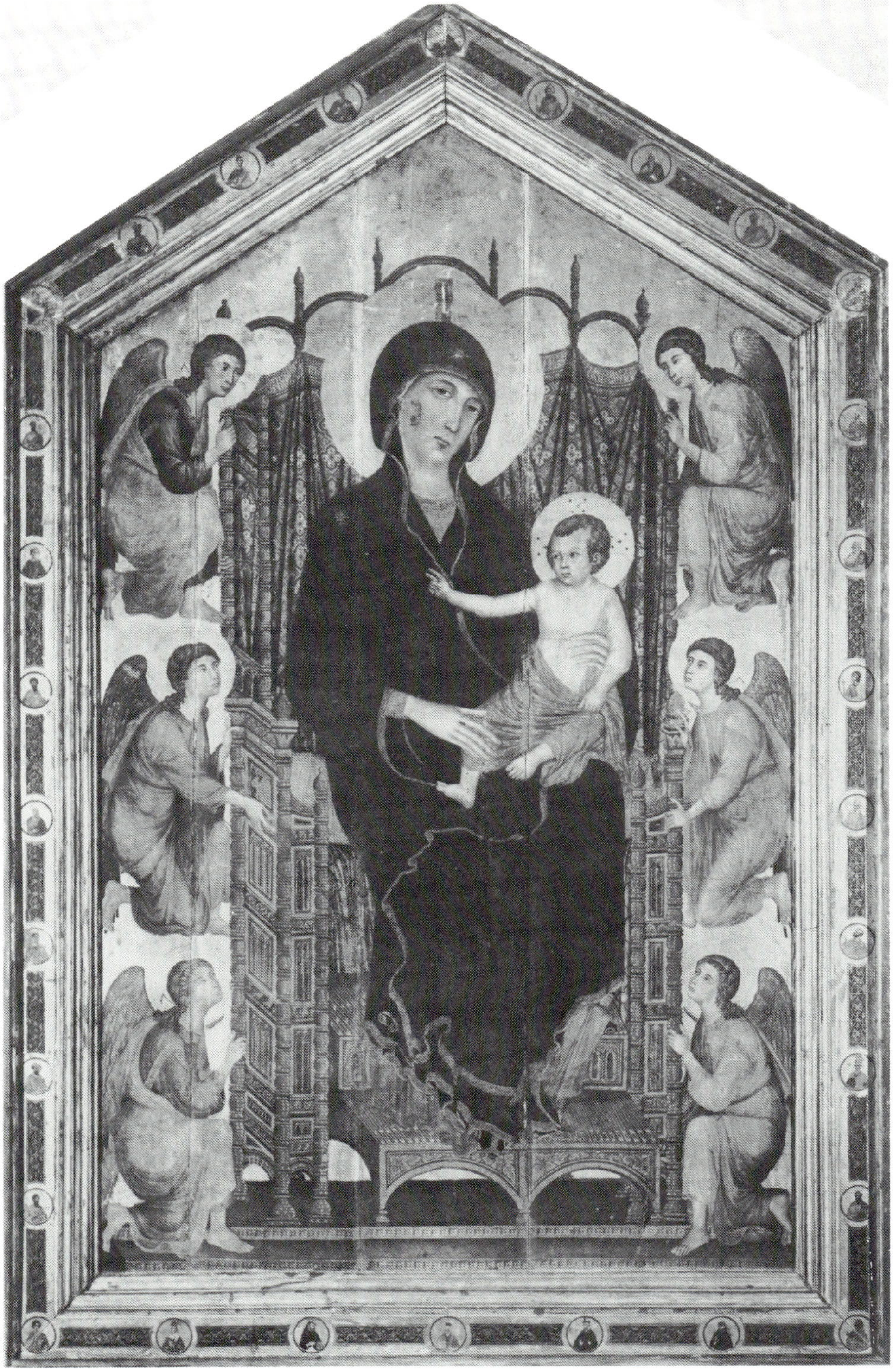

30 Duccio, 'Rucellai Madonna', 450 x 290 cm, 1285, Galleria degli Uffizi, Florence.

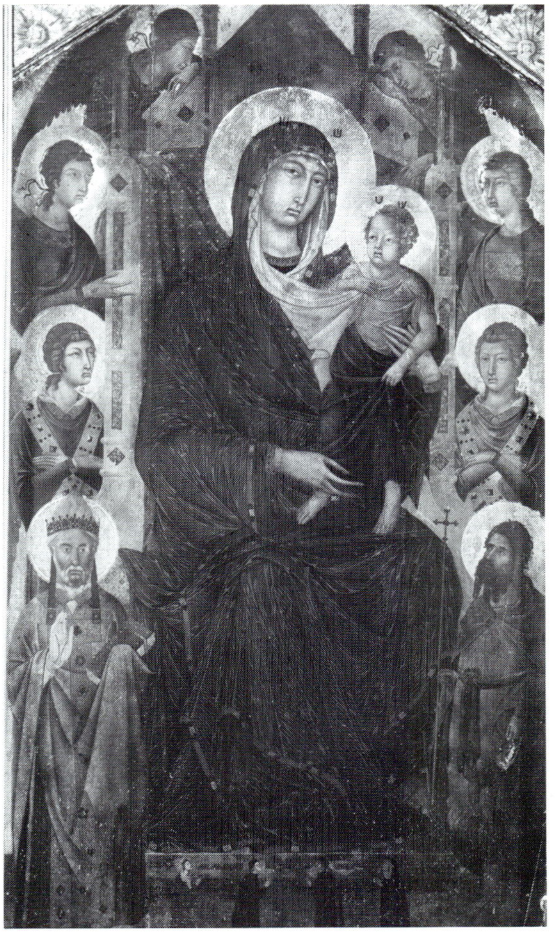

31 Segna di Bonaventura, Madonna with donors, 244 x 140 cm, Collegiata di S. Giuliano, Castiglion Fiorentino.
32 Cimabue, Madonna with St Francis, Lower church of S. Francesco, Assisi.

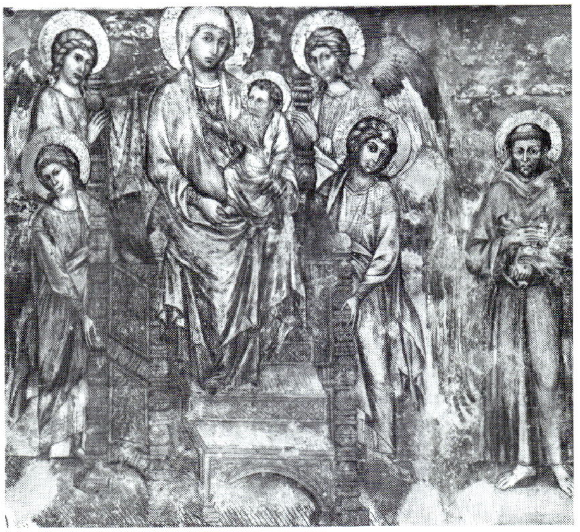

high altar of Santa Trinità, which probably predates the *Rucellai Madonna* by a few years. Cimabue's work is still very sculptural, with its tall, narrow format and the grouping of the figures within the picture surface. The Madonna of the Laudesi represents a new departure, not only because it is relatively broad, but also because of the way in which the artist has deliberately exploited that width, filling it with the broad throne, the figures of the Madonna and Child, who are sitting almost side by side, and the angels kneeling against the gold ground. They have been reclaimed from the spandrels they occupied in Guido's altarpieces, and now surround the Madonna in majesty, creating an atmosphere of glorification and worship. To a certain extent the wooden throne can be regarded as an extremely elaborate variant of the thrones presented in side view in earlier altarpieces. However, there are no precedents in the Sienese tradition for the open lower structure and the footstool, which elevate the Madonna to the centre of the picture surface. For these elements we must turn to Assisi, where Cimabue painted his famous fresco of the *Madonna and Child with angels and St Francis* around 1280 (fig. 32).

There is, of course, far more to the *Rucellai Madonna* than its size alone. It is a painting in which Duccio, 'pictor de Senis' as the contract calls him, transformed the youthful artistic tradition of his city. We need only recall the angular arrangement of the drapery in earlier works, and the striations used to suggest folds. It is as if Duccio is freeing the forms, movements and attitudes from the rigid programmes in which they had been frozen. What was once stiff and unyielding has been transformed into flowing movement. The relationship between the Mother and Child is unremarkable. The traditional structure can still be discerned in their faces, but it has been softened by subtle modelling. The new plasticity and freedom are seen to best effect in the clothing of the Christ Child. He is still making the traditional gesture of the Saviour, but the robe he wears as Christ Logos has slipped. It now hangs loosely around his waist, revealing a thin, delicately depicted undergarment. The present state of the painting prevents us from fully appreciating one feature which must have been particularly impressive at the time. The harsh, contrasting colours of the past have given way to subtly balanced, tender shades like mid-blue, rose-pink and a pinkish lavender. As far as one can judge from the present surface of the painting, Duccio introduced a completely new palette which imparted great sensitivity and decorative beauty to the scene.

It could be said that thirteenth-century Sienese painting reached its peak with the *Rucellai Madonna*.

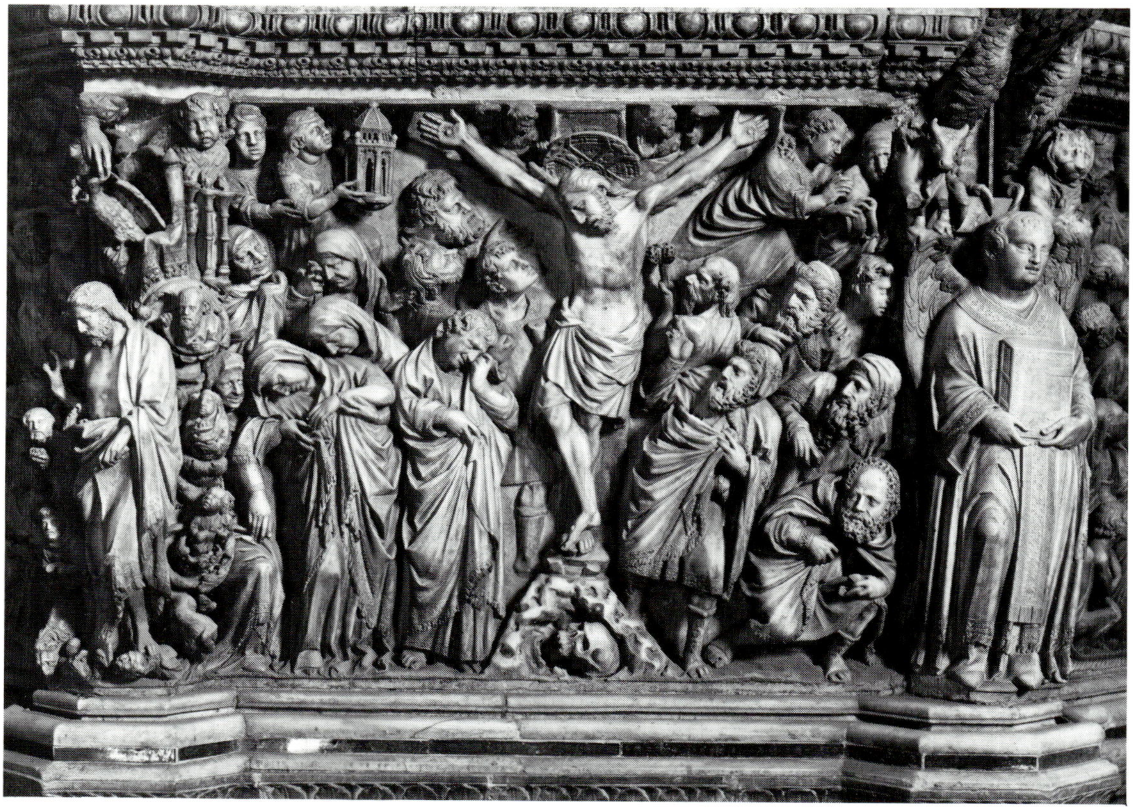

33 Nicola and Giovanni Pisano, Crucifixion panel on the pulpit, Duomo, Siena.

The difficulty is explaining exactly how it came about. We know almost nothing about Duccio's work before the *Rucellai Madonna*. The small *Madonna of the Franciscans* and the so-called *Crevole Madonna* (fig. 34) are the only works which are generally regarded as early. Even allowing for the give and take in the relationship with Cimabue there is a fundamental difference between the plastic and sculptural organisation of the Santa Trinità Madonna and the decorative composition of the Laudesi altarpiece. Is it a question of a happy interaction between Byzantine and Gothic art? We must not overlook the influence of the sculptors Nicola and Giovanni Pisano. Their pulpit had been standing in Siena cathedral since 1268 (fig. 33), and the mass of impressive sculpture which they had executed for the facade of the cathedral must also have had an effect on local artists. The figures and drapery of their statues have the same suppleness of movement we find in the *Rucellai Madonna*, and also the same expressiveness and sensibility. However, one is immediately struck by the very direct link with Byzantine art in the saints and Old Testament figures at the edge of the frame of the *Rucellai Madonna*. It is therefore better to think not in terms of an interaction between Byzantine and Gothic art, but of a specifically Sienese development of Byzantine art in which familiarity with such works as the Pisani sculptures may well have played a vital role.

The significance of the *Rucellai Madonna* for the development of the altarpiece becomes apparent when we compare it with Cimabue's altarpiece of 1301 for San Francesco in Pisa (fig. 36). The donors or the artist (or both) quite clearly preferred the *Rucellai Madonna* type of painting and frame to the far narrower type represented by Cimabue's Santa Trinità Madonna. It is a question of content as much as form. Duccio's work had evidently become a compositional model. The only difference in the Pisan altarpiece is that the angels are no longer kneeling ethereally on either side of the throne, but have come down to earth. Only very early altarpieces have angels floating against the gold ground (cf. figs. 1, 21).

All Duccio's commissions for altarpieces prior to his *Maestà* came from the Dominicans and their followers. He painted an altarpiece for Perugia's church of San Domenico of which the Madonna survives (fig. 37). There is another altarpiece attributed to the artist in the Pinacoteca in Siena (fig. 38). Its provenance is unknown, but since it has St Dom-

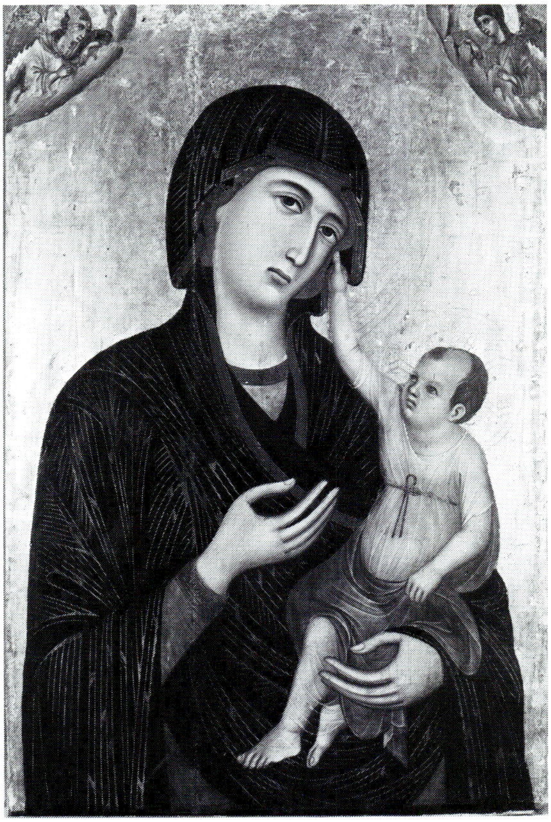

34 Duccio, 'Crevole Madonna', 89 x 60 cm, Museo dell'Opera del Duomo, Siena.

35 Duccio, 'Rucellai Madonna', framing (detail).

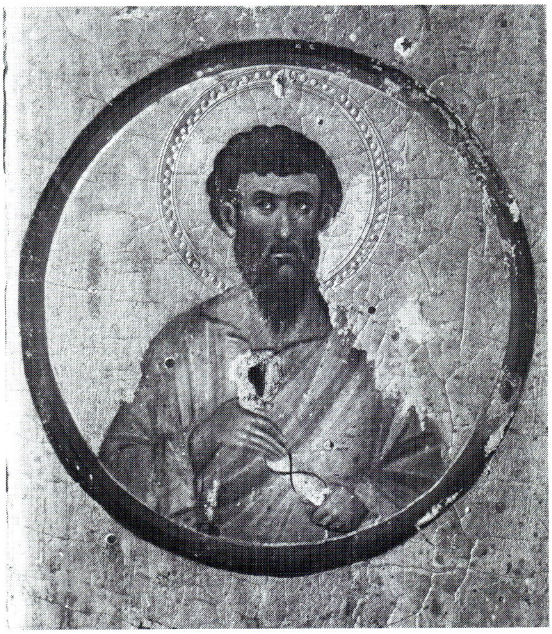

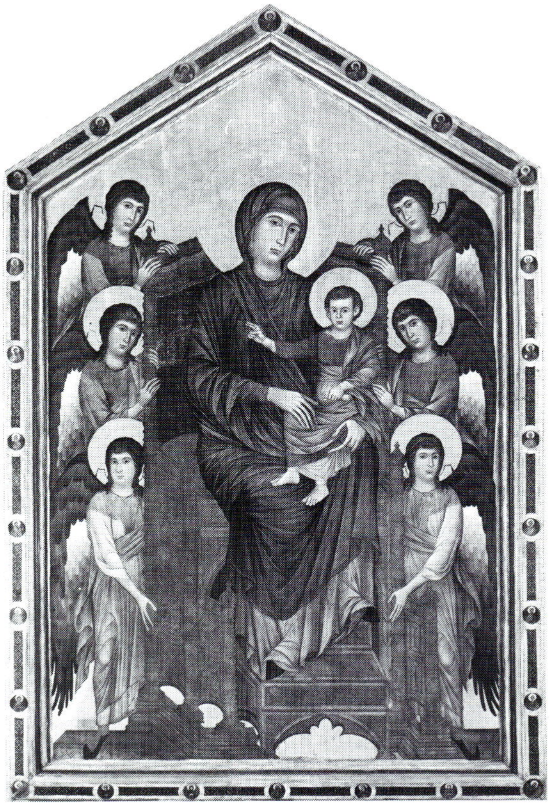

36 Cimabue, Madonna, 424 x 276 cm, Musée du Louvre, Paris.

inic on the right and St Augustine, whose rule the Dominicans followed, on the left, it can safely be assumed that the donors were Dominicans. The form of these altarpieces will be discussed in the next chapter. The point of particular interest here is that the Dominicans were evidently as important to Duccio as the Servites had been to Coppo. This brings us to an intriguing question concerning the creation of works of art. Why is there so little evidence of Duccio's activity in Siena prior to the *Maestà*? Why is his most important early work an altarpiece in Florence? This introduces a phenomenon which has never yet been investigated, despite the fact that it is probably vital to any understanding of the way works of art were produced in Siena. It is a fact that, from Duccio's day onwards, the major early works of important Sienese artists are almost always found outside Siena itself. Ambrogio Lorenzetti worked in the province near Greve before he received a major commission in his native city, and his brother Pietro worked in Cortona and Arezzo. Simone Martini never seems to have settled anywhere for very long. Guido's workshop was probably able to cope with local demand in Duccio's day, just as Duccio's own workshop would later force ambitious young artists

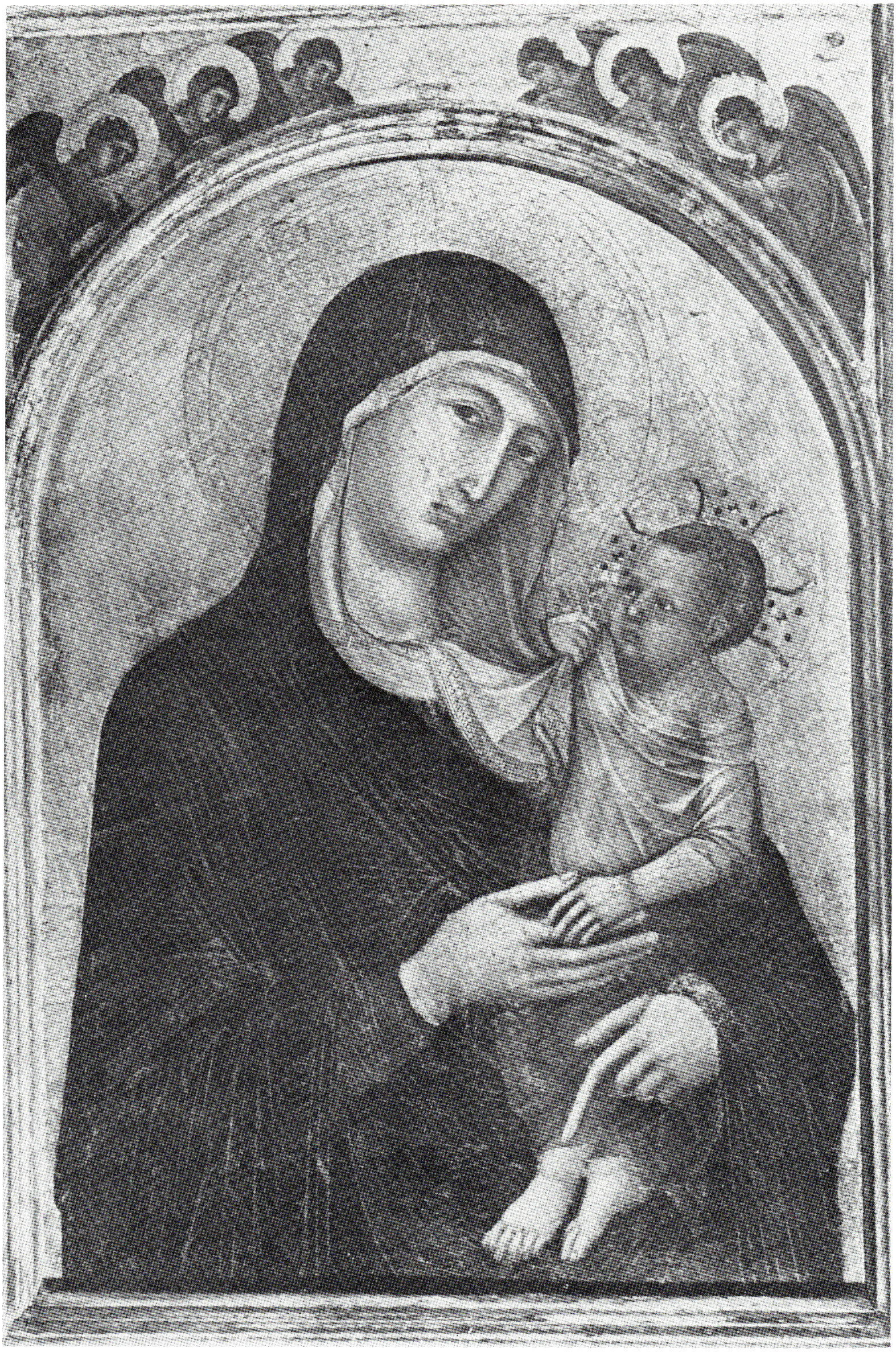

37 Duccio, Madonna, 98.5 x 63.5 cm, Galleria Nazionale dell'Umbria, Perugia.

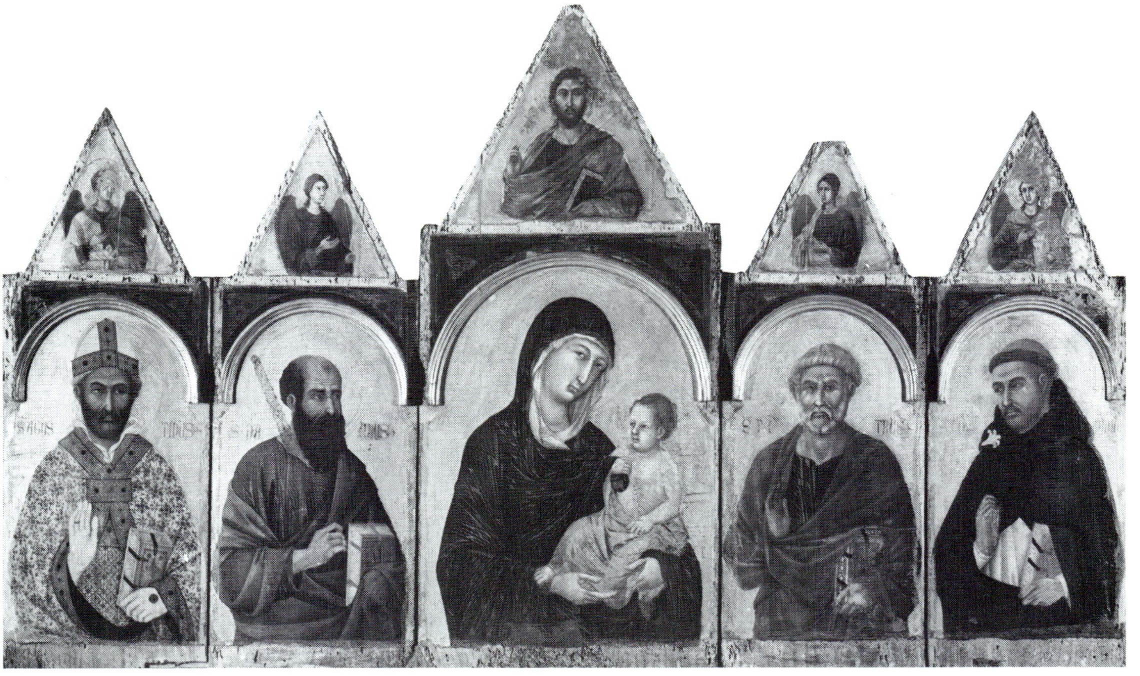

38 Duccio, Madonna with Sts Augustine, Paul, Peter and Dominic, 139 x 241 cm, Pinacotéca Nazionale, Siena.

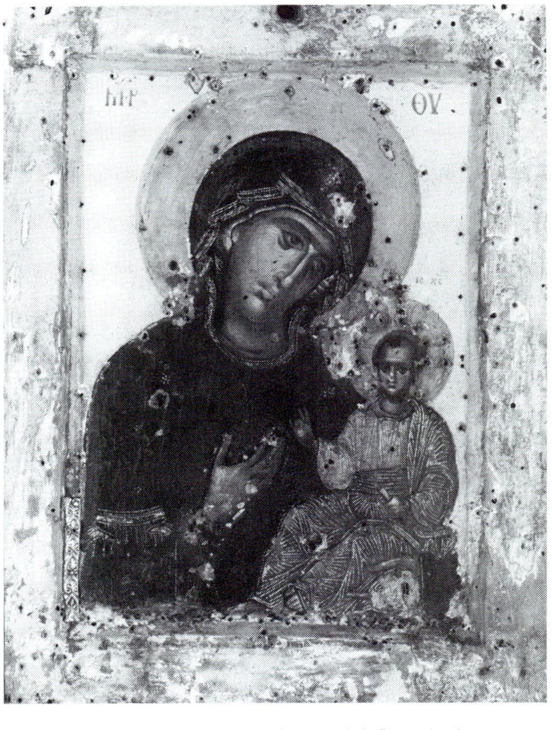

39 Byzantine ca. 1300, 'Madonna del Carmine', 28 x 22 cm, S. Niccolò del Carmine, Siena.

to seek employment elsewhere.[29] Here, admittedly, we are entering on an area of surmise and hypothesis, but conjecture can serve a useful purpose in suggesting lines for further research.

To return to Siena. There is one monastic order which deserves closer scrutiny, and that is the Carmelites. They were not important patrons in the thirteenth century, so historians of art and culture have tended to overlook them.[30] Nevertheless, they had an important influence on the religious life of Siena, and they did own works of art which enjoyed great prestige at the time. Legend had it that the Madonna on their high altar had been painted by St Luke himself (fig. 39). There are literally scores of 'St Luke Madonnas' known to history, but what makes this one stand out is that, according to early Sienese sources, it was a focus of local veneration. It is a thirteenth-century icon,[31] but its putative origin gave it a cachet which raised it far above all those other altarpieces, however large they may have been. Art history, which is concerned solely with artistic trends and developments, has virtually ignored this Madonna. Nevertheless, it is indispensable to any historical account of the earliest altarpieces in Siena.

Strangely enough there is another icon-like Madonna in the Carmine which was also the object of especial veneration, and that was the *Madonna dei Mantellini* (fig. 40). There is not a mention of this work before 1585, when Francesco Vanni was commissioned to create an altarpiece around it. This is one of the earliest examples of the Counter-Refor-

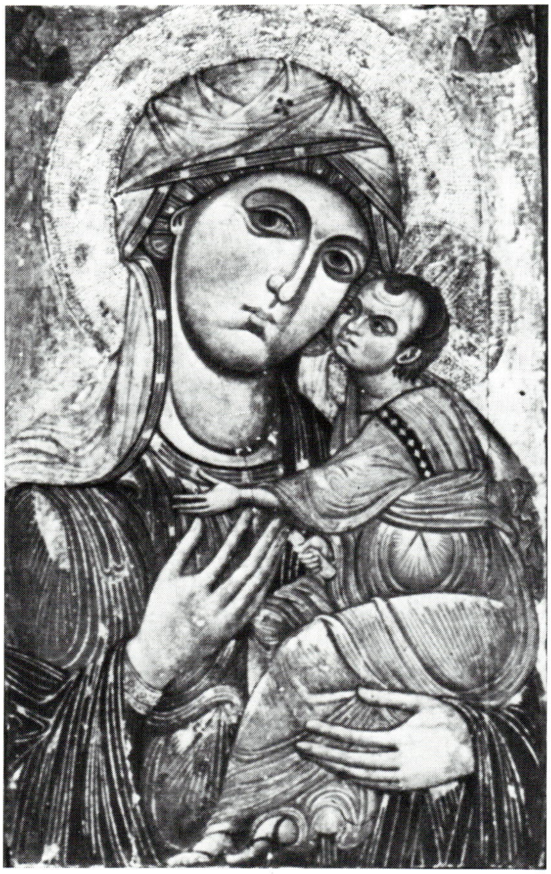

40 Pisan (?) ca. 1280, 'Madonna dei Mantellini', 78 x 49 cm, S. Niccolò del Carmine, Siena.

mation practice of re-using old Madonna panels, particularly those which had been intensely venerated.[32] These two Madonnas suggest that the Carmelites were expert at getting the best propaganda value out of their icons. They had originally lived as hermits on Mount Carmel, but around 1240 many of them left as the Saracen menace became more acute. They came to Europe, where they settled in the cities, and in 1247 their rule was modified, enabling them to organise their order along the lines of the other mendicants. Franciscan propaganda focussed on the person of St Francis. The Dominicans prided themselves on being the intellectual defenders of the true Christian doctrine, and they had called on the city-dwellers to support them in their struggle against heresy. The Carmelites claimed to be the oldest of all the monastic orders, and portrayed themselves as the true heirs of the great hermits. Antiquity as a guarantee for authenticity. A Madonna painted by St Luke himself was the ideal reinforcement of those claims. In the middle of the thirteenth century they placed another Madonna on the high altar of their church in Siena. It may be larger than the Siena icon, but is has such a Byzantine appearance that it is still a mystery where and by whom it was painted. Art historians regard it as a dreadfully old-fashioned altarpiece, and that it certainly is. But perhaps the antique look was just what the Carmelites wanted, if only to bolster their claim that they had been living in ascetic communion with the Virgin long before anyone else.

III

DUCCIO'S MAESTÀ

On 9th July 1311 a solemn procession wended its way through the city. The devout inhabitants of the 'Civitas Virginis' were carrying a massive altarpiece to the place which had been reserved for it: the high altar of the cathedral (figs. 41, 42). 'Trumpeters, players of a horn and a kettledrum' went out to meet the procession.[33] Forty years later the chronicler Agnolo di Tura described the events of that day, which had evidently made a deep impression on him.

'This [the *Maestà*] was painted by master Duccio di Niccolò, painter of Siena, who was in his time the most skillful painter one could find in these lands. The panel was painted outside the Porta a Stalloreggi in the Borgo a Laterino, in the house of the Muciatti. The Sienese took the panel to the cathedral at noontime on the ninth of June [1311], with great devotions and processions, with the bishop of Siena, Ruggero da Casole, with all of the clergy of the cathedral, and with all the monks and nuns of Siena, and the Nove, with the city officials, the Podestà and the Captain, and all the citizens with coats of arms and those with more distinguished coats of arms, with lighted lamps in hand. And thus, the women and children went through Siena with much devotion and around the Campo in procession, ringing all the bells for joy, and this entire day the shops stayed closed for devotions, and throughout Siena they gave many alms to the poor people, with many speeches and prayers to God and to his mother, Madonna ever Virgin Mary, who helps, preserves and increases in peace the good state of the city of Siena and its territory, as advocate and protectress of that city, and who defends the city from all danger and all evil. And so this panel was placed in the cathedral on the high altar. The panel is painted on the back with the Old Testament [sic] with the Passion of Jesus Christ, and on the front is the Virgin Mary with her son in her arms and many saints at the side. Everything is ornamented with fine gold; it cost three thousand florins.'[34]

This spectacle of an urban community bearing an image of the Madonna to its cathedral has fired the imagination of many a romantic, for it was a perfect answer to a deep-seated desire – the complete integration of art and society. A story of this kind proved that that integration had once been reality and not some unattainable dream. Lord Leighton, the famous Victorian artist, actually executed a painting based on Vasari's description of the *Rucellai Madonna* being carried in procession through Florence, [35] and in those days it was still thought that the *Rucellai Madonna* had been painted by Cimabue. It is still not clear whether Vasari based his account on Agnolo di Tura, but the only known story of a community which held art in such high esteem comes from this Agnolo, and concerns Siena and Duccio's *Maestà*.

The *Maestà* was indeed a unique altarpiece. It was painted on both sides, and was larger than any other painting of its day. In fact, very few panel altarpieces ever approached it for size. The donors who commissioned Duccio and his atelier must have been bordering on megalomania. The *Rucellai Madonna* had shown that Duccio was capable of handling a major commission, and in 1302 he had painted a *Maestà* for the chapel of the Nine in the town hall, the Palazzo Publico.[36] Now, though, he was being asked to produce something on a far more ambitious scale for the high altar of the cathedral. The contract for the painting has survived. It is dated 9th October 1308, and in it Duccio accepted the task from the Opera del Duomo 'of painting a certain panel to be placed on the high altar of the church of S. Maria of Siena'. He undertook 'to make the said panel, as well as ever he was able and knew how to and the Lord bestowed upon him – and to work continuously upon the said panel at such times as he was able to work on it – and not to accept or receive any other work to be carried out until the said panel shall have been made and completed.' He was to be paid a salary for every day that he worked on the panel 'with his own

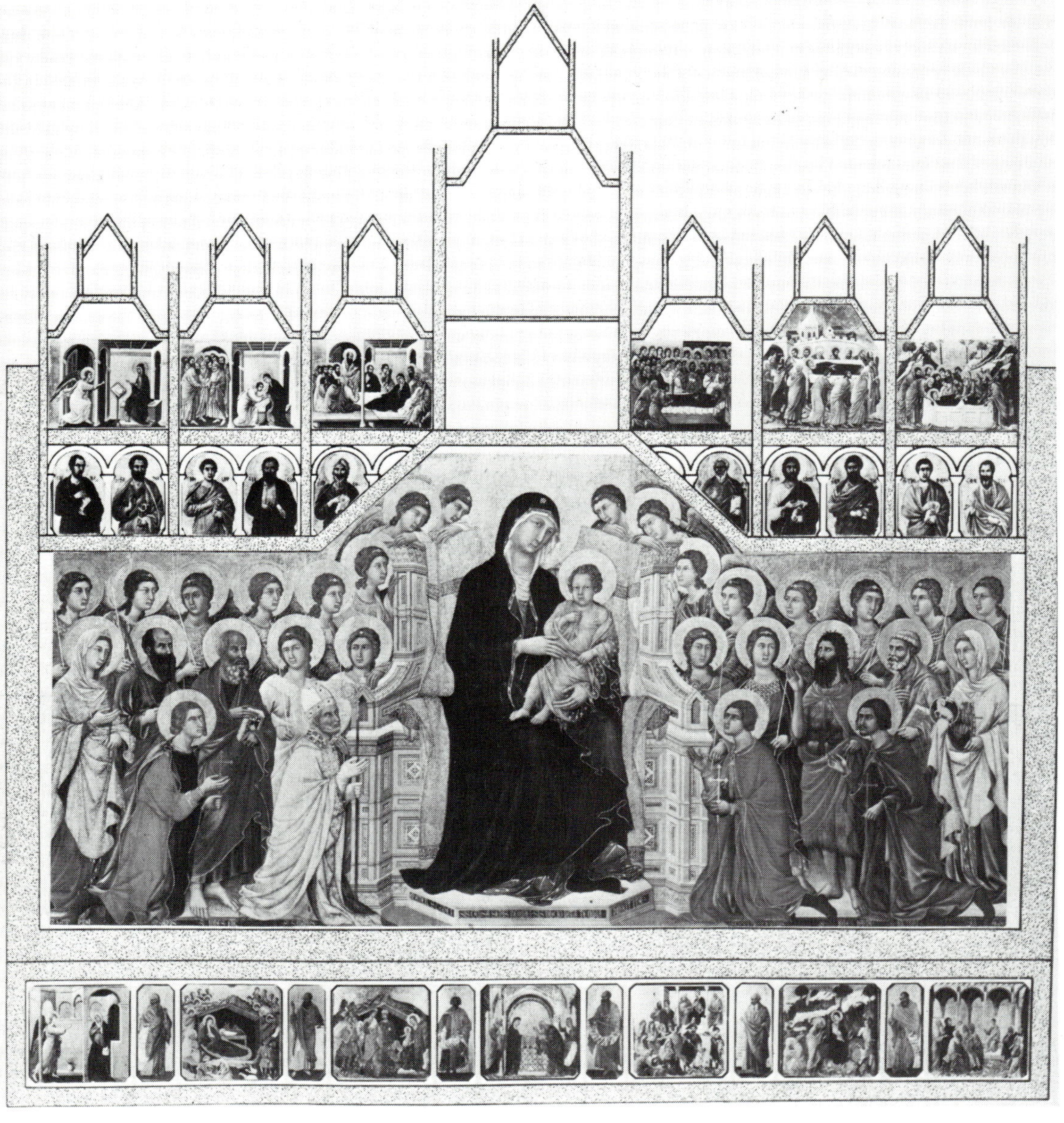

41-42 Duccio, Maestà, front and back (reconstruction after White), original dimensions ca. 500 x 470 cm, 1311. Main panel and most of the scenes now in Museo dell'Opera del Duomo, Siena.

hands'. There were clauses stipulating a reduction in salary 'should he lose any part of the day'. The client undertook 'to supply and to give all those things which shall be needed for the working of the said panel, so that the said Duccio shall be bound to put nothing into it except his person and his work.' After agreeing to a penalty clause in the event of default 'the said Duccio for greater precaution swore voluntarily on the Holy Gospels of God, physically touching the book, that he would observe and implement everything in good faith and without fraud'.[37]

The difference between this contract and the one for the *Rucellai Madonna* is that Duccio was to be paid a straight salary. The materials on this occasion were to be provided by the Opera del Duomo. The phrase 'suis manibus' ('with his own hands') has given rise to a certain amount of confusion. Some authors have interpreted it as meaning that pupils were expressly prohibited from working on the painting. That, of course, is quite incorrect. The sentence is concerned solely with the salary which Duccio was to receive for

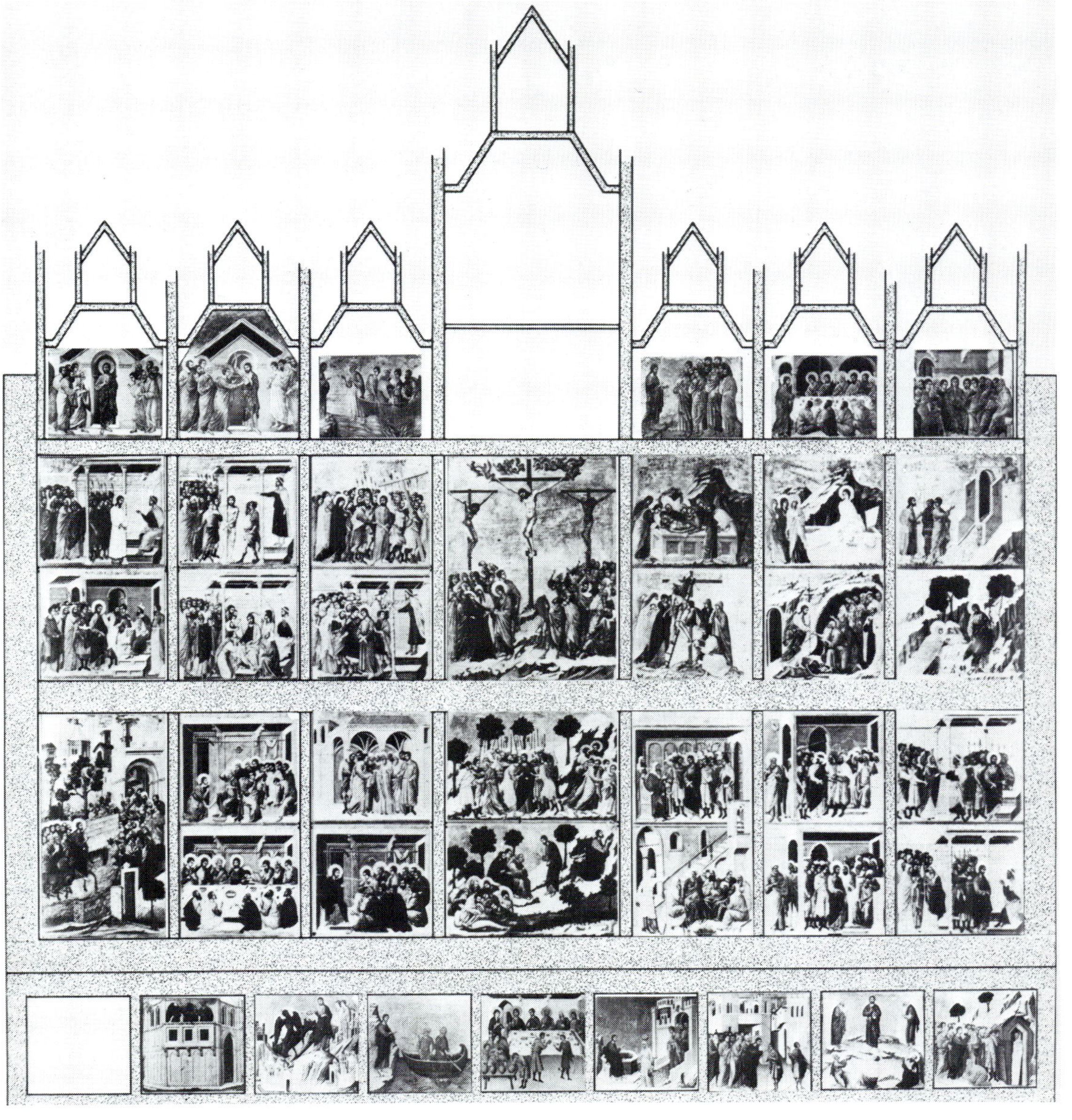

work on the altarpiece, and in fact it could be read as evidence that pupils would actually be involved. Given the size of the work Duccio would almost certainly have needed the continuing assistance of a number of pupils. It is also clear from the wording of the contract that a distinction was made between the panel to be painted and the actual painting of that panel, and in that respect it is similar to the contract for the *Rucellai Madonna*. In other words, it is not self-evident that the 'pictor' was also involved in the design of the altarpiece, although it is certainly probable. He may well have supplied sketches of a type of altarpiece, similar to those which we know from a far later period.[38]

We also have a document dating from one or two years after this contract in which two outside assessors present an agreed estimate of the amount that should be paid for work on the rear face of the altarpiece. 'They understand that there are thirty-four histories principally, which they estimate, for the majority of any of the same histories, at the common figure, and for the little angels above, and for any other works, if they should be required of the brush, that the said histories shall be thirty-eight. He shall be paid for thirty-eight and he shall have and must have for each history two and a half gold florins, the same Master Duccio furnishing all that

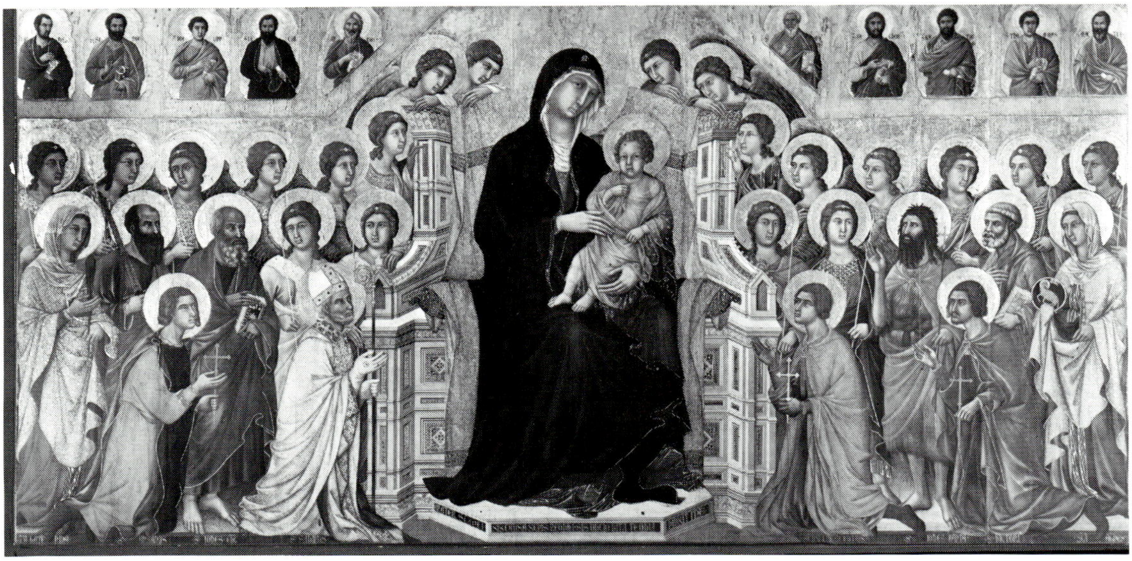

43 Duccio, Maestà, detail of front.

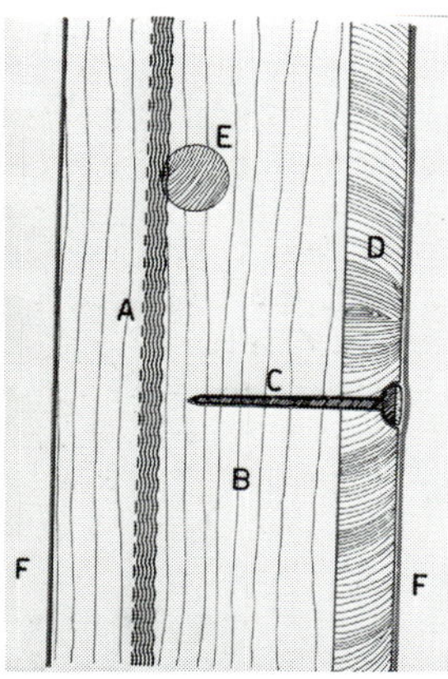

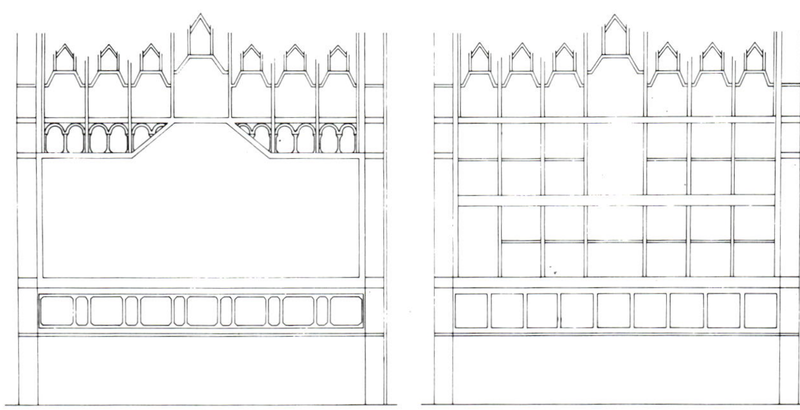

44 Original attachment of front and rear panels of the Maestà; A = sawcut (after Brandi).
45 Schematic reconstruction of the Maestà (after White, modified by Gardner-von Teuffel).

which pertains to the craft of the brush, and the master of works must furnish colours and whatever else may be needed.'[39] In fact there are thirty-two 'principal histories', excluding the predella, and not thirty-four. However, two of them are twice the size of the others: the *Entry into Jerusalem* and the *Crucifixion*. Payment seems to have been based on the number of scenes rather than their size, for with six angels at the top we arrive at the correct figure of thirty-eight.

A third document associated with the *Maestà* deals with the management of the Opera del Duomo. The city authorities had examined its accounts and were disturbed by some items of useless expenditure. They demanded better progess of the works, and this also applied to the 'new and great panel of the blessed and glorious Virgin Mary'. They came to the following decision: 'For the doing of all these works and for their completion, there shall stay and remain only ten of the best and most useful masters of the said Opera, so many and no more, the means, income and provision for the said works being considered; to all the other masters, indeed, they give leave of absence and [decree] that they be removed from the undertakings of the aforesaid Opera, since the income of the same Opera and its means and provision are not sufficient to sustain such and so great and so intolerable burdens'.[40] It is clear from this attempt to eliminate inefficiency and curb uncontrolled growth that the Opera del Duomo had developed into a complex organisation.

In its original form the altarpiece consisted of a main panel with the Madonna enthroned amidst saints and angels (fig. 43), and with the four patron saints of Siena kneeling at her feet. Along the border at the top are the ten apostles (shown half-length) who do not appear in the main scene. This panel consisted of eleven vertical planks approximately seven centimetres thick. Nailed to the back were five horizontal planks which were only one centimetre thick, forming the support for the scenes of Christ's Passion. There was also a predella, or strip of paintings, running along the base of the main panel. The paintings on the front of the predella dealt with Christ's early life, and those on the back with his ministry. Prophets holding Biblical texts alternated with the scenes on the front of the predella. This is the oldest painted predella to have come down to us, although it was certainly not the first. We know from documentary evidence that there was a painted predella below Duccio's *Maestà* of 1302 for the chapel of the Nine, and that Cimabue's altarpiece for Santa Chiara in Pisa was also meant to have a predella.[41] Above the main panel of the *Maestà* in Siena cathedral were pinnacles depicting, on the front, the last days of the Virgin, and on the reverse the glorification of Christ. Each scene, front and back, was crowned with the figure of an angel.

Thanks to the work done by van der Ploeg (see Appendix) we now know a great deal more about the interior arrangement of the cathedral in 1311, when the *Maestà* was installed on the high altar. The civic pride of the Sienese was continually finding an outlet in new and grandiose plans for enlarging the cathedral. This urge to expand reached its peak with a megalomaniac design for turning the existing building into the transept of a truly gigantic church. Although work only started on that plan in 1339, masons had been remodelling the inside of the church since 1317, enlarging the choir and demolishing the crypt in order to create a single, unified space along the lines of the great French cathedrals. Just as the *Madonna del voto* (fig. 9) must be viewed in relation to the rebuilding which took place around 1260, so the commission for the *Maestà* must be seen as a prelude to the remodelling of the interior which began in 1317. In 1311, however, the *Maestà* was ceremoniously installed on Nicola Pisano's high altar, which stood over the crypt. The new altarpiece replaced the dossal, of which only the *Madonna del voto* has survived. The new Madonna gazed out over the congregation, while the scenes of Christ's Passion and glorification on the reverse served to inspire the canons in their devotions.[42]

The *Maestà* stood on the high altar of Siena cathedral for close on two hundred years. We have come to regard it as the most splendid adornment for a high altar, and it is hard to imagine that anyone could ever have thought otherwise. Nevertheless, it was removed in 1506 on the orders of Pandolfo Petrucci, the tyrant of Siena. A new high altar was built, and on it was placed the bronze tabernacle which Vecchietta had made in 1472 for the main altar of the Hospital Church of Santa Maria della Scala, opposite the cathedral. The *Maestà* was moved to a side altar. Then, in 1711, fate struck, as we learn from a cathedral inventory of 1776. 'The said panel was sawn into several pieces and they were transported to the last room of the mezzanine of the Rector's quarters to be made into various pictures. One is on the altar of Sant Ansano, the other is near the altar of the Sacrament.'[43] The main panel was cut into seven vertical pieces, each of which was then sawn down the middle, separating the front from the back surface. The parts of the front and back of the main panel were put together as two separate paintings. The predella and pinnacles had been removed before this operation was carried out. This crude surgery should not necessarily suggest any lack of respect for Duccio the artist. On the contrary, Siena often showed that it knew how to honour its past masters. It was more a sign of indifference towards an altarpiece which had long outlived its original function. It was thus that sections of the altarpiece came to be sold separately, finding their ways into a number of different collections. The later task of conservation was complicated by the way in which the main panel had been separated into two parts. Removal of the nails attaching the rear panel to the front of the altarpiece would have caused irreparable damage to the Passion scenes. Instead the fairly thick front panel was sawn through the middle, avoiding the points of the nails (fig. 44) and leaving it so thin that it was no longer an adequate support for the large painting. The rear face. however, was now supported on two separate layers of wood which began to work against each other, creating internal stresses. Moreover, the operation was done so crudely that the saw slipped at the height of the Madonna's face, damaging a considerable area of paint. New wood was added behind the Madonna during the ambitious restoration of 1953-58, and the entire structure was ingeniously cradled. The extra layer of wood was also removed from behind the Passion scenes. The Madonna's face was restored, but in such a way that it became rather more sentimental than Duccio could ever have intended, if we are to judge by his other Madonnas.[44]

The great problem is to visualise the original form of the predella, and above all of the superstructure. The *Maestà* is a sublime altarpiece, which is why it was the first painting to be subjected to a scholarly analysis of its original form and function. An account of the many attempts to reconstruct the *Maestà* would be both fascinating and instructive, for it would show

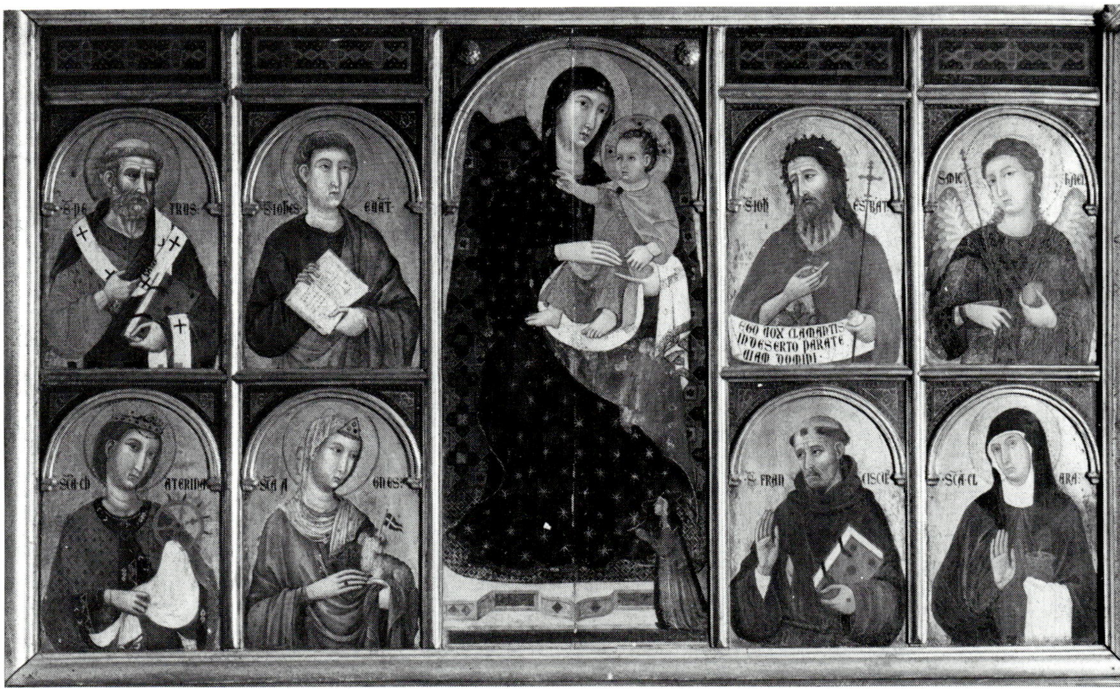

46 Memmo di Filippuccio, Madonna with Sts Peter, John the Evangelist, John the Baptist, Michael, Catherine, Agnes, Francis and Clare, 120 x 127 cm, Museo Civico, San Gimignano.

how much more meticulous we have become in the reassembly of panels. Physical and technical examination and pinpoint measurement have only become common in recent years. Even more remarkable, though, is the fact that the latest attempts at reconstruction have been the first to give due weight to the history of this specific type of object: a liturgical artefact known as an altarpiece. It was John White who ultimately arrived at a convincing reconstruction which also covers the original arrangement of the scenes above and below the main panel. He assumes that one predella scene has been lost, along with a tall pinnacle in the centre, the front of which would have had scenes of the Virgin's glorification, such as the Dormition, the Assumption or the Coronation, while the reverse might have had an Ascension and a Christ Logos. The fact that these important scenes are missing is inexplicable on any other grounds. The original framing is the only remaining problem. White believes that the altarpiece was encased in the usual framing box, but Christa Gardner-von Teuffel has put forward the more plausible suggestion that the *Maestà* was the first altarpiece to be supported by lateral buttresses (fig. 45).[45] This disposes of the problem raised by the presence of a predella below White's proposed framing box. Altarpieces either had a framing box or a predella and piers.

Any discussion of the design of the *Maestà* is complicated by the fact that it was such an unusual commission. Exceptional commissions produce exceptional paintings, and it is notoriously difficult to fit exceptions into an organic development. The *Maestà* stands alone. In terms of form it is related not only to the monumental Madonna panels of the Dugento, but also to Trecento polyptychs (see Chapter IV). For this reason I will be referring both backwards and forwards in time in the following discussion.

There is a great deal to be said for treating Duccio's creation as a sublime synthesis of the formal and thematic developments which took place in altarpiece painting in the course of the thirteenth century. Moreover, Duccio has succeeded brilliantly in bringing to panel painting the effect of unity through variety, the finest medieval examples of which are to be found in the thirteenth-century sculptural programmes for cathedrals. There is also a synthesis of the horizontal format of the dossal and the verticality of the Madonna altarpiece. Evidence that other attempts were being made to achieve this synthesis (but at a far more primitive level) is provided by Memmi di Filippuccio's altarpiece for the monastery church of Santa Chiara in San Gimignano (fig. 46).

Since 1280 there had been a type of altarpiece in which the upper contour was broken by gables, in the tradition of the dossal (fig. 47). The question of whether the *Maestà* fits into the tradition of the double-sided altarpiece must remain unresolved until it is decided whether Giotto's *Stefaneschi altarpiece* for the high altar of the old St Peter's in Rome should be dated early or late. Not that it makes a great deal of difference, really, for Giotto's altarpiece had a totally different form, content and function.[46] It is also worth bearing in mind that Guido's original dossal with the *Madonna del voto* may well have been painted on both sides. As we have seen, painted predellas were probably known by the time of the *Maestà*, as was the combination of a Madonna with scenes from Christ's early life and Passion (fig. 28). It was also a perfectly natural development for the themes of incarnation and sacrifice to be united in a single, vast altarpiece. The emphasis in all those varied scenes on the reverse is on Christ's redemptive death, culminating in the central scenes of the *Crucifixion*. The association with the Eucharist is subtly accentuated by placing the *Marriage at Cana* in the centre of the predella. The *Presentation* in the middle of the predella facing the congregation emphasises the relationship with the ritual taking place at the altar.

The traditional type of Madonna altarpiece has been extended with the addition of companies of angels and saints on either side of the Mother and Child. The half-length saints of the dossal have now made way for full-length figures. The two saints standing nearest the throne are John the Evangelist and John the Baptist. This was by no means uncommon in Sienese iconography (cf. fig. 46), but it is unusual to find the evangelist depicted as the aged visionary of Patmos rather than as a beardless young man. Duccio's models evidently differed from those available to Guido, his predecessor. The evangelist and the Baptist are inviting the faithful to witness the scene, and behind them come the two saints who endorse the authority and doctrine of the church: Peter and Paul. They are followed by two female martyrs – St Catherine on the left and St Agnes on the right. These six saints are not arranged in discrete groups but are part of the serried ranks of angels and saints which run more or less parallel to the picture plane. Duccio is in effect presenting no more than a fragment of the heavenly hosts. The four figures kneeling in the foreground are the patron saints of Siena. They are dedicating the community under their protection to the Madonna, thus making it the 'Civitas Virginis'. Immediately to the left and right of the throne are Savinus, the first bishop of Siena, and Crescentius, a Roman martyr whose relics were preserved in the cathedral. Behind them are Ansanus, the son of a Roman nobleman, who was martyred near the city, and Victor of Siena, who won his

47 Vigoroso da Siena, Madonna with Sts Mary Magdalen, John the Baptist, John the Evangelist and Giuliano, 153 x 232 cm, Galleria Nazionale dell'Umbria, Perugia.

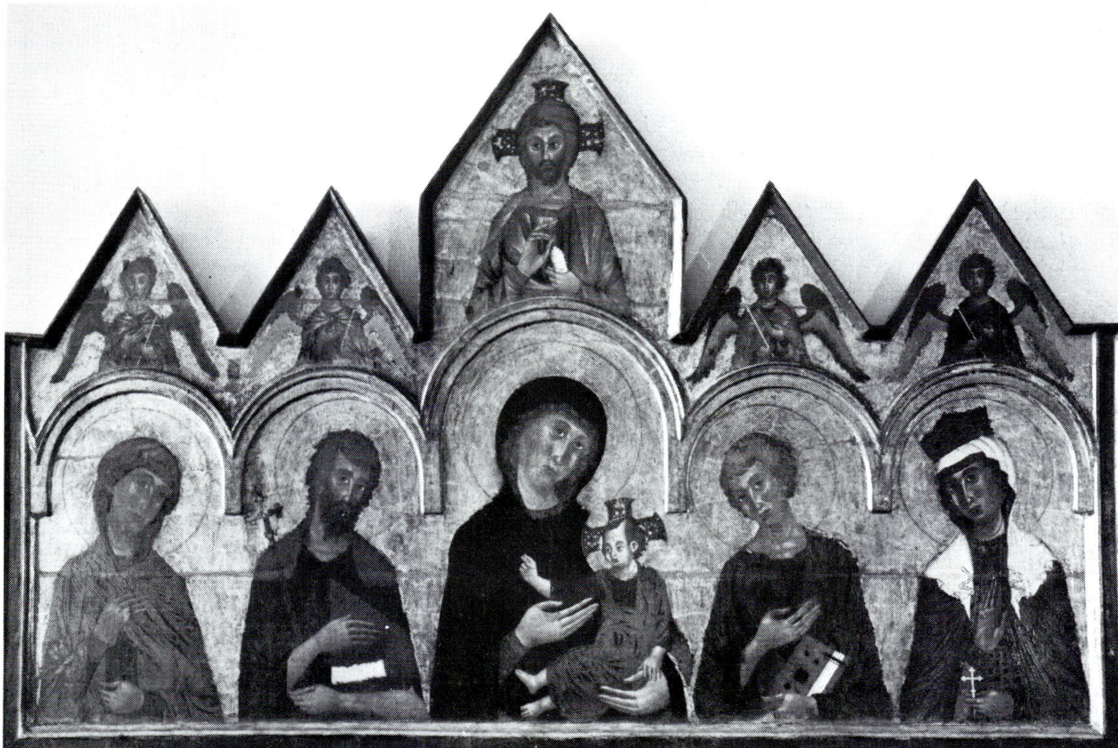

martyr's palm in Egypt. Savinus suffered death by scourging, the other three were beheaded. Their most important relics were kept in Siena cathedral.[47]

The Madonna is seated on an ornate stone throne decorated with Cosmati work. The angularity of the structure is softened by the flowing lines of the gold brocade cloth against which she is framed, setting off the plain blue of her robe to brilliant effect. The Christ Child, who faces the viewer, is neither blessing the faithful nor reaching out a hand towards his mother, as he does in Guido's Madonnas. Duccio places all the emphasis on the majesty and the representative function of the figures. The composition owes its unity not to any interplay of looks or gestures, or to a powerful three-dimensional organisation of the groups, but to the flowing movements of the robes, which unite the figures into an organic whole. The colours, too, contribute to this harmony. Not only are the two groups flanking the throne in perfect colour balance but there is a subtle harmony of colour within each group.

Should one seek the origin of this grand design in French monumental sculpture, as some authors have done? It is true that a certain 'Duch de Siene' appears on the Paris tax-roll for 1296, but there is nothing to show that this was the Duccio of the *Maestà*. It has also been suggested that Duccio travelled to Rome and visited Santa Maria in Domnica, where he was supposedly inspired by the apse mosaic with its majestic group of figures surrounding the Madonna.[48] The difficulty with hypotheses of this kind is that they fail to take two basic factors into account. In the first place it was the donors who decided that they wanted an enormous altarpiece, and we can safely assume that they had some idea, however vague, of the kind of painting it should be. Secondly, the various elements of the *Maestà* were already well-established in the Sienese altarpiece tradition. Some interpreters have probably been misled by the scale enlargement required by the donors and by the high artistic standard of Duccio's workshop. In art history it seems almost axiomatic to attribute excellence to the influence of outstanding works of art created elsewhere. However, as with any other craft product, the quality of late medieval art has to be seen in the context of increasing rivalry between competing workshops which owed their vigorous growth to a favourable combination of circumstances. The ambitious commissions awarded to artists are just one indication that conditions in Siena were extremely favourable in the period when Duccio executed the *Maestà*.

The scenes on the front of the predella were the *Annunciation*, the *Nativity*, the *Adoration*, the *Presentation in the temple*, the *Massacre of the innocents*, the *Flight into Egypt*, and *Jesus among the doctors*. These scenes were

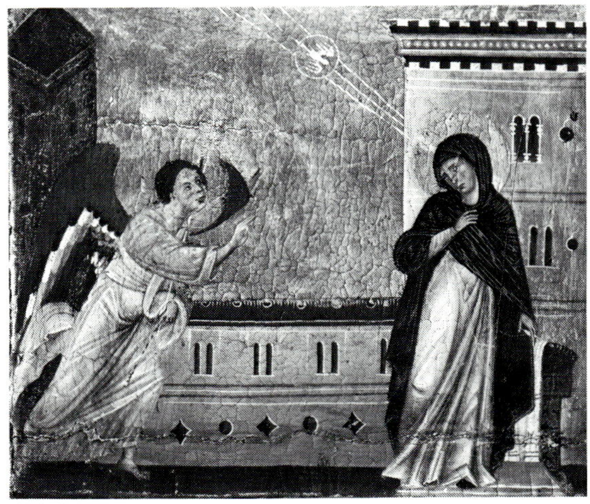

49 St Peter Master, Annunciation, detail of the Antependium of St Peter, Pinacoteca Nazionale, Siena.

interspersed with prophets holding texts foretelling the Incarnation, which set the narrative of the Virgin's motherhood and Christ's early years in a theological framework. The only pinnacle scene to have survived in its original form is the *Apostles bearing the Virgin's body to the tomb*. All the others have been reduced to a rectangular format. Reading from left to right they were the *Annunciation of the Virgin's death and glorification*, the *Return of the apostles*, the *Death of the Virgin*, the *Dormition* (when Christ gathered the Virgin's soul), the *Apostles bearing the Virgin's body to the tomb*, and the *Entombment of the Virgin*. Rather than discuss all these predella and pinnacle scenes individually I have singled out one which I believe to be the most representative. The *Annunciation* on the predella is ideal for the purposes of comparison, if only because it is matched by a second *Annunciation* on one of the pinnacles (figs. 48, 50).

Early Sienese art adhered to a rigid visual programme for the Annunciation. It consisted of two standing figures frozen in expressive poses (fig. 49, cf. fig. 25). The angel appears to be rushing full tilt towards the Virgin, who shrinks back in fright. The two figures do not have exactly the same weight. This is because the dove of the Holy Ghost is seen descending on the Virgin at the very moment when the angel makes his announcement, illustrating the words of the scriptures that she was overshadowed by the Holy Spirit. Both the angel and the dove draw our attention to the figure of the Virgin. The architecture, too, tends to emphasise her rather than the angel. It is totally two-dimensional, its purpose being to reinforce the composition of the figures and to define their positions. Gabriel's approach is made even more expressive by the emphatic verticals of the building behind him, while the low wall gives the figures greater cohesion. However, the architecture is not solely a compositional device. The colourful arched windows and the dentils heighten the decorative aspect of the scene.

The angel's haste and Mary's fright are based on an interesting theological construct. The angel says 'Mary, do not be afraid', so we know immediately that she started back in fright when he appeared before her. Thirteenth-century theologians interpreted this as a sign of her humility. She knew that she had been chosen by God and yet she was so unassuming that she was still frightened by the apparition of the angel – the outward manifestation of her selection. Truly a holy woman. But how did she know why she had been chosen? The gospels are silent on this point, so it is hardly surprising to find it expounded at length in the apocrypha. The *Meditationes vitae Christi*, which was an extremely popular Tuscan adaptation dating from the end of the thirteenth century, goes into great detail on Mary's special relationship with God prior to her visitation by the angel. In fact, his arrival was inevitable, for she had already shown that she was worthy of this sign of divine favour. What it amounts to is that man owes God's arrival on earth to Mary. However heretical that may sound, it was the firm conviction of many a medieval theologian. It also explains why the angel had to hurry. The writer of the *Meditationes* relates how Gabriel set out on his mission. 'Then he arose cheerfully and gaily and flew down from heaven and in a minute stood in human form before the Virgin, who was in a room of her little house. But his flight was not so swift that God did not enter before him, and thus the Holy Trinity was present, entering before his messenger.'[49]

Duccio's *Annunciation* basically follows the traditional formula (fig. 48). The angel approaches from the left, and Mary draws back, making the same gesture with her right hand as she does in Guido's version. The architecture articulates these movements and gives added emphasis to Mary's position. The figures once again act out the scene against the backdrop of a wall. However, the difference in interpretation, thirty years on, is startling. Gone are the isolated, expressive figures, seemingly knocked off

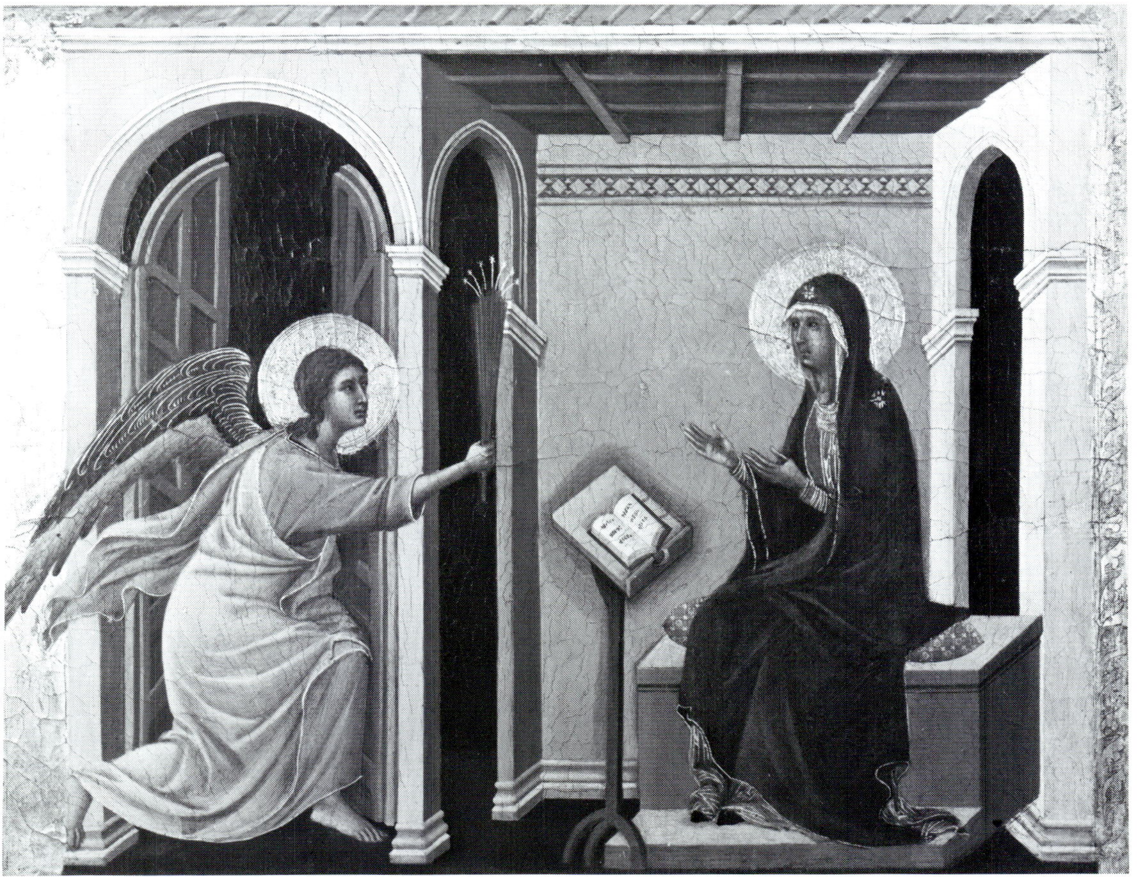

50 Duccio, Annunciation of the death and glorification of the Virgin from the Maestà, 41 x 54 cm, Museo dell'Opera del Duomo, Siena.

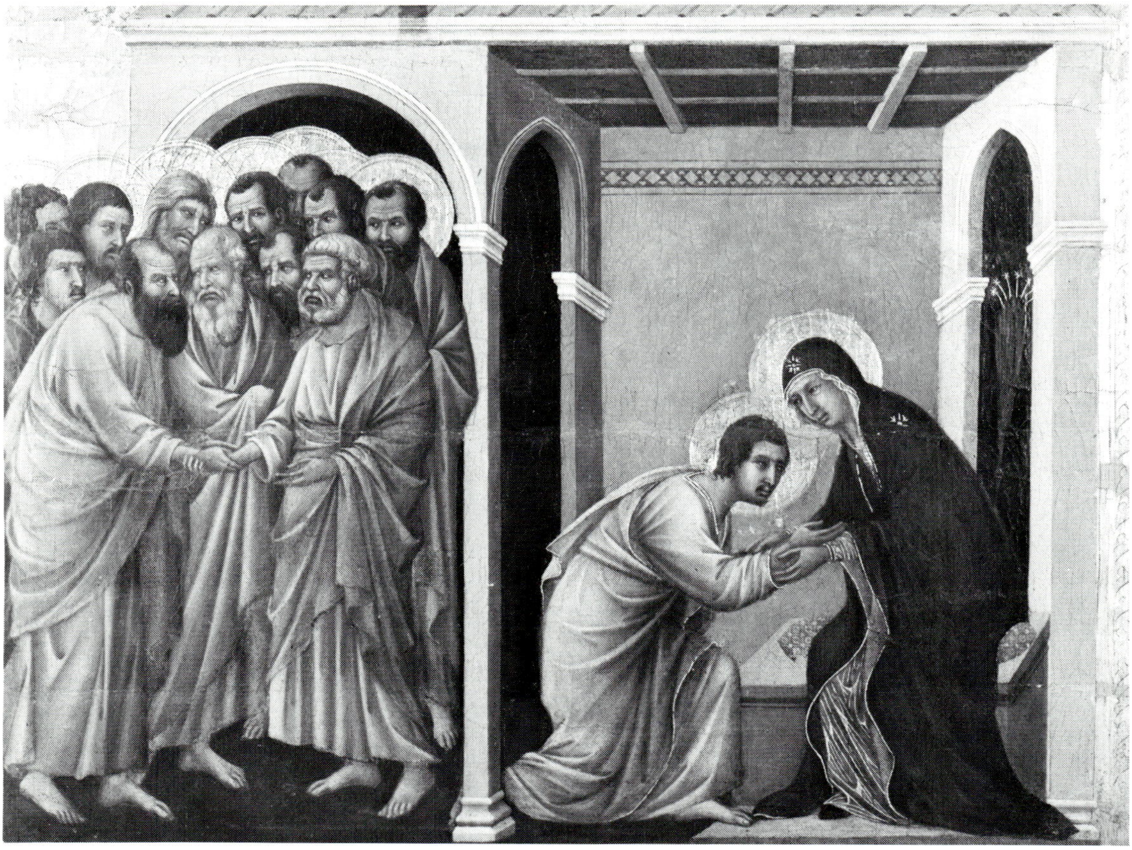

51 Duccio, Gathering of the Apostles from the Maestà, 41 x 54 cm, Museo dell'Opera del Duomo, Siena.

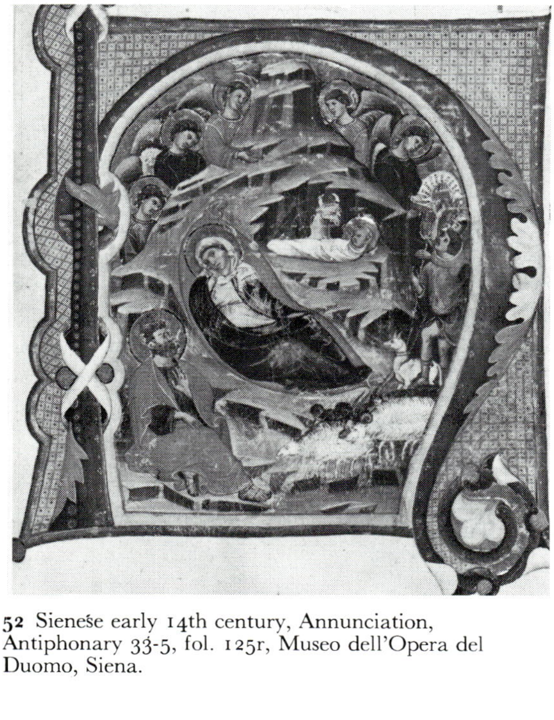

52 Sienese early 14th century, Annunciation, Antiphonary 33-5, fol. 125r, Museo dell'Opera del Duomo, Siena.

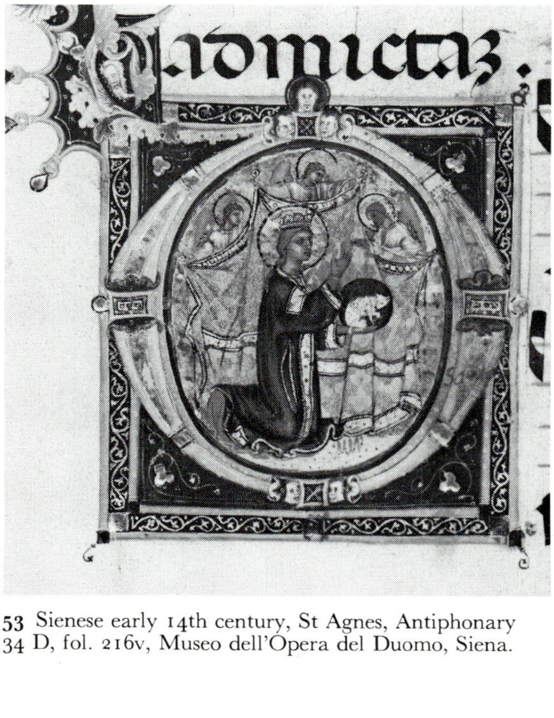

53 Sienese early 14th century, St Agnes, Antiphonary 34 D, fol. 216v, Museo dell'Opera del Duomo, Siena.

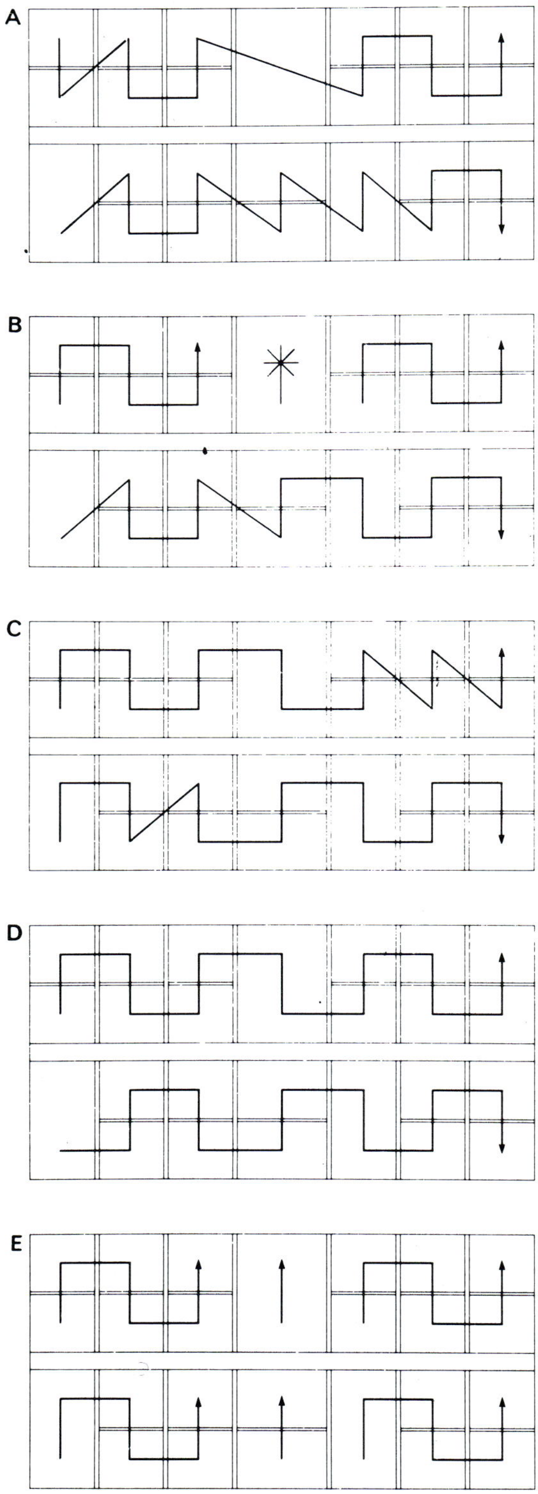

54 Diagrams of the chronological sequence of the Passion cycle of the Maestà (after Deuchler 1981); A = Cooper 1965, B = Carli 1979, C and D = White 1979, E = Deuchler.

balance by the awe-inspiring divine message of salvation, and gone are the dramatic, angular gestures and poses. Both Gabriel and Mary play their roles without losing their composure. The Annunciation and its reception are perfectly balanced. The architectural setting has become a complex spatial structure without any bold, contrasting colours. A muted hue sets the tone of the scene, bringing harmony to the different colours. The architecture looks more like a superbly painted cardboard set than solid stone. This is also the first appearance in Sienese art of the angel's staff, the pot of lilies and the Virgin's book, which is open to display the prophecy of Isaiah (7:14): 'Maid shall be with child'. Duccio was the first to enrich the *Annunciation* with attributes which were later to become such important adjuncts in Sienese treatments of the scene.

The composition of the *Annunciation of the Virgin's death and glorification* is totally different (fig. 50). The angel, who is kneeling before the seated Virgin, holds out a flowering palm frond, the symbol of her victory through virtuousness. The architectural setting is far simpler than in the Annunciation, and the figures are totally divorced from the three-dimensional space behind them. The angel's extended right arm actually passes in front of the structure. One feature of the pinnacle series which is in marked contrast to the predella scenes is the repeated use of the same architectonic elements (cf. fig. 51). This was probably done to enhance the visual unity of this upper register. In this particular case the setting is a small building which, in itself, creates a strong illusion of depth. It is all the more noticeable, therefore, that the architecture merely articulates the organisation of the figures *on the plane*, and in that respect the scenes of the Virgin's glorification do not differ from those of her motherhood on the predella. A closer look at the Virgin's position in the predella *Annunciation* reveals that there too the figures have not been conceived within the architectural setting but against it. The predella scenes, however, do display a far greater variation and refinement in the relationship between figural composition and architectonic background. This kind of stylistic difference between the various scenes on the *Maestà* has prompted attempts to explore working methods, to postulate participation, and even to identify pupils. Such exercises, however interesting in themselves, have not led to any hard-and-fast conclusions. Indeed, the identification of pupils is a particularly hazardous undertaking. However, it is quite clear from these two Annunciation scenes that a whole team of collaborators worked on the *Maestà*, and that although they shared a common grammar their articulation often differed quite markedly.[50]

That being said, we have still not accounted for the

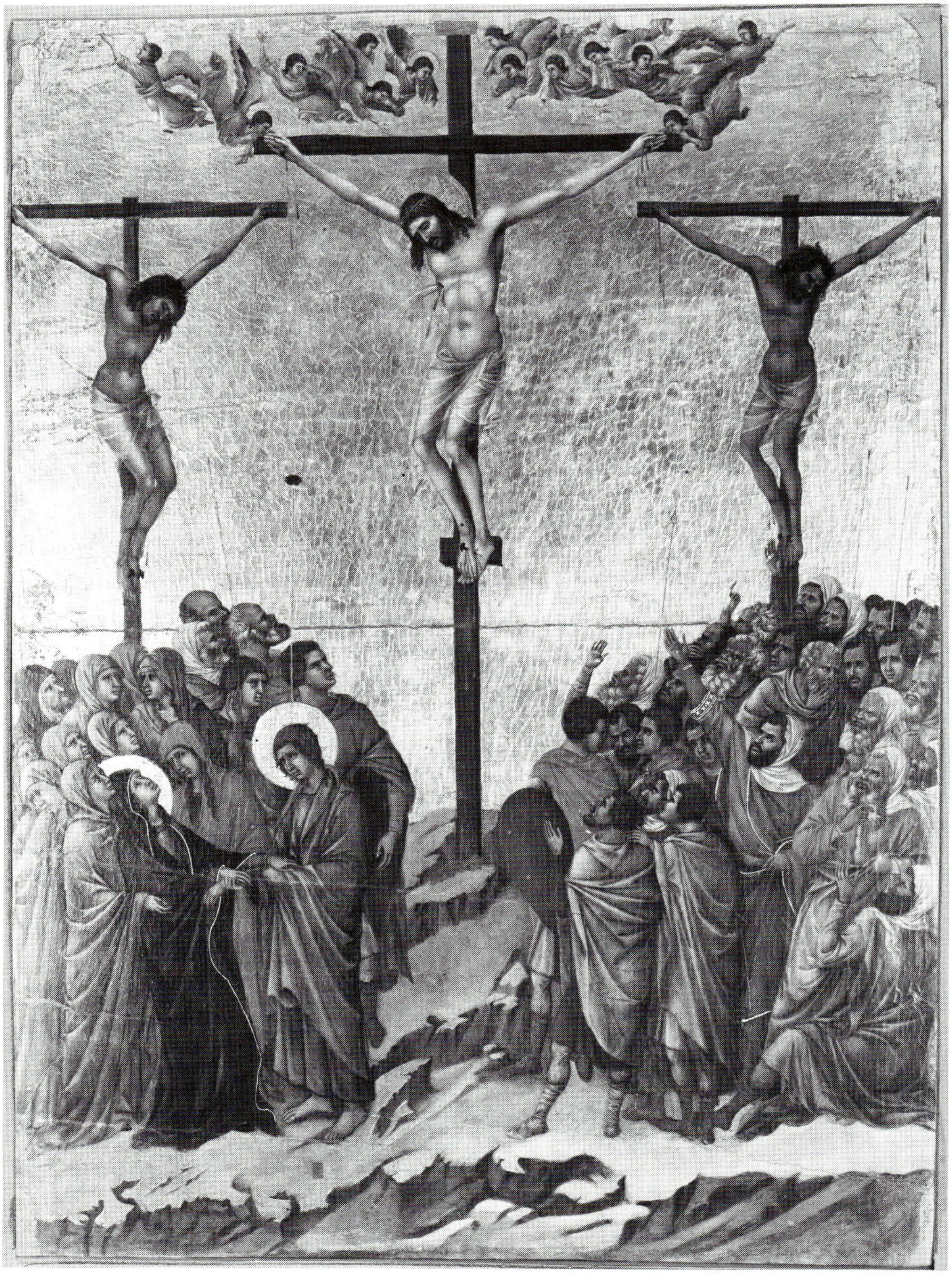

55 Duccio, Crucifixion from the back of the Maestà, 100 x 76 cm, Museo dell'Opera del Duomo, Siena.

remarkable difference between the narrative styles of Guido and Duccio. Had there been new developments in Byzantine art? Did Duccio's workshop have a Byzantine manuscript which was consulted rather like a pattern book? It is certainly worth noting that there were a number of liturgical manuscripts in Siena with miniatures of approximately the same date as the *Maestà* (figs. 52, 53). Although there are parallels between the *Maestà* and Byzantine miniaturist art of the period, there are no truly striking similarities. Nevertheless, the narrative scenes of the *Maestà* are definitely part of a Byzantine tradition,[51] and although their execution betrays a wide range of other influences, including that of Giovanni Pisano's sculptures, this does not detract from the fact that Duccio's workshop created a style which was so individual as to obscure its origins.

The canons seated in the choir looked on the back of the *Maestà*. The scenes of Christ's ministry, passion and glorification would have formed an edifying visual accompaniment to the reading of divine office. There is a certain visual unity to these scenes, despite their number. In the first place, of course, this is due to the clearly defined central axis, with the *Crucifixion* as the largest scene, but it is reinforced by Duccio's consistency in using approximately the same architectonic or landscape setting for events which take place in the same location. There are various opinions on the way the cycle should be read. One recent suggestion, by Deuchler, is that the central axis should be read from bottom to top as a self-contained set of essential scenes (fig. 54).[52]

Analysis of the individual scenes on the reverse of the *Maestà* reveals a number of general compositional features which deserve closer examination. In the first place Duccio has managed to strike an extremely subtle, if fragile, balance between group and individual. This is well illustrated in the *Crucifixion* (fig. 55), where the mourning angels above the Cross enhance the emotional impact of the scene. The spectators at the foot of the Cross have been arranged in two stacked groups, in accordance with the Byzantine custom. On the left is sorrow, and on the right a mixture of fear and aggression. These emotions pervade the entire group, as they do in earlier works like the sculptures by Nicola and Giovanni Pisano on the cathedral pulpit (fig. 34). The difference there is that the bystanders at the foot of the Cross are literally 'struck all of a heap'. Malicious scribes are whisked out of the picture by superhuman forces. Disciples are overcome by grief, and the Virgin collapses in a swoon. In Duccio's paintings not even groups lose

56 Cimabue, Crucifixion, Upper church of S. Francesco, Assisi.

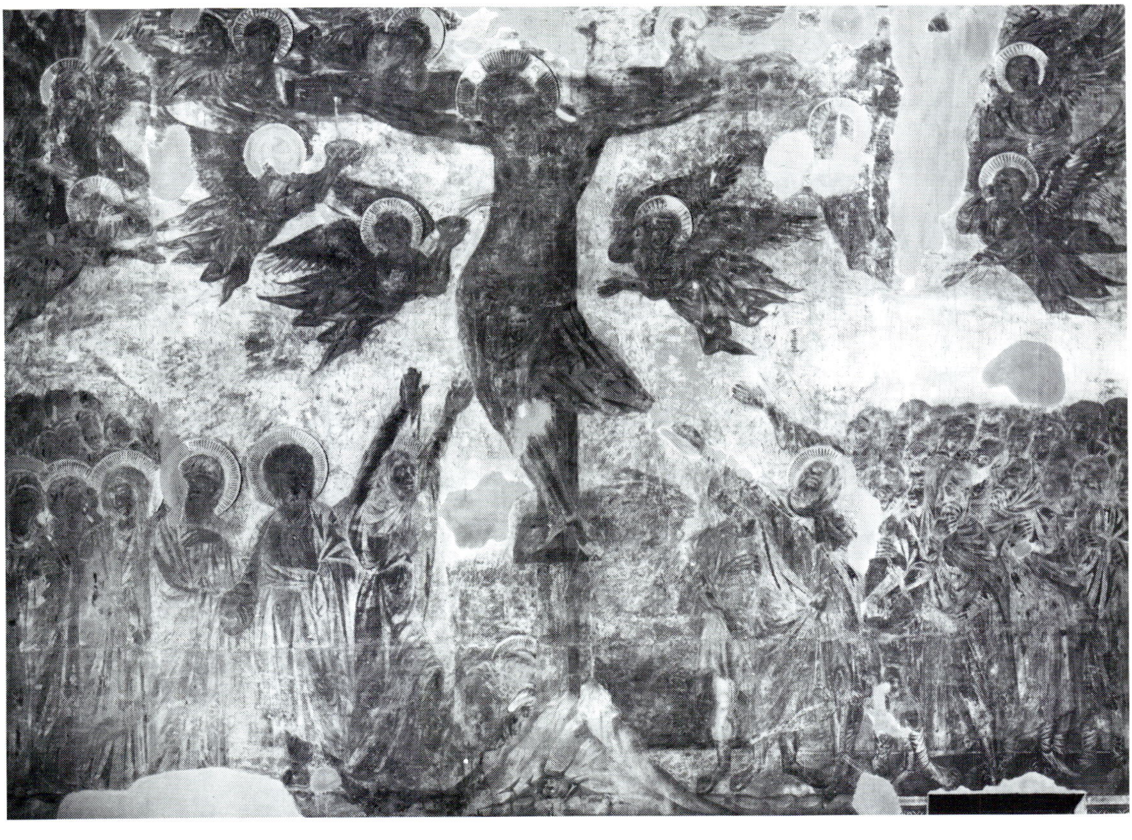

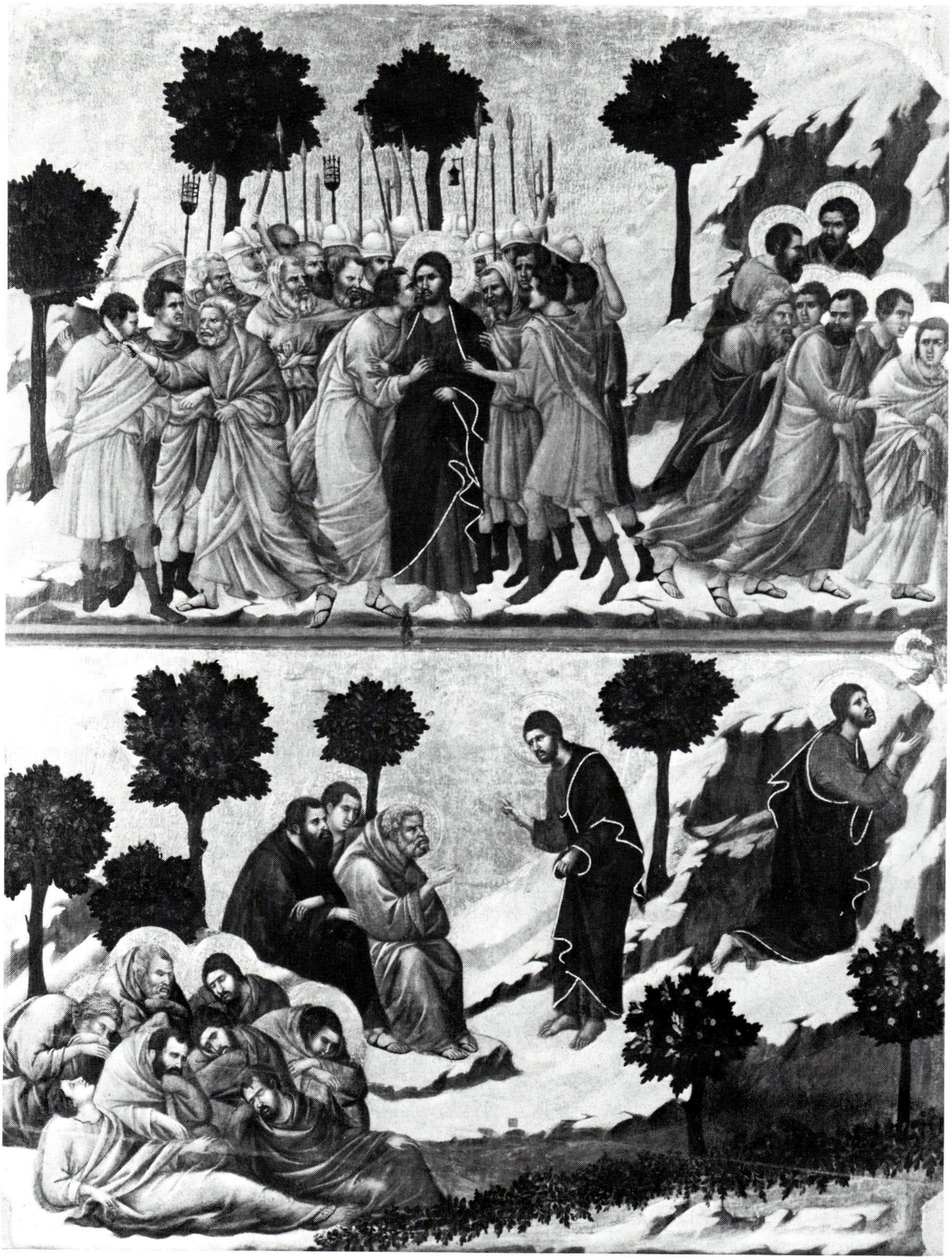

57 Duccio, Gethsemane and Betrayal from the Maestà,
50.5 x 77.5 cm, Museo dell'Opera del Duomo, Siena.

their *maintien*. Equilibrium prevails. In the *Crucifixion* he manages to keep the two most emotional reactions within the compositional confines of the group. The Virgin is depicted as the spiritual martyr – a sword pierced her heart, as the evangelist says. But she remains upright, and it is mainly the colour of her cloak which makes her stand out. The centurion is the only member of the fearful, hate-crazed crowd on the right to recognise Christ as his Lord. He does not shrink back, but boldly stands his ground. His gesture is one of greeting, not rejection or fear. Yet despite this contrast with the other figures he remains an integral part of the group. Cimabue's fresco in the upper church at Assisi provides us with a very different conception of this scene (fig. 56). There the two people with the most emotional reactions to the event, Mary Magdalen and the centurion, have been removed from the groups of onlookers and placed in highly expressive poses in the foreground.

The subtlety of the equilibrium in Duccio's work becomes apparent when we compare his *Kiss of Judas* with the same scene painted by his pupil, Ugolino di Neri, on the predella of the altarpiece for Santa Croce in Florence (fig. 57, 58). The apostles have already absented themselves in Ugolino's painting. In the *Maestà* they are seen leaving in a body, fleeing the scene of betrayal. Duccio has established a harmony of movement by balancing the group of apostles on the right with Peter's action on the left. He is moving in the opposite direction, lunging forward to cut off Malchus's ear. Malchus himself is a compositional part of the group which has come to seize Christ, surrounding him and Judas in a single cohesive cluster. This compositional balance is lacking in Ugolino's painting, and there is no cohesion of movement. Each figure moves independently of the others, immersed in his own action. This imparts a greater individuality to each separate incident; it becomes a narrative in itself. Judas kisses Christ, a soldier moves forward menacingly, Peter cuts off Malchus's ear. Duccio brings a visual cohesion to all these separate instants, establishing a balance not only between the individual and the group, but also between individual actions or emotions and the totality of the event. The essence of the scene is expressed in the interrelated movement of groups of figures.

An impressive example of this is the *Entombment* (fig. 59), in which the disciples around the tomb bend further and further forwards, culminating in the almost horizontal figure of the Virgin leaning down to kiss Christ. Her pose is also a formal intensification of this stooping motif, for there is a gradual transition from the attentive onlooker on the right to the prone figure of the dead Christ. Mary Magdalen's despair, as she raises her arms to heaven, is tempered by the fact that her stance has been carefully designed to

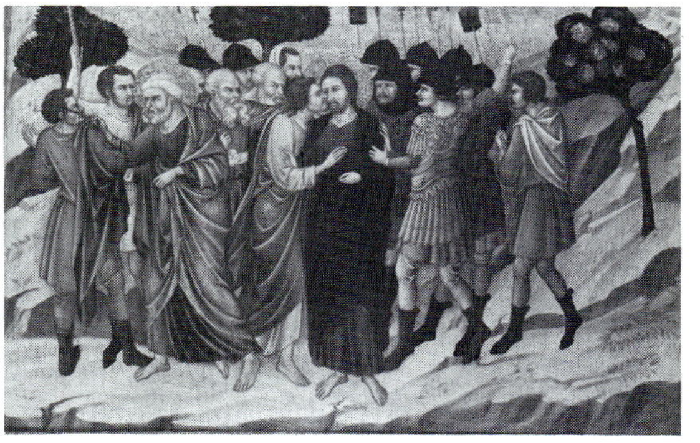

58 Ugolino di Neri, Betrayal, 34.5 x 53 cm, National Gallery, London.

provide a formal counterbalance to the stooping of the other figures. The entire figural composition is in effect a superb, unified ornament balanced subtly against the landscape background. What a contrast with Guido's organisation of this scene (fig. 25). There the disciples swoop over Christ in panic-stricken grief, with the sole exception of a figure who is probably meant to be Joseph of Arimathaea. Ugolino, in his version of the scene, once again disrupts the cohesion of the group around the tomb (fig. 60). Mary Magdalen's 'hands up' gesture is more reminiscent of the dramatic expressiveness of Guido's Magdalen than of her sorrowing pose in Duccio's *Entombment*.

The *Entry into Jerusalem*, which is the starting point of Duccio's Passion narrative, is the only scene apart from the *Crucifixion* to extend over two registers, and for that reason alone deserves closer examination (fig. 61). It is generally assumed, and rightly so, that Duccio was influenced by Guido da Siena's version of the scene, which was painted (on canvas, strangely enough) on a form of antependium which probably served as a Lenten hanging (fig. 62). Guido shows Christ riding in at bottom left on a she-ass accompanied by her foal. The apostles follow in a body behind Christ. The hills leading up to the city are packed with the inhabitants of Jerusalem, who have come to honour their king. Young boys spread out their cloaks before him. The onlookers wave palm fronds, which some children are tearing from the trees. The only motif omitted by Duccio is the mother who is holding up her child to Christ. Duccio, in his version, makes Guido's spatial organisation more explicit. A road flanked by walls leads up to the city gate. Beyond the walls are gardens with trees. We know that Duccio was deliberately trying to create a suggestion of depth from his own overpainting (*pentimento*) of a female figure (fig. 63) which would have destroyed the overall legibility of the scene as an assembly of superimposed zones. Duccio has given

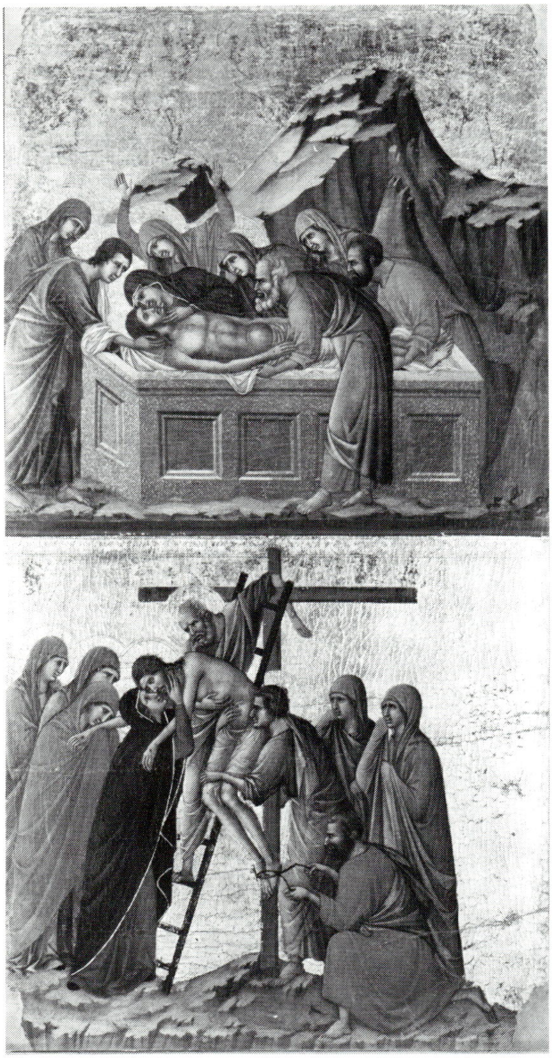

59 Duccio, Deposition and Entombment from the Maestà, 101.5 x 53.5 cm, Museo dell'Opera del Duomo, Siena.

the traditional programme an almost topographical realism, but we should exercise more caution than has been shown by many art-historical interpreters. In the first place Duccio enlivened an existing programme; he did not create a new one. Secondly, his realism operates on two levels, and this is typical of the Trecento. His city is both Jerusalem and Siena. We find a similar awareness of place in a passage in the *Meditationes vitae Christi* describing how Mary and Joseph set out to search for Jesus, not knowing that he was lecturing the doctors in the temple. 'Very early the next morning they left the house to look for Him in the neighbourhood, for one could return by several roads; as he who returns from Siena to Pisa might travel by way of Poggibonsi or Colle or other places. Therefore they searched on other roads, asking acquaintances and friends.'[53] The object is to give the story greater conviction by relating the geographical setting to a topography known to the reader or viewer. However, the most important feature of Duccio's *Entry into Jerusalem*, and the one that sets it apart from Guido's version, is the overall organisation of the scene. The narrative owes its expressive value to the actions of the separate, coherent groups. The fact that those groups are directly related to the architecture greatly enhances the visual expression of the scene. The narrative acquires its shape from the way in which the groups are related to the gate of Jerusalem. Most of them are going into the city, but others are waiting at the gate to honour their Messiah. Others are content merely to look on. All these actions are expressed by group behaviour which has been deliberately related to the architecture.

The very essence of Duccio's narrative skill is displayed in the scene with the fewest figures – *The three Marys at the sepulchre* (fig. 64). It is a scene almost totally devoid of action. The angel gestures in one direction and the women react by moving back very slightly the other way. The white marble of the tomb gives off a lambent sheen, and the hills are bathed in a soft, gentle light. We learn of Christ's triumph over death from the minimal actions of the angel's tender gesture and the slight withdrawal of the women.

Let us return to the Madonna on the front of the altarpiece (figs. 41, 43). On the footrest of the throne there is an inscription which is so prominent and so unusual that it warrants a closer look. It reads: MATER SCA DEI / SIS CAUSA SENIS REQUIEI / SIS DUCCIO VITA / TE QUIA PINXIT ITA ('Holy Mother of God be thou the cause of peace for Siena, and, because he painted thee thus, of life for Duccio'). Now some authors see this as an early manifestation of a growing self-awareness on the part of the artist, but in that they are mistaken.[54] The name of the artist is often found on important and costly works of art from the middle ages. For example, many goldsmiths signed their creations. Nor was it uncommon for Sienese artists to sign important paintings, as Guido da Siena did with his *Madonna* for San Domenico. On those grounds alone we cannot regard this signature as a portent of a new breed of self-aware artist. Duccio was painting the supreme guardian of his city, and he took the opportunity to place his own life under her protection.

As we have seen, it is difficult to visualise the effect which the *Maestà* must have had when it stood on the high altar of the cathedral. On the cover of a municipal accounts book of 1482 there is a depiction of a renewed dedication of Siena to the Virgin and, in the background we can just glimpse the *Maestà*. Although there is too little detail to aid any

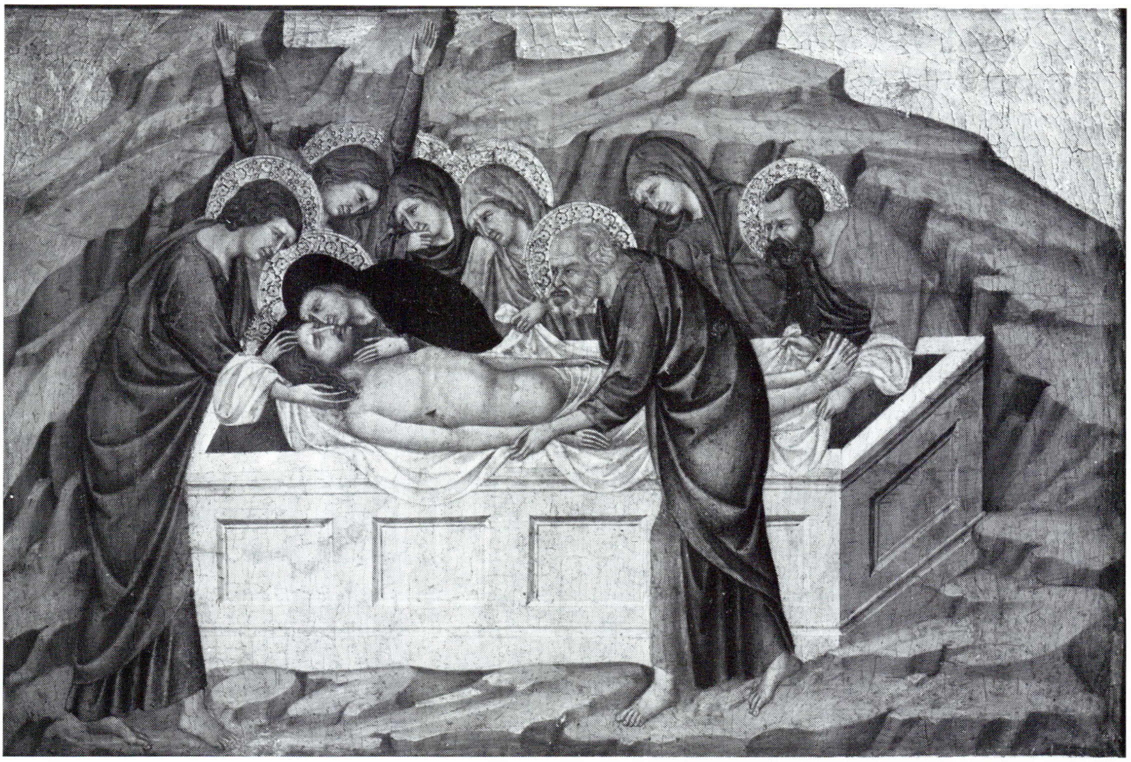

60 Ugolino di Neri, Entombment, 34.5 x 53 cm, Staatliche Museen, Gemäldegalerie, Berlin-Dahlem.

attempt at reconstruction, this illustration does tell us that there was a canopy over the altarpiece. We also know from the record of a payment made in 1339 that angels with candlesticks had been commissioned in order to give added lustre to the painting. A cathedral inventory of 1435 gives a good idea of the embellishment of the high altar. 'A high altar of marble with a panel on it which is painted on both sides, with the figure of Nostra Donna and several saints and with all of the Passion of Jesus Christ, with the canopies (suspended) from above on four iron poles, with three little tabernacles inside of which are three little carved and gilded angels that descend for the administration of the sacred mass, with the host and with cups and with covering for the hands, and four more little angels with candlesticks in hand who serve the altar behind and in front, and for the singing at the said altar are two iron grilles, with a vermilion cloth to cover the said altar, with fringe of silk and painted in the centre, two angels who hold a tabernacle painted with the body of Christ, and two little boxes painted with the coat of arms of the Opera that sit on the said altar, in which are placed alms, and two ostrich eggs in front of the said altar, hung from on high, with five iron candlesticks. Four little, carved angels are suspended with iron candlesticks in their hands, of which two are in front of the altar and two behind, that hold candles which light up the altar.'[55]

The *Maestà*, in other words, gave rise to a host of ancillary furnishings: a canopy, legions of angels holding candlesticks or tabernacles, ostrich eggs and so on. All these embellishments served to underscore the sacral nature of the high altar. The liturgical objects mentioned in the first chapter were still present, but they now acquired their proper significance against the backdrop of this massive altarpiece. The use of ostrich eggs is not as strange as it might seem. In Hagia Sophia, for instance, there were large numbers of them set in chandeliers. They were placed in chapels and near altars not only as curiosities but also because they embodied the hope of eternal life and symbolised the virgin birth.[56] The candles highlighted the painted figures against the gold ground of the altarpiece. At one time it was thought that the oculus of 1287 had dictated the iconography of the *Maestà*, which stood beneath it (fig. 65). This window consists of three scenes of the Virgin's glorification, flanked by the evangelists and the patron saints of Siena. The implausibility of that theory will strike anyone who has tried to determine the function of the altarpiece. The *Maestà*, with its myriad scenes, was a self-contained world, a sort of eucharistic event in itself, and the addition of all the embellishments

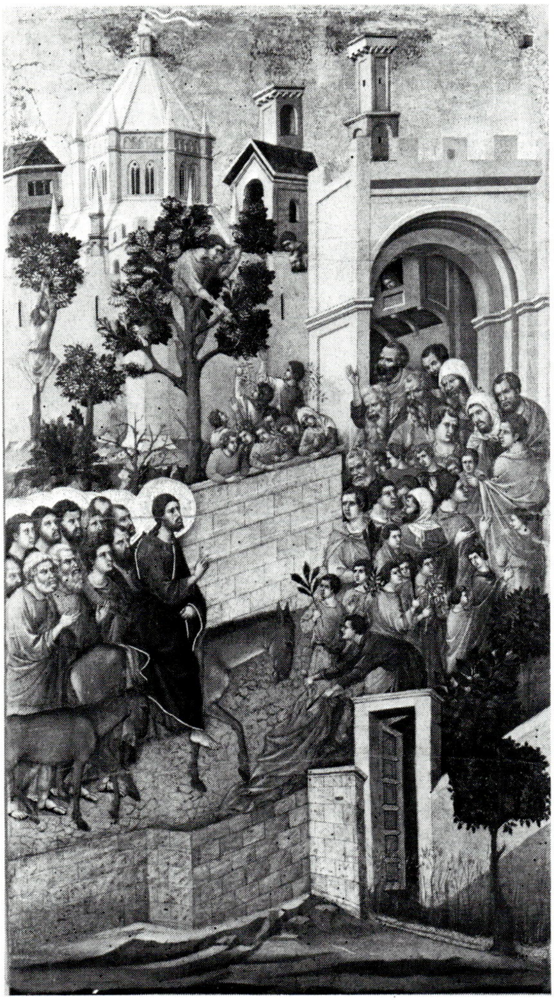

61 Duccio, Entry into Jerusalem from the Maestà, 101 x 56.5 cm, Museo dell'Opera del Duomo, Siena.

made it an object which totally dominated the space around it. The window above the canopy had a completely different visual significance. Maria Assunta, flanked by Siena's patron saints, was a radiant seal which the city government had ordered to be placed on the building.[57]

People have often been suprised that the *Maestà* had so little influence on later works. The high altar of Siena cathedral now had an altarpiece which could be regarded as a synthesis of the various developments in thirteenth-century art, and yet it was never widely imitated.[58] Once again, this reveals a tendency to think in terms of artistic conception without examining the specific background to the commission for an altarpiece. The *Maestà* was quite simply too expensive for most churches, and anyway, what workshop could possibly carry out such a commission? There was only one attempt to follow the example set by Siena. It was probably around 1315 that Duccio's workshop, or a group of its affiliated artists, was asked to execute a *Maestà* for the high altar of the cathedral in Massa Marittima (figs. 66, 67), together with a large crucifix for the wall above the altar (fig. 68). The cathedral choir had been enlarged a short time before, and these two commissions must be seen in relation to the modification of the interior, which may have been carried out by artisans from Siena's Opera del Duomo. The new choir was so deep that it called for a double-sided altarpiece like the *Maestà* to close off the space for the canons and to serve as a fitting visual accompaniment to the liturgy. The panel was later trimmed around the figure of the Virgin, leaving a Madonna altarpiece which was relegated to a side chapel, where it became known as the *Madonna delle grazie*. Little remained of the scenes on the back. The painting was restored in 1947 and the front and back were separated. A second restoration had to be carried out in 1980 to correct damage resulting from the 1947 operation.[59]

A document has come down to us which provides indirect confirmation that the reason why there were so few imitations of the *Maestà* was that it was too ambitious for most communities. In 1316 Massa found itself in financial difficulties. 'Since the work on the new panel of the Blessed Virgin Mary cannot be completed and brought to a conclusion so long as there is not enough money with which to pay expenses involved in the project, and since, by any further delay in the project, that part which has been done might be more easily damaged, it was ordered by the nine Lords etc. that Master Peruccio, the director of the Opera of San Cerbone [sc. the Opera del Duomo], should lend the necessary money for doing the work of the panel and that, as surety for the loan, a gift of all the wax that is offered on the feast day of Saint Mary in August should be pledged to Master Peruccio, receiving it on behalf of the Opera of San Cerbone. And until he has been paid back all of this money, the gift of the wax will remain his for this reason.'[60] The Nine of Massa approved the loan for the simple reason that the altarpiece would never have been finished otherwise. The security was the wax for the candles to be used at the feast of the Assumption. The Madonna's majesty was a prize dearly bought.

A *Nativity* and an *Adoration* (figs. 69, 70) by Duccio's school undoubtedly belonged at one time on the pinnacles of an altarpiece modelled on the Siena *Maestà*,[61] but it is difficult to say whether they actually came from the *Maestà* of Massa Marittima. Their style is not very close to that of the surviving scenes,

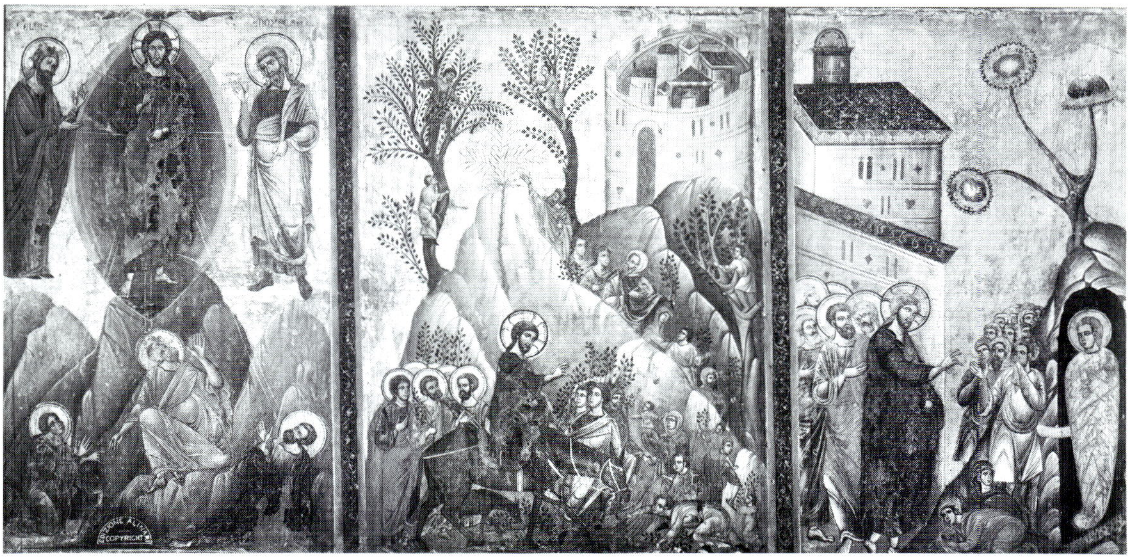

62 Guido da Siena, Transfiguration, Entry into Jerusalem, Raising of Lazarus, 90 x 186 cm, Pinacoteca Nazionale, Siena.

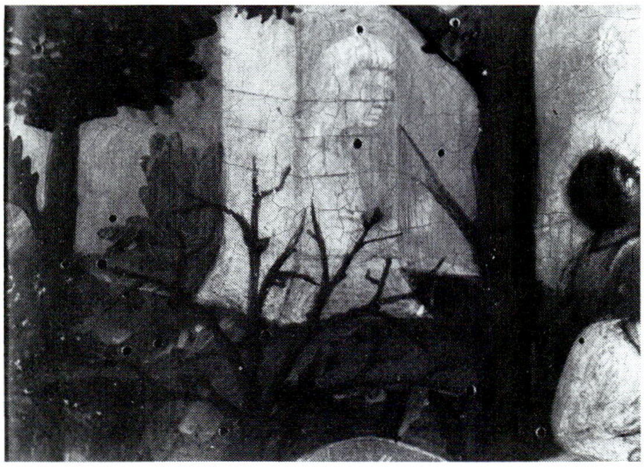

63 Duccio, Entry into Jerusalem (infrared detail).

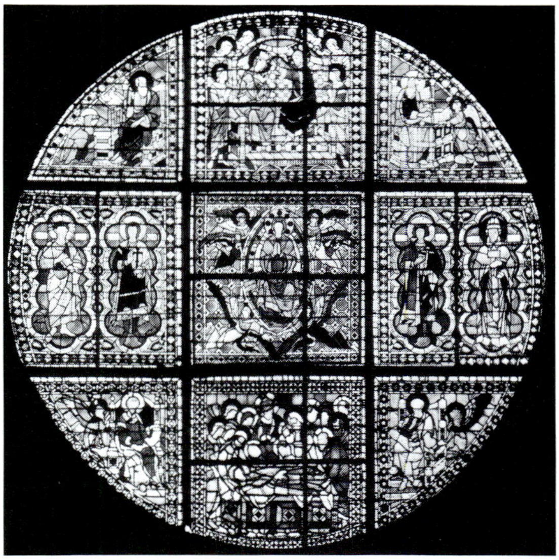

65 Duccio (?), Stained glass window, diameter ca. 700 cm, Duomo, Siena.

but that is hardly conclusive evidence, given the major stylistic inconsistencies among those scenes. This lack of stylistic cohesion suggests that the master's supervision of the work was rather lax. Duccio was an old man by now, and we know that he died between 1315 and 1318. It is now generally accepted that the soldiers at the foot of the Cross, with their oriental features and exotic fashions, are additions made twenty years later, but even if one disregards them the differences in figure types are so great as to detract from the work as a whole. The figures surrounding Christ in *Christ before Annas* are a hotchpotch of facial types and movement motifs compared to the group in the same scene by Duccio.

There is another imitation of Duccio's *Maestà*, but since it is not an altarpiece it really lies outside the scope of this book. It is the fresco of the *Maestà* which Simone Martini painted in 1315 for the great council chamber of Siena's Palazzo Pubblico (fig. 71). This is Simone's earliest known work, and it is immediately apparent that he had set out to implant Sienese art in the French Gothic tradition. The fresco itself bears little resemblance to an Italian mural, suggesting rather a sumptuous tapestry designed to cover an entire wall. The Madonna is seated on a Gothic throne beneath a canopy, rather like an earthly queen attending a tournament. The Child is depicted in a pose which was unknown in Italy at the time, and it is one which cannot be traced to any of the known Byzantine programmes governing the relationship between Mother and Child. French sculpture provides the only source for a frontal Christ standing on his mother's lap. The kneeling patron saints of the city are preceded by angels who are proferring dishes laden with flowers. What makes this fresco so interesting is that it shows that Duccio's *Maestà* had immediately acquired a political significance, with the result that it could appear a mere four years later in the guise of a monumental seal of the 'Civitas Virginis' in the most important civic hall of Siena.

The political function of Simone's *Maestà* is spelled out explicitly in the lengthy inscriptions, some of which are supposedly spoken by the Madonna herself. This is her reply to the gift of flowers.

The angelic flowers, the rose and lily
With which the heavenly fields are decked
Do not delight me more than righteous counsel.
But some see who for their own estate
Despise me and deceive my land
And are most praised when they speak worst.
Whoever stands condemned by this my speech take heed.

She addresses the saints as follows.

My beloved bear it in mind
When your just devotees make supplication
I will make them content as you desire,
But if the powerful do harm to the weak
Weighing them down with shame or hurt
Your prayers are not for these
Nor for whoever deceives my land.[62]

Let us now return to Massa Marittima. Since 1299 the Augustinians had been building a church there, which they finally completed in 1348.[63] Ambrogio Lorenzetti, who also worked for the Augustinians in Siena, was evidently commissioned around 1335 to produce a painting for the high altar in Massa (fig. 72). When he arrived there he found that lone imitation of Duccio's *Maestà* on the high altar of the cathedral. It evidently provided him with his inspiration, for he proceeded to create a painting which was based on that altarpiece. To use a modern

66-67 Duccio (shop), Maestà (fragments), front and back, 179 x 99 cm, Duomo, Massa Marittima.

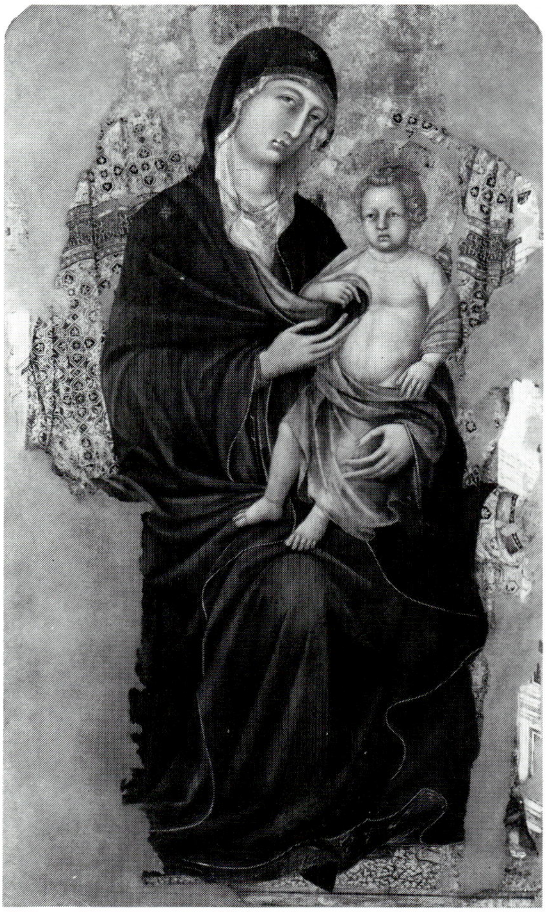

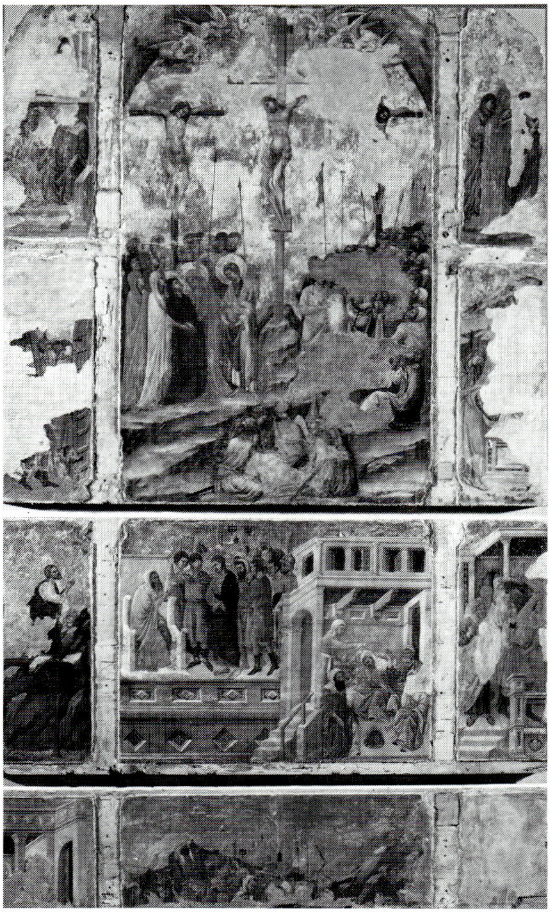

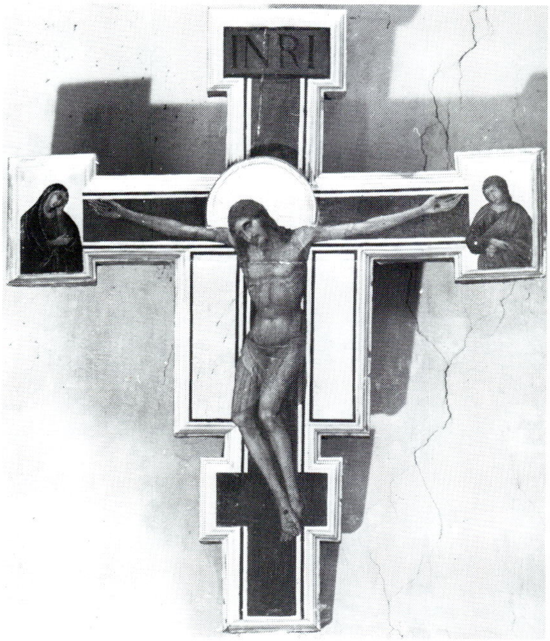

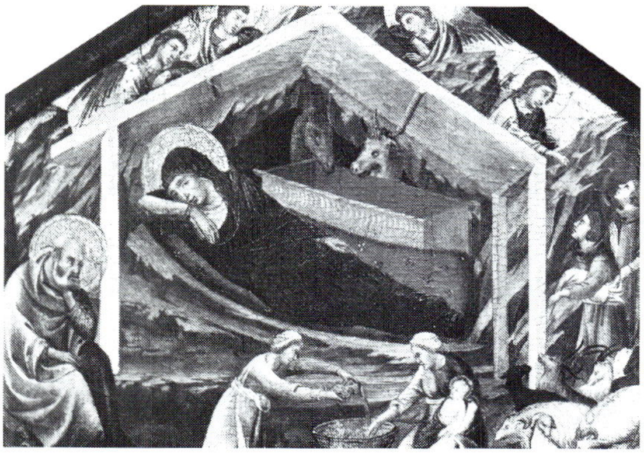

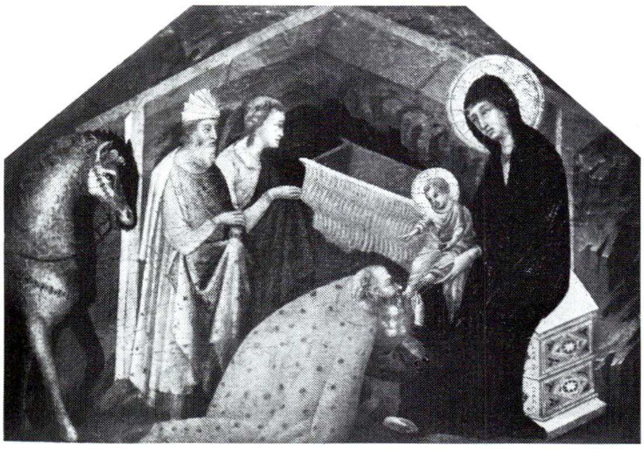

68 Duccio (shop), Crucifix, 218 x 175 cm, Duomo, Massa Marittima.
69 Duccio (shop), Nativity, 26 x 38 cm, Private collection, The Hague.
70 Duccio (shop), Adoration, 28 x 40 cm, Private collection, Eindhoven.

phrase, he painted an alternative *Maestà*, producing a radical reinterpretation of Duccio's vision of the heavenly hosts. Here we have a solid, plastic Madonna framed by angels' wings and seated on a spatial throne of steps. She and her Child are oblivious of the outside world, so absorbed are they in their intimate cheek-to-cheek. In terms of Byzantine formulae this relationship is known as the Eleousa type.

The Madonna is presented as the loving mother whose virtue invites imitation. On the white step at the foot of the throne sits Faith, gazing at his reflection in an image of the Trinity. To the left, on the second, green step, Hope stares up at the tall spire he holds in his hands. But the greatest of these (in this case the highest) is Charity, who sits at the Virgin's feet holding a flaming red heart. Ambrogio was rather fond of adding allegorical figures to his depictions of the Madonna. Various authors have investigated the individual significance of those figures,[64] but seldom does one find any reference to a totally different meaning which the Madonna acquires from this particular context. Ambrogio has placed a liturgical motif in a moralistic exegesis. He is rather like a preacher, enumerating the virtues inherent in the Virgin's motherhood. The effect of this painting is to turn the altar into a pulpit from which an appeal is made not only to the piety of the congregation but also to its intellect and knowledge of theology.

Even more surprising than the central group of this altarpiece is the organisation of the surrounding saints. They are no longer arranged in ranks parallel to the picture surface but in three-dimensional groups literally clustered around the throne. The picture surface for this celestial vision is organised according to human ideas of space, and here the haloes play a particularly important role. In principle a halo presses the figure against the flat surface, but here Ambrogio has used a series of haloes one behind the other in order to reinforce the suggestion of depth. They are also very ornate haloes. Duccio and his pupils usually decorated their haloes with painted ornamentation, but Ambrogio's workshop used a variety of punch-marks. These punched haloes and the decoration of the clothing make the altarpiece look extremely costly. The golden sheen of the haloes serves to connect figures which are otherwise in marked colour contrast – sometimes as markedly as the white, green and red of the steps at the foot of the throne.

It is unnecessary for our purposes to identify each of the saints in this altarpiece. At the top are patriarchs and prophets. Below and to the left are the principal saints of the western church: John the Evangelist, Peter and Paul. The figures on the right

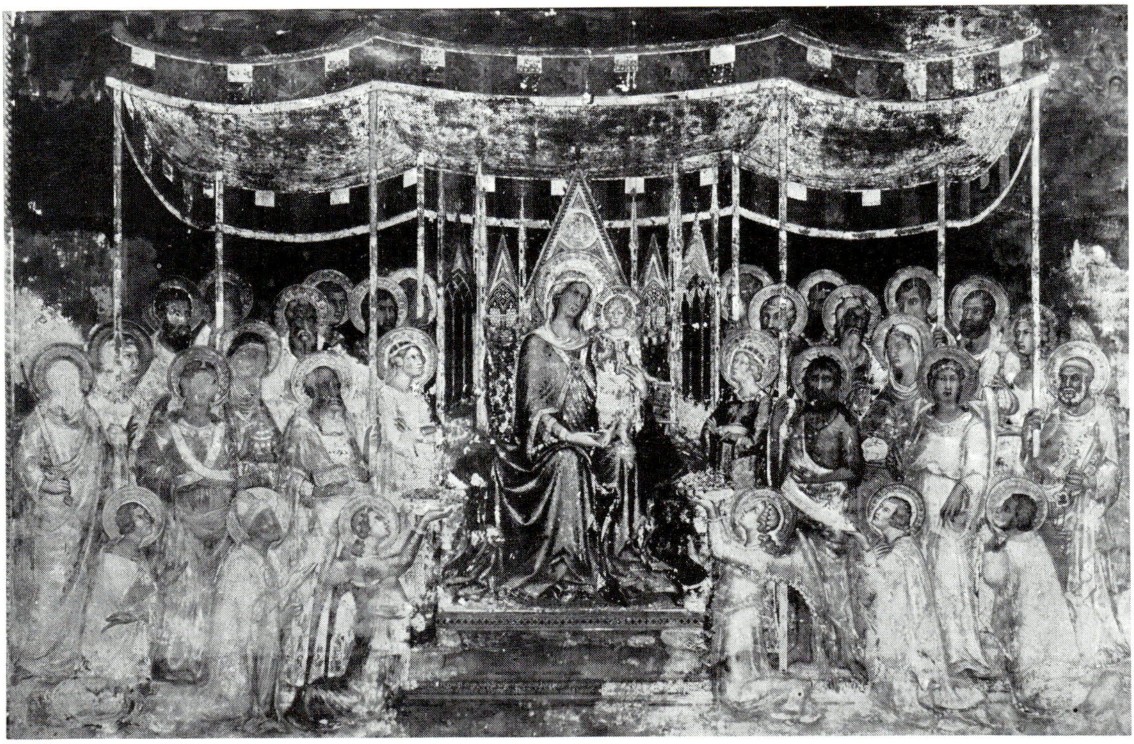

71 Simone Martini, Maestà, 1315, Sala della Pace, Palazzo Pubblico, Siena.

of the throne are probably the great saints of the eastern church: Andrew, Matthew and Matthias. At the bottom stand the saints who were especially revered by the Augustinians, and by the Augustinians of Massa Marittima in particular. On the right, for example, is Cerbone, the patron saint of Massa and the first bishop of the old Etruscan town of Populonia, to which diocese Massa belonged. Around 500, so the story goes, Cerbone was summoned to Rome by the pope to account for his actions. When he arrived at the gates of the city, after a long and arduous journey, he discovered that he had forgotten to bring a present for the Holy Father. But the bishop was a countryman, at home in the wilds of the Maremma, and he solved his little embarrassment by calling down a pair of geese which were flying by and taking them in to the pope as his gift. Cerbone is portrayed in an active rather than a representative attitude, as are most of the other saints in Ambrogio's *Maestà*. They really are looking at the Madonna and worshipping her. The angels, too, are active, presenting lilies and playing musical instruments. This is the first appearance of angels honouring the Madonna with their music. Later they were to become one of the established motifs of Sienese art.

Ambrogio's *Maestà* marks the culmination of this visual theme. A *Maestà* like Duccio's was just too expensive for most altars. Moreover, its content no longer appealed. Representative images of that kind belonged to the past, as did heavenly hosts, and Ambrogio's inclusion of that message in his *Maestà* was almost certainly deliberate. The individuality of a new breed of artist is revealed not in the inscription on the throne of Duccio's *Maestà* but in the complex, antithetical altarpiece of San Agostino in Massa Marittima. It was not without reason that two later writers, Ghiberti and Vasari, presented Ambrogio as the prototype of the learned painter, the 'pictor doctus'. By taking a cool, critical look at a traditional form he acted like a true intellectual, and that was very unusual for an artist of his period. What prompted this analytical approach? Perhaps we can regard Ambrogio as the artistic exponent of the secular intelligentsia which Siena had gained when it lured so many scholars away from the University of Bologna. The transfer fee, needless to say, was considerable. Siena owed the foundation of its own university to this 'migratio Bolognese' of 1322. It is almost impossible to overstate the importance of a university for the cultural life of a medieval city. It is certainly reflected in Ambrogio's art. He almost certainly consulted Bolognese jurists for the huge fresco programme with the *Allegory of good government*, which he executed in the same period as the Massa altarpiece. The virtues we see seated on benches and

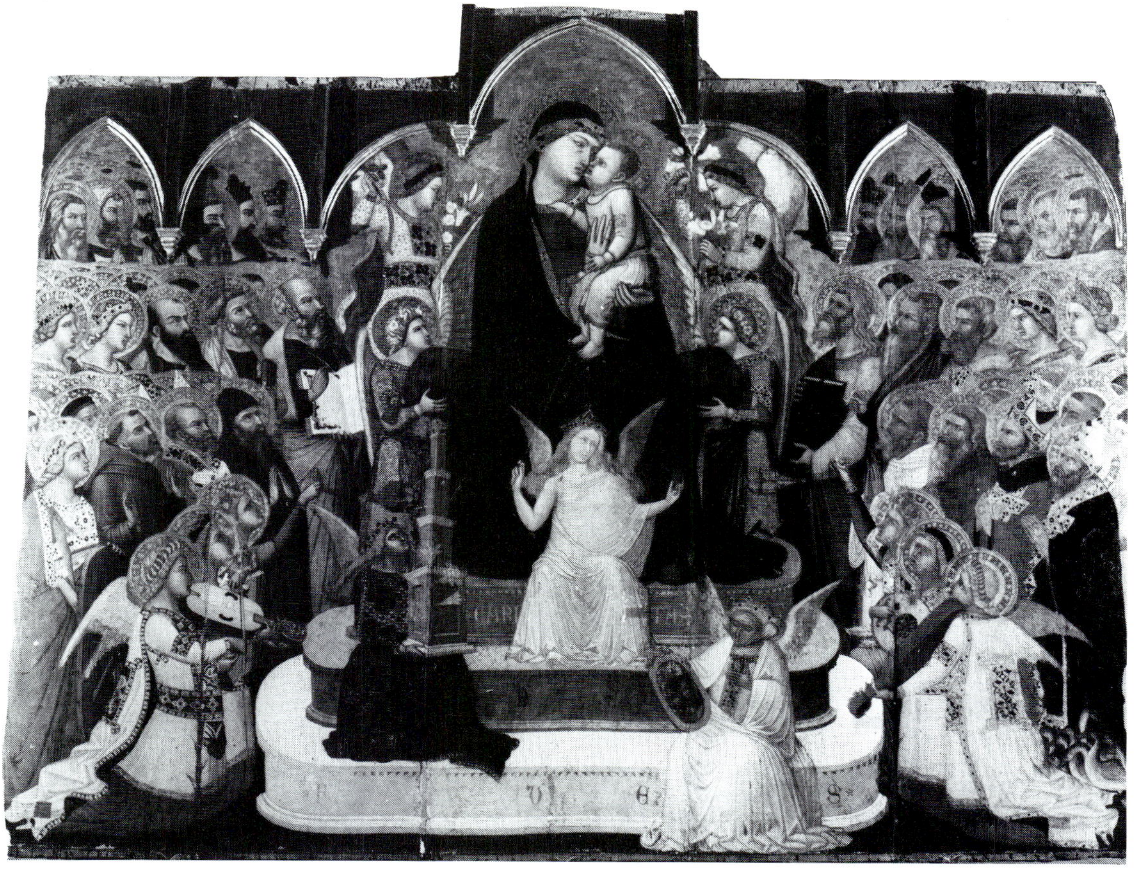

72 Ambrogio Lorenzetti, Maestà, 155 x 206 cm, Municipio, Massa Marittima.

thrones in Bolognese illuminations of fourteenth-century legal manuscripts are the keys to Ambrogio's *Allegory of good government*, and it is they who present the maternal Madonna in a didactic role in the altarpiece in Massa Marittima.

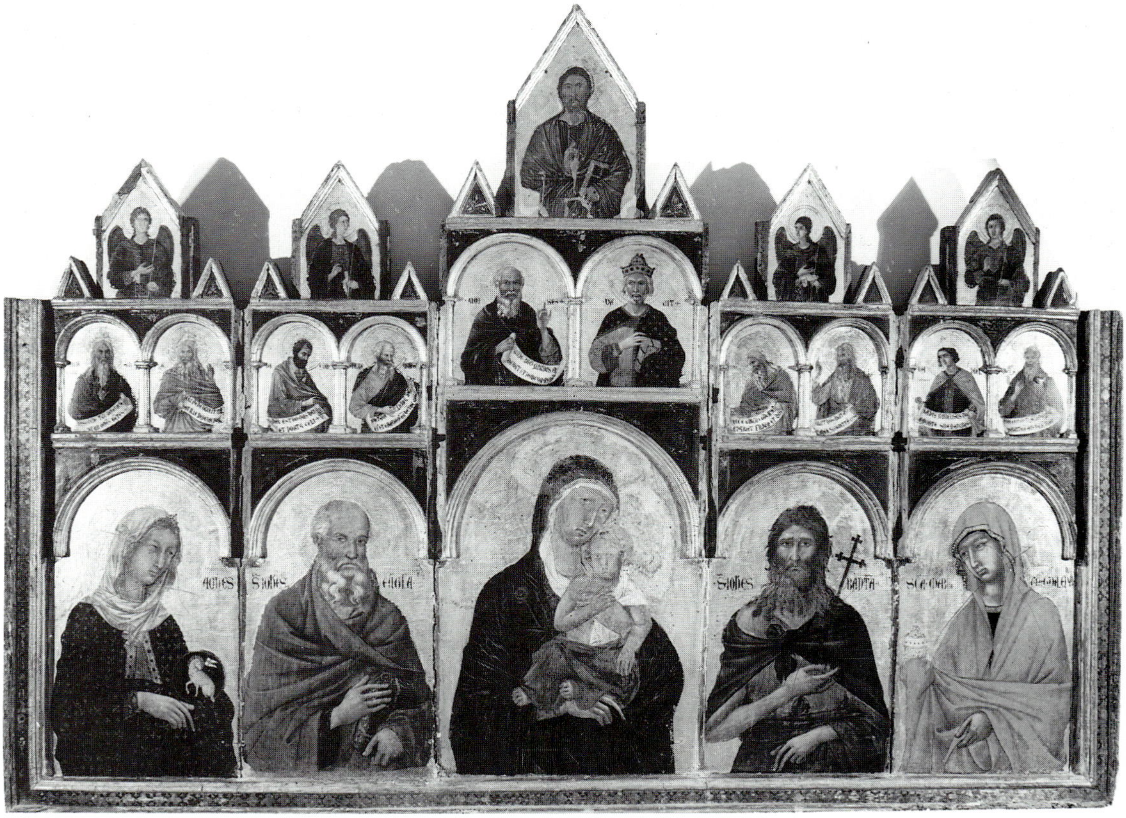

73 Duccio, Polyptych, 185 x 257 cm, Pinacoteca Nazionale, Siena.

IV

EARLY SIENESE POLYPTYCHS

One of the many commissions which Duccio received from the Dominicans resulted in the painting now known as polyptych. no. 28 in the Pinacoteca in Siena, which we have already touched on in passing (fig. 38). It is a work which occupies a key position in altarpiece development. At first sight it appears to be a variant of the dossal which had been developed in Guido da Siena's workshop. It is a type of altarpiece made to fit the width of the altar table. The half-length figures occupy arches, and the Madonna in the centre takes up more space than the flanking saints. It is slightly higher than a dossal, due to the presence of Christ Logos and angels above the Madonna and saints – a motif already encountered in the upper register of altarpieces by Guido da Siena (figs. 24, 29). Above the Christ Child in the arms of his Mother there is a heavenly Redeemer. The arches are part of the wooden structure of the panel, and both they and the surface of the panel have been covered with a preparatory layer of linen. The raising of the gesso at the edges shows that the main frame and the framing of the angels and the Redeemer were an integral part of the structure before the gesso and paint were applied. The piers and pinnacles separating the figures, however, were added afterwards.

Closer inspection reveals that there is one fundamental difference between this altarpiece and a dossal, notwithstanding all the apparent similarities. The wooden support of a dossal consisted of horizontally grained planks, whereas here it is a structure of five separate panels with the grain running vertically which are held together by a kind of frame box and are subdivided by piers and pinnacles. The entire structure has been put together in accordance with a specific system of proportions. The ratio between height and width is the same as that between the width of the central panel and a side panel. In Perugia there is an altarpiece by Vigoroso da Siena of ca. 1280 which represents an interesting intermediate stage between dossal and polyptych (fig. 47). Although it is composed of horizontally grained planks its upper contour is broken by five gables cut from a single plank.[65] This gave the altarpiece a new form which echoed its architectural setting. Although Duccio's altarpiece adhered fairly closely to the standard ratio between height and width it was no longer a straightforward horizontal strip closing off the back of the altar table. The polyptych in its frame box was soon abandoned in favour of the polyptych supported by lateral buttresses, and it was this type, in numerous shapes and variants, which remained customary throughout the Trecento.

The fact that a polyptych consists of several more or less self-contained elements not only creates problems for the restorer. It also entailed a change in production methods. The standard procedure in a large workshop was to allocate individual panels to several collaborators, each of whom worked on his own under the overall supervision of the master. The degree of supervision varied from altarpiece to altarpiece, with the result that connoisseurs have developed a passion for attributing different parts of a polyptych to different hands. In the case of polyptych no. 28, for instance, it is believed that the supposedly inferior outer panels are the work of a second artist. However, this distinction has little historical relevance, for at the time the altarpiece went under the name of just one artist, and that was undoubtedly Duccio. Unfortunately it is very easy to break a polyptych down into its component parts, and this is exactly what happened to many of them, with disastrous results. In some cases we no longer know where a particular segment belonged in the overall composition, a case in point being the Pisa polyptych by Simone Martini, for which two reconstructions have been proposed (figs. 78, 79). A far more common, and far more damaging practice was to sell off the parts of a polyptych separately, as we saw in the case of altarpieces by both Guido and Duccio. It is

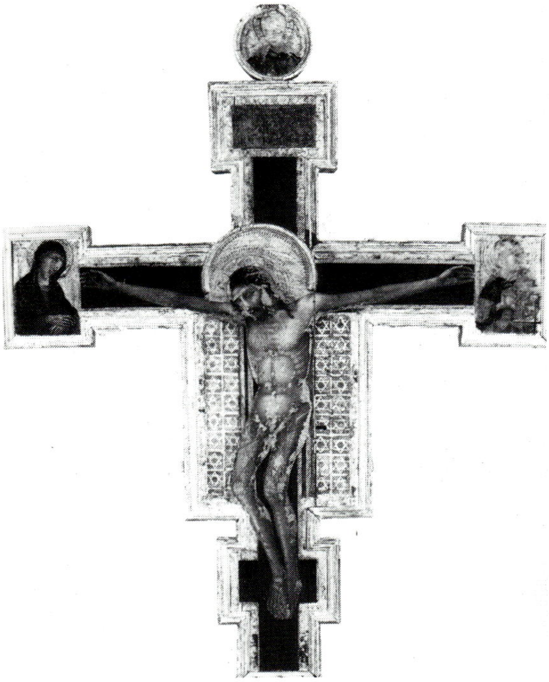

74 Duccio (shop), Crucifix, 235 x 187 cm, S. Maria Annunziata (Ospedale della Scala), Siena.

often necessary to reconstruct an altarpiece before it can be allocated a place in the development of this art form. This used to be done by associating certain panels with others bearing a signature or a date, or both. This evidence, circumstantial as it may have been, provided the 'proof' for attributions and datings. Nowadays the main purpose of reconstruction is to get an idea of the original form of the altarpiece. As a result modern reconstructions tend to be less a matter of incidental accumulations of panels around a single dated or signed work. A sound modern reconstruction involves painstaking physical examination and a great deal of detective work in tracking down the provenance of the various fragments, sifting through old records, and searching for old drawings and photographs.

Another work in the Pinacoteca in Siena which is attributed to Duccio is polyptych no. 47 (fig. 73). Its date is uncertain, partly because of the poor state of conservation. Some date it shortly before and others shortly after the *Maestà* of 1308-11. Whatever its precise date it is certainly the oldest surviving polyptych with a structure extending over three registers. It originally came from the hospital church of Santa Maria della Scala – so called because it stands at the foot of the steps leading up to the cathedral. The cathedral was dedicated to the Assumption of the Virgin (Maria Assunta), and the hospital church to the Annunciation (Maria Annunziata). At that time the hospital was still the responsibility of the cathedral canons, so both the polyptych and the *Maestà* actually come from the same milieu. The original hospital church was demolished in the fifteenth century to make way for a new church on the same site, and at that time the orientation of the building was changed from east-west to north-south.[66] The polyptych undoubtedly stood on the high altar of the old church, below a crucifix from Duccio's workshop which can still be seen in the church, although it has unfortunately been damaged in the interim (fig. 74).

Remarkably enough, the framing elements of the polyptych are still in good condition, and it also has its original wrap-around pictorial frame. The piers and pinnacles, which can only be surmised in polyptych no. 28, are also in place. The structure in three zones has been created by the insertion of a middle register of Old Testament figures between the glorified Christ at the top and the Madonna with saints. At extreme left is Abraham with the text 'In semine tuo benedicentur omnes gentes' ('All the races of the world shall find a blessing through thy posterity'; Genesis 22:18). Then comes Isaac with a scroll reading 'Qui benedixierit tibi sit ille benedictus' ('A blessing on those who bless thee;' Genesis 27:29). He is followed by Jacob with the text 'Hec est domus Dei et porta celi' ('This can be nothing other than the house of God; this is the gate of Heaven;' Genesis 28:17). Then comes Jeremiah: 'Mictamus legnum in partem eius et eradamus eum dextra' ('Let us give him a taste of the gallows-tree; let us rid the world of him;' Jeremiah 11:19). In the centre are Moses: 'Videbam quod rubus ardebat et non comburebatur' ('It seemed that the bush was alight, yet did not burn;' Exodus 3:2), and King David, who is the only figure without a legend. To the right of the central compartment Isaiah displays his prophecy: 'Ecco Virgo concipiet et pariet filium et vocabitur Emanuel' ('Maid shall be with child, and shall bear a son, that shall be called Emmanuel;' Isaiah 7:14). Beside him Elijah says: 'Vivit Dominus vivit anima me si dimittam vos' ('As the Lord is a living God...and thy soul a living soul, I will not part from thee;' 4 Kings 2:2). The last two prophets are Daniel and Malachi. The first holds a scroll with the words 'Lapis imprecisus de monte sine manibus' ('This is that stone... none ever quarried, that fell from the mountain-side;' Daniel 2:45), while Malachi says: 'Ecce ego mitto angelum meum qui parabit viam ante faciem tuam' ('See where I am sending an angel of mine, to make the way ready for my coming;' Malachi 3:1).

I have quoted these inscriptions in full because they are essential to our understanding of the world of ideas underlying this polyptych. In terms of

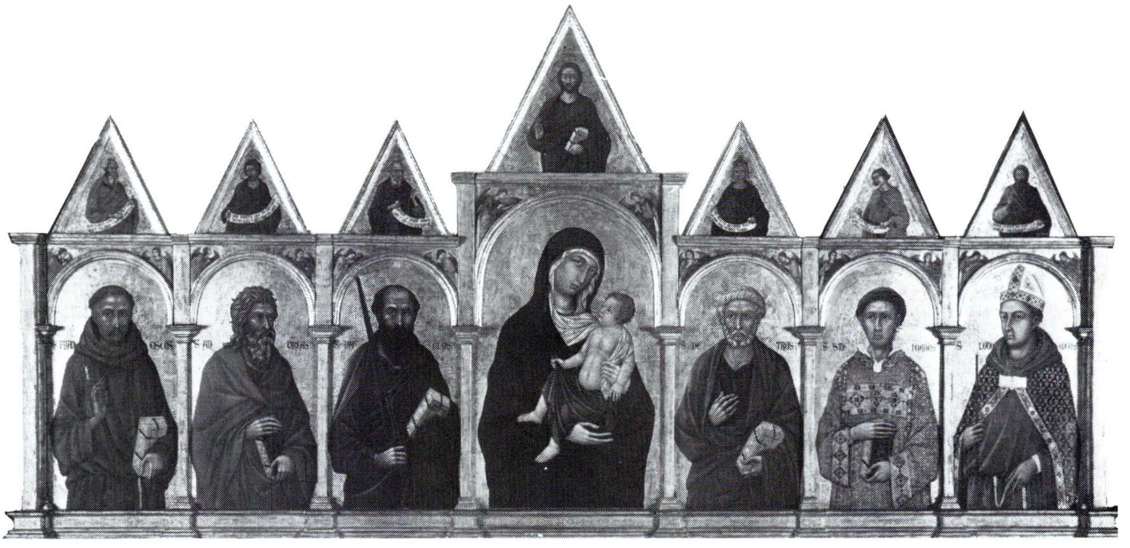

75 Ugolino di Neri, Polyptych, 164 x 341.5 cm, Sterling and Francine Clark Art Institute, Williamstown (Mass.).

medieval theology all these figures and their texts refer to the Incarnation. David is the direct ancestor of Christ, Moses sees the burning bush which is not consumed by fire as a sign of the virgin birth. Malachi foretells the Annunciation, Isaiah and Abraham predict the Incarnation. The others hold texts glorifying Mary as the Mother of God. Most of them face the central axis and look down at the Virgin and her Child. Some, though, are addressing the viewer directly, thus involving the 'reader' of the altarpiece in a message which links all the figures in their separate compartments. In a way it is a cartoon strip without a narrative. As the viewer meditates on the figures and their texts he penetrates to the meaning of the polyptych.[67]

The polyptych of Santa Maria della Annunziata is a gloss on the Incarnation, which was a basic theme of eucharistic symbolism. However, this is by no means a unique configuration of saints and texts. The same theme is depicted in a polyptych by Duccio's pupil Ugolino, but this time in two rather than three zones (fig. 75). The fact that Christ Logos is higher than all the other figures once again creates the impression of a company of patriarchs and prophets amplifying the theme of the Incarnation. Most of them are the same figures as Duccio used, and they hold the same texts. The saints in Duccio's polyptych are in effect half-length versions of the figures flanking the Madonna in the *Maestà* (fig. 43). The Magdalen has a double in the *Mary Magdalen* in the Museum of Fine Arts, Boston (fig. 76), and Daniel is the very image of the *Daniel* in the Johnson collection, Philadelphia (fig. 77), which was originally part of Ugolino's altarpiece for Santa Croce in Florence, the predella of which has already been mentioned. There are also various other parallels. The figures in altarpieces from Duccio's workshop look as if they have been produced from established models, as do the overall designs. The only specific relationship is that between the Mother and Child in the Ospedale polyptych. The Madonna clasps the Child to her, placing her left hand on his chest. He, in turn, presses his hand over hers. However, despite this physical intimacy there is no eye contact between them. They are both looking outwards, at the spectator.

Polyptych design may have become standardised in Duccio's workshop, but this still leaves the question of where the visual idea originally came from. It is perfectly possible, of course, to trace a genetic evolution from dossal to multi-storeyed polyptych, but no matter how meticulously it is done it cannot account for the fact that polyptych no. 47, with its cusped arches, piers, pinnacles and colonettes is a totally different kind of altarpiece from a dossal. It is not merely an altarpiece which stands in a new relationship to the architectural setting – it has itself become architecture. The protagonists are holy men standing in niches. Were there others of their kind in Siena at this time? Indeed there were. All one had to do was walk out of the hospital church and there, on the majestic facade of the cathedral, were Giovanni Pisano's statues set in niches.[68] But that was not all. All the figures on that facade are united in a single theme, and once again it is the theme of the Incarnation as expressed by prophets with text scrolls. The polyptych as an organisation of figures in separate compartments presenting a single message would have been inconceivable were it not for the sculptural programme on the facade of Siena cathedral.

In 1319 Simone Martini painted a polyptych for

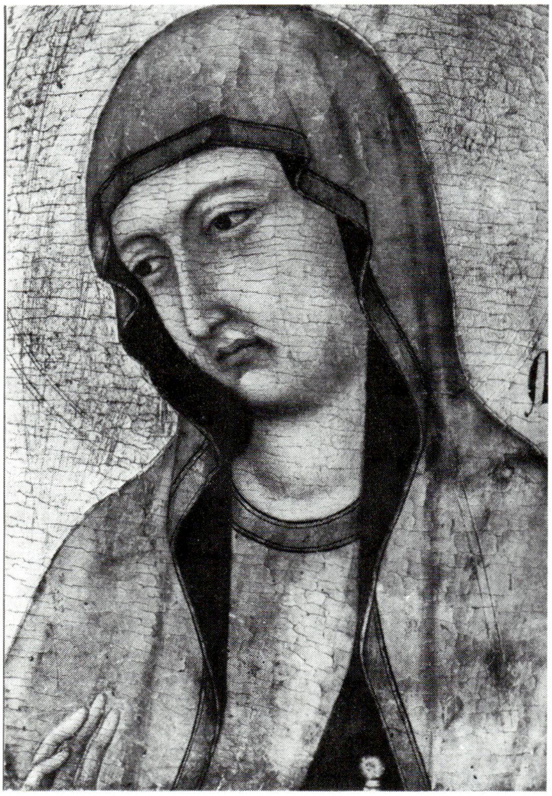

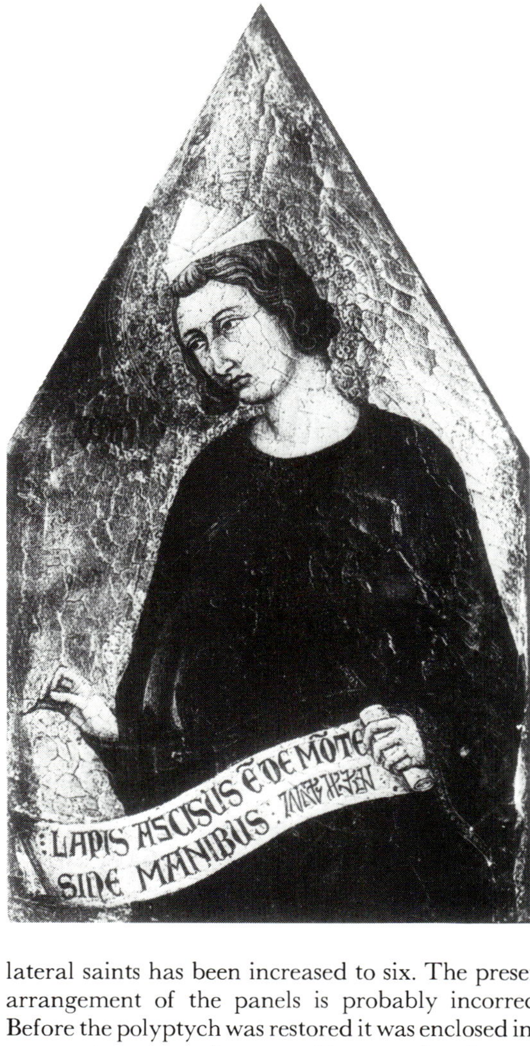

76 Ugolino di Neri, St Mary Magdalen, x x 29 cm, Museum of Fine Arts, Boston.
77 Ugolino di Neri, Daniel, 46.5 x 25.5 cm, John G. Johnson Collection, Philadelphia.

Santa Caterina, the Dominican church in Pisa (fig. 79). Although the original framing of the various panels and the supporting buttresses have been lost, the inner framing and ornamentation show that the artist was striving for a greater decorative refinement than we see in Duccio's polyptych. This was almost certainly Simone's own invention, for this sort of ornamental refinement is a distinguishing feature of all his work. The Santa Caterina polyptych is adorned with spiral colonettes supporting trefoil arches inscribed within round arches. The frame has a *pastiglia* decoration. The effect of the painted surface is greatly enhanced by the use of punch marks to enliven the gold of the saints' haloes. Simone was the first to use ornamental punches on a large scale in the haloes and along the edges of the painted surface. This gave the altarpieve an added sheen and sparkle which heightened the suggestion of costliness.

The Dominicans of Pisa clearly spent more on their altarpiece than the donors of Duccio's polyptych for the hospital church in Siena. Apart from anything else, it was to stand in a far larger church. There are now four registers, and the number of lateral saints has been increased to six. The present arrangement of the panels is probably incorrect. Before the polyptych was restored it was enclosed in a non-contemporary frame, and it seems that the panels were then in the right order, with the patron saints of the Dominicans furthest from the Madonna (fig. 79).[69] As usual the figures nearest the Madonna are John the Evangelist and John the Baptist. Interestingly enough Simone has depicted the evangelist as a young man, whereas on his *Maestà* fresco of 1315 he appears as St John of Patmos. The central saints of each group are female martyrs, but in this case the counterpart to Mary Magdalen is not St Agnes but St Catherine of Alexandria. That is not in the least surprising, for she is the titular saint of the church. St Catherine was blessed with a penetrating intellect and great rhetorical gifts, which enabled her to rout the heathen philosophers produced by emperor Maxentius. She was naturally held in high regard by the Dominicans, whose self-appointed task was to defend the true faith.

Christ Logos at the top of the altarpiece is displaying an open book with the words 'Ego sum alpha et

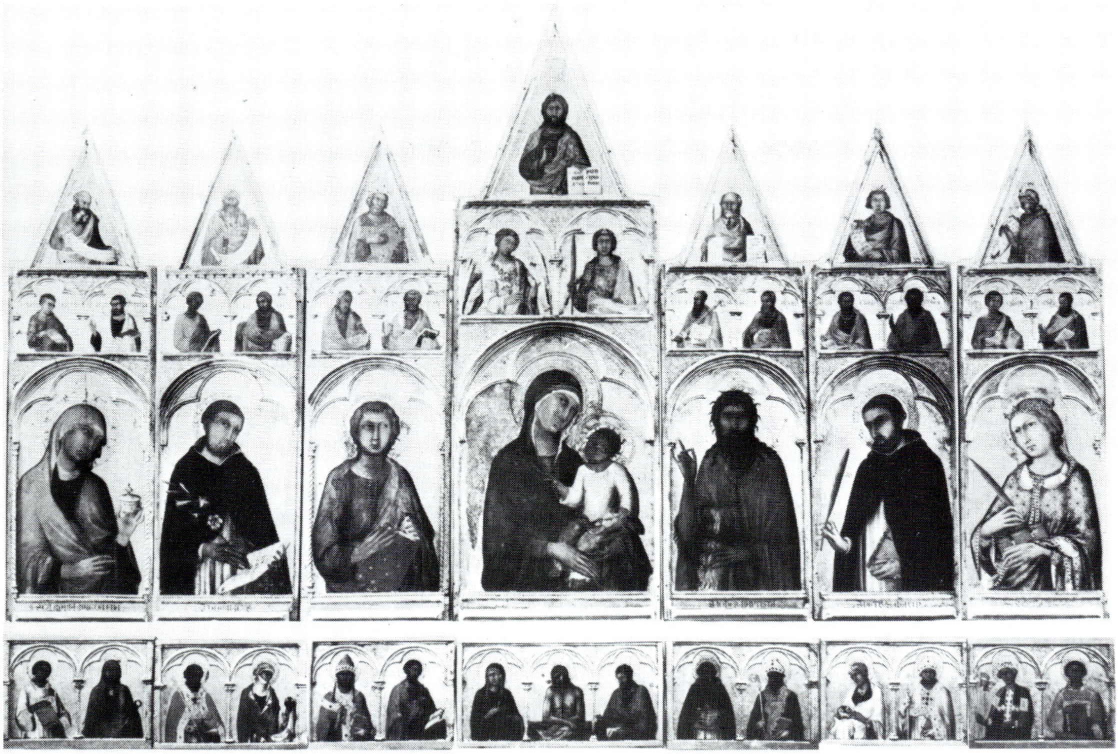

78 Simone Martini, Polyptych, 195 x 340 cm, Museo Nazionale di Matteo, Pisa.

omega, principium et finis' (fig. 80). The triangular pinnacles contain the usual row of Old Testament figures with texts alluding to the Incarnation. The register below them is occupied by the twelve apostles. The figures separating Christ Logos from the Madonna and Child are particularly interesting. They are not David and Moses, but the two archangels who are responsible for communications between heaven and earth. One holds a scroll with the words 'Angelus qui nuntiavit', so this must be Gabriel. The other is more readily identifiable as Michael from the text 'Michael princeps magnus'. Gabriel holds an olive branch, and Michael a palm frond. Palm and olive trees found a fertile soil in the imagination of medieval theologians. The branches of both trees were associated with the Incarnation, although of course the palm frond is also the badge of martyrs in their paradoxical victory over death. Here the olive branch undoubtedly stands for peace and reconciliation, as expressed by Christ's arrival on earth, and the palm frond for Mary's virginity.[70] The inscriptions may also be intended as a gloss on the Alpha and the Omega, the beginning and the end, which Christ Logos is displaying to the viewer.

The lowest of the four registers is a predella. It is no longer an unrelated strip running along the base of the altarpiece but is an integral part of the overall arrangement of half-length figures within arches. The saints on the predella are evangelists, female martyrs and fathers of the church. They also include that great Dominican scholar, Thomas Aquinas, although he had not yet been canonised. In the centre of the predella we see Christ as the Man of Sorrows between the Virgin and St Mark (fig. 81). The Man of Sorrows is a 'compendium' image combining different moments from the narrative of the Passion: the deposition from the Cross, the entombment and the Resurrection. It was intended to inspire meditation on Christ's sufferings, so it was the perfect image to accompany the sacrifice of the mass. A Man of Sorrows flanked by two figures is more commonly found on triptychs used by Dominicans for private devotion. It is not known whether a crucifix ever hung above Simone's polyptych; the Man of Sorrows on the predella may have served the purpose instead.[71] It is certainly a fitting conclusion to the central axis, for it integrates the moment of sacrifice with the Incarnation in the visual programme accompanying the celebration of the Eucharist.

The Dominican approach to religion is decidedly meditative, whereas Franciscan devotion tends to favour the more active, narrative aspects. One is therefore tempted to think that the Dominicans were

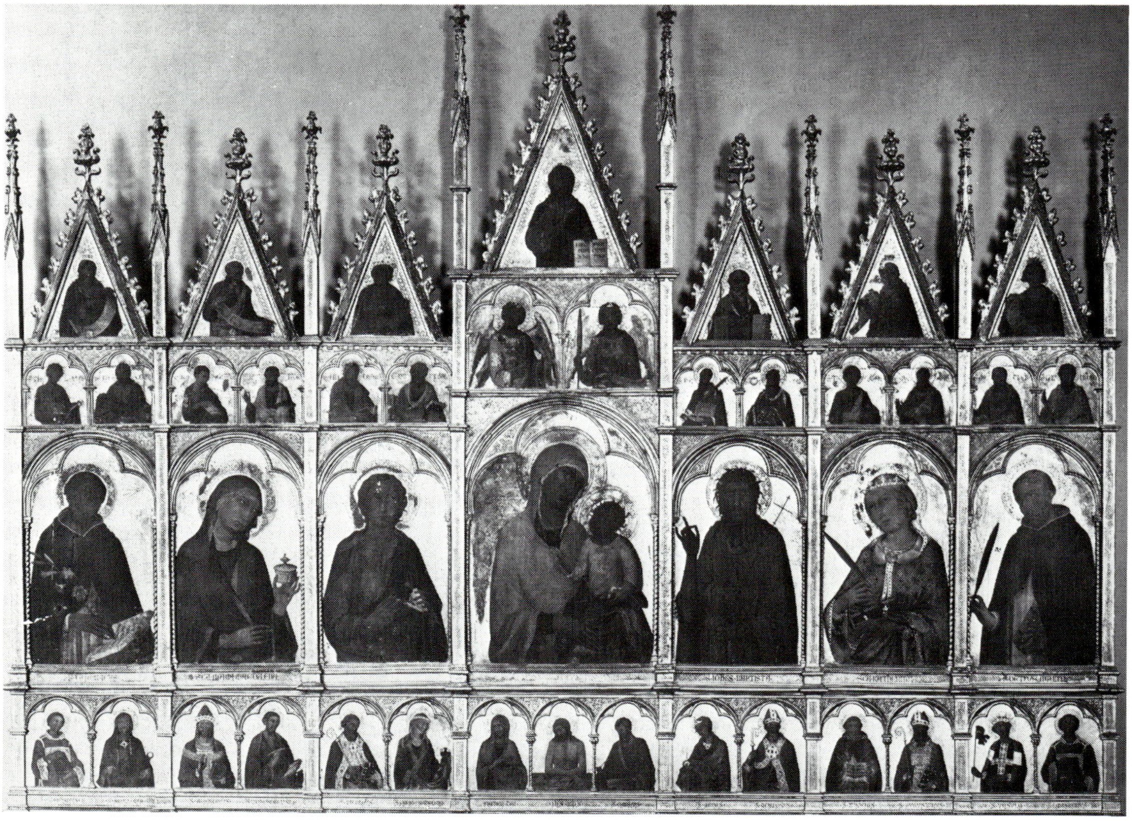

79 Simone Martini, Polyptych, arrangement in a modern frame of 1949.

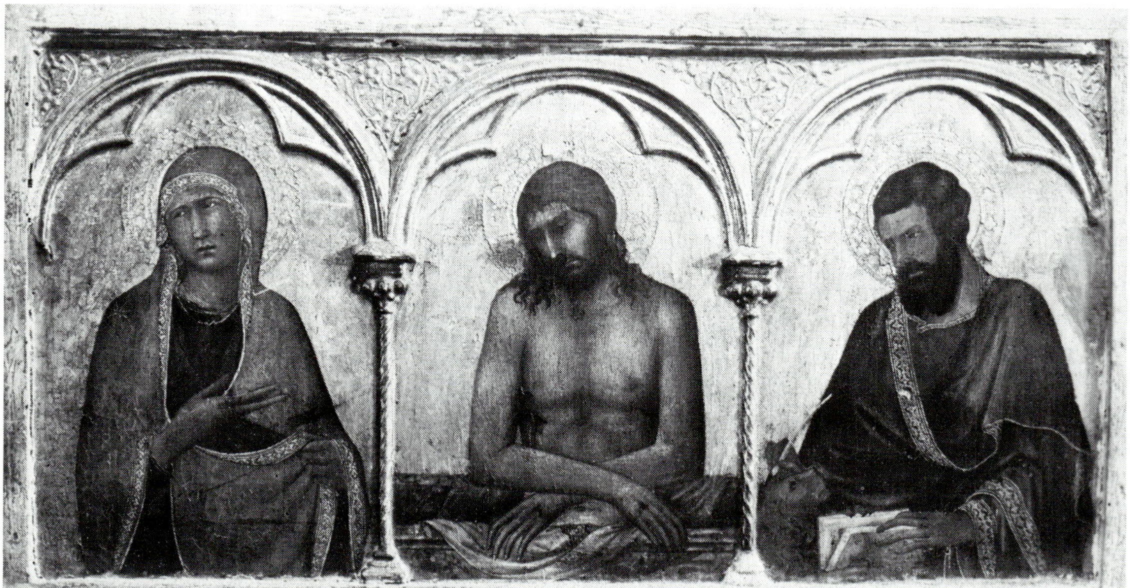

81 Simone Martini, Man of Sorrows between the Virgin and St Mark, detail of fig. 79.

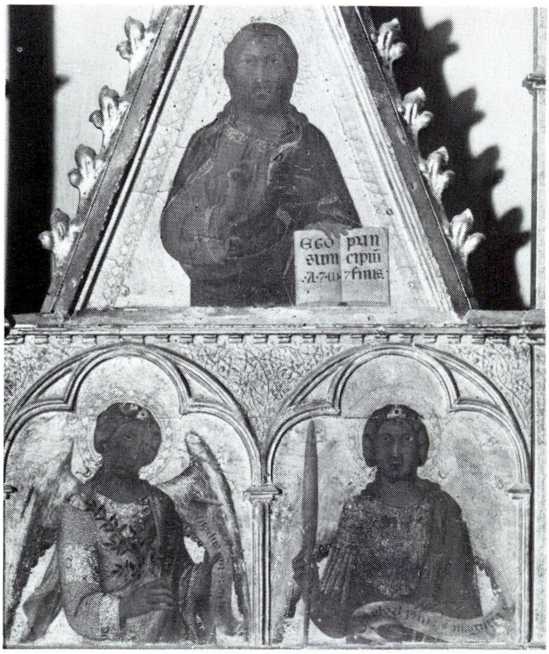

80 Simone Martini, Christ Logos with the archangels Gabriel and Michael, detail of fig. 79.

the ideal order to decipher the reading matter of Simone's polyptych, and even that their religiosity actively encouraged complicated symbolic games involving archangels with palm fronds and olive branches. There is no way of proving this, but it is quite clear that the Dominicans of Pisa were impressed by Simone Martini, for he went to work of the Domenicans Orvieto immediately afterwards (fig. 82). The polyptychs he painted for them and for the Franciscans were far simpler than his altarpiece for Santa Caterina. In Pisa he left behind a flourishing workshop under the direction of his brother-in-law, Lippo Memmi.[72]

On 17th April 1320 Guido Tarlati, bishop of Arezzo, commissioned Pietro Lorenzetti to paint a 'tabula Beate Virginis Marie' with very beautiful figures for the high altar of the Pieve (fig. 83). The bishop undertook to supply the actual panel, while Pietro agreed not to work on any other commissions until the altarpiece was completed. The contract gives the following specifications for the altarpiece: '... in the middle of which panel must be the image of the Virgin Mary with her Son and with four collateral figures to the wishes of the Lord Bishop; to be worked in the fields and spaces of these figures with the best gold at one hundred leaves to the florin, and the main parts and fields of these figures with the aforesaid gold, and with other ornaments of the best silver, and putting in these five figures select ultramarine blue, and in the others round about, and in the circumferences and spaces of this panel are to be painted images of prophets and saints in good and select colours to the wishes of the said Lord Bishop. It must be VI braccia long and V braccia high in the centre, apart from two columns, of which each must be half a braccio wide, and in each of which must be six figures worked with the aforesaid gold'.[73]

As we have already seen in the contract between the Laudesi and Duccio, aesthetic appreciation in this period was largely determined by purely material considerations. The 'lord bishop' wanted the best gold leaf, silver and costly pigments like ultramarine

82 Simone Martini, Polyptych, 113 x 257 cm, Museo dell'Opera del Duomo, Orvieto.

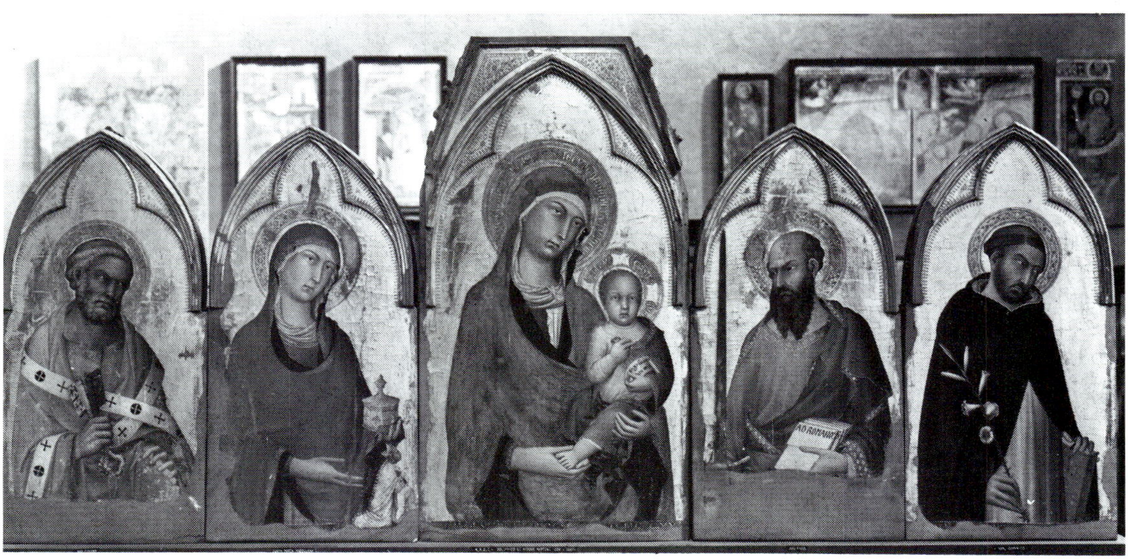

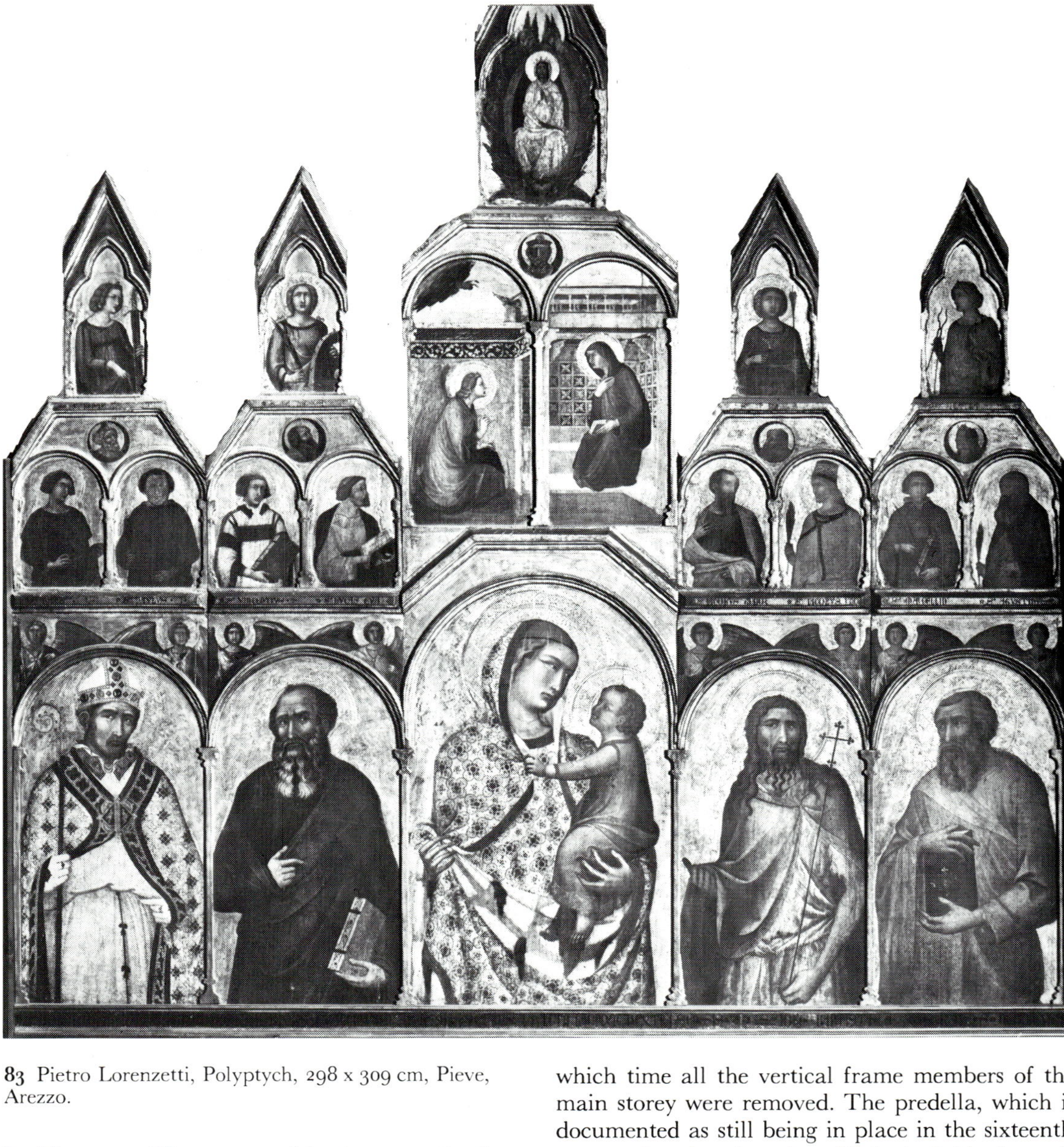

83 Pietro Lorenzetti, Polyptych, 298 x 309 cm, Pieve, Arezzo.

for his money. There were evidently supporting buttresses on either side of the altarpiece, and in fact each of these 'columnae' was to be decorated with six figures so as to form an integral part of the painting. The polyptych was removed from the high altar to a smaller altar in the Pieve in the sixteenth century, at which time all the vertical frame members of the main storey were removed. The predella, which is documented as still being in place in the sixteenth century, has since been lost. All the individual panels of the polyptych were trimmed at the sides, with the result that the figures are now crowded too close together. The most striking feature of the present structure is the broad horizontal band above the arches containing the principal figures, which ap-

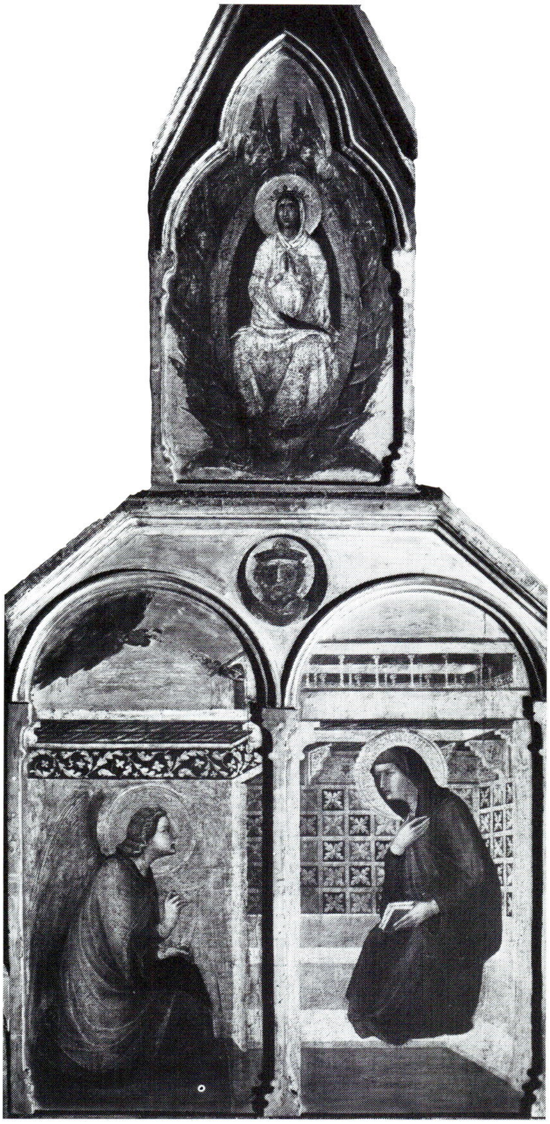

84 Pietro Lorenzetti, Annunciation and Maria Assunta, detail of fig. 83.

pears to group the Madonna and the large lateral saints in a single unit.

It is clear from the contract that the bishop was responsible for the iconography of the polyptych, and this is also reflected in the choice of saints. At the extreme left there is the figure of St Donatus, the mythical first bishop of Arezzo, and in the register above there are several saints whose cult was so specific to Arezzo that they appear nowhere else. At the extreme left of this central register are Sts John and Paul, two Christian brothers who were put to death for refusing to serve the emperor. At the extreme right are Sts Marcellinus and Augustinus, two early Christian martyrs from Monterongrifoli near Arezzo, whose relics are preserved in the Pieve.[74] The paired arrangement of this register was dictated by the structure of the polyptych, and the donor put it to good use by choosing saints whose names were coupled: two brothers and two fellow-martyrs. This was continued next to Marcellinus and Augustinus with two apostles who were namesakes: James the Greater and James the Less. The system breaks down with Sts Vincent and Luke, to the left of the central axis, but it seems that they were not intended to be a pair. St Luke has his back to St Vincent and is devoting his entire attention to the Annunciation in the centre. This is hardly surprising, since his is the gospel which gives the most graphic and detailed account of the Virgin's motherhood. This subtle positioning of St Luke suggests that St Matthew has been placed next to John the Baptist in the main register because he is commonly regarded as the genealogist of the Virgin and her Child.

Taking the iconographical structure as a whole we see that it differs fundamentally from the polyptychs by Duccio and Simone Martini in the message of the central axis. It is interrupted in the middle by a large narrative scene (fig. 84). At first sight, though, it seems that there is no very great difference. The allusion to the Incarnation is achieved by means of a narrative rather than by individual figures.[75] David in the oculus above the scene confirms this function of the Annunciation, as do the prophets in the other oculi, who are facing the centre as if foretelling the event. Added emphasis is given to the *obumbratio*, the overshadowing by the Holy Ghost, by the hand of God emerging from a large cloud. However, the use of the Annunciation to represent the Incarnation imparts a very special theological significance to the thematic programme, for it gives pride of place to the Virgin, rather than to Christ.

The Mariological interpretation is reinforced by the fact that the angel is kneeling before the Virgin, as in Duccio's *Annunciation of the Virgin's death and glorification*. This is one of the earliest scenes in which the angel of the Annunciation kneels in front of the seated Virgin, altering the entire nature of the image. Gabriel has evolved from a messenger into a worshipper. He has hastened to bring the message to Mary, only to find that his announcement has been overtaken. All he can do is kneel before the one who is already filled with God's grace. The choice of the Annunciation for this key position, and its unusual presentation, could have left the viewer in no doubt about the Virgin's importance. This is elaborated by the figure at the very top of the altarpiece. It is no longer Christ Logos, but Maria Assunta, the motif of the Virgin's glorification which had first appeared on the window in Siena cathedral (fig. 65). The final

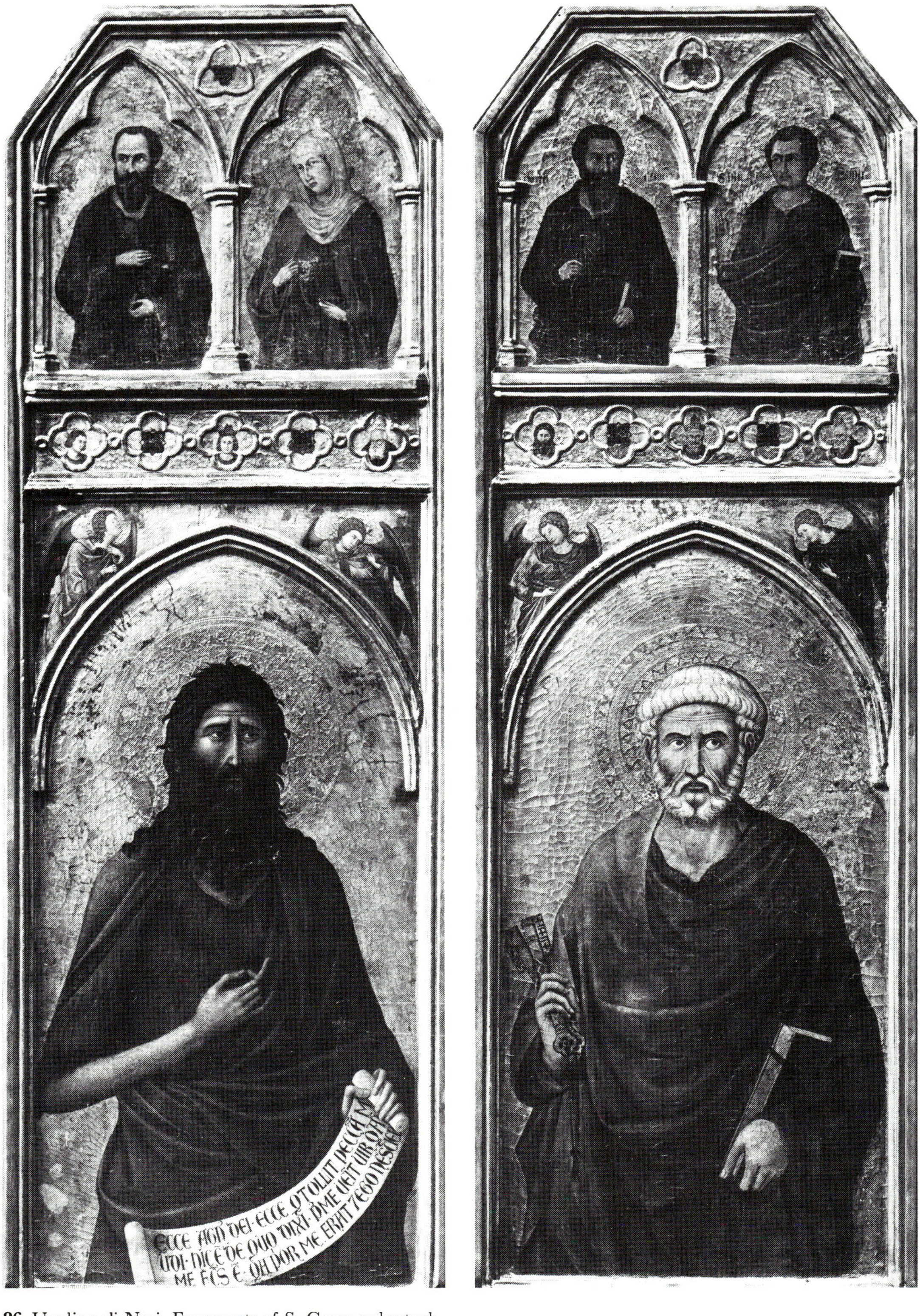

86 Ugolino di Neri, Fragments of S. Croce polyptych, each 137 x 57 cm, Berlin (DDR), Staatliche Museen.

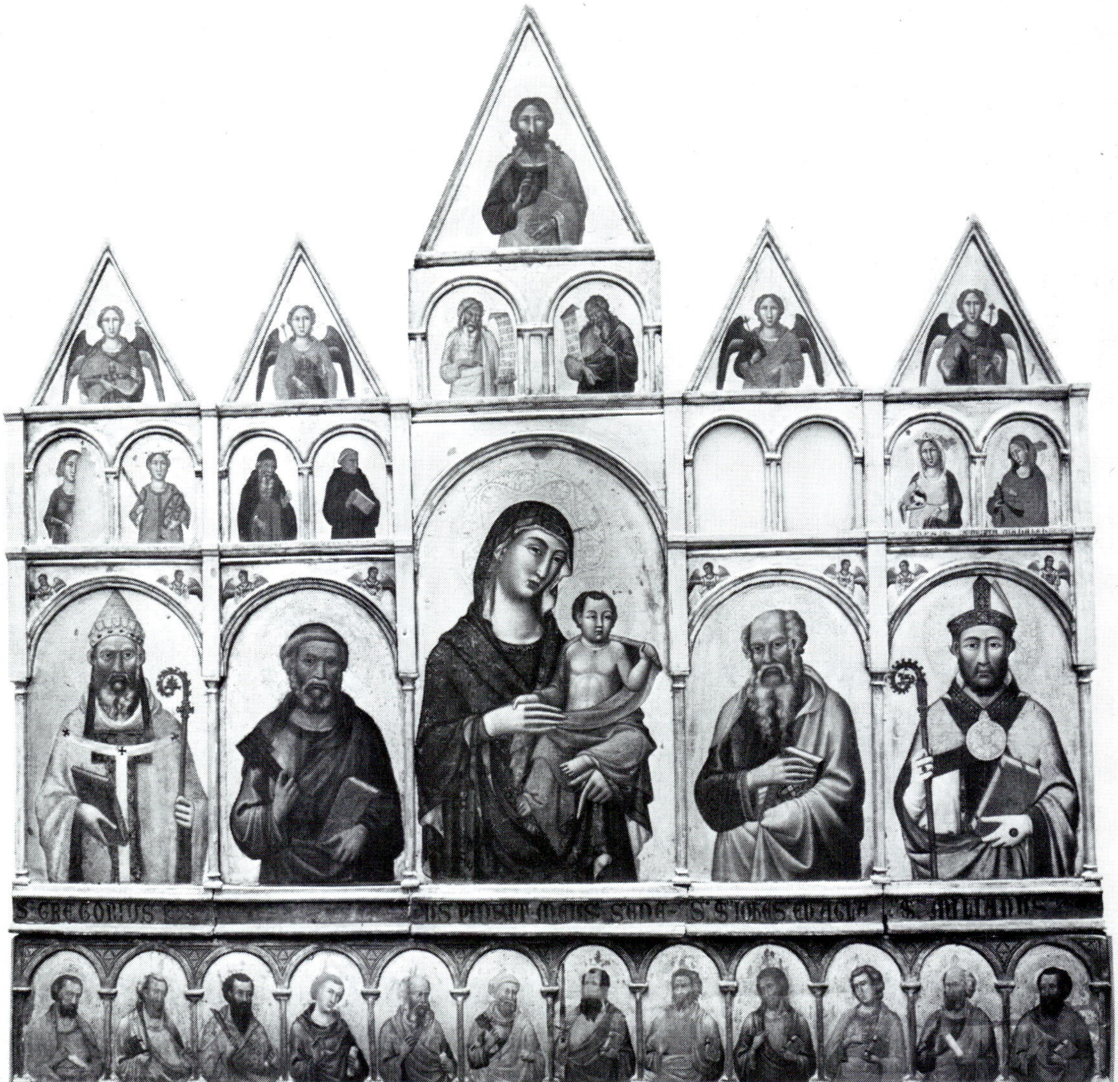

85 Meo da Siena, Polyptych, 233 x 242 cm, Galleria Nazionale dell'Umbria, Perugia.

theological subtlety of Pietro's polyptych is provided by the four female martyrs flanking Maria Assunta.[76] In the middle ages the Virgin was considered to have been a martyr herself, even if she had not been the victim of some cruel heathen ruler. After all, the evangelists had said that she felt a sword pierce her breast as she stood at the foot of the Cross. Was that spiritual martyrdom not a more grievous suffering than even the physical torments of her sisters? She was therefore placed at the head of the female martyrs as the holiest of them all, and that is how she is portrayed here.

The donor may have played an important part in the planning of the thematic programma of this altarpiece, but it was Pietro's invention and interpretation which turned it into such a superb work. We need only mention the monumental effect of the figures, the powerful impact of the evangelists John and Matthew, the spatial organisation of the Annunciation scene, and above all the new intimacy of the Virgin's relationship with the Christ Child. Mother and Child are totally engrossed in each other, and Mary is holding the infant realistically. The slight twisting of her upper torso creates space for the plastic portrayal of the Child, but the compensating inclination of her head towards Christ gives an added intensity to their relationship. The Child's action in grasping the Virgin's robe is traditional, but here it is given a spatial and expressive significance never

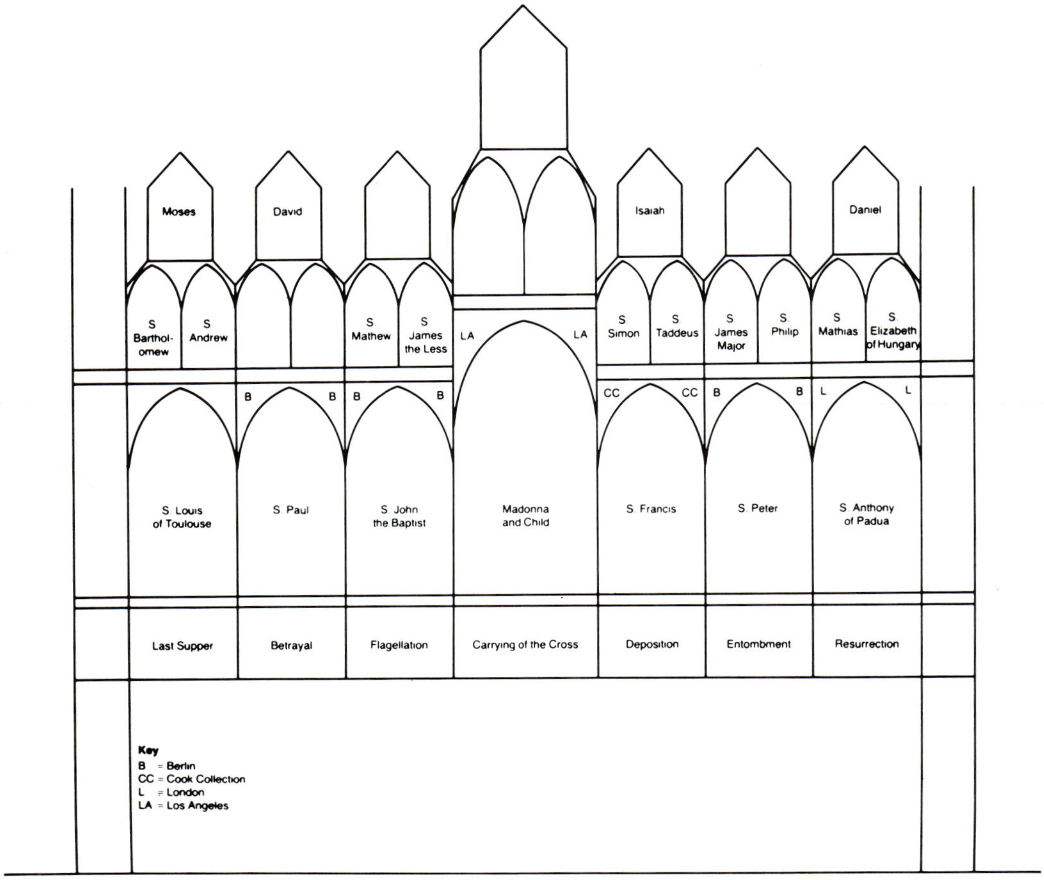

87 Reconstruction of S. Croce polyptych (after Gardner-von Teuffel).

before encountered in Sienese Madonnas. This new portrayal of the Virgin and Child has distinct sculptural overtones (cf. fig. 84). The ornate rendering of architecture and of figures in architectural settings may have been derived from the murals in San Francesco in Assisi, where Pietro had worked before he went to Arezzo.[77]

The early Sienese polyptychs discussed in this chapter will have to suffice as a guide to the form, content and function of this type of altarpiece. Not only were there far more of these polyptychs, but far more of them have survived than we have room to discuss here. I have restricted myself to the most important and well-documented commissions of the period. Surveying the large number of polyptychs one is struck by the fact that around 1320 Sienese artists were being commissioned to produce multi-storeyed polyptychs with half-length figures throughout the whole of central Italy, and not just in Pisa, Orvieto and Arezzo. In Perugia there is a polyptych which Meo da Siena executed for the abbey church of Montealabate in 1320 (fig. 85). Ugolino di Neri, a pupil of Duccio, painted polyptychs for Santa Maria Novella and Santa Croce in Florence. The altarpiece for the Dominicans is now lost, but as we have seen there are still fragments of the polyptych for the high altar of Santa Croce (figs. 58, 60. 86, 87).[78]

Simone Martini related the subject matter of his altarpiece to the idea of the eucharistic sacrifice by introducing the Man of Sorrows on the predella. Ugolino did the same in his altarpiece for the Franciscans by using a series of Passion scenes.

Whatever the differences between these polyptychs we can only conclude that around 1320 donors in central Italy evidently felt that a Sienese polyptych was the finest object that could be placed on a high altar. The Sienese dominated panel painting around this period, but what was it that made the Sienese polyptych so special? The answer becomes clear if we take a representative early Venetian altarpiece for comparison (fig. 88). Although it lacks the

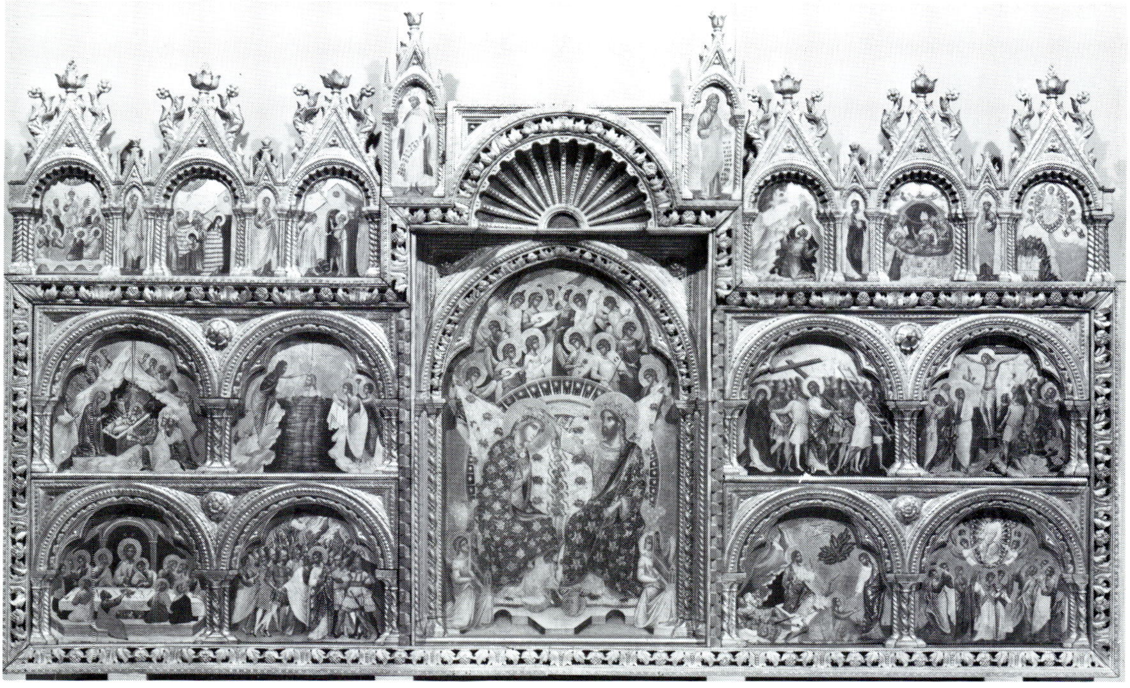

88 Paolo Veneziano, Polyptych, 128 x 251 cm, Galleria dell'Accademia, Venice.

topmost element and some parts of the frame are damaged, this is quite obviously an object which created a very different effect. The painted scenes are quite literally overshadowed by the ornamentation. It is a precious gold box decorated with intricate, curly motifs to which the scenes add a colourful lustre. The workmanship suggests that it should really be regarded as an inexpensive version of precious metalwork. First the framework was made, and then the scenes were added rather like incidental illustrations. One has to get close to read them. Sienese polyptychs consist of large, painted panels. The framing may be attractive, but it is still an adjunct whose prime purpose is to unite the scenes into a whole. The use of buttresses on either side made it possible to create what the Germans call a *Bilderwand*. That wall with the figures of saints is more a piece of architecture than a precious object, and the figures on a Sienese polyptych are more reminiscent of monumental sculpture, not craft products.

One wonders why Siena had so many good artists at this particular time. Attemps to answer that question often amount to the notion that 'art was second nature to the Sienese'. That, of course, is not only unverifiable but is also the sort of interpretation which has come to be regarded as highly suspect, and rightly so. In fact, there is no single, clear-cut explanation, although there are certain suggestive pointers. At an early and crucial moment in their history the Sienese had discovered the importance of what one might call 'visual material', and they used visual images as a channel for their urban chauvinism. This is best illustrated by the history of the altarpieces on the high altar of the cathedral. A grandiose project like the *Maestà* obviously gave many Sienese artists an expertise in panel painting, and particularly in the painting of altarpieces. This must have created a large reservoir of painters in the city, just as the building of the cathedral created a large pool of good stonemasons.[79] It seems very likely that many of the artists who worked on the *Maestà* later found employment elsewhere. After 1350, when socio-economic conditions no longer favoured large commissions, the hegemony of the Sienese altarpiece came to an end. This is a question to which I will be returning in the second volume of this study.

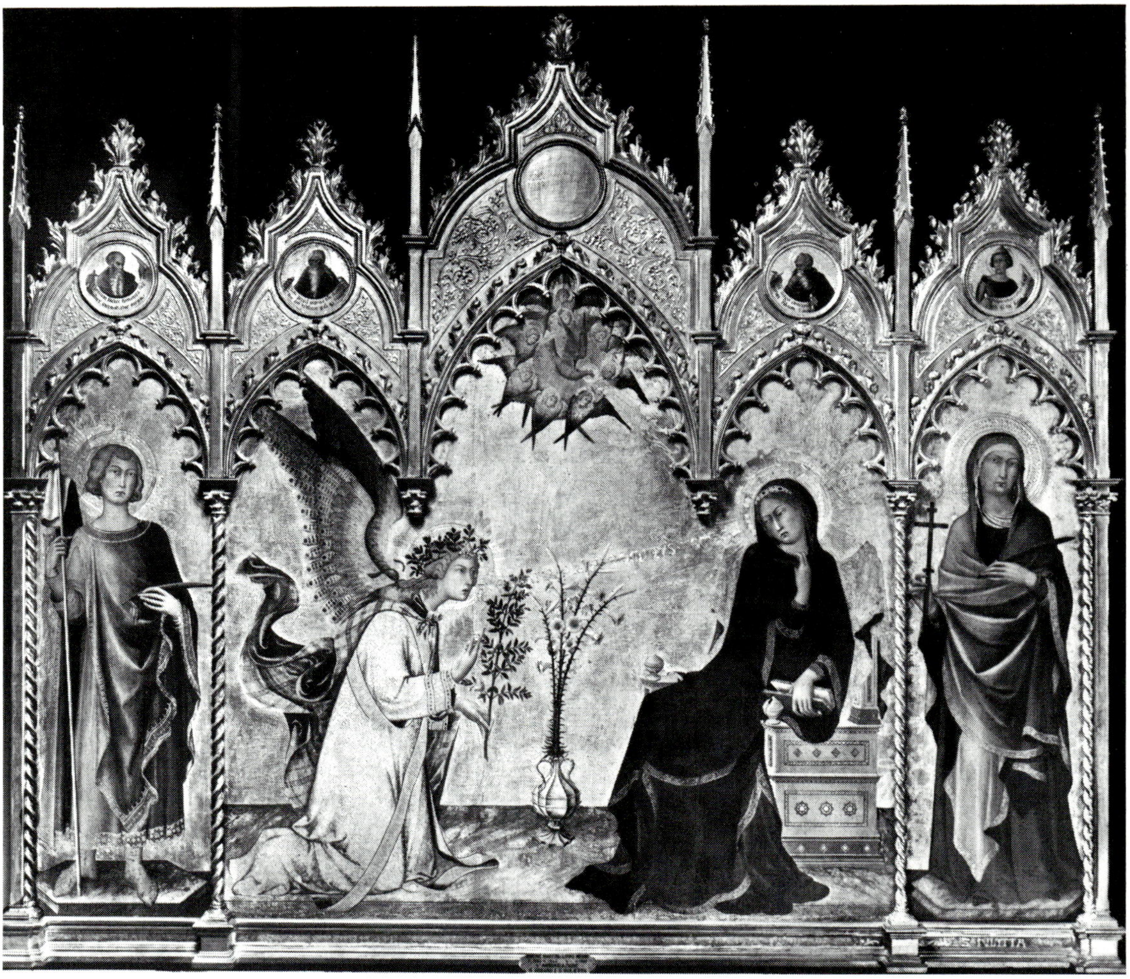

89 Simone Martini, Annunciation with Sts Ansanus and Margaret, 184 x 210 cm, 1333, Galleria degli Uffizi, Florence.

V

THE PATRON SAINTS OF SIENA AND THEIR ALTARS IN THE CATHEDRAL

The various plans for remodelling Siena cathedral naturally gave rise to new ideas on the organisation of the liturgy, which also involved such questions as the dedication of altars and commissions for altarpieces. It was not simply a matter of enriching the cathedral with more beautiful and ambitious works, as one might have expected from the foregoing account of the altarpieces for the high altar. The rapid succession of new plans for the fabric of the building made it necessary to draw up coordinated programmes for the altars and their decoration. In late medieval churches this was often done on a fairly haphazard basis, with one corner being given over to a saint who had suddenly become popular, another being furnished for the veneration of newly acquired relics, while elsewhere chapels and altars were built for the propagation of new feasts in honour of the Virgin. Most of the comprehensive, large-scale plans for altars and altarpieces date from the period of the Counter-Reformation, and it is noteworthy that the altarpieces were frequently being moved and rearranged. It was one such plan for Siena cathedral that led to the dispersal of the church's medieval altarpieces, with the result that it was only realised recently that there had been an impressive and coherent plan for the liturgy in the cathedral as early as the fourteenth century. Documentary evidence has revealed that Simone Martini's *Annunciation* (fig. 89), Ambrogio Lorenzetti's *Presentation* (fig. 90) and Pietro Lorenzetti's *Birth of the Virgin* (fig. 91) were all part of a single programme. These paintings of three feasts of the Virgin stood on altars dedicated to Siena's patron saints.[80]

Even in the old, early thirteenth-century cathedral there had been a cult of Savinus, Ansanus and Crescentius, each of whom had his own altar and feast-day. We know little about Crescentius beyond the fact that he was beheaded in Rome. In 1058 Bishop Antifredus of Siena obtained the saint's remains from the pope, and as far as we know the acquisition of those relics is the only scene relating to Crescentius ever to have been depicted in Sienese art. The work in question, by Martino di Bartolommeo, is a fresco of 1405 in the cathedral sacristy.[81] Crescentius was the usual kind of local saint. As urban communities began to evolve in Italy the local bishops saw the advantage of encouraging the veneration of early Christian martyrs, which is probably why Bishop Antifredus applied to the pope for the remains of this particular champion of the faith. At the time Savinus was already being venerated as the first bishop of Siena. Savinus is to Siena what Zenobius is to Florence and Donatus to Arezzo. And yet there is something a little odd about Savinus, for he owed his cult to the misconception that he was the city's first bishop. He may have been bishop of Faenza, but he had nothing whatever to do with Siena, and although his remains are preserved in the cathedral the Sienese did not have a monopoly of his veneration, for he was also honoured in Assisi, Spoleto and Chiusi. He was evidently a favourite of the Benedictines, for they had dedicated a Pisan abbey to him at the early date of 780.[82] His presence in the Sienese pantheon was probably due to the leading role which the Benedictines played in the religious life of the eleventh century.

The cathedral window of 1287 (fig. 65) reflects Savinus's rather misty origins, for he is on the extreme right rather than in a position of honour beside the Virgin. In Duccio's *Maestà*, on the other hand, he kneels right next to the Madonna (fig. 43), in a position which incorrectly gives the impression

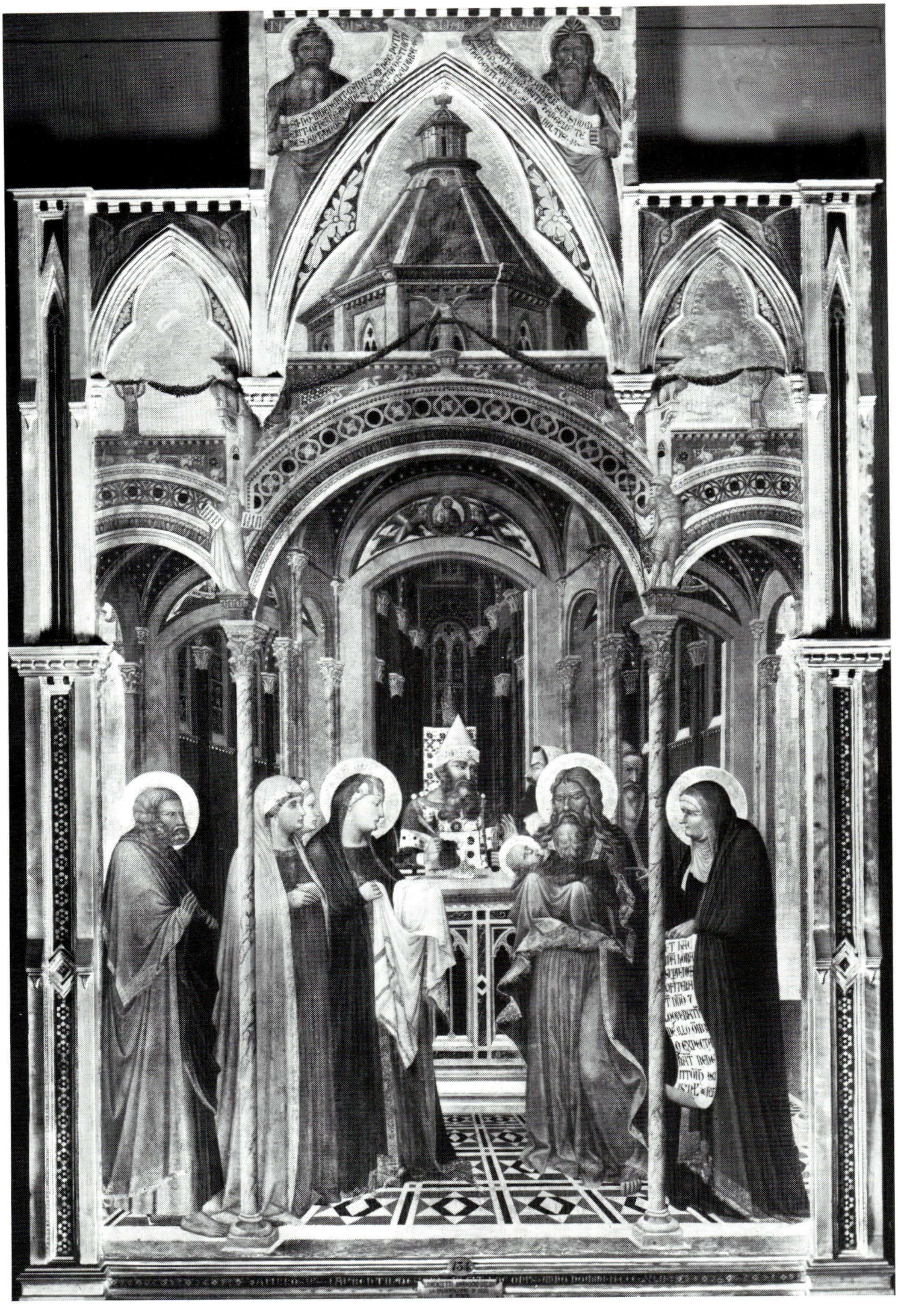

90 Ambrogio Lorenzetti, Purification, 257 x 168 cm, 1342, Galleria degli Uffizi, Florence.

that he was Siena's first bishop. The fact that two saints like Crescentius and Savinus could become the city's patron saints shows how hard pressed Siena was to find suitable candidates. What other course was open to a city which had neither a Roman nor an early Christian past of any significance but which had become an important population centre by the late middle ages? One way out of the impasse was to assemble relics which would establish a respectable pantheon of early Christian martyrs, and at the same to urge humanists to portray Siena as a second Rome. The most striking example of this kind of local saint whose relics were acquired with the sole object of sparking off a cult was St Victor of Siena, who makes his first appearance in the *Maestà*. He is not present in the window of 1287, his place being taken by the apostle Bartholomew, who had long been venerated in Siena, particularly in the northern part of the city.[83] Like the previous two saints, Victor is a nondescript figure whose veneration in Siena failed to give rise to any exciting mythopoeia. Interest later shifted to the many devout citizens of Siena itself, of whom Sts Catherine and Bernardino were to become the best known. It was only in the cathedral that the veneration of the city's original patrons continued unabated.

There was, however, one exception to these rather dubious claims, and that was St Ansanus, whom the Sienese regarded as their John the Baptist. A scion of the Anicii, a patrician Roman family, he moved to Tuscany, where he was extremely successful in converting and baptising the heathen. He acquired his martyr's crown in 303 when he was beheaded near the river Arbia in the inhospitable region between Arezzo and Siena. According to the legend his body was discovered by a shepherdess on 6th February 1107. The bishop of Arezzo immediately claimed the saint's head, but the bishop of Siena responded by sallying forth from the city accompanied by the entire clergy in order to collect the saint's remains. The citizens waited eagerly at the gate for their return. When the procession came in sight a cry of joy went up: 'il Santo viene' (The saint is coming), and to this day the gate has been known by that name. No fewer than three feast-days were instituted for the city's new saint: the translation of the body on 6th February, the martydrom on 1st December, and on the Tuesday after Pentecost his right arm (the one with which he had baptised the heathen) was borne in procession through the city. Ansanus became the most Sienese of the city's four patrons, although he was also venerated elsewhere in Tuscany.[84]

Some time after the *Maestà* had been completed it must have been decided to commission paintings for the altars of these saints. The first, predictably, was for the altar of St Ansanus, and it was to become one of the best-loved of all late-medieval altarpieces. It was Simone Martini's *Annunciation*, which is now in the Uffizi in Florence (fig. 89). The frame was completely refurbished in the nineteenth century working from late fourteenth-century models; the original was undoubtedly far less ornate (fig. 92).[85] The inscription beneath the central scene reads: SYMON MARTINI ET LIPPUS MEMMI DE SENIS ME PINCXERUNT ANNO DOMINI MCCCXXXIII ('I was painted by Simone Martini and Lippo Memmi of Siena in the year of Our Lord 1333'). This is borne out by records of payments made in 1333 to Simone, his brother-in-law and business partner Lippo, to carpenters and even to porters. It is noteworthy that this is the first work to be signed by two artists, indicating that Lippo had graduated from pupil to associate. Not unexpectedly, art historians have taken this opportunity to indulge in a debate which is as lengthy as it is tedious in an attempt to establish who painted what. Did Lippo paint the lateral saints and Simone the *Annunciation*, or was one of them responsible for the two female figures and the other for Gabriel and Ansanus? Or did Lippo do the ornamentation while Simone painted the scenes? Although we know from a document of 1333 that Lippo was indeed paid for the ornamentation, he was also paid another sum of money by Simone. He was undoubtedly more than just the ornamenter, but it is unclear precisely what his contribution was. It is reassuring to know that not even the most determined and sophisticated efforts of modern scholarship have been able to shatter the unity of a late medieval workshop method.[86]

The most remarkable feature of the painting is that, although it belonged on a patronal altar, it is not the altarpiece of a saint (cf. figs. 16 and 17). The principal subject is not Ansanus but the Annunciation – one of the feasts of the Virgin. It was followed by an altarpiece of the *Presentation in the temple* by Ambrogio Lorenzetti for the altar of St Crescentius (fig. 90). A commission was also awarded to Pietro Lorenzetti for a *Birth of the Virgin* to adorn the altar of St Savinus (fig. 91). Both these altarpieces were completed in 1342, but at some later date they lost their lateral saints. We know that those saints existed from fourteenth and fifteenth-century inventories, and that in each case one was the patron to whom the altar was dedicated. It was a brilliant idea, for it enabled these saints, who had little appeal on their own, to bathe in the reflected glory of the Virgin, the supreme protectress of the city. This project is an important milestone in altarpiece history, for it is the first time that narrative scenes are given pride of place in the centre of an altarpiece.

The structure of this new type was in fact derived from the polyptych with full-length standing figures.

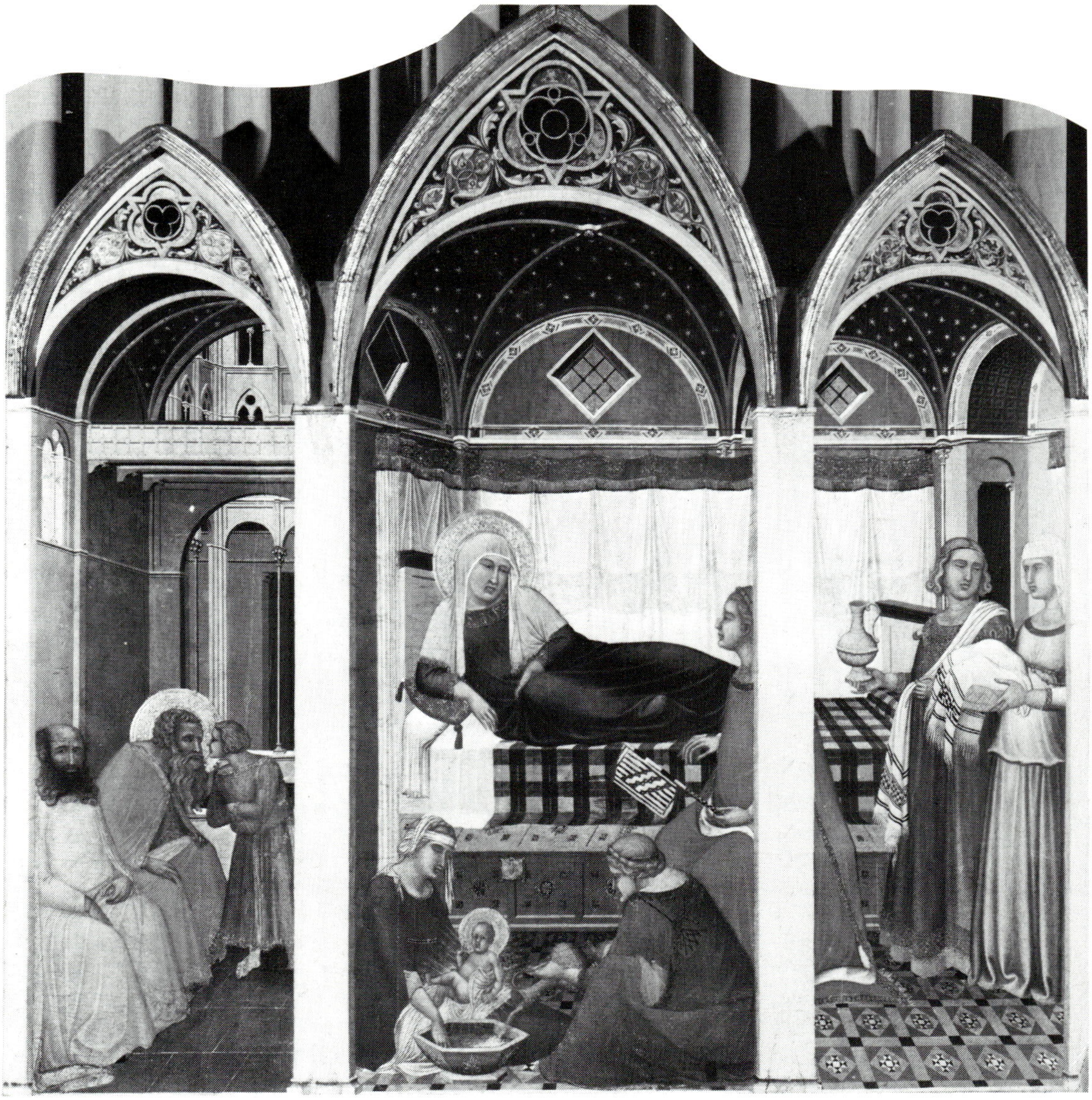

91 Pietro Lorenzetti, Birth of the Virgin, 187 x 182 cm, 1342, Museo dell'Opera del Duomo, Siena.

The trouble is that there are no extant Sienese examples of that kind of polyptych from the early fourteenth century. The dominant fashion was evidently the polyptych with half-length figures. However, there are such altarpieces from other centres, and in some cases they are by painters whose style was influenced by Sienese artists (fig. 93).[87] The effect of the framing is to form niches for the figures. The central panel usually consists of a *Madonna enthroned*, and it is flanked by matching arcades containing saints. In the altarpieces for Siena cathedral two of those arcades serve to increase the width of the central section; the innermost columns have simply been omitted. The vertical wooden planks of the central section have been carefully crafted to form a single picture surface without any visible seams. Pietro Lorenzetti's *Birth of the Virgin* consists of five vertical planks which cannot be distinguished even when one examines the planed reverse (fig. 94). At the edges there are long grooves for the wooden dowels attaching the lateral saints to the central panel. This did leave a visible join, but it was masked on the front by a pillar.[88]

Simone's *Annunciation* has all the usual iconographic elements of the scene. Gabriel's fluttering cloak shows that he has arrived in a hurry, and his wings are still extended. However, there is little left for him to do but kneel before the Virgin. The Holy Ghost has pre-empted him yet again. He holds an olive branch as a sign of peace, and points to the descending dove. His words, accordingly, are both a

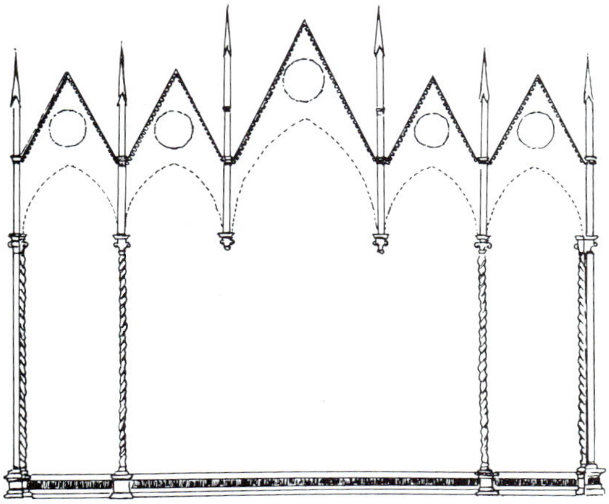

92 Original framing of Simone Martini's Annunciation (after Cämmerer-George).

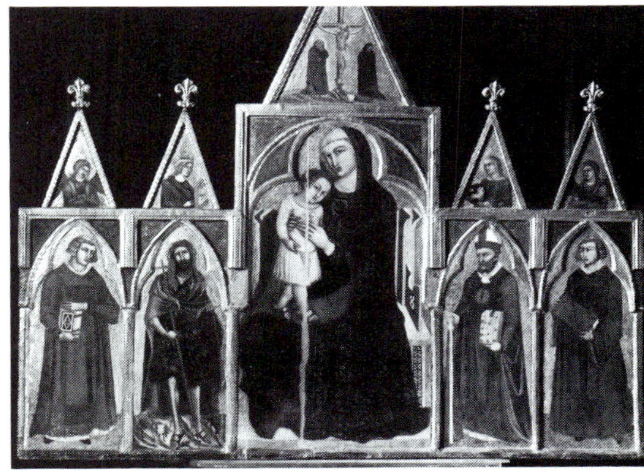

93 Meo da Siena (school of), Polyptych, 164.5 x 231.5 cm, Museo Civico, Gubbio.

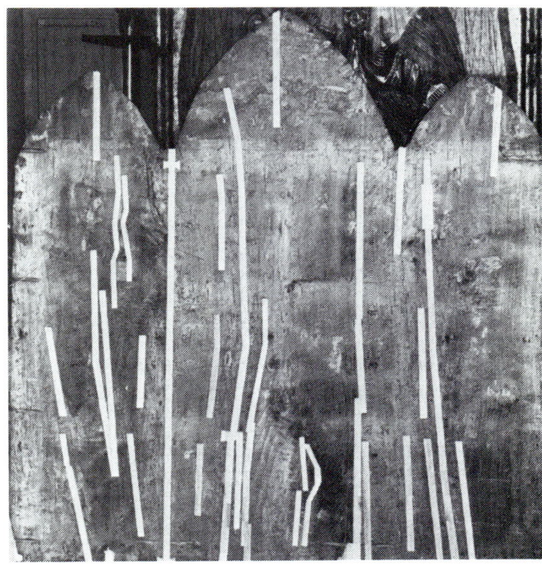

94 Back of Pietro Lorenzetti's Birth of the Virgin (fig. 91).

greeting and a respectful observation: 'Ave Maria. Gratia Plena. Dominus Tecum' ('Hail Mary, full of grace, the Lord is with thee'). The Virgin is seated on a throne and is quite clearly startled by this sudden apparition. She recoils in fright, and this gives her a twisted pose, turned away form the angel and towards the viewer. She is holding the book in her left hand. The prophets with their texts in the roundels are squarely in the tradition of the polyptych, confirming that this is a scene of the selection of the Virgin and the Incarnation of Christ. The centre roundel, which is now lost, undoubtedly contained the figure of Christ Logos. Ansanus, who is shown as a youthful warrior martyr, stands on the left holding a banner with the black-and-white colours of Siena and a palm frond with the dates still attached. Attempts to identify the female saint on the right have caused a certain amount of confusion. The nineteenth-century frame bears the legend 'Giulitta', but it soon became clear that this obscure saint was a most unlikely contender. Another suggestion was that the lady, who is holding a cross and a palm frond, was St Maxima, the mother of Ansanus, but that too is highly implausible, for there is not a single depiction of Maxima in Tuscan art. In fact this female martyr is the absolute image of the customary depiction of St Margaret, who was held in high esteem in Siena. It is hardly surprising, then, to find the figure identified as St Margaret in a cathedral inventory of 1458.[89]

In this altarpiece Simone Martini has transformed the Annunciation from a narrative scene into a devotional image. He has omitted all superfluous detail and has done away with the architectonic setting which was so scrupulously depicted by Duccio and, above all, by Pietro Lorenzetti (figs. 48 and 84). Duccio accentuated the interplay of arrival and recoil by means of the architecture, but here it is articulated by the frame. The movements of the angel and the Virgin are once again in perfect counterpoise, but there is now a greater intensity to the scene. The angel's message and the Virgin's reaction may be theologically motivated, but there is also a certain intrinsic, personalised significance to their attitudes, which are highlighted by the isolation of the two figures against the gilt ground.

It has rarely been pointed out that this *Annunciation* must have astonished the contemporary viewer with its display of illusionistic effects, which were well in advance of their time. Although the scene is set on a shallow proscenium, the robes trailing over the edge of the picture plane bring the figures into the spectator's world. Ansanus and Margaret play no part in the evocative events of the Annunciation, but nor are they relegated to the flat gold background. They stand there like statues on low pedestals. The throne, the vase of lilies and the olive branch are depicted with a realism which is quite remarkable for the period. These large and lifelike attributes almost force the viewer to contemplate the scene in terms of symbols. Our attention is also drawn to the rendering of fabrics. No expense or effort has been spared to make the robes as true to life as possible in their movement, colour and trimmings. But that is not all. The supple, flowing drapery which is familiair to us from the work of both Simone and Duccio has here become a means of expression. The angel's haste and the Virgin's fright are expressed by their clothing, and one could therefore describe these figures as the perfect culmination of gothic 'Gewandfiguren'.

Simone's *Annunciation* could also be described as a scene with two actors flanking a central section containing Christ Logos, the descent of the Holy Ghost, attributes and a text. Simone has made an altarpiece out of a narrative by emphasising theological motifs and symbols, both in his composition and execution. The text 'Ave Maria. Gratia Plena. Dominus Tecum' ('Hail Mary, full of grace, the Lord is with thee') plays a key role in this process. The other words spoken by Gabriel are woven into the edges of his robes: 'ne timeas' and 'ecce concipies, Spiritus Sanctus superveniet in te, virtus Altissimi obumbrabit tibi' ('Do not be afraid...behold, thou shalt conceive...the Holy Spirit will come upon thee, and the power of the most High will overshadow thee'). But the faithful have not just read the 'Ave Maria', they have also recited it as a prayer, probably adding the words spoken by Elizabeth at the Visitation: 'Blessed art thou among women, and blessed is the fruit of thy womb.' From the end of the thirteenth century these words were joined together to form the first half of the ritual 'Hail Mary', which has since become one of the most important prayers in the daily devotions of Catholics. By 1332 those words of Gabriel and Elizabeth were being repeated every day at the tolling of the Angelus. This custom was probably introduced by Bonaventure, the great Franciscan theologian and mystic.[90] In Simone's painting the angel Gabriel is not so much a messenger bringing news to Mary as a model for the viewer. He kneels and adores the person who is filled with God's grace.

The alterpiece of the *Birth of the Virgin* (fig. 91) is signed 'PETRUS. LAURENTII. DE SENIS. ME PINXIT A MCCCXLII' ('Pietro Lorenzetti of Siena painted me in the year 1342') Pietro's commission was similar to Simone's, but he set about it in a very different way – so much so that one suspects a deliberate antithesis. In Simone's painting there is a shallow proscenium, with the gold ground closing off the rear of the picture space. Pietro opens up that space. The three arcades provide a view of a realistically painted delivery room with adjoining chambers. In the centre foreground the newborn Virgin is being given her first bath, regardless of her aura of sanctity. The monumental matron lying on the childbed in the background is St Anne, who is being attended by a midwife with a fly whisk in her left hand. To the right are two other midwives holding objects used in post-natal care. Joachim, who is waiting outside the delivery room, is just being told that he is a father.

Pietro could have found the models for his monumental figures in sculpture. St Anne, for instance, bears a striking resemblance to figures by the Florentine sculpture Arnolfo di Cambio and by the Sienese Tino da Camaino. Even more remarkable than Pietro's references to sculpture, which have already been noted in connection with his polyptych for Arezzo, is his concern for the realistic depiction of space. He has gone to great lengths to give each of the architectural units its own identity. Floor tiles suggest depth. Drapery, objects and architectural details reflect great skill in the realistic handling of textures. Bold, local colours create marked contrasts and contribute to the illusion of the presence of real people and objects. The most remarkable feature, though, is the continuity of the framing and the pictorial space, which serves to bring the Virgin forward towards the viewer.

It appears from fifteenth-century inventories that Pietro's *Birth of the Virgin* was flanked by Sts Savinus and Bartholomew, so it was evidently decided to give Siena's favourite apostle a place of honour in this programme of altarpieces for the city's patron saints. There is a record of payment involving this altarpiece dated as early as 1335, but it is not for an artist or a carpenter, but for a scholar: 'To master Ciecho de la Grammatica, for translating the story of St Savinus from the Latin so that it may by recorded on panel.'[91] The conclusion to be drawn from this is that the altarpiece probably had a predella with scenes from the saint's life. Although several attempts have been made to identify those scenes they all lack conviction. The only work which may well have come from that predella is a painting from the workshop of Pietro Lorenzetti which is now in the National Gallery, London. There is some doubt about the subject, but it could be Venustianus, the Roman governor of Tuscany, vainly ordering Bishop Savinus and his deacons to worship a statuette of Jupiter (fig. 95).[92]

One of the most important feasts of the Virgin was the Purification, which took place at the same time as the Presentation in the temple. This was when

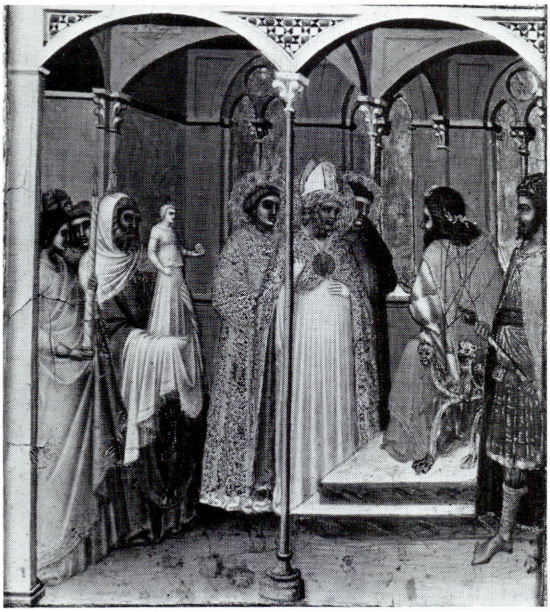

95 Pietro Lorenzetti, St Savinus before the Roman governor (?), 30.5 x 27 cm, National Gallery, London.

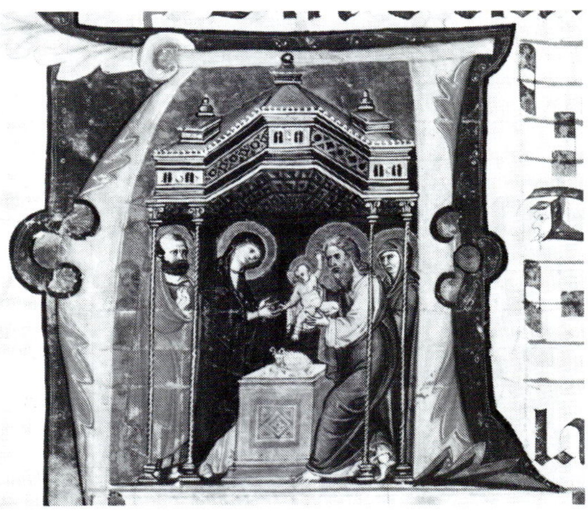

96 Sienese early 14th century, Purification, Antiphonary 34 D, fol 254r, Museo dell'Opera del Duomo, Siena.

Joseph, Mary and Jesus appeared before the priests in obedience to Mosaic law. Joseph bought two turtle doves, the sacrifice prescribed for poor people, and gave them to the priest. Jesus was then consecrated to the Lord and was received again 'from His hands'. As the writer of the *Meditationes* says: 'If you wish to learn about humility and poverty, consider in the aforementioned events the donation, the redemption, and the observation of the law and you can easily perceive them.'[93] This feast of the Virgin was dipicted on the central section of the altarpiece of St Crescentius, which was ordered from Ambrogio Lorenzetti. We know that work had already started on the *Presentation in the temple* by 1339, for there is a record of money being paid to a carpenter, Maestro Paolo Bindi, for the material and work on the predella of the 'tavola di San Crescenzo'. The signature tells us that the painting was completed three years later: 'AMBROSIUS. LAURENTII. DE . SENIS . FECIT . HOC OPUS . ANNO DOMINI MCCCXLII' ('Ambrogio Lorenzetti of Siena executed this work in the year of Our Lord 1342'). Inventories and old descriptions tell us that Crescentius was depicted on the left 'carrying his head in his hands', while on the right was the archangel Michael, the weigher of souls and warrior leader of the heavenly hosts, who was riding a crest of popularity at this period. This may have been the first time that Crescentius was shown as a head-bearer ('cephalophorous'). Ambrogio had a definite penchant for realistic overstatement when it came to depicting martyrs' attributes.[94]

The structure of this altarpiece relative to the architectonic setting of the scene is quite remarkable. The central section is very high, with a very different height-to-width ratio from that of the previous two works. The three arcades consist of heavily moulded, narrow pointed arches containing Gothic trefoils. This pronounced verticality contrasts with the emphatically horizontal dentils at the very top of the altarpiece. The capitals halfway up the side framing reinforce this horizontal effect. The altarpiece owes its pronounced architectonic character to the pointed arch shapes in the wood, the dentils and, above all, to the heavy pilasters. It is difficult to imagine how the lateral saints would have looked alongside this massively framed central section. The ornate architectural framing is in marked contrast to the painted architecture, where there is no continuity at all of framing with pictorial space, but rather a sophisticated interplay of tripartite architecture vis-à-vis a tripartite frame. Pointed arches as against low arcades, and the world of gold and two-dimensional ornamentation as against the painted illusion of depth. That depth is not the result of a more or less intuitive organisation of the pictorial space, as in Pietro's altarpiece. Ambrogio's tiled floor follows the laws of perspective, with a single vanishing point,[95] so that the figures appear to have solid ground beneath their feet. This is the first painting to display this kind of scientific treatment of the painted space, adding further weight to Ambrogio's claims as a 'pictor doctus'.

The depiction of the temple building with three bays open towards the viewer was not uncommon in *Presentation* scenes (cf. fig. 96). What is new, though, is Ambrogio's realistic treatment of the building. The

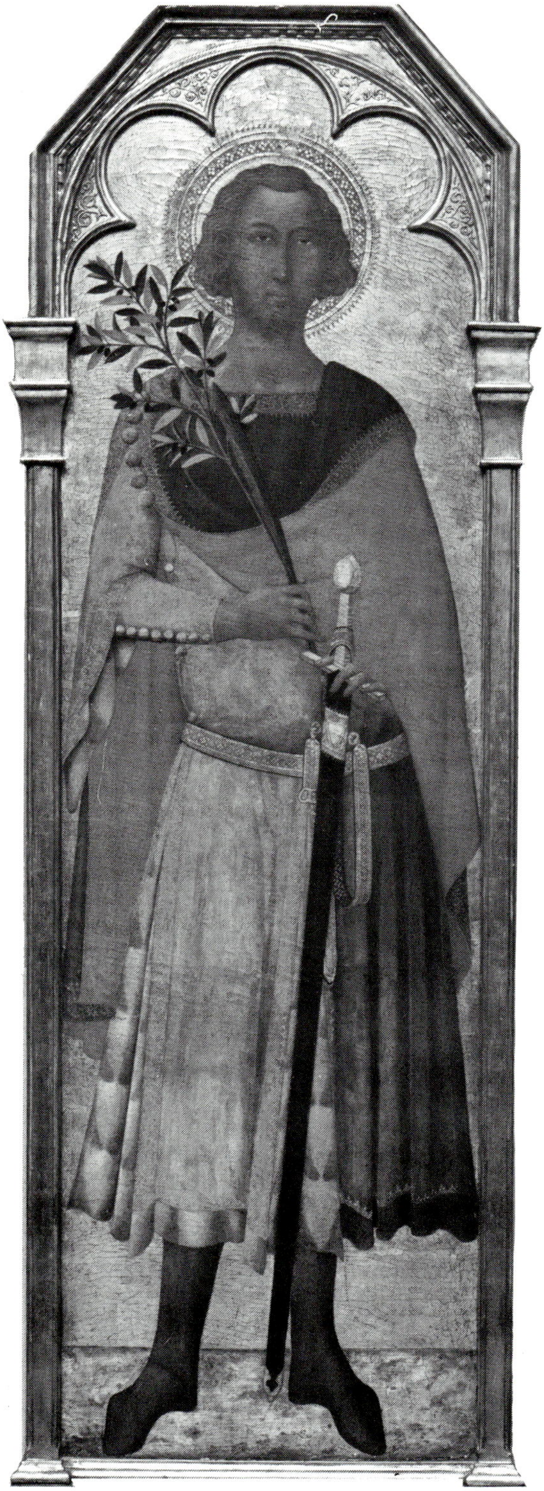

97 Sienese ca. 1340, St Victor of Siena, 160 x 50 cm, Royal Museum of Fine Arts, Copenhagen.

painstaking rendering of pillars, capitals, tiled floors, ornamental borders and other elements create a 'lifelike' effect which had never been achieved by any other artist. This striving for realism was the feature which so impressed Ghiberti and Vasari, who were the first to describe Ambrogio's art. He has also included a number of details which are designed to identify the building specifically as a temple. David and Moses stand on the capitals of the two pillars in the foreground, and Moses appears again in a tympanum in one of the aisles, this time as a counterpart to Malachi. The same two Old Testament figures are also found at the very top of the altarpiece, on either side of the pointed arch. Moses is holding up a scroll with the words 'SI NON INVENERIT MANUS EI [US] NEC POTUERIT OFFERRE AGNIUM SUMET DUOS TURTURES AUT DUOS PULLOS CHOLUNBE' ('If she cannot lay her hand on a lamb fit to be offered, she must bring two turtle doves or two young pigeons', Leviticus 12:8), while Malachi prophesies: 'ET STATI VENIET AD TEMPLUM SUUM DOMINATUR QUEM VOS QUAERITIS ET ANGELUS TESTAMENTI QUEM VOS VULTIS' ('All at once the Lord will visit his temple; that Lord, so longed for, welcome, herald of a divine covenant', Malachi 3:1).[96] The figure of the Messiah in a clipeus on the tympanum of the nave may well be an allusion to this prophecy. The Messiah is borne aloft by winged victories, demonstrating Ambrogio's knowledge of classical images. The victories in a row supporting garlands on the roof of the temple are a further display of the artist's erudition.[97]

The figures inside the temple form a balanced composition within the three bays. On the left is Joseph and on the right Anna. The Virgin in the centre is accompanied by two midwives. Opposite her is Simeon, with the Christ Child cradled in his arms. Standing behind the altar is the high priest with the doves, and in his left hand he holds the circumcision knife. His attention has been distracted by a figure who is the fourteenth-century stereotype of the Jewish scribe. A similar figure can be seen peering round a pillar at the back of the right aisle. One of the most interesting aspects of this altarpiece is that the cohesion of the figural composition is due not only to the arrangement within the architecture but also to the contact between the figures. Their gestures and glances show that they are involved in each other's actions. It is a typically Ambrogian touch to use human relationships to highlight the significance of a traditional image. An excellent illustration of this device is the prophetess Anna, who has been vouchsafed a glimpse of salvation in her old age. Her gesture and gaze show her total absorption in Jesus, who appears in the endearingly naturalistic pose of an infant with a finger in his mouth. In her

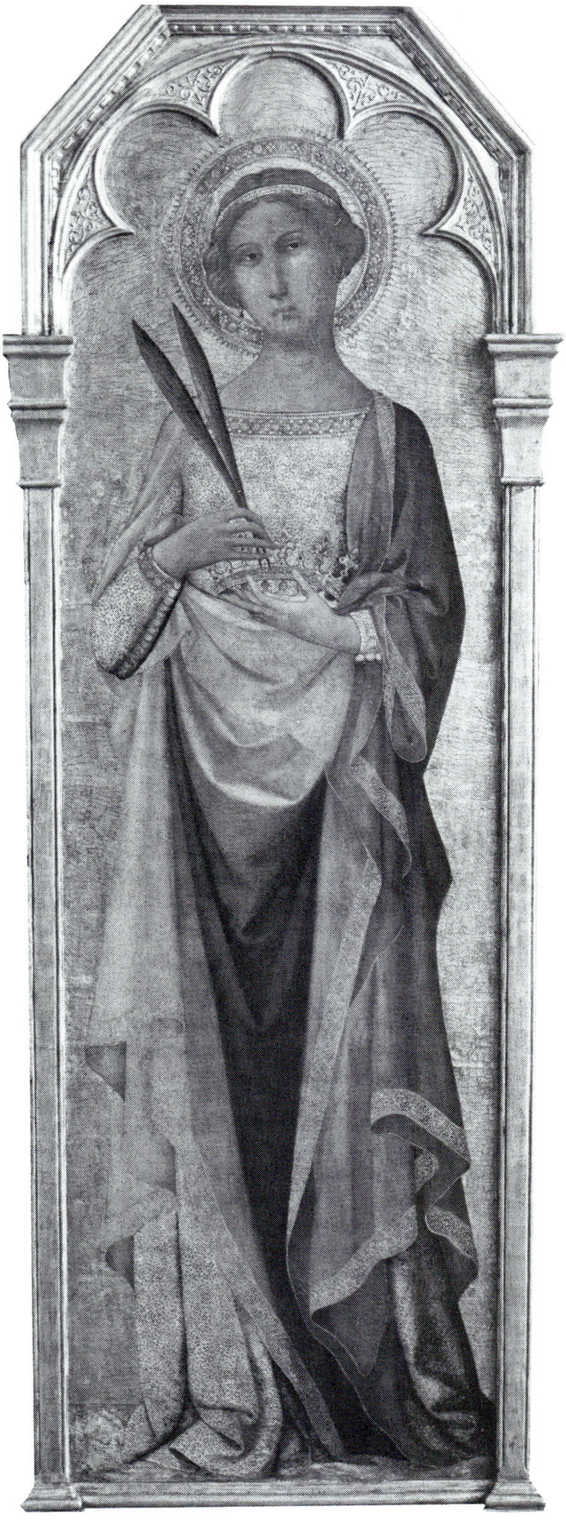

98 Sienese ca. 1340, St Catherine of Alexandria, 155 x 50 cm, Royal Museum of Fine Arts, Copenhagen.

left hand Anna holds a large scroll which tells us how she reacted to this sight of Jesus. 'Et haec ipsa hora superveniens confitebatur domino et loquebatur de illo omnibus qui expectabant redemptionem Israel' ('She too, at that very hour, came near to give God thanks, and spoke of the child to all that patiently waited for the deliverance of Israel', Luke 2:38). Ambrogio was clearly concerned with that single moment of prophecy which comes at the end of the story of the Presentation, and was not following the usual course of combining the crucial moments of the episode. Joseph has already handed over the doves, and Jesus has been circumcised. The aged Simeon has seen 'that saving power', as he puts it in his paean of praise, and holds the child in his arms. Now it is Anna's turn to speak. This eighty-four-year-old widow 'abode continually in the temple, night and day, serving God with fasting and prayer', and like Simeon she recognises the child as her Saviour. In the background the scribes are coming forward to comment on these prophecies. It can be no accident that it was Ambrogio, the 'pictor doctus', who outstone his contemporaries in creating a unity of time and action which later theorists were to prescribe as essential to the success of a painting.

Until now it had been thought that the painting for the altar of St Victor of Siena had vanished without trace. We know from various inventories that it was a *Nativity* with St Victor and another saint. There are also financial records which show that Andrea di Bartolo painted murals in the chapel of St Victor in 1405.[98] There is a painting in Copenhagen which gives us an idea of how St Victor was portrayed ca. 1340 (fig. 97). The companion piece is a female saint who has traditionally been identified as *St Catherine of Alexandria* (fig. 98). Victor is shown with the instrument and mark of his martyrdom: the sword and the palm branch. He also holds an olive branch, which was awarded to saints on whose feast day a victory had been won,[99] and it was on 15th May 1229, the feast of St Victor, that Siena conquered Sarteano.

It was once suggested that the Sts Victor and Catherine in Copenhagen originally flanked a *Madonna* which is now in the Berenson collection (fig. 99),[100] but this reconstruction is obviously quite untenable. It is inconceivable that the arcades containing the two saints could ever have been placed next to the pointed arches above the Madonna. In addition, the dimensions of the three panels and the differences in scale between the saints and the figures on the Madonna panel completely rule out any association. Nevertheless, there are ample grounds for believing that the Copenhagen panels are the ones mentioned in the inventories as flanking the *Nativity* on the altar of St Victor in Siena cathedral. That was the only

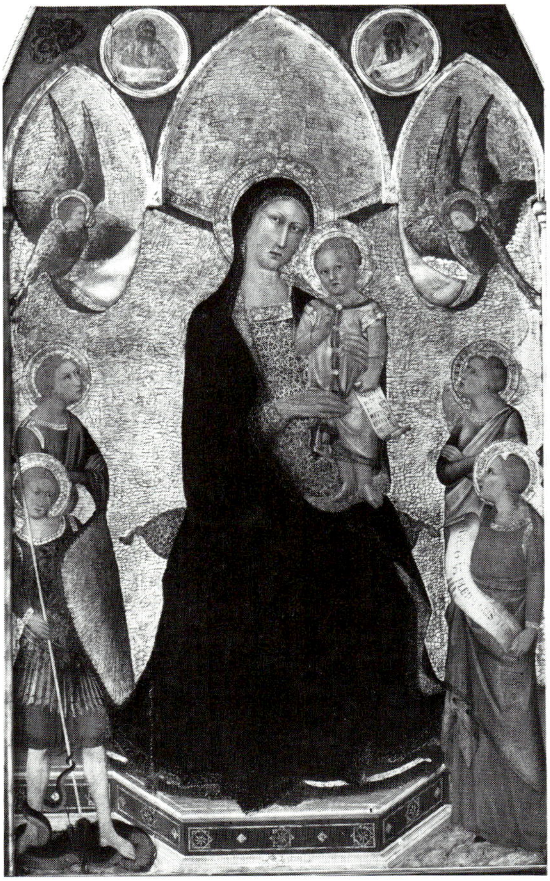

99 Master of the Palazzo Venezia Madonna, Madonna with archangels and angels, Berenson Collection, Settignano.

place in the city where St Victor would have been venerated at that particular time, so it is virtually inconceivable that a Sienese painting of the saint from this period could ever have stood anywhere else.

Might it yet be possible to identify the central panel of St Victor's altarpiece? There cannot be all that many Sienese paintings of the Nativity from the 1330s to choose from, for after all we are dealing with the earliest altarpieces to have a narrative scene in the centre. As it happens there is a Sienese *Nativity* from the right period. With the exception of the three works by Simone Martini and the Lorenzetti brothers it is virtually the only narrative altarpiece to have come down to us from the first half of the fourteenth century. I am referring to the *Nativity* in the Fogg Museum in Cambridge, Massachusetts, which is attributed to Bartolommeo Bulgarini (fig. 100). Unfortunately it has been mutilated at the sides. The arm protruding through the doorway on the right, for instance, tells us that there must have been at least one more shepherd. The top has also been sawn into a different shape, presumably to fit the painting into its present frame. As a result it is no longer possible to envisage the original structure of the altarpiece.

As with Simone's *Annunciation* it is fascinating to see how a traditional image which would normally belong in a narrative series has been transformed to suit it to its new function as the central scene of an altarpiece. In the first place the Madonna has been moved to the centre of the composition in order to present the Nativity as a feast of the Virgin. She is seated in the foreground rather than lying down, which was her more usual pose in Sienese treatments of the theme (cf. fig. 25). This is also a very rare, early representation of the *Adoration of the shepherds*, who were usually shown hearing of Christ's birth from the angel. They have already arrived at the birthplace, and like the kneeling Gabriel in scenes of the Annunciation they have adopted the pose which the viewer is expected to imitate when approaching the Virgin. In Mary's halo are the words 'Ave Maria. Gratia plena', from the prayer which the faithful should use when addressing her. The second unusual feature of this painting is the emphasis on the theological and liturgical essence of the Nativity: the incarnation of the Logos ('And the Word was made flesh'). The dove of the Holy Ghost and the group of seraphim with Christ Logos in their midst transform the story into a theological event. Bartolommeo Bulgarini has adapted the Nativity for the devotion of the faithful, just as Simone did with his *Annunciation*.[101]

The architectural setting of the Fogg *Nativity* can only be explained by assuming that the painting was originally part of a series of altarpieces for Siena cathedral. A *Nativity* was normally set in a cave or a manger, or a combination of both. Here, though, it takes place in a hall facing the viewer which is divided into three by slender pillars. This arrangement matches perfectly with the altarpieces by Pietro and Ambrogio Lorenzetti. This is the only instance of a Nativity being set in such a hall. The mutilation of the top of the painting has destroyed what was undoubtedly the artist's intention – to organise the pictorial space in depth based on the subdivision of the altarpiece, just as the Lorenzetti had done.

There have been considerable difficulties with the attribution of this *Nativity*. It belongs to a group of superior works executed by an excellent but anonymous pupil of Pietro Lorenzetti who was dubbed the Master Pietro a Ovile after a *Madonna* in the Sienese church of that name. Millard Meiss proposed the name of Bartolommeo Bulgarini for this homogeneous group of paintings, which are related to the work of Pietro Lorenzetti.[102] Seventeenth and eighteenth-century authors tell us that Bartolommeo was an associate of Pietro's and that he was regarded as an important artist in his day. The relationship between the two must have been comparable to that between Lippo Memmi and Simone Martini. There is documentary evidence that Bartolommeo painted two altarpieces for the church of the Ospedale Santa Maria della Scala. All three altarpieces by the Ovile Master in the Pinacoteca in Siena originally came from the Ospedale, and it is extremely unlikely that any other pupil of Pietro's executed altarpieces for that rather small church. The obvious assumption is that Bartolommeo's two documented paintings for the hospital church should be sought among the three works by the Ovile Master in the Pinacoteca. The difficulty, of course, is that we have no work by Bartolommeo which is either signed or clearly documented. There is a Biccherna panel which must have been painted by Bartolommeo, going by the documentary evidence, but it is quite impossible to compare that miniature scene with a large altarpiece. The most that can be said is that the style of the Biccherna panel does not preclude the identification of the Ovile master with Bartolommeo Bulgarini, for which there is anyway considerable supportive evidence. All in all there are good grounds for agreeing with Meiss's identifications.

However, that still does not tell us whether the Sts Victor and Catherine in Copenhagen could have flanked the *Nativity* in Cambridge. We no longer know the original dimensions of the *Nativity*, so there would appear to be little hope of making a convincing reconstruction on the basis of physical evidence. Style criticism has condemned the two saints to a rather peripatetic existence. It is true that there are affinities with the early work of Bartolommeo Bulgarini, particularly in the treatment of drapery and hands, but they could not in any way be described as characteristic of that master's style. Of course there is no reason why the lateral saints should not have been executed by a second artist. The suggestion that the two saints are connected with the *Nativity* rests on functional and historical considerations rather than on grounds of style. Nevertheless, the panels with the two saints do have one formal feature which is also found in altarpieces by Bartolommeo Bulgarini, and that is the framing. The semi-circular arch enclosing five smaller semi-circular arches appears on almost all the early altarpieces attributed to the artist. Moreover, this type of framing is rarely found outside his workshop.[103] Taken as a whole these arguments constitute a strong case for believing that the two saints in Copenhagen once flanked the Fogg *Nativity* on the altar of St Victor in Siena cathedral.

What, though, was the connection between the building programme for Siena cathedral and this series of four altarpieces for the city's patron saints and feasts of the Virgin? The various plans which were put forward from 1317 onwards had one factor in common. The crypt was to go. Architectural historians have commented widely and variously on those plans, but amidst all the astonishment at the megalomania of the Sienese it has been forgotten that even megalomaniac plans have their functional side. The cathedral may be a tower of Babel, but the Sienese had their reasons. They wanted to create a new space which would show off the ideological function of the church to the best possible advantage. Van der Ploeg is therefore right to point out that the removal of the crypt affected one of the essential functions of the original church.

Siena's mediators, who knelt at the feet of the city's patroness in Duccio's *Maestà* above the crypt, were to be honoured in a new way. No longer were they to be hidden away in the crypt. They were brought out of the shadows and put on display in a new, spacious church in relic altars, with their likenesses to identify them. A depiction of one of the feasts of the Virgin would directly associate each saint with the city's protectress. This programme demanded a new and very different visual approach. In a crypt the veneration of relics tends to be an intimate, personal affair. Mass interest could be aroused by a temporary exhibition of the relics outside the crypt or by carrying them in procession. The installation of relic altars in the main body of the church turned the veneration of the city's patron saints into a far more public occasion in which the altarpieces played a key role.

Van der Ploeg is the first person to have noticed that the patronal altars are the only ones to be referred to by name on the original plan for the 'Duomo Nuovo', and he argues that this should be taken into account when interpreting the function of the proposed church. Personally I am convinced that the most important reason for the rebuilding from the liturgical point of view was to present the patron saints in a new way. The crypt was still demolished, even after the plans for the Duomo Nuovo had been abandoned, and the authorities went ahead with their new presentation of the saints. In 1405, thirty years after the rebuilding had been completed, murals were commissioned for the sacristy and for those chapels which had already been completed. The subjects included the translation of the saint's relics. We only know of these paintings from documents,[104] but what concerns us here is the fact that the visual propaganda for the city's patron saints had been a factor in the liturgical history of the cathedral since 1215 and in the associated commissions for its rebuilding and decoration. Antje Mitteldorf-Kose-

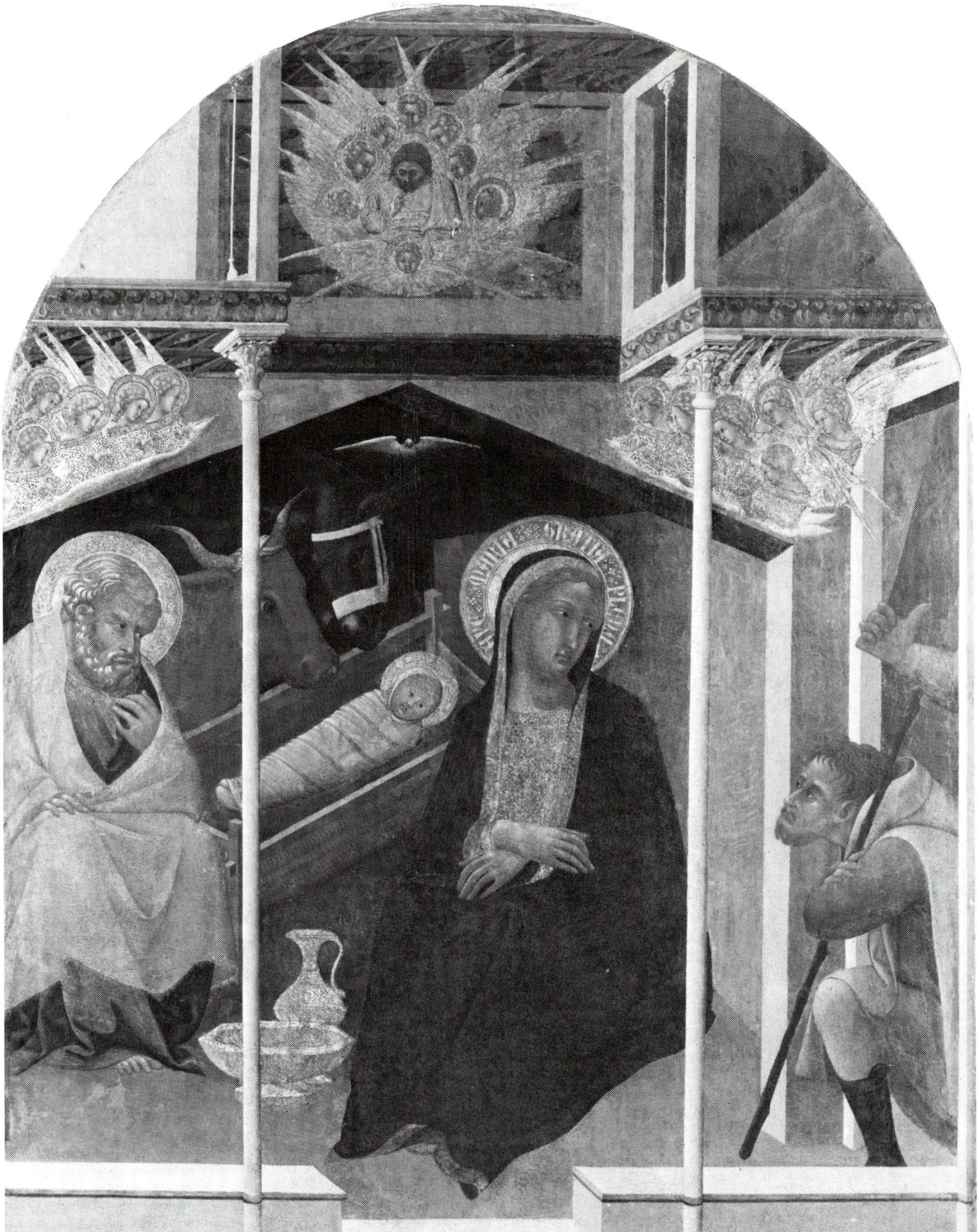

100 Bartolommeo Bulgarini, Nativity, 170.5 x 123 cm,
Fogg Art Museum, Cambridge (Mass.).

garten has suggested that the huge dome was conceived as a fitting structure to crown the high altar with its altarpiece of the Madonna. One may perhaps be a little sceptical about such 'ideologising of architectonic space', but the fact remains that the veneration of the city's saints led to the installation of life-size images in the pendentives of the dome at the end of the fifteenth century. Advantage was taken of the dome's hexagonal shape to add two new saints: Catherine and Bernardino. The Opera del Duomo, with its stream of new commissions, demonstrated that the cathedral was to be regarded and experienced as the city's pantheon. Butzek's exemplary study of sixteenth and seventeenth-century statues of Sienese popes makes it clear that the cathedral retained this role of a pantheon, even if family interests had by then superseded those of the city itself.[105]

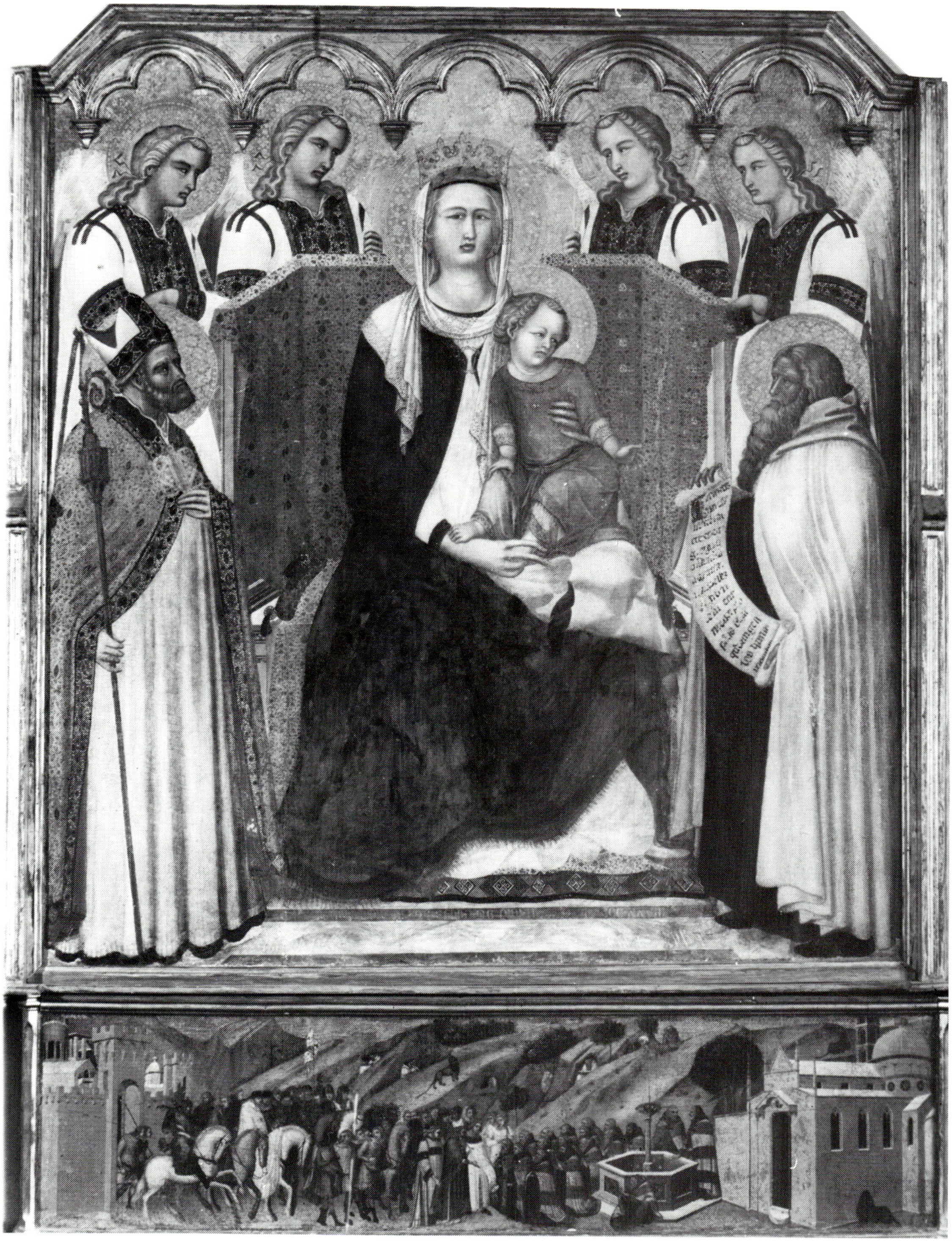

103 Pietro Lorenzetti, Carmelite Madonna,
169 x 148 cm, 1329, Pinacoteca Nazionale, Siena.

VI

PIETRO LORENZETTI'S CARMELITE ALTARPIECE OF 1329

Although polyptychs with full-length figures flanking a central Madonna were being produced elsewhere in Italy from the beginning of the fourteenth century (fig. 93), Siena had a marked preference for half-length figures. The occasional altarpieces depicted in paintings by Sienese artists all have half-length figures (cf. fig. 101). It is true that there are individual Madonnas which probably came from altarpieces with standing figures, but it is by no means clear that they were executed for Sienese patrons. There are full-length saints in Duccio's *Maestà*, of course, but they are not enclosed in separate compartments. It was only at a fairly late date that the Sienese began introducing the polyptych with full-length figures, and it was not until around 1370, when Lippo Vanni painted a sort of 'al fresco' ideogram of this form of altarpiece in the church of San Francesco, that it became a standard type in Sienese painting (fig. 102).[106] Pietro Lorenzetti's Carmelite altarpiece of 1329 marks the very beginning of this development (figs. 103-115).

The full reconstruction of Pietro's altarpiece was recently made possible by the discovery of two full-length saints who clearly belong with the known fragments of the work.[107] They are the prophet Elisha (fig. 105), with a scroll bearing the text. 'ASCENDIT HELIAS PER TURBINEM IN CELUM HELISEUS AUTEM VIDEBAT ET CLAMABAT PATER MI PATER MI CURRUS I [SRAEL]' ('Elias went up on a whirlwind into heaven. Elisha watched it, crying out, My father, my father, Israel's chariot'; 4 Kings (2:11-12), and John the Baptist (fig. 106), who stands in his characteristic 'hitch-hiking' pose, jerking his right thumb towards the Christ Child on Mary's lap.[108] Together with Sts Agnes and Catherine (figs. 107, 108) in the Pinacoteca in Siena they originally flanked a large squarish panel with the enthroned Madonna (fig. 103). Standing next to the Madonna are St Nicholas and the prophet Elijah, who has a halo. Like Elisha on the lateral panel he has been placed on a par with the saints. He too holds a scroll, with a quotation from 3 Kings 18:19: 'VERUMTAMEN NUNC MITTE ET CONCREGA AD ME UNIVERSUM ISRAEL IN MONTE CARMELO ET PROPHETAS BAAL QUADRINGENTOS QUINQUAGINTA' ('Gather me all Israel on mount Carmel, with Baal's four hundred and fifty prophets'). Four angels wearing white robes with ornate trimmings stand behind the Madonna's throne, gracefully arranged beneath the cusped arcades of the framing. Below the throne are the signature and date: 'PETRUS LAURENTII DE SENIS ME PINSIT A.D. MCCCXXVIII[I]' ('Pietro Lorenzetti of Siena painted me in the year 1329').

The composition of the central scene can be regarded either as a Madonna altarpiece of the same type as Duccio's *Rucellai Madonna* (fig. 30), but with the addition of full-length saints, or as a simplified version of the *Maestà* (figs. 41, 43). The central panel has been augmented with lateral saints in individual compartments. This sense of augmentation is reinforced by the broad, heavily moulded framing of the central panel, the sides of which are very similar to the framing of Ambrogio's *Presentation in the temple* (fig. 90). There is also a sophisticated use of scale, with the lateral saints being the same size as the figures of St Nicholas and Elijah on the central panel. Pairs of half-length apostles above the lateral saints make up for the difference in height between the central and side panels. This was the customary position for apostles, as we saw from the *Maestà* and from polyptychs with half-length figures (cf. fig. 73). The predella scenes mirror this arrangement, consisting of a very wide composition in the centre flanked by four smaller scenes (fig. 114). The disparity between the width of the central predella scene

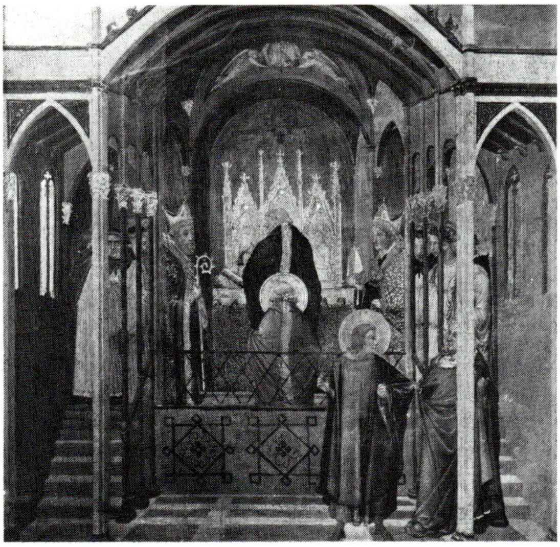

101 Ambrogio Lorenzetti, St Nicholas consecrated bishop, 48 x 53 cm, Galleria degli Uffizi, Florence.

and those on either side is slightly tempered by the fact that it is in effect a series of five scenes which modulate smoothly from left to right (fig. 115).

The commission for such a large altarpiece evidently proved too ambitious for the donors, for in 1324 they applied to the city government for a subsidy. The Commune eventually agreed to provide the necessary funds, demonstrating yet again how eager the urban community was to encourage mendicant orders to settle in the city. On 26th October 1329 the Consiglio Generale della Campana voted fifty pounds for the completion of the painting with 'Virgin, apostles, martyrs, confessors and holy virgins'.[109] Nicholas was the only saint to be mentioned by name, but since he was the titular saint of the Carmelite church there is nothing surprising in that. The Carmelites, like so many mendicant orders in the fourteenth century, had settled on the site of an ancient oratory, in this case a small church dedicated to St Nicholas.[110] They thus profited from their association with an established, local veneration, and at the same time utilised it to present themselves as the restorers of a neglected religiosity. This claim of restoration, in the most literal sense of repairing shrines, was a common thread running through the propaganda of almost every mendicant order. St Francis, for example, was constantly initiating rebuilding and restoration projects. The purpose of this kind of propaganda was to show that the mendicants were working for the church as an institution and that their activities were not part of some sinister modernism but were solely intended to restore an ecclesiastical heritage which was in danger of being lost through the ravages of time.

In their decision to grant a subsidy the Consiglio Generale spoke of Pietro's altarpiece in the most glowing terms. It was a painting which was 'honorabilis', 'valde pulcra', and even 'multa pulcerima'. It was certainly a remarkable painting for its day, not only because of its size (it measured at least 169 by 332 centimetres), but also because of its structure, the richly ornamented gold of the haloes, and the colourfulness of the predella narrative. Pietro Lorenzetti's Carmelite altarpiece is an extremely important document on the stylistic evolution of Sienese art. The spatial structure of the central section displays a compositional finesse formerly found only in Florentine Madonnas. When the altarpiece was in place it must have seemed that the altar table continued upwards into the stone floor of the painting, uniting the world of the spectator with that of the Madonna and her attendants. The figures stand firmly on solid ground and are clearly differentiated within the pictorial space. One typically Sienese feature is the visual significance of the Madonna's throne, which is very different from the function it had in many Florentine works. In the art of Giotto and his pupils, for example, the space is defined chiefly by the plastic figures of the Madonna and Child. The throne serves merely as a compartment to hold the Madonna, whereas in Pietro's painting it has a specific spatial and colouristic significance as a setting within and against which the Madonna and Child are outlined.

The role of the architectonic setting emerges even more clearly in the predella scenes (figs. 109-113), where Pietro has created extremely complex structures with a distinct colouristic and narrative value. He gives a strikingly bravura display of how figures can be disposed in depth within the confines of architecture (figs. 112, 113). Considering that only twenty years had elapsed since Duccio painted his *Maestà*, this was certainly a remarkable innovation in Sienese art. The same applies to the organisation of figures in a landscape, for which the hermits in their hilly retreat provided ideal material (figs. 110, 111). It is noteworthy that both Pietro and Ambrogio used contours to achieve the spatial effect of their figures, rather than modelling or the plastic development of those figures. They acquire their depth from the asymmetrical contours, and it is this that creates the illusion of space. The actual drawing in the Carmelite altarpiece differs quite considerably from that in Pietro's earlier work. The Arezzo polyptych (fig. 83) has sharp, thin lines, but here the drawing is rather thick and loose (so much so that at times it is almost absorbed in the modelling), as in the *Birth of the Virgin*.

Recent authors have rightly made great play of the fact that Pietro's altarpiece of 1329 was intended

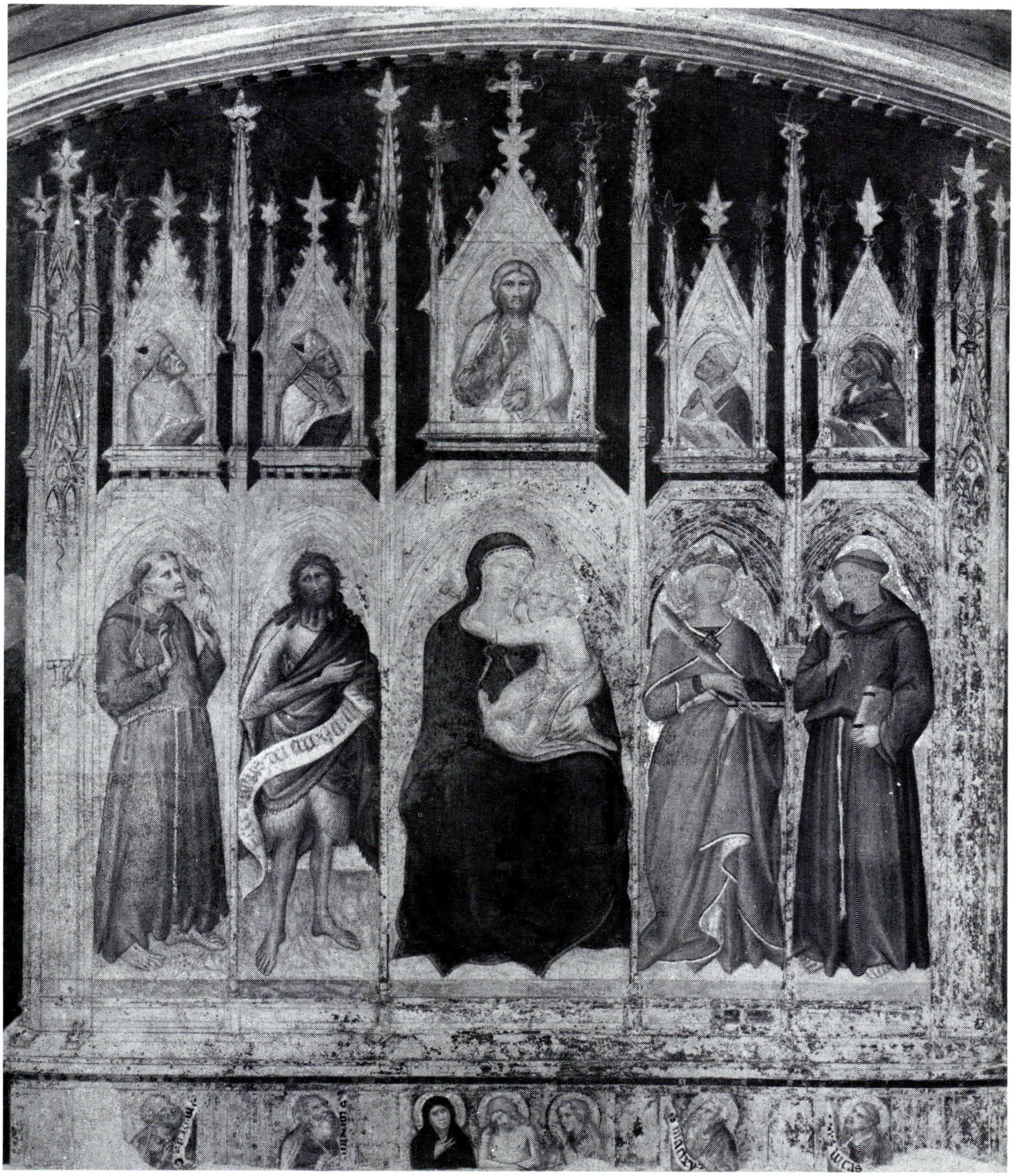

102 Lippo Vanni, Fictive polyptych, the Madonna with Sts Francis, John the Baptist, Catherine of Alexandria, and the Blessed Peter of Siena, 290 x 260 cm, S. Francesco, Siena.

as visual propaganda for the Carmelites.[111] Before going on to discuss that aspect of the painting it is worth reiterating that the chief function of any altarpiece was liturgical and that any altarpiece can be interpreted as a propagandist statement on the basis of the choice of scenes and saints, the size of the work, and its ornateness and resplendence. Pietro's painting is rather different, though, in that it expresses highly specific issues of Carmelite propaganda by iconographic means. It also predates any mention of those issues in the literature.

As we have seen, the choice of saints almost invariably reflects a specific relationship with the world of

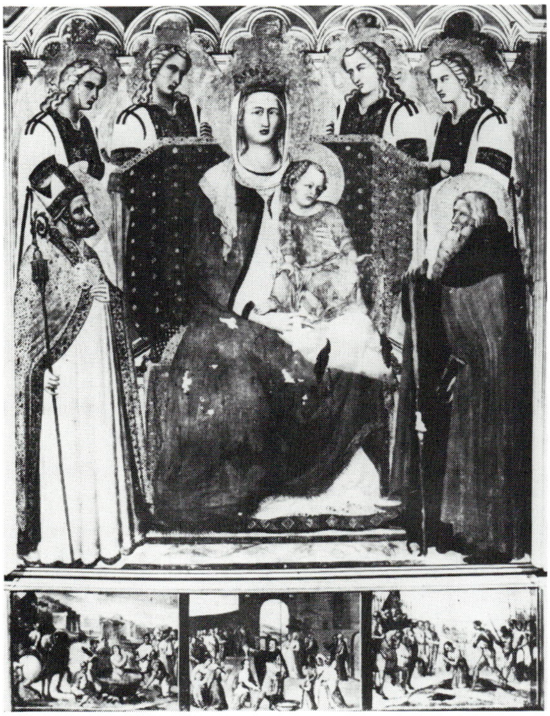

104 19th-century photograph of Pietro Lorenzetti, Carmelite Madonna with St Anthony painted over Elijah and scenes from the life of St Ansanus painted over the scene of Patriarch Albert consigning the rule to Brocardus, a 16th-century adaptation which stood on the high altar of the church of S. Ansano la Dofana.

the donor. This is particularly apparent in the case of the Carmelite altarpiece, for two of the 'saints', Elijah and Elisha, are not saints at all, but prophets. They are presented as the putative antecedents of the order, which is why they are wearing the white mantle which Pope Honorius IV granted the order in 1287 (fig. 113). The scrolls which they are holding refer to the two key events which associate them with Mount Carmel. Elijah calls the people together in order to demonstrate the power of his God to the priests of Baal, and Mount Carmel was the place chosen for the holocaust. Elijah prayed to God, who responded by sending down a bolt of lightning which consumed the burnt offering, after King Ahab's priests had vainly slashed themselves with knives to induce Baal to perform a similar miracle. Carmel was also the place where Elisha saw Elijah carried up to heaven, as described on his scroll. When Elijah had vanished Elisha 'caught at his own clothes, and tore them across; then he took up the mantle of Elias, that had fallen from him; and when he reached Jordan bank again...' (4 Kings 2:12-13). According to the Carmelites their mantles were originally striped to commemorate the fact that Elijah's mantle

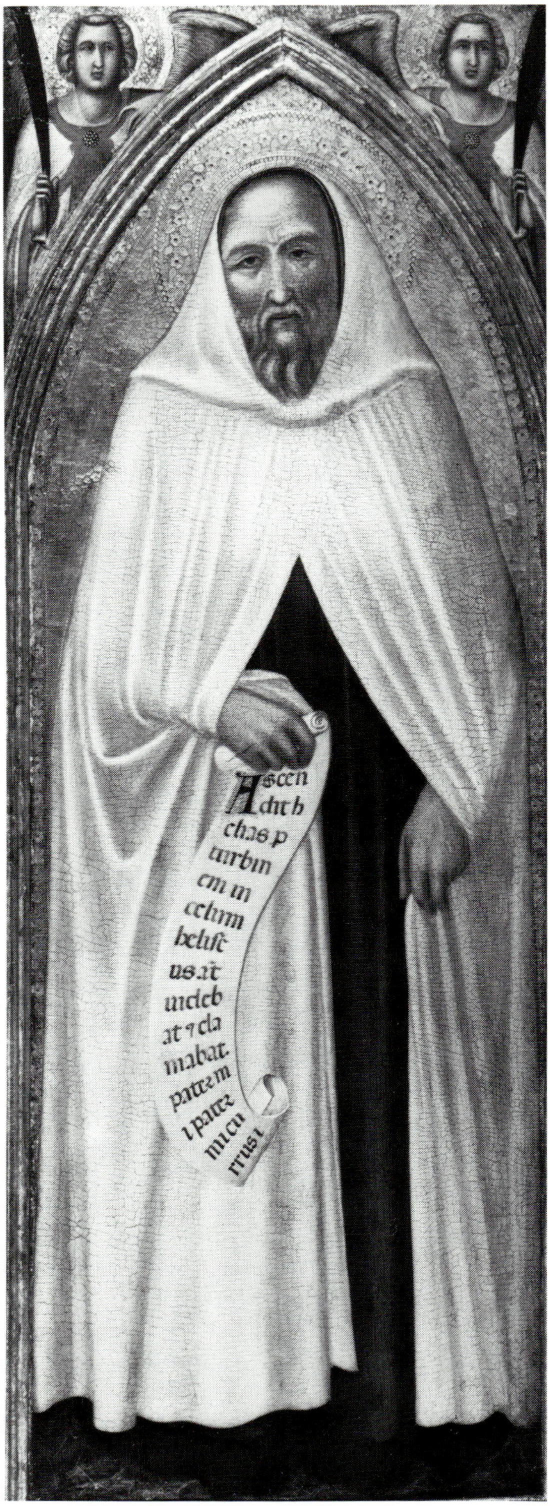

105 Pietro Lorenzetti, Elisha, 124 x 44.5 cm, University Art Museum, Princeton (Norton Simon Foundation loan).

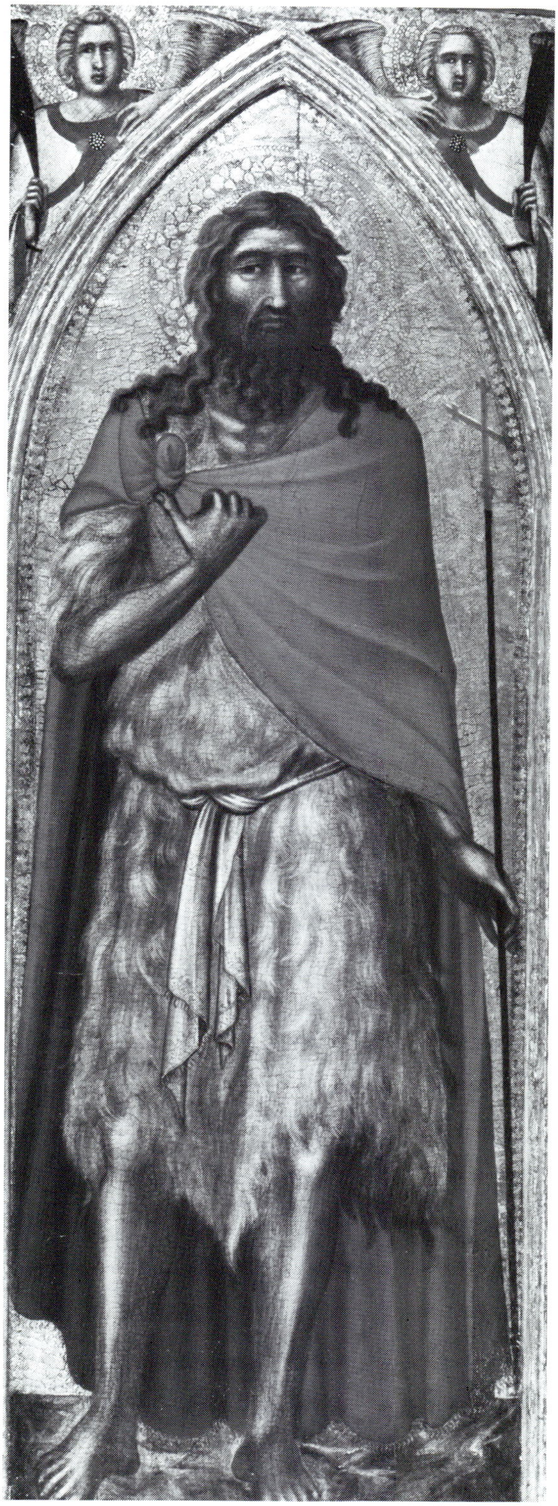

106 Pietro Lorenzetti, St John the Baptist, 123 x 44.5 cm, University Art Museum Princeton (Norton Simon Foundation loan).

had been scorched by the fiery chariot which took him up to heaven. This explains the 'pallium barratum' in Pietro's altarpiece (figs. 109-112). And who was the hermit who stood on the bank of the same Jordan to baptise the Redeemer? None other than John the Baptist, who was Elisha's counterpart on Pietro's Carmelite Madonna.

The Carmelites were not the only order to enlist Elijah's aid in their propaganda. St Francis was proclaimed as a second Elijah ('alter Helias'), and there is a story that one night several of the friars saw their beloved founder ride by in a fiery chariot. That, though, was merely a late medieval typological construct. The Carmelites go a great deal further by claiming Elijah as the actual founder of their order, and they have created a sort of spiritual pedigree linking them to him.[112] Pietro's altarpiece spells out that descent in unequivocal terms. Elijah and Elisha are portrayed as saints, although the Carmelites only venerated them as such at a much later date. Beliefs concerning the origins of the Carmelites and the miraculous history of their habit are well known, but they have to be gleaned from the works of various Carmelite mythographers.[113] Writings can be challenged and arguments rebutted, but images simply exist. That is why this altarpiece is more explicit than most contemporary Carmelite writers dared to be.

However, there was one difficulty about this mythical continuity of the Carmelites. Although their origins were supposed to be lost in the very dawn of asceticism there was a specific, historical moment when they were officially recognised as an order. That was in 1226, when Pope Honorius III gave them their rule. The Carmelites countered this argument by pointing out that Honorius had merely ratified an older rule conferred in 1209 by Patriarch Albert of Jerusalem on a group of hermits who had been living 'by the fountain of Elijah' on Mount Carmel since approximately 1185 under the leadership of St Brocardus. That would have made them even older than the Dominicans and the Franciscans, and it is this prior recognition of the order which is depicted so extensively (in the literal sense of the word) on the central section of the predella (fig. 110).

Pietro Lorenzetti gave his imagination free rein in this frieze-like scene beneath the Madonna. The medieval Tuscan city on the left must be Acre. Patriarch Albert has just sallied forth into the desert accompanied by a large retinue. The region around Acre was extremely popular with ascetics and hermits, who withdrew into the stark landscape populated by wild animals in order to practise the self-mortification which would ensure them of their place in heaven. To put it in terms of their own ascetic imagery, they were climbing the ladder which would

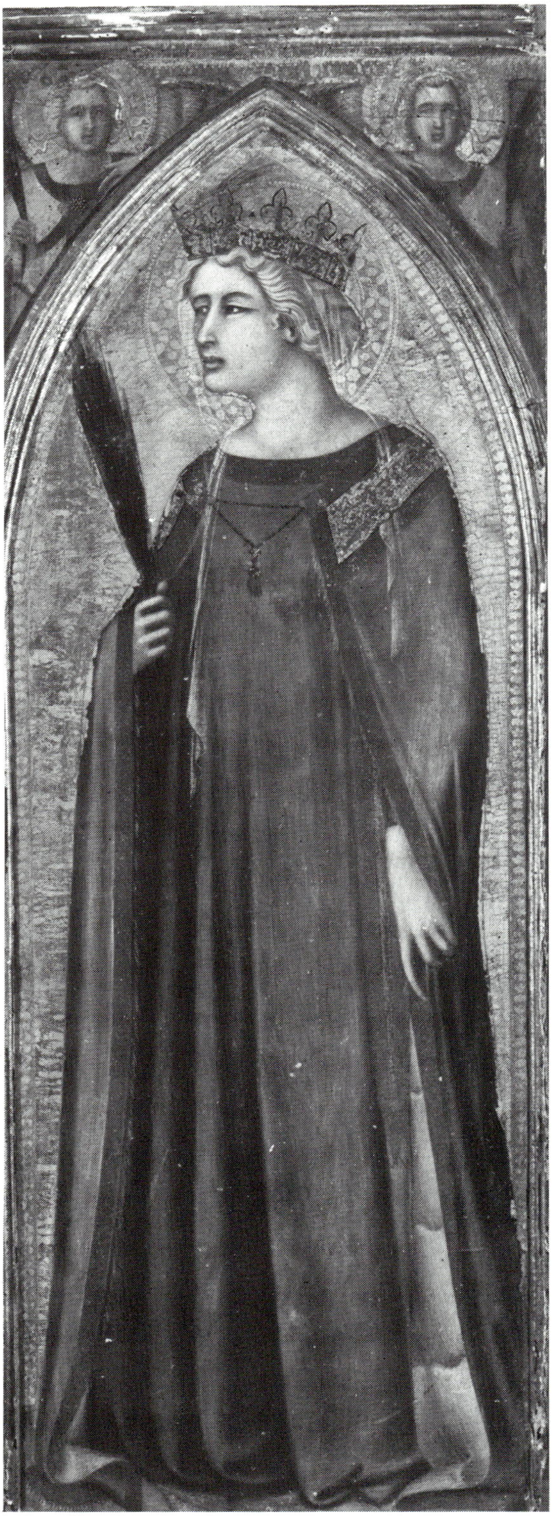

107 Pietro Lorenzetti, St Catherine of Alexandria, 127 x 46 cm, Pinacoteca Nazionale, Siena.

ultimately bring them to the perpetual vision of the Most High. Pietro's predella, however, shows little of the harsh and heroic life of rigorous asceticism. In his vision man and beast lived peaceably side by side in idyllic surroundings. This idealised view of the anchorite's life was the first of many such scenes in Italian art. On the right Brocardus and his followers kneel beside the fountain of Elijah. They are not solitary hermits living in individual seclusion, but a community of ascetics. Their oratory, a splendid Trecento church, stands behind them, with a stray lion posed decoratively against the side wall. The prominence given to this oratory reflects the Carmelites' claim that their church on Mount Carmel had been dedicated to the Virgin since time immemorial. In other words they were not just the oldest of all monastic orders, they were also the first to venerate the Virgin. Hence this church beside the 'fons Heliae'.

The date of 1209 for the approval of the Carmelite rule was certainly a competitive claim among the mendicant orders, but that was not enough for the Carmelites. Honorius III had not merely ratified a rule first conferred by Patriarch Albert, but earlier popes too had supposedly granted rules to the order which went back to the ninth century. This is illustrated in the predella scene of Pope Honorius awarding the rule (fig. 112) by three other popes who come flying down with earlier rules in their hands. Not surprisingly, this distortion of historical facts for propaganda purposes aroused considerable criticism, even in the fourteenth century. It was only in 1477, after powerful lobbying in the Vatican, that Sixtus IV recognised this extravagant claim.[114] In Siena, anyway, the Carmelite propaganda was successful, for by the beginning of the fifteenth century Sienese authors were convinced that the Carmelites had settled in the city in 797.[115]

The first two scenes on the predella are intended to illustrate the great antiquity of the order and its origins on the sacred mount. The first shows an angel with a scroll hovering over a sleeping man (fig. 109). For a long time no one was very sure what this scene was meant to represent, but it is now generally assumed that the subject is the dream of Sobac. Sobac was the apocryphal father of Elijah, and to the best of my knowledge he exists only in Carmelite writings. The text on the angel's scroll, which is in rather ungrammatical Latin, translates as follows: 'Before Elijah was born, and while he lies asleep, he sees men greeting each other, clad in white raiment'. This text is found in better Latin in a history of the Carmelites written by one John of Kermaten, the earliest manuscript of which dates from around 1337. John added that this was an incontrovertible portent of the many who would follow Elijah. The

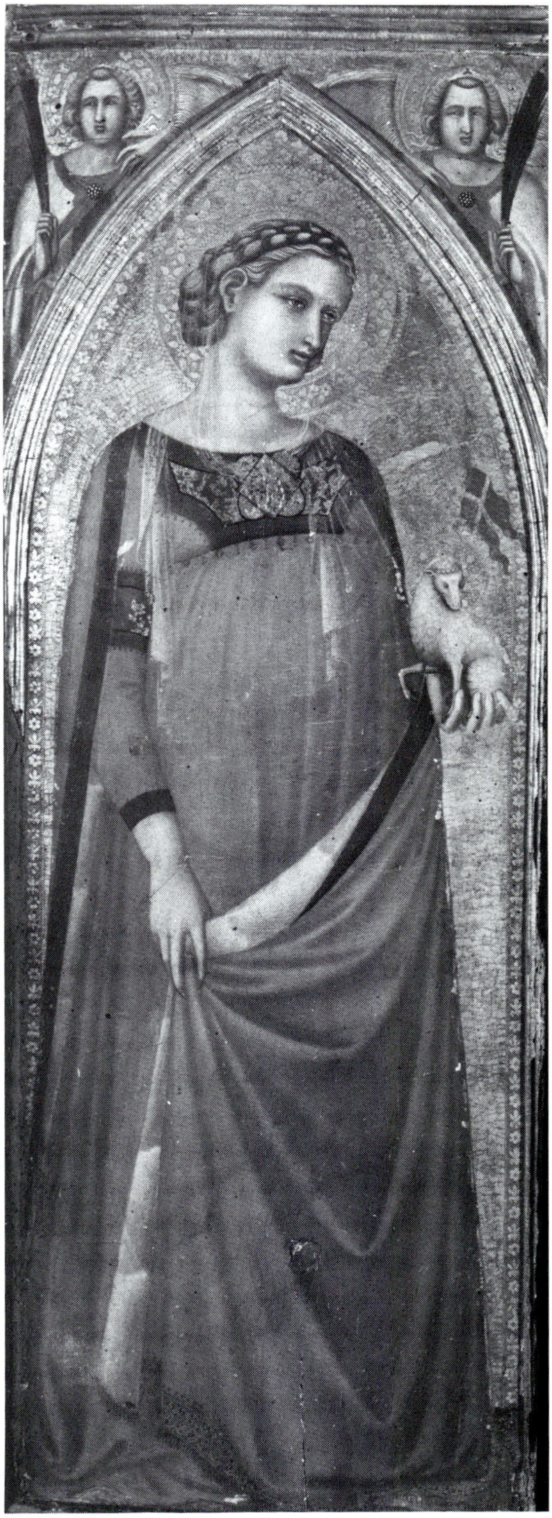

108 Pietro Lorenzetti, St Agnes, 128 x 44.5 cm, Pinacoteca Nazionale, Siena.

men 'clad in white raiment', of course, were the Carmelites. This story of a vision experienced by an apocryphal father of Elijah was due solely to the Carmelite obsession with their origins.[116]

The second scene is not really a depiction of a specific event, and it has never been regarded as such. It appears to be a general portrayal of the ascetic life of the first Carmelites (fig. 110), but in fact it has a very specific significance. The focal point is the fountain of Elijah, which was a key motif in Carmelite thought of the fourteenth century and which gave rise to a whole series of miraculous stories. Water was a miracle in the desert, and was essential to the hermits who lived there. The Carmelites had a symbiotic relationship with Elijah's fountain. Whenever they left it dried up, and when they returned the water began to flow again. It was in this way that Elijah identified his true followers. John of Venice, another fourteenth-century Carmelite writer, relates that this miracle was constantly repeated for the Carmelites when they had spread throughout western Europe. Water began to flow wherever they prayed, and it was there, beside that living water, that they settled.[117]

There was a direct connection between this story of Elijah's fountain and one of the urban myths of Siena. Water supply was a major problem in this hillside city, just as it had been in the desert fastness of Mount Carmel. The Sienese not only had no wells, they also lacked a waterway link with the sea which was essential to the survival of a medieval city. An entire history could be written about Siena's fierce and costly fight for water and harbours.[118] The myth was designed to compensate for the water shortage, for it told that in fact there was a river, called the Diana, which flowed beneath the city. In the soil beneath the city of the Virgin, in other words, were the wells of antiquity, and that underground river linked Siena with the sea. Dante, too, heard of this story. In his *Purgatory* a Sienese lady speaks to him about her fellow-citizens: '... that vain multitude, who set their hope / On Talamone's haven; there to fail / Confounded, more than when the fancied stream / They sought, of Dian called...' (Purg. XIII, 141-44). To date, though, authors have paid little heed to the people who discovered that underground stream. According to the earliest versions of the story it was none other than the Carmelites. When they were digging a well in Siena they once again struck their 'fons Heliae', but to the Sienese it became the 'fancied stream' Diana.[119]

The reason why I have discussed the visual programme of Pietro Lorenzetti's Carmelite altarpiece at such length is that this incidental but important commission illustrates the degree of control which donors could have over the execution of an altar-

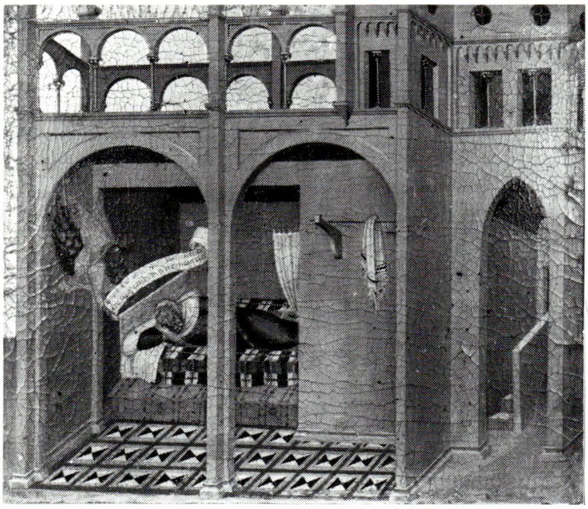

109 Pietro Lorenzetti, The dream of Sobac, 38 x 46 cm, Pinacoteca Nazionale, Siena.

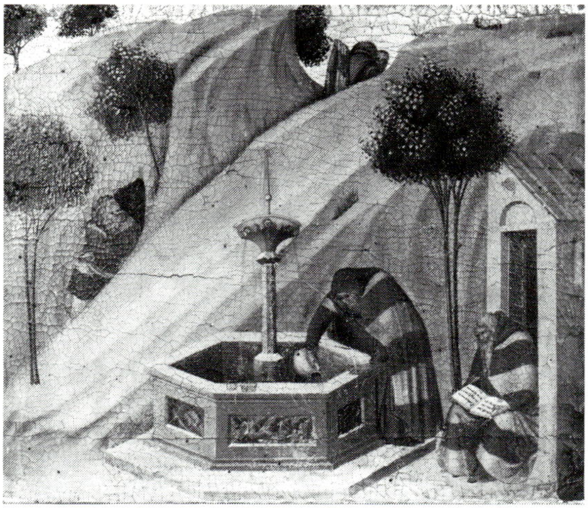

110 Pietro Lorenzetti, The fountain of Elijah, 38 x 47 cm, Pinacoteca Nazionale, Siena.

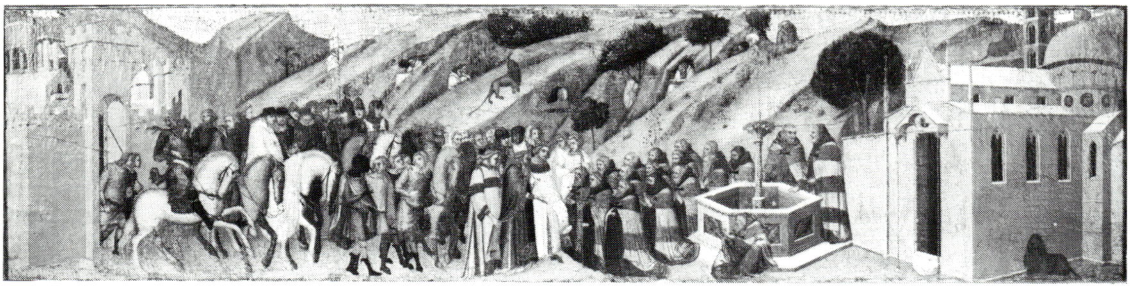

111 Pietro Lorenzetti, Patriarch Albert consigning the rule to Brocardus, 37.5 x 154.5 cm, Pinacoteca Nazionale, Siena.

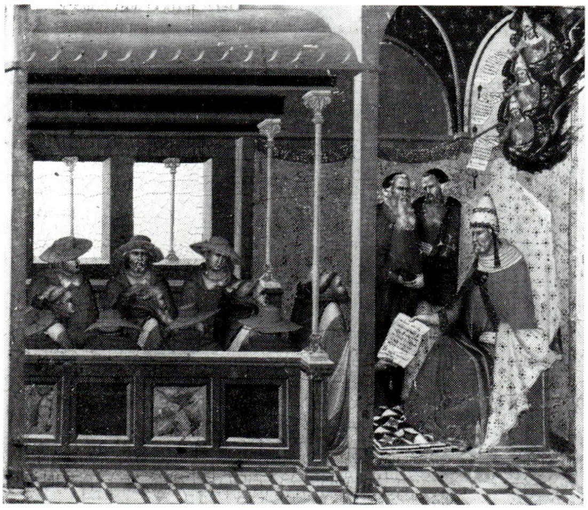

112 Pietro Lorenzetti, Pope Honorius III approving the rule of Albert, 37.5 x 47 cm, Pinacoteca Nazionale, Siena.

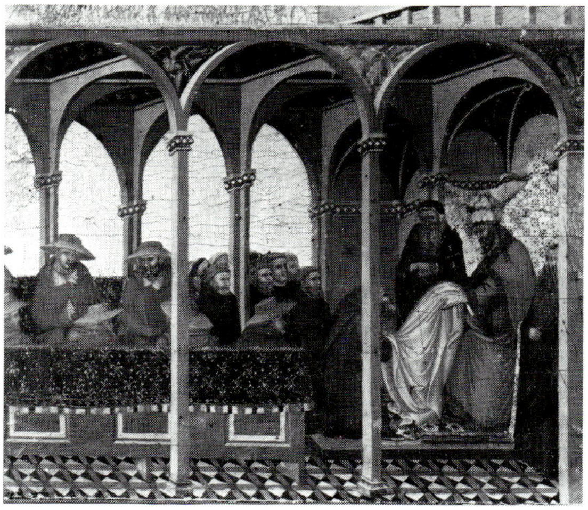

113 Pietro Lorenzetti, Pope Honorius IV granting the white mantle, 37.5 x 47 cm, Pinacoteca Nazionale, Siena.

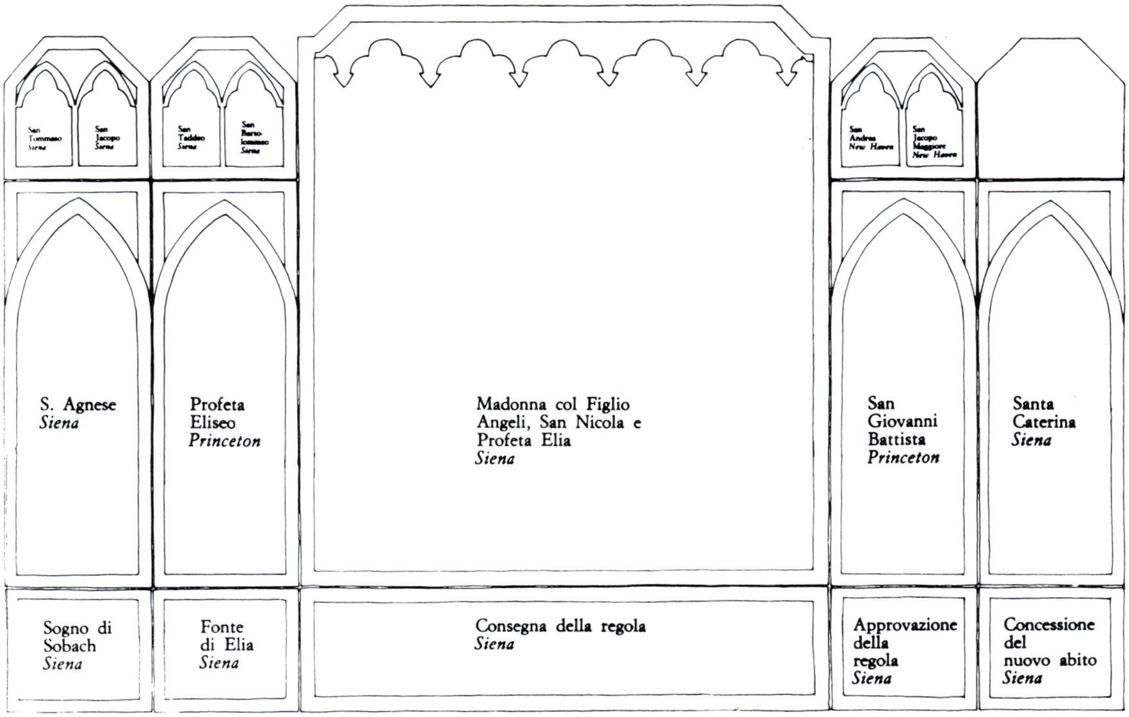

114 Reconstruction of Pietro Lorenzetti's Carmelite altarpiece (after Torriti).

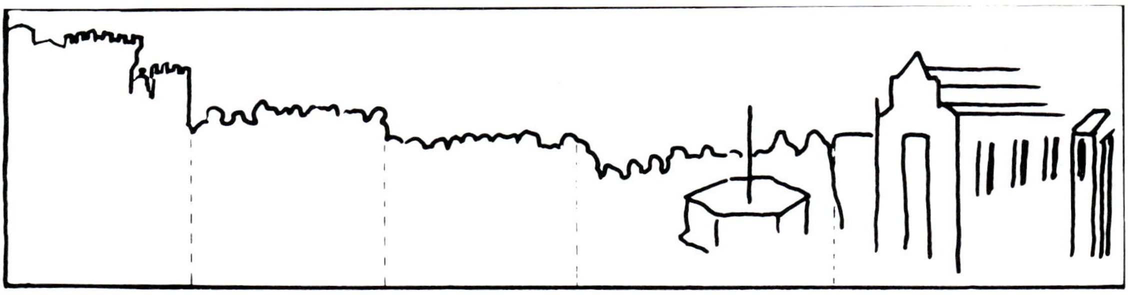

115 Compositional structure of the central predella scene of Pietro Lorenzetti's Carmelite altarpiece (after Preiser).

piece. Elijah and Elisha with their portentous texts, the abstruse scenes of Sobac and the 'fons Heliae', and such touches as the flight of popes above Honorius III are evidence that the Carmelites were concerned with every detail of the design and execution of the work they had commissioned. When 'Maestro Ciecho della Grammatica' provided Pietro with the story of St Savinus it was presumably left to the artist to treat that story in his own way. That was definitely not the case with the Carmelite altarpiece. It undoubtedly stood on the friars' high altar, and it was a declaration of pre-eminence and antiquity which differed in every conceivable way from iconic St Luke Madonnas. It was no longer the age of cult objects that mattered, but their visual programme.

NOTES

1 E.B. Garrison, 'Sienese historical writings and the dates 1260, 1221, 1262 applied to Sienese paintings', *Studies in the history of medieval Italian painting* 4/1 (1960-62), pp. 23-58.

2 E.B. Garrison, 'Toward a new history of the Siena Cathedral Madonna's', *Studies in the history of medieval Italian painting* 4/1 (1960-62), pp. 5-22. [P. Torriti], exhib. cat. *Opere d'arte restaurate nelle provincie di Siena e Grosseto*, Siena (Pinacoteca) 1979, p. 16.

Garrison is being needlessly critical when he suggests that the relief Madonna never stood on the high altar. Hager has satisfactorily rebutted this viewpoint, see H. Hager, *Die Anfänge des italienischen Altarbildes: Untersuchungen zur Entstehungsgeschichte des toskanischen Hochaltarretabels*, Munich 1962, pp. 79, 92, 104-08, 113, 115, 124, 128, 134, 152-53, fig. 144.

3 P. Torriti, cat. *La Pinacoteca Nazionale di Siena: i dipinti dal XII al XV secolo*, Genoa 1977, pp. 20-22. Hager, op. cit. (note 2), pp. 79, 103, 105, 113, 115, figs. 142, 234-36. For the *Tressa Madonna* see [P. Torriti], cat. *Opere d'arte*, cit. (note 2), p. 18. On the ornamentation: M.S. Frinta, 'Raised gilded adornment of the Cypriot icons, and the occurrence of the technique in the West', *Gesta* 20 (1981), pp. 333-47.

4 See, for example, M.M. Gauthier, 'Du tabernacle au retable: une innovation limousine vers 1230', *Revue de l'Art* 27 (1978), pp. 23-42.

5 I.H. Forsyth, *The throne of wisdom: wood sculptures of the Madonna in romanesque France*, Princeton 1972, pp. 31-60.

6 Cf. E. Kleineidam, 'Die Nachfolge Christi nach Bernhard von Clairvaux', *Amt und Sendung*, Freiburg 1950, p. 444.

7 See p. 134.

8 H.W. van Os, *Vecchietta and the sacristy of the Siena hospital church: a study in Renaissance religious symbolism*, The Hague 1974, pp. 47-49.

9 See pp. 134-35.

10 It was around 1200 that the Badia ran into financial difficulties, see P. Bargellini, 'Abbadia a Monastero d'Ombrone Castelnuovo Berandenga', *Bulletino di Storia Patria* 3 (1932), p. 295.

It is more likely that Cardinal Alessandro Zondadari had the altarpiece removed from Siena to the new altar in the church, which he had rebuilt in 1720 and had rededicated as his family church to S. Salvatore e S. Alessandro (sic).

11 A good survey of the literature on canonical reform will be found in L.K. Little, *Religious poverty and the profit economy in medieval Europe*, Ithaca 1978, pp. 240-41.

12 J.H. Stubblebine, *Guido da Siena*, Princeton 1964, figs. 14, 32, 39, 43, 54, 60.

13 Hager, op. cit. (note 2), pp. 83, 106, 130, 134-37, 152, 153, figs. 187-89.

14 Stubblebine, op. cit. (note 12), pp. 72-75, figs. 37, 38, 40.

15 D. Gordon, 'A Perugian provenance for the Franciscan double-sided altarpiece by the Maestro di S. Francesco', *The Burlington Magazine* 124 (1982), pp. 70-77.

16 Little, op. cit. (note 11), pp. 146-219, with extensive bibliography.

17 For the obligatory, general reference to the special significance of the Franciscans as donors: J. White, *Duccio: Tuscan art and the medieval workshop*, London 1979, p. 54; Hager, op. cit. (note 2), p. 163. For the source of this notion see H. Thode, *Franz von Assisi und die Anfänge der Kunst der Renaissance in Italien*, Berlin 1885. Until recently there was no good study of the Dominicans as donors, but that lack has now been filled by J. Cannon, *Dominican patronage of the arts in Central Italy: the Provincia Romana, c. 1220-c. 1320*, typescript Ph.D. thesis, University of London 1980. For a general survey of ecclesiastical patronage by the Commune: J. Larner, *Culture and society in Italy 1290-1420*, London 1971, pp. 65-86.

18 C. Gomez-Moreno, E.H. Jones, A.K. Wheelock and M. Meiss, 'A Sienese St. Dominic modernized twice in the thirteenth century', *The Art Bulletin* 51 (1969), pp. 363-66.

19 G. Coor-Achenbach, 'A visual basis for the documents relating to Coppo di Marcovaldo and his son Salerno', *The Art Bulletin* 28 (1946), p. 234.

20 B. Cole, 'Old and new in the early Trecento', *Mitteilungen des Kunsthistorischen Institutes in Florenz* 17 (1973), pp. 229-48.

21 H. Belting, 'The "Byzantine" Madonnas: new facts about their Italian origin and some observations on Duccio', *Studies in the History of Art. National Gallery of Art Washington (D.C.)*, 12 (1982), pp. 7-21.

22 Cole, op. cit. (note 20), p. 232 for the repainting. On the problem of the inscription see J. Gardner, 'Guido da Siena, 1221, and Tommaso da Modena', *The Burlington Magazine* 121 (1979), pp. 107-08.

23 [C. Ressort], exhib. cat. *Retables italiens du XIIIe au XVe siècle*, Paris (Musée de Louvre) 1978, pp. 7-9, for an up-to-date resumé of the literature.

24 [G. Borghini], cat. *Opere d'arte*, cit. (note 2), pp. 20-22.

25 Cf. White, op. cit. (note 17), pp. 186-87. See also J.H. Stubblebine, *Duccio di Buoninsegna and his school*, vol. l, Princeton 1979, pp. 192-94.
26 H.W. van Os, 'The literature of art: Duccio', *The Burlington Magazine* 123 (1981), p. 166; C. Gilbert, 'Peintres et menuisiers au début de la Renaissance en Italie', *Revue de l'Art* 37 (1977), pp. 9-28.
27 White, op. cit. (note 25), pp. 36-37; Stubblebine, op. cit. (note 25), pp. 22-23. The payments for 'oil to burn in the lamps on altars' are equally uninformative on the original location of the *Rucellai Madonna*. It is perfectly possible that Duccio executed the *Madonna* for the high altar and that it was replaced by a new polytych forty years later (see Chapter IV).
28 M.B. Hall, 'The Ponte in S. Maria Novella: the problem of the rood-screen in Italy', *Journal of the Warburg and Courtauld Institutes* 37 (1974), pp. 157-73.
29 I owe this hypothesis to Miklos Boskovits, who repeatedly relates the actual economic conditions in the city to the operation of artists' workshops in his *Pittura fiorentina alla vigilia del Rinascimento 1370-1400*, Florence 1975; see pp. 18-19 for Sienese artists in Florence.
30 A survey of the literature in C. Gardner-von Teuffel, 'Masaccio and the Pisa altarpiece: a new approach', *Jahrbuch der Berliner Museen* 19 (1977), pp. 23-68.
31 [M. Bonfioli], cat. *Opere d'arte*, cit. (note 2), pp. 104-05. F. Bossi, *Visita apostolica di monsignor Bossio 1575*, Archivio arcivescovile di Siena, Ms 21, fol. 689v: 'Icona vero erat parva cum imagine Gloriosissime Virginis Mariae magnae devotionis piam deferri asseruit dictus Provincialis quandoque processionaliter per Civitatem pro obtinere aliquid gratia.' It was flanked by statues of St Luke and of St Antony, whose feast was celebrated at this altar.

Before its recent restoration the *St Luke Madonna* hung in the apse behind the high altar.
32 M. Warnke, 'Italienische Bildtabernakel bis zum Frühbarock', *Münchner Jahrbuch der bildenden Kunst* 19 (1968), pp. 76-77, fig. 13. See also M. Ingendaay, *Sienesische Altarbilder des sechzehnten Jahrhunderts*, Bonn 1976, vol. l, fig. 70, vol. 2, pp. 609-10. Ingendaay incorrectly identifies the male saint kneeling in the foreground as St Antony. It is clearly either St Stephen or St Laurence, for he is wearing the robes of a deacon. As yet there has been no study of the history of the two Carmelite icons. For attributions see E.B. Garrison, *Italian romanesque panel painting: an illustrated index*, Florence 1949, nrs. 125, 126.
33 Cf. Stubblebine, op. cit. (note 25), p. 205.
34 Cf. Stubblebine, op. cit. (note 25), pp. 33-34.
35 L. and R. Ormond, *Lord Leighton*, New Haven & London 1975, pp. 26-31, figs. 33-37.
36 J. Stubblebine, 'Duccio's Maestà of 1302 for the Chapel of the Nove', *Art Quarterly* 35 (1972), pp. 239-68. A question as yet unresolved is whether it would be possible to reconstruct this *Maestà* purely on the basis of documents and other paintings by Duccio and his pupils.
37 Cf. White, op. cit. (note 17), p. 193. As to whether this contract was the first agreement concerning the *Maestà* see F. Deuchler, 'Duccio et son cercle', *Revue de l'Art* 51 (1981), pp. 20-21.
38 See for example M. Baxandall, *Painting and experience in fifteenth century Italy*, Oxford 1972, fig. 1.
39 Cf. White, op. cit. (note 17), p. 195.
40 Cf. White, op. cit. (note 17), p. 196.
41 On this predella see A. Preiser, *Das Entstehen und die Entwicklung der Predella in der italienischen Malerei*, Hildesheim & New York 1973, pp. 200-02.
42 See p. 139.
43 Cf. Stubblebine, op. cit. (note 25), pp. 35-36.
44 C. Brandi, *Il restauro della Maestà di Duccio*, Rome 1959.
45 C. Gardner-von Teuffel, 'The buttressed altarpiece: a forgotten aspect of Tuscan fourteenth century altarpiece design', *Jahrbuch der Berliner Museen* 21 (1979), pp. 36-44, fig. 14.
46 White, op. cit. (note 17), pp. 140-50; J. Gardner, 'The Stefaneschi altarpiece: a reconsideration', *Journal of the Warburg and Courtauld Institutes* 37 (1974), pp. 57-103; idem, 'Fronts and backs: setting and structure', *La pittura nel XIV e XV secolo: il contributo dell'analisi tecnica alla storia dell'arte*, ed. H.W. van Os and J.R.J. van Asperen de Boer, Atti del XXIV Congresso del Comitato Internazionale di Storia dell'Arte, Bologna 1979, vol. 3, pp. 297-322.
47 G. Kaftal, *Iconography of the saints in Tuscan painting*, Florence 1952, nrs. 23, 78, 277, 310; E. Carli, *Vetrata duccesca*, Milan 1956, passim.
48 Stubblebine, op. cit. (note 25), pp. 38-39.
49 *Meditations on the life of Christ*, ed. I. Ragusa and R.B. Green, Princeton 1977, p. 16; H.W. van Os, *Marias Demut und Verherrlichung in der sienesischen Malerei 1300-1450*, The Hague 1969, pp. 35-57.
50 One such attempt to identify the various hands will be found in Stubblebine, op. cit. (note 25), pp. 39-45. On this point I am in complete agreement with White, op. cit. (note 17), p. 103.
51 Stubblebine, op. cit. (note 25), pp. 50-52.
52 F. Deuchler, 'Duccio doctus: new readings for the Maestà', *The Art Bulletin* 61 (1979), pp. 541-50.
53 *Meditations*, cit. (note 49), p. 89; F. Deuchler, 'Siena und Jerusalem: Imagination und Realität in Duccios neuem Stadtbild', *Europäische Sachkultur des Mittelalters*, Vienna 1980, pp. 13-20.
54 Van Os, op. cit. (note 26), p. 167.
55 Cf. Stubblebine, op. cit. (note 25), pp. 34-35.
56 I. Ragusa, 'The egg re-opened', *The Art Bulletin* 53 (1971), pp. 435-43.
57 White, op. cit. (note 17), pp. 137-40, van Os, op. cit. (note 49), pp. 157-62.
58 Hager, op. cit. (note 2); p. 154.
59 [P. Torriti], *Opere d'arte,* cit. (note 2), p. 25.
60 Cf. Stubblebine, op. cit. (note 25), p. 206.
61 Stubblebine, op. cit. (note 25), p. 141, attributes both panels to the school of Segna and groups them in an *oeuvre* which he gives to an artist he calls the Seminary Madonna Master. His idea of the original form of the *Maestà* of Massa (his fig. 159) is very different from mine, and in my view it is not warranted by the available facts. He believes that it had a gable or a truncated gable, and as a result does not associate either panel with the Massa *Maestà*. However, it is far more probable that the Massa altarpiece bore an even closer resemblance to the Siena *Maestà* than Stubblebine realises. The *Nativity* and the *Adoration* certainly suggest that such an altarpiece existed.
62 Cf. White, op. cit. (note 17), p. 96; E. Borsook, *The mural painters of Tuscany*, ed. Oxford 1980, pp. 19-23.
63 E. Carli, *L'arte a Massa Marittima*, Siena 1976, p. 27.
64 A recent publication on Virtues of this sort is G.A. Schüssler, 'Zum Thomasfresko des Andrea Bonaiuti in der spanischen Kapelle am Kreuzgang von Santa Maria Novella', *Mitteilungen des Kunsthistorischen Institutes in Florenz* 24 (1980), pp. 251-74. For a rather peculiar and far-fetched political interpretation of Ambrogio's *Maestà*: A. Perrig, 'Formen der politischen Propaganda der Kommune von Siena in der ersten

Trecento-Hälfte', *Bauwerk und Bildwerk im Hochmittelalter. Anschauliche Beiträge zur Kultur- und Sozialgeschichte*, Gieszen 1981, pp. 232-34.

65 White, op. cit. (note 17), p. 69. His Chapter V is a brilliant exposition of the development from dossal to polyptych. A recent examination of fourteenth-century Sienese altarpieces in the form of a description of individual examples is F. Leroy, *Les retables siennois du 14ᵉ siècle: les modèles, les styles, l'organisation des formes*, Mémoire de Maîtrise, Paris I 1974.

66 Van Os, op. cit. (note 8), pp. 4-14. See also U. Morandi and A. Cairola, *Lo Spedale di Santa Maria della Scala*, Siena 1975, pp. 94-100.

67 Van Os, op. cit. (note 49), pp. 22-24. Chapter 1, § 2 presents an interpretation of the iconographic structure of this polyptych which is worked out in greater detail in the present volume. In the interests of clarity the texts are given without abbreviations or word breaks. They are followed by the English translation from the Vulgate of Ronald Knox, ed. Cambridge 1956.

68 Borsook, op. cit. (note 62), p. 47.

69 A. Caleca, 'Tre polittici di Lippo Memmi, un ipotesi sul Barna e la bottega di Simone e Lippo', *Critica d'Arte* 41 (1976), nr. 150, pp. 49-59, and, *Critica d'Arte* 42 (1977), nrs. 151-53, pp. 55-80. M. Eisenberg recently published a fascinating article entitled 'The first altar-piece for the "Cappella de'Signori" of the Palazzo Pubblico in Siena...tales figure sunt adeo pulcre...', *The Burlington Magazine* 123 (1981), pp. 134-48, in which he points out that Simone had probably painted a polyptych for the Cappella de'Signori in 1319 which is now only known from documents.

70 Van Os, op. cit. (note 49), pp. 24-26.

71 On the Man of Sorrows between two secondary figures see H. Belting, *Das Bild und sein Publikum im Mittelalter: Form und Funktion früher Bildtafeln der Passion*, Berlin 1981, pp. 61-68.

H.W. van Os, 'The discovery of an early Man of Sorrows on a Dominican triptych', *Journal of the Warburg and Courtauld Institutes* 41 (1978), pp. 65-76.

72 For the polyptychs in Orvieto: G. Contini and M.C. Gozzoli, *L'opera completa di Simone Martini*, Milan 1970, nrs. 4-12. On the subject of Simone and Lippo in Pisa see note 69.

73 Cf. White, op. cit. (note 17), p. 35.

74 Kaftal, op. cit. (note 47), nrs. 33 and 197.

75 On the Annunciation as a representation of the Incarnation see van Os, op. cit. (note 49), pp. 37-74. The theological aspect is discussed by E. Gössmann, *Die Verkündigung an Maria im dogmatischen Verständnis des Mittelalters*, Munich 1957.

76 From left to right they are Sts Reparata, Catherine, Ursula and Agatha.

77 For a detailed stylistic analysis of Pietro's polyptych see H.B.J. Maginnis, *Pietro Lorenzetti and Assisi: the study of a problem*, master thesis, Princeton 1976, pp. 18-24.

78 For the reconstruction: Gardner-von Teuffel, op. cit. (note 45). For a diagram of the proportions: N. Finet, *L'organisation et la fabrication des retables siennois pendant la première moitié du XIVᵉ siècle*, Mémoire de Maîtrise, Paris I 1974, pp. 131-40.

79 There is now an excellent account of the socio-economic context of cathedral building: W. Vroom, *De financiering van de kathedraalbouw in de middeleeuwen*, Maarssen 1981.

80 M.B. Hall, *Renovation and Counter-Reformation: Vasari and Duke Cosimo in Sta Maria Novella and Sta Croce*, Oxford 1979.

81 G. Gigli, *Diario senese*, vol. 2, Siena 1854 (2nd ed.), pp. 355-56.

82 Kaftal, op. cit. (note 47), nr. 277.

83 Carli, op. cit. (note 47), pp. 45-49.

84 Kaftal, op. cit. (note 47), nr. 23; Gigli, op. cit. (note 81), vol. 1, pp. 58, 560-61, and vol. 2, pp. 575-76.

85 M. Cämmerer-George, *Die Rahmung der toskanische Altarbilder im Trecento*, Strasbourg 1966, pp. 153-55.

86 This question has been reopened by J. Polzer in a forthcoming study. See further Contini and Gozzoli, op. cit. (note 72), nr. 25. For a summary of the various opinions contained in earlier literature see L. Marcucci, cat. *Gallerie Nazionali di Firenze: i dipinti Toscani del secolo XIV*, Rome 1965, pp. 149-52.

87 Gardner-von Teuffel, op. cit. (note 45), p. 47.

88 C. Gardner-von Teuffel, 'Ikonographie und Archäologie: das Pfingsttriptychon in der Florentiner Akademie an seinem ursprünglichen Aufstellungsort', *Zeitschrift für Kunstgeschichte* 41 (1978), p. 29.

89 Van Os, op. cit. (note 49), p. 40. Thirteenth-century sculpture provides several examples of Annunciations with a marked emphasis on the descent of the Holy Ghost. The dove, and the words 'Ave Gratia Plena', are found beneath a canopy, see J. Pope-Hennessy, cat. *Italian sculpture in the Victoria and Albert Museum*, vol 1, London 1964, pp. 20-22, fig. 35.

An intriguingly different example of an *Annunciation* with the hurrying angel and a frightened Virgin enthroned is the fresco in Santa Sophia, Trebizond: V.J. Djurić, 'La peinture murale byzantine: douzième et treizième siècles', *Rapports et co-rapports du XVᵉ congrès international d'études byzantines*, Athens 1976, p. 56, pl. IX, nr. 17.

90 Van Os, op. cit. (note 49), pp. 43-44.

91 Preiser, op. cit. (note 41), pp. 297-302, fig. 297c.

92 M. Davies, cat. *National Gallery: the earlier Italian schools*, London 1961, pp. 300-01.

93 *Meditations*, cit. (note 49), p. 65.

94 The most remarkable example of this practice is the 'al fresco' *Maestà* for San Agostino; see M. Seidel, 'Die Fresken des Ambrogio Lorenzetti in S. Agostino', *Mitteilungen des Kunsthistorischen Institutes in Florenz* 22 (1978), pp. 185-252.

95 J. White, *The birth and rebirth of pictoral space*, London 1968, pp. 99-102, for the perspective construction of the two altarpieces by Pietro and Ambrogio.

96 For the correct transcription see Marcucci, op. cit. (note 86), p. 164. See also note 67 above.

97 C.H. Krinsky, 'Representations of the Temple of Jerusalem before 1500', *Journal of the Warburg and Courtauld Institutes* 33 (1970), pp. 1-19.

98 G. Milanesi, *Documenti per la storia dell'arte senese*, vol. 2, Siena 1854, p. 26.

99 Kaftal, op. cit. (note 47), nr. 310.

100 See, *inter alia*, H. Olsen, *Italian paintings and sculpture in Denmark*, Copenhagen 1961, p. 75, and C. de Benedictis, *La pittura senese 1330-1370*, Florence 1979, p. 44, fig. 79.

101 There is a fourteenth-century embroidery which shows that this treatment of the Nativity was soon being imitated, see B. Kurth, 'Florentiner Trecento-Stickereien', *Pantheon* 8 (1931), pp. 455-62. The composition, but remarkably enough without the architecture, is also found on a predella panel in Altenburg which is attributed to Paolo di Giovanni Fei, see R. Oertel, *Frühe italienische Malerei in Altenburg*, Berlin 1961, pp. 80-81.

102 For an assessment of the art-historical discussion see M. Franken, in H.W. van Os, J.R.J. van Asperen de Boer and C. Wiethoff, *Sienese paintings in Holland (1250-1500)*, Florence 1984, nr. 5.
103 Cf. Torriti, op. cit. (note 3), nrs. 59, 76, 80.
104 For the paintings of Sts Crescentius and Victor see notes 81 and 98 respectively. In the sacristy there were also frescoes of St Savinus, see Kaftal, op. cit. (note 47), nr. 277.
105 M. Butzek, 'Die Papstmonumente in Dom von Siena', *Mitteilungen des Kunsthistorischen Institutes in Florenz* 24 (1980), pp. 15-78.
106 See note 67 above.
107 Torriti, op. cit. (note 3), pp. 97-103, with full bibliography.
108 For a reconstruction and a discussion of various iconographic problems surrounding this altarpiece see H.B.J. Maginnis, 'Pietro Lorenzetti's Carmelite Madonna: a reconstruction', *Pantheon* 33 (1975), pp. 10-16.
109 Maginnis, op. cit. (note 108), p. 10.
110 See for example Gigli, op. cit. (note 81), p. 27.
111 Maginnis, op. cit. (note 108), p. 12. At the annual meeting of the Association of Art Historians in London on 4th April 1981 Joanna Cannon gave further details on the relationship between the iconography and the history of the Carmelites. Her research and the work I did for this chapter ran parallel at several points.
112 R. Hendriks, 'La succession héréditaire (1280-1451)', in *Elie le prophète*, vol. 2 (Etudes carmélitaines 35), 1956, pp. 34-42; P. Kallenberg, 'Le culte liturgique d'Elie dans l'ordre du Carmel', ibid., pp. 134-51. Erasmus was one of the people who ridiculed these pretensions, see H.T. van Veen, 'Erasmus on the "Carmelite taboo"', *Bibliothèque d'Humanisme et Renaissance* 43 (1981), pp. 335-39.
113 The work of B. Zimmerman is essential reading for those wishing to learn more about the history of the order, see his *Monumenta historica carmelitana*, Lérins 1907, and his articles in the *Catholic Encyclopedia*, the *Dictionnaire de Théologie Catholique*, and the *Dictionnaire d'Archêlogie Chrétienne et de Liturgie*. For an excellent concise account see G. Mesters, s.v. Karmeliten, in *Lexikon für Theologie und Kirche* 5 (1960), cols. 1366-72.
114 See note 112.
115 See note 110.
116 C. Weigelt, *Die sienesische Malerei des vierzehnten Jahrhunderts*, Leipzig 1930, was the first to identify the old man as Sobac and to direct attention to Carmelite sources. For further information on Sobac see Hendriks, op. cit. (note 112), p. 49, and T. Spasky, 'Le culte du prophète Elie et sa figure dans la tradition orientale', in *Elie le prophète*, vol. 1 (Etudes carmélitaines 35), 1956, p. 220.
117 Zimmerman, *Monumenta*, cit. (note 113), p. 281, quotes the *Speculum* of John of Venice for the fountains that dried up.
118 W.M. Bowsky, *A medieval Italian Commune: Siena under the Nine 1287-1355*, Berkeley, Los Angeles & London 1981.
119 Gigli, op. cit. (note 81), p. 28; G. Rondoni, *Tradizioni popolari e leggende di un commune medioevale e del suo contado*, Florence 1886, pp. 49-50.

PHOTO AND FIGURE CREDITS

Alinari, Florence: 6, 8, 9, 12, 18, 19, 20, 24, 29b, 30, 31, 32, 33, 34, 35, 43, 49, 50, 51, 52, 53, 55, 56, 57, 59, 61, 62, 65 (Anderson), 71, 79, 80, 81, 83 (Brogi), 84 (Brogi), 89, 90 (Anderson), 91, 93, 94, 96, 101
Bibliotheca Apostolica Vaticana, Rome: 4
The Burlington Magazine, London: 14 - 15
Courtauld Institute of Art, London: 26
Fogg Art Museum, Cambridge (Mass.): 17, 100
Foto Grassi, Siena: 1, 40
Instituut voor Kunstgeschiedenis der Rijksuniversiteit, Groningen: 13, 28, 37, 69, 70, 76, 77
Musée du Louvre, Paris: 25, 36
National Gallery, London: 48, 58, 95
National Gallery, Washington (D.C.): 21, 22
Norton Simon Foundation, Pasadena: 105, 106
Royal Museum of Fine Arts, Copenhagen: 97, 98
Scale, Florence: 64
Soprintendenza di Monumenti e alle Gallerie dell'Umbria, Perugia: 5, 27, 47, 85
Soprintendenza alle gallerie, Florence: 99
Soprintendenza alle gallerie, Venice: 88
Soprintendenza per i beni artistici e storici delle provincie di Siena e Grosseto, Siena: 2, 3, 7, 10, 11, 16, 23, 29a, 38, 39, 46, 66, 67, 68, 72, 73, 74, 102, 103, 104, 107, 108, 109, 110, 111, 112, 113
Staatliche Museen, Berlin-DDR: 86
Staatliche Museen preussischer Kulturbesitz, Gemäldegalerie, Berlin-Dahlem: 60
Sterling and Francine Clark Art Institute, Williamstown (Mass.): 75
John White, London: 41, 42

Figs. 44, 63 from: Brandi, 1959
Figs. 45, 87 from: Gardner-von Teuffel, 1979
Fig. 54 from: Deuchler, 1981
Fig. 92 from: Cämmerer-George, 1966
Fig. 114 from: Torriti, 1977
Fig. 115 from: Preiser, 1973

ARCHITECTURAL AND LITURGICAL ASPECTS OF SIENA CATHEDRAL IN THE MIDDLE AGES

KEES VAN DER PLOEG

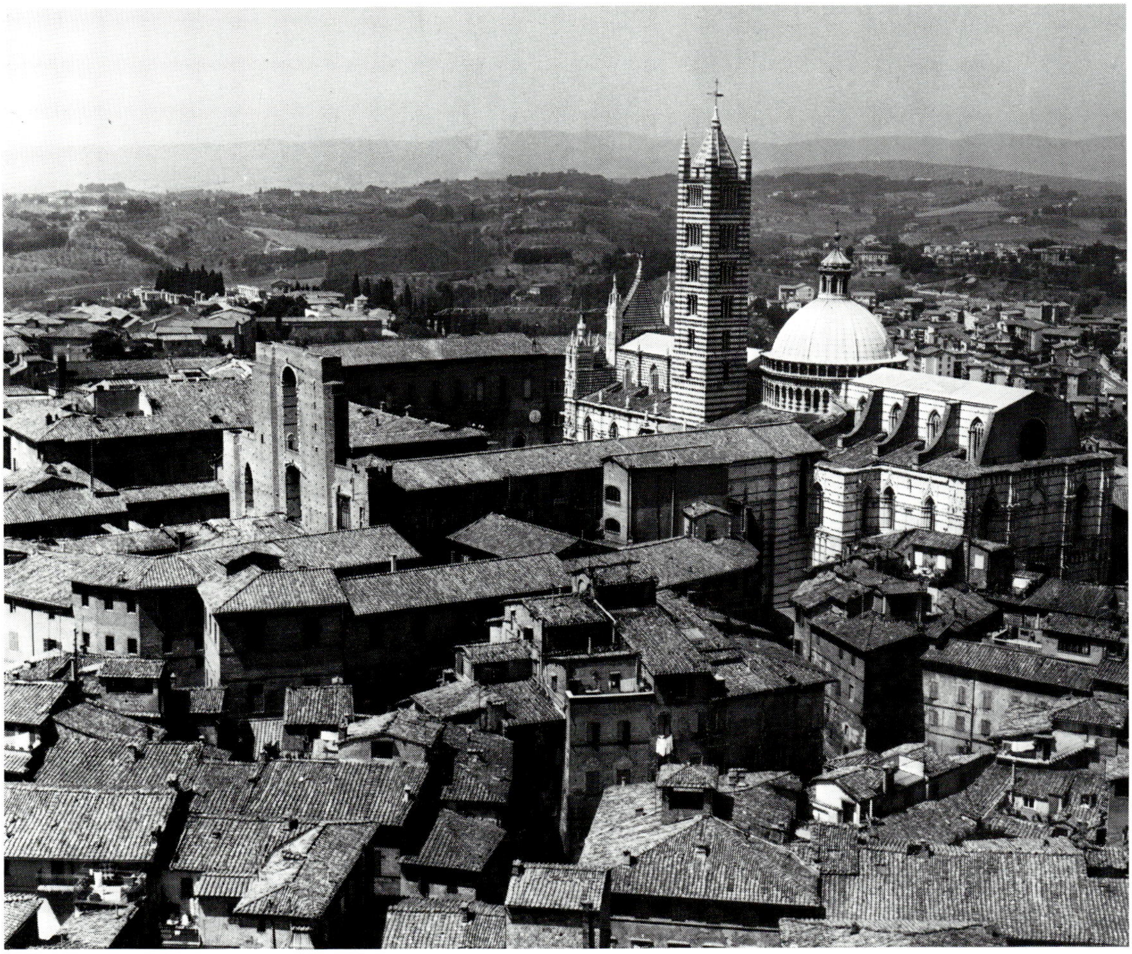

1 Siena cathedral seen from the tower of the Palazzo Pubblico. Between the church and the *facciatione* are the remains of the projected nave of the Duomo Nuovo.

INTRODUCTION

Siena cathedral is the focal building of the 'Civitas Virginis', and as such it has a historical significance which transcends by far its purely architectonic importance (ills. 1, 11; diags. 1, 2). This makes it all the more remarkable that so little is known of its early history. Some of the reasons for this gap in our knowledge must be laid at the door of art historians, who have always been more interested in the isolated works of art which stood or hung in the church than in investigating the relationship between those works and their architectural setting. Questions such as 'Why was this particular altarpiece placed here, and not somewhere else?' or 'Why did this painting have this specific form and content?' were never posed until fairly recently.[1] While the work of art was almost always regarded as a cause for predominantly aesthetic and stylistic observations, the function of the building which housed it was reduced to little more than Herington's definition of a Greek temple: 'a weather-proof statuebox'.[2]

Architectural historians, too, have tended to treat the cathedral in much the same way as students of painting look at an altarpiece – as an isolated work of art. It is true that Lusini unearthed a great deal of archive material for his monumental monograph on Siena cathedral, but he never really marshalled it in such a way as to provide a real interpretation of the building as such.[3] He was followed by Carli and Wagner-Rieger, each of whom made valuable contributions to the architectural history of the cathedral.[4] These and other authors have uncovered and described numerous stylistic affinities, but it is not until 1953 that we at last find a work which sets out to analyse the cathedral's role as the focal point of an urban organism. Braunfels was the first to tackle this task, and his study has considerably enriched our understanding of the background of early Tuscan art – not just its architecture, as the title of his work might suggest, but sculpture and painting as well.[5] Middeldorf-Kosegarten displayed considerable originality when she attempted to explore the underlying significance of the cathedral architecture by emphasising the possible symbolic associations of the dome.[6]

However, our comparative ignorance of the history of Siena cathedral is not entirely due to the rather narrow view adopted by most art historians. The superb inlay floor makes it impossible to carry out excavations which might reveal earlier foundations and enable us to make deductions from soil discolouration. And yet another factor which complicates any study of the cathedral is the strong sense of history of the Sienese themselves, for they based all subsequent modifications on the distinctive style of the fourteenth-century exterior. The archiepiscopal palace against the south side of the cathedral was demolished in the seventeenth century, and it was necessary to put a new outer cladding on the wall of the nave.[7] The architects elected for a fourteenth-century design, and they imitated it so faithfully that without the documentary evidence it might never have been realised that it was a seventeenth-century addition. The adviser called in by the Sienese was none other than Bernini, the master of Roman Baroque.[8]

The object of this study is to gain a clearer idea of the interaction between architecture and liturgy and specifically of the significance of the altars, drawing on contemporary documents and on the information which can be deduced from the actual fabric of Siena cathedral.

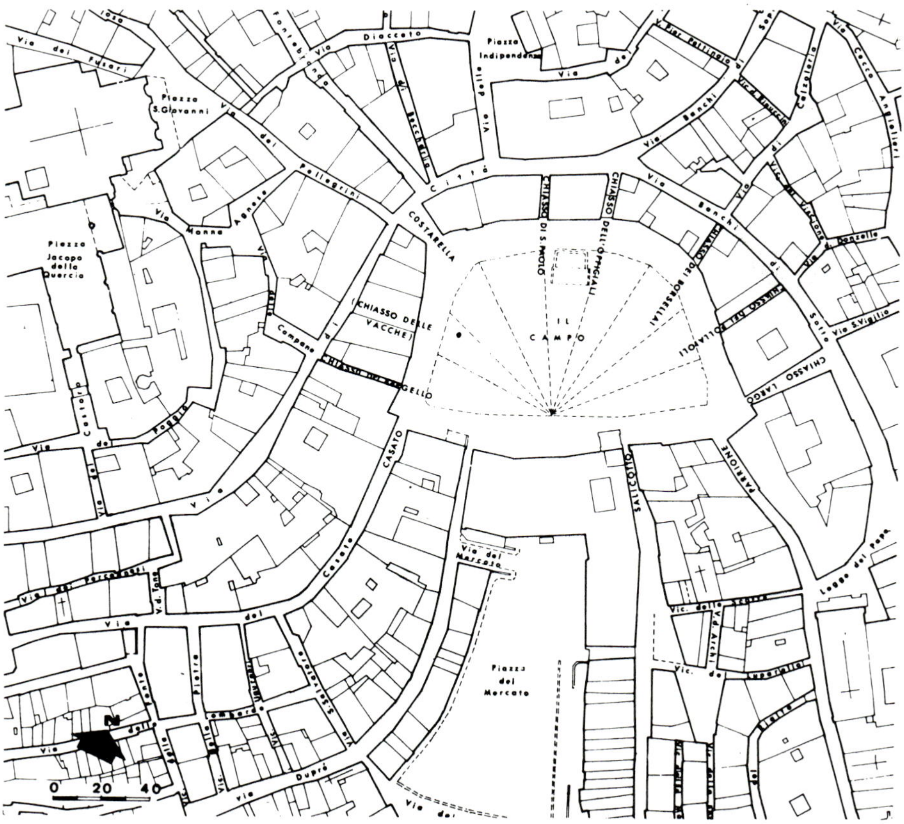

Diag. 1 The centre of Siena. Map showing the Cathedral, Campo and Palazzo Pubblico.

1
THE EARLY HISTORY OF THE CATHEDRAL – A RECONSTRUCTION

If we are to understand the liturgical operation of Siena cathedral we must inevitably focus on the choir, for it was here that the liturgy was concentrated. First, though, we must try and reconstruct the entire edifice as accurately as possible. The following reconstruction is based on evidence from documentary sources and from the physical structure of the building.

Work apparently started on the new church around 1220.[9] Lusini was the first to propose a reconstruction for this thirteenth-century cathedral, but the welter of unresolved problems makes his suggestion highly implausible.[10] It seems that Lusini (motivated, one suspects, by a local chauvinism) proposed his system of radiating chapels in order to make the Siena choir the prototype of that in Florence (diag. 4).

Carli demolished Lusini's reconstruction and proposed another, eminently plausible one in its place (diag. 5).[11] On the basis of the remains of the crypt beneath the south aisle of the choir he created transepts two bays wide and one bay deep (fig. 3). Beyond the crossing was a tripartite choir two bays deep. The available evidence suggests that the choir was straight-ended. The remains of a wall in the crypt indicate that, if there ever was an apse, it could only have extended from the central choir aisle. Secondly, the ground falls away so sharply behind the choir that massive foundations would have to have been built to support an apse. Finally, stained glass was ordered for the large round window in the choir in 1287,[12] shortly after the church had been completed.[13] This window virtually rules out the presence of an apse, certainly when one remembers that the choir was not as high as it is now.[14] The lower zone would have been pierced by narrow windows, as in the case of Laon and Vercelli cathedrals. The probable involvement of the Cistercians in this design is made all the more plausible in the case of Siena by the fact that the *operaio*, who was responsible for the supervision of the building work, was chosen from 1258 to 1305 from the monks of the nearby Cistercian monastery of San Galgano (ill. 2).[15]

Wagner-Rieger supplements this picture of the choir with a detailed discussion of the nave.[16] She believes that Siena cathedral was modelled on Notre-Dame-la-Grande in Poitiers, which is a pseudo-basilica with columns, groined vaulting in the aisles and a barrel vault over the nave (diags. 6, 7). Notre-Dame-la-Grande dates chiefly from the second quarter of the twelfth century,[17] and it certainly has much in common with Siena cathedral in both design and proportions. Wagner-Rieger extends that similarity to the facade on the basis of structural type and decoration (ill. 3).[18]

According to Wagner-Rieger the thirteenth-century nave at Siena would have had a barrel vault springing immediately above the cornice, which was part of the original design. That vault supposedly joined up with the massive arch opening onto the hexagon,[19] while transverse arches sprang from the clustered piers protruding into the nave. However, a barrel vault would have been very old-fashioned by the mid-thirteenth century. Moreover, the marked similarity of the nave and dome capitals to the classicist style of Nicola Pisano precludes an earlier date for the vault.[20] In addition, the intercolumniation is unusually wide for such a heavy structure, and the large round window in the choir also militates against it on constructional grounds. It is more probable that there were rib vaults between the transverse arches, and this appears to be borne out by a document of 1260 (1259 Sienese style).[21]

Since the external arcade of the dome was built almost immediately on top of the massive arch to the nave, the apex of the nave must have overlapped some of the arcading of the drum.[22] This was not exceptional in Italian architecture, as we can see from Pisa cathedral (ill. 5). We know that the nave and the dome at Pisa were part of a single plan dating from the second half of the eleventh century, yet despite that the roof of the nave does extend into the zone of the drum.[23] It was not until 1369 that work started on raising the nave of Siena cathedral as part of the rebuilding programme begun in 1317. It was once again given rib vaulting,[24] and from 1377 the

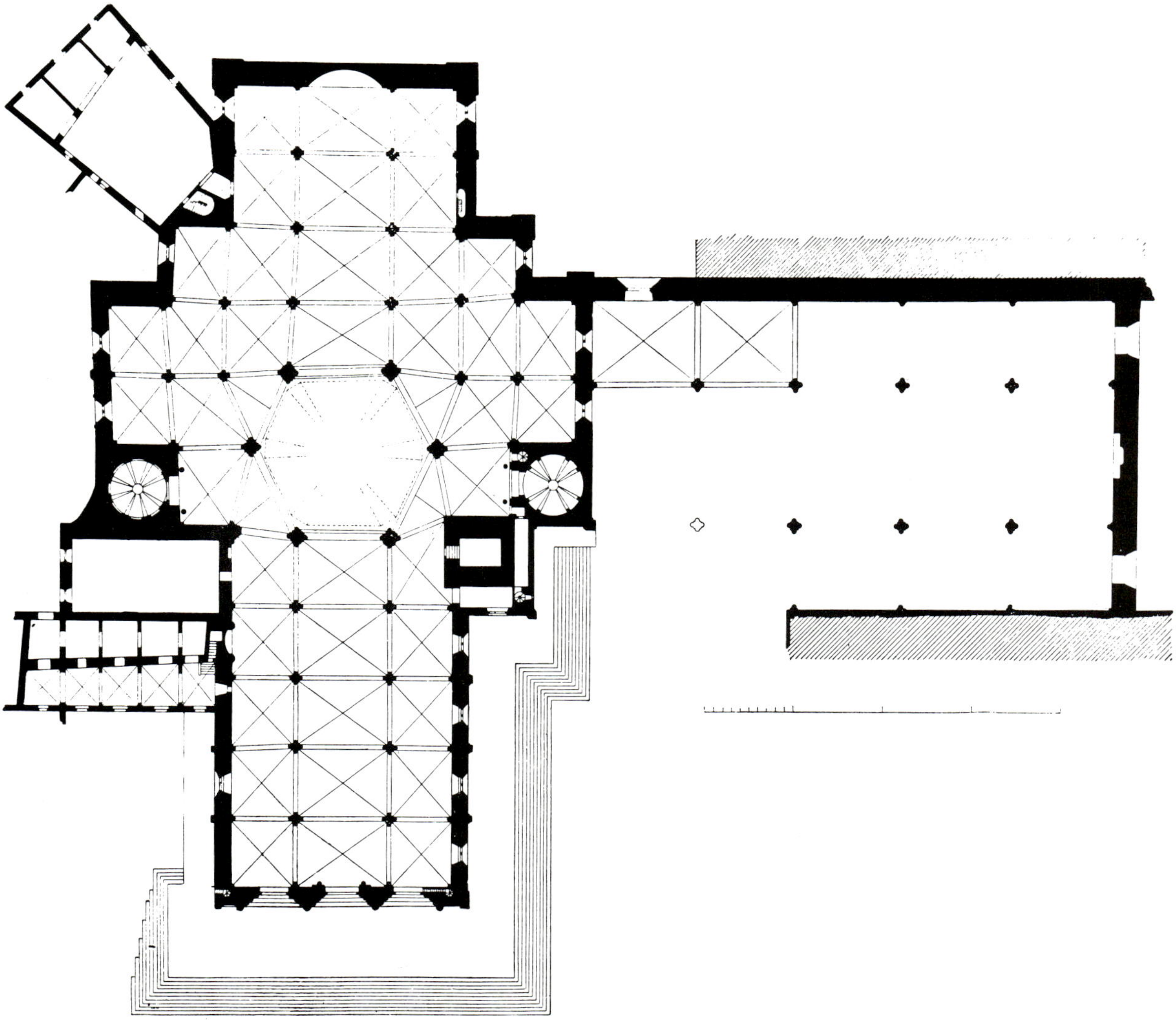

Diag. 2 Siena, Cathedral, Ground plan of the present church.

facade was also heightened to match the nave.[25]

We can see from the arch between the hexagon and the choir that the vaulting of the thirteenth-century choir was originally lower than that of the nave, and although this is also found in Poitiers and in other churches in Poitou, there are several examples in Tuscany itself (ill. 4).[26] The choir, like the nave, would have had a rib vault.[27] This shallow choir with its low roof must have been a far humbler structure than the present choir, which is the result of rebuilding and enlargement in the Trecento. It is possible that the thirteenth-century choir did not even have a clerestory. In the course of the fourteenth-century extension the cornice supported by consoles was raised to the level of the nave cornice, and the insertion of imposts above the capitals made the aisle vaults of the choir slightly higher than those of the nave aisles. The clerestory, too, was extended above that in the nave, thus reversing the thirteenth-century relationship between the height of the choir and the nave.[28]

Another similarity with Poitou is the arrangement of clustered columns with a demi-column extending upwards to support the cornice over the nave arches, the Duomo of Sovana (Sorano), which was built in the third quarter of the twelfth century (ill. 7).[29] We find a similar arrangement in the Pieve di San Giovanni Battista in Ponte allo Spino (Sovicille), which dates from the end of the twelfth century (ill. 8).[30] Both churches have a crossing tower, the one in Ponte allo Spino taking the archaic form of a high barrel vault over the sanctuary. The rib vaults in Sovana

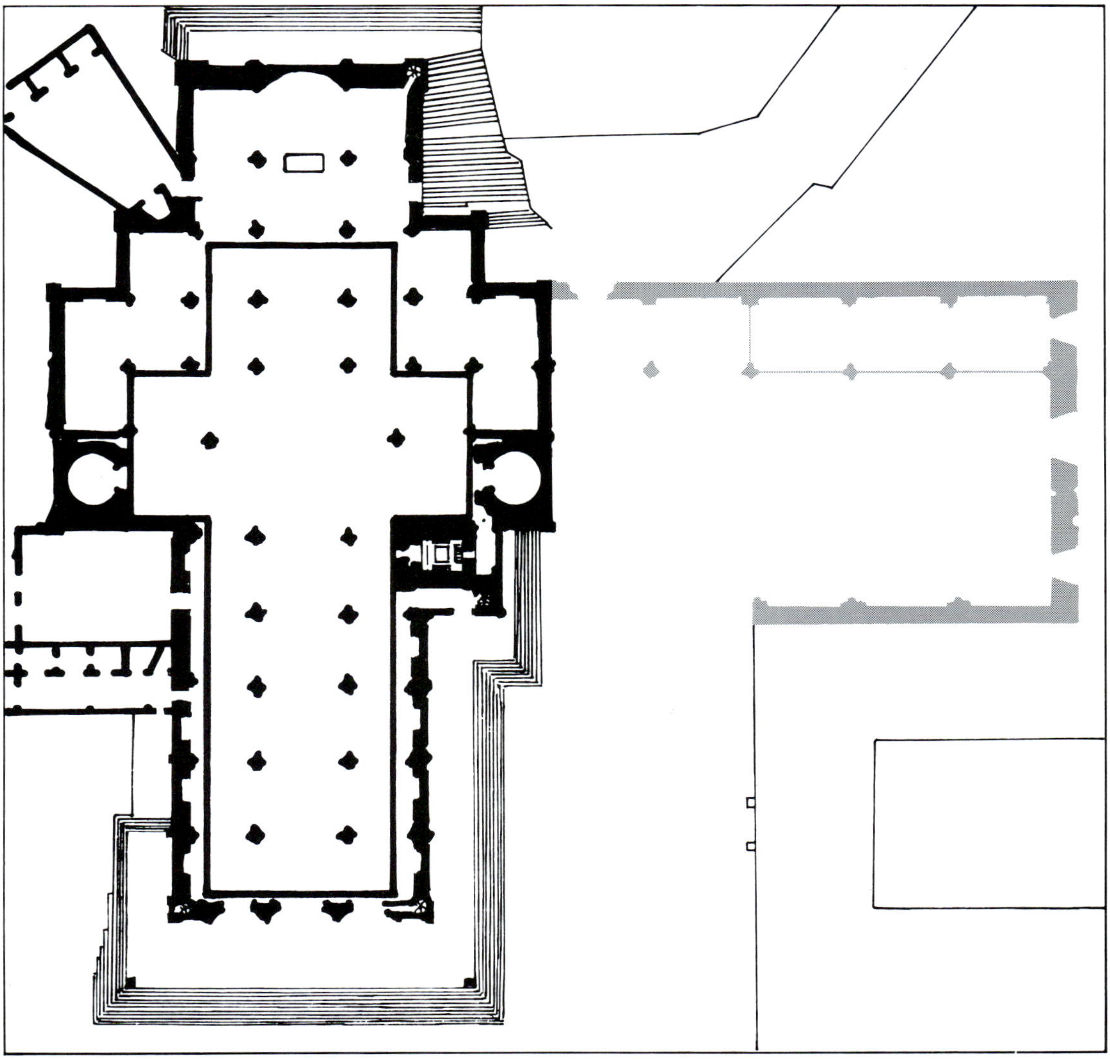

Diag. 3 Siena, Cathedral. Ground plan of the twelfth-century cathedral superimposed on the present church. The remains of the crypt lie below the shaded bays.

date from the thirteenth century.[31] Before that time the nave probably had an open-trussed wooden roof. Ponte allo Spino still has an open wooden roof, although both Salmi and Moretti argue convincingly that the original intention was probably to build a stone barrel vault.[32] Both these examples show that the thirteenth-century nave in Siena was not some sudden innovation, and that the influence of Poitou is already discernible in the twelfth century. What is new is the far more monumental treatment of the design,[33] and the greater prominence of the cornice above the nave arches.[34]

At first sight the dome between the choir and the nave gives a distinctly odd impression, but there can be no doubt that it was an integral part of the design for the thirteenth-century church. The pillars, and especially the capitals, in the nave, hexagon and the adjoining transept bays are stylistically and structurally related. The internal and external galleries with their early Gothic crocket capitals and depressed Gothic arches are part of the thirteenth-century formal vocabulary, as are the three-light windows below them. Those windows originally served to light the crossing when the transepts were only one bay deep.[35] In the Dugento, when the nave and the choir were considerably lower, the dome would have had a far stronger centralising effect, certainly with a choir which was not only two bays shorter than the present one but was also lower than the original nave. In

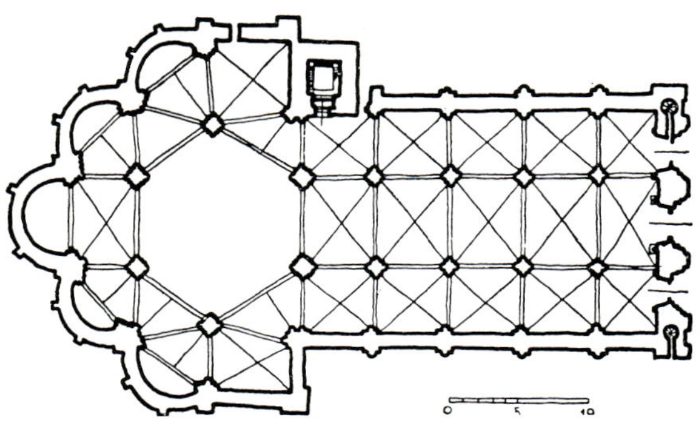

Diag. 4 Lusini's reconstruction of the thirteenth-century cathedral with radiating chapels (1911).

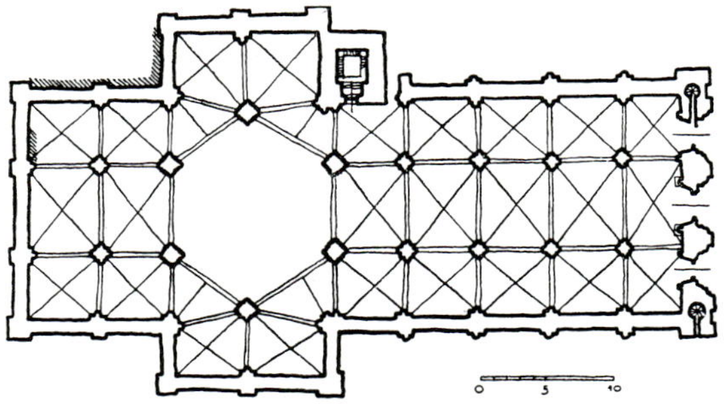

Diag. 5 Carli's reconstruction of the thirteenth-century cathedral with straight-ended choir (1946).

addition, the shallow transept arms did not extend above the aisles.[36]

Nevertheless, it is odd that the northern and southern dome pillars stood in the sight-line of the aisles. It is unlikely that the aisles were originally intended to be narrower, since the engaged columns belong to the same building phase as the free-standing piers, as we can see from the sculpting of the capitals and the black-and-white banding. Moreover, the Romanesque window in the north transept is precisely on the central axis of the bay (ill. 9). There are other examples of almost square aisle bays in Tuscany (diag. 8).[37] It is true that the lateral portals are not aligned with the centres of the aisles, but that is due to the position of the flanking towers. We find a similar arrangement in Poitiers (ill. 3).[38] We know from the receipt for the bronze ball on the dome that the church was virtually complete by 1264, so the aisles must have acquired their final form before that date.[39] The reason why the campanile encroaches onto the aisles is that it was built around an earlier *torre*.[40]

It is not impossible that the dome resulted from a change in the construction plans, and the same may be true of the many other irregularities in the ground plan and elements around the crossing. It is also noteworthy, given the system of measurements used in the thirteenth-century cathedral, that the eastern and western dome piers are exactly two bays apart. It is possible that the foundations for the piers had already been laid when it was decided to built a far larger dome. The simplest solution would than have been to move the two central piers further apart, creating a hexagonal ground plan and making the 'side walls' shorter at the same time. This in turn affected the construction of those walls, with an extra three-light window being inserted above the necessarily narrower and lower arches.

That being said, it is perfectly possible that the thirteenth-century designers deliberately intended to give the crossing a centralising effect, but they would have been far more likely to have chosen a modest crossing tower. There are numerous such towers in Poitou, and as we have seen there was a relationship between Poitou and Siena,[41] but it is also a fact that many Italian Cistercian churches built after the second half of the twelfth century also had a crossing tower (ill. 12).[42]

The crossing dome, albeit fairly small, is found at an early date in Pisan-Tuscan architecture,[43] and the dome space in the cathedral at Massa Marittima is an interesting case in point (ill. 5, 13, diag. 9). Work started on Massa cathedral in the second half of the twelfth century,[44] and the dome over the crossing extends over two bays, just as we had assumed in the case of the original plan for Siena.[45] The Pisan influence on Massa's drumless dome on pendentives is unmistakable. The domes in Pisa also have an elongated ground plan. However, the external arcades, both in Massa and Siena, are markedly reminiscent of Lombardic dwarf galleries, such as those around the tall crossing tower of the Cistercian abbey in Chiaravalle Milanese (ill. 12).[46]

The posited enlargement of the dome at Siena could be seen as a demonstration of civic pride.[47] This in no way debars the Mariological interpretation put forward by Middeldorf-Kosegarten, but it is unlikely that the dome was built in order to express that kind of symbolism.[48] In 1375, when the choir extension was almost finished, the altar which had stood near the dome was moved back,[49] stripping the dome of any possible symbolic significance as a canopy sheltering the Mother of God, who was venerated on the high altar.

The crypt is vital to our understanding of the function of the thirteenth-century church (diag. 10).[50] As already noted, there are remains of the crypt beneath the south aisle of the thirteenth-century choir. The present space beneath the choir consists of two bays separated by a wall (ill. 14). The innermost area is known as the 'Cripta degli affreschi', and the outer one as the 'Cripta delle statue'. The entrance to the crypt is on a landing halfway down the large staircase leading from the baptistery

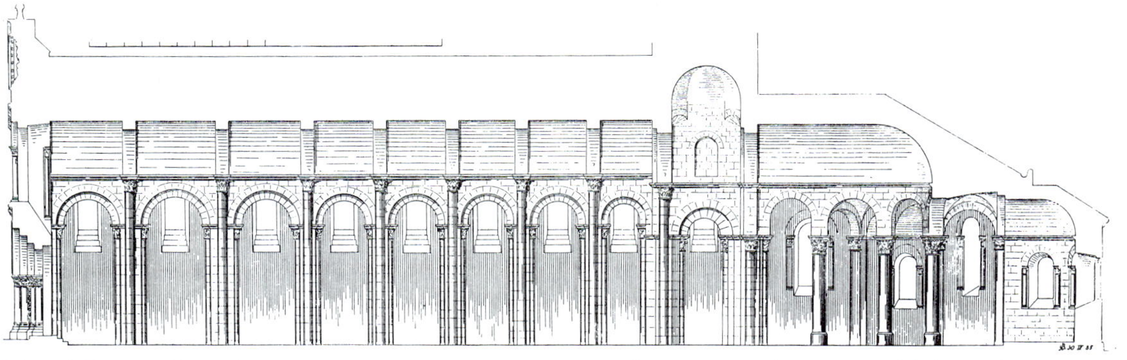

Diag. 6 Poitiers, Notre-Dame-la-Grande. Longitudinal section.

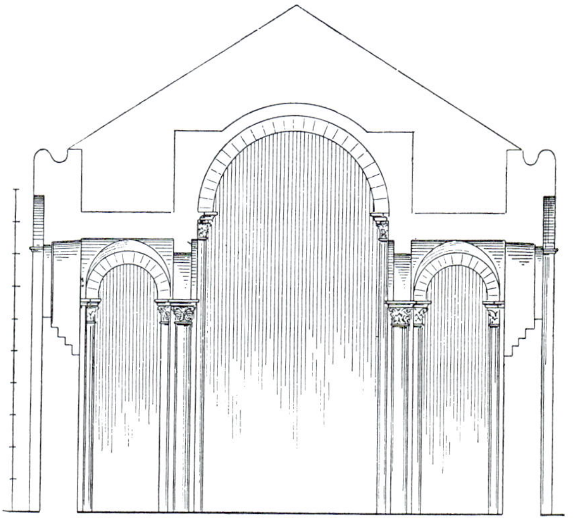

Diag. 7 Poitiers, Notre-Dame-la-Grande. Transverse section through the nave.

to the great door of the Duomo Nuovo. Little remains of the original subdivision and roofing of the crypt apart from the vestiges of two pillars and the lower parts of two vaults. Carli gives a plausible date of ca. 1270-80 for the murals in the earliest of the two bays, which provides us with a *terminus ante quem* for the construction of that bay.[51] There are various passages in the *Ordo officiorum* for the cathedral which point to the existence of a crypt in the twelfth-century church.[52] The smaller crypt module indicates that this space was retained below the church built in the thirteenth century. It is unlikely that the choir of the Dugento cathedral had the same smaller size of bay. The round window would have to have been proportionately smaller, and the stained glass is certainly based on a thirteenth-century design.[53] Moreover, we can see from the capitals which were reused in the fourteenth-century enlargement of the choir that there was no change in the diameter of the pillars (ills. 15, 17).[54] If the bays had been smaller the thirteenth-century columns would have been correspondingly narrower. The remains of the pillars in the crypt belong to an earlier period than the thirteenth-century columns, and are of a different design.[55] This leads us to the conclusion that the crypt was the only part of the old church to be retained in the thirteenth-century structure.[56] As can still be seen, massive supports were built in the crypt at a subsequent date to take the weight of the columns in the present, fourteenth-century choir.[57] All that remains of the entrance on the Valle Piatte side, where the baptistery was later built, is the door-sill, which tells us that the floor of the crypt stood at approximately its present level. This is borne out by the fresco decoration of the walls, which consists of figural scenes above a simple plinth motif.[58] It can also be deduced from these frescoes that the crowns of the crypt vaulting were considerably higher than that of the present barrel vault.[59] The conclusion to be drawn from these facts is that the choir in the thirteenth-century church must have been elevated several steps above the floor of the remainder of the building.[60]

We have a description of the choir from the beginning of the sixteenth century which states that the church had a 'confessio', 'supported by fifteen pillars and with three chambers'.[61] Now as it happens fifteen pillars is exactly the number necessary to divide the space beneath the choir so that there were four vault bays below each choir bay, which was the customary arrangement in the middle ages (diag. 11).[62] There are also traces of a staircase, and Carli believes that, in addition to the entrance on the Valle Piatte, the crypt could be reached from the transept (ill. 14).[63] There would have been a similar staircase around a column on the other side, creating a route from the church, down into the crypt, and then back up again.[64]

During the enlargement of the church which began in 1317 the floor of the two old choir bays was lowered to the level of the nave and the hexagon, which must have entailed the demolition of the crypt vaulting and the total reconstruction of the choir.[65]

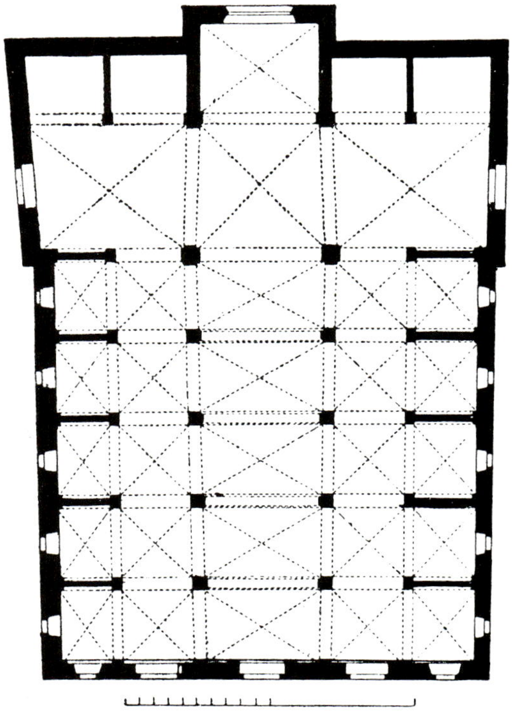

Diag. 8 Florence, Santa Trinità. Plan.

The relics of the city's patron saints must have been removed from the crypt and brought up into the body of the church before this was done.[66] The history of the construction and remodelling of Siena cathedral falls into perspective when the elevation of the relics and the subsequent demolition of the crypt are seen conjointly as the first step in the fourteenth-century building programme. The thirteenth-century church, embodying the twelfth-century crypt, still adhered to the programme of the large Romanesque churches, where relics were venerated in a space set apart from the church proper, namely the crypt.[67] The design for the fourteenth-century enlargement of the choir was based on a totally different conception of architectonic space. The object was to create a single spatial unit such as had been developed in the great French cathedrals from the twelfth century onwards, and there was no place in that scheme for enclosed spaces within the cathedral as a whole.[68] The rebuilding of 1317 therefore marks the point when Sienese architecture turned from a traditionally Romanesque approach to the acceptance of Gothic principles. The Duomo Nuovo, which was begun in 1339 but never completed, was to have been the fulfilment of that Gothic conception of space.

One chamber of the crypt survived (although not intact) after 1317, and two bays were added to it beneath the new part of the choir. They were used by the 'Compagnia di S. Giovanni Battista della Morte',[69] and the alterations to the lower parts of the murals would have been made during this rebuilding.[70] Since the present side entrance was only built during the construction of the large staircase in 1451, and since the door to the Valle Piatte disappeared during the construction of the baptistery, the single entrance from the transept to what remained of the crypt must have been in use until the middle of the fifteenth century.[71] The steeply shelving terrain necessitated the construction of a massive substructure to take the lateral extension of the transept and choir on the side where the archiepiscopal palace now stands (diag. 15). Despite the fact that it was evidently left unfinished, and although it was modified at a later date, it is still possible to make out much of the design of this semi-subterranean space. The shapes of the windows are typical of the fourteenth century, and the lines of the steep rib vaults can be traced from the grooves.[72] They were able to rise so high because the floor of the substructure lay below that of the old crypt, on approximately the same level as the baptistery. This rules out the possibility that the two spaces, the vestiges of the crypt and the new substructure, ever formed a single space. In other words, after 1317 Siena cathedral no longer had a real crypt.

The conclusions, then, are as follows. The thirteenth-century church consisted of a tripartite nave, five bays deep, roofed with a rib vault. There were transepts on either side of the crossing, which was enlarged into an irregular hexagon. The transepts were two bays wide and one bay deep. Behind the crossing dome there was a rectangular choir, two bays deep and of the same tripartite design as the nave. It too had rib vaults, but they were considerably lower than in the nave. The choir floor was several steps higher than that of the nave due to the retention of the crypt from the previous, twelfth-century church. The end of the choir was pierced by a large round window in the vault zone. Beneath it there may have been three tall, narrow windows. The crypt below the choir consisted of a space measuring three by six bays which could be reached from the transepts.

Most of the crypt was closed off when the church was enlarged. This programme began in 1317 and entered its final phase in 1375 with the relocation of the high altar. Between 1339 and 1348 work was carried out on the planned Duomo Nuovo. The choir was heightened considerably with the addition of a clerestory and was extended a further two bays over a substructure which served as a baptistery. Two new vault bays were built on either side of the bays of the old choir. The transepts were made twice as deep and acquired an extra bay on the choir side. The nave was given a new, taller clerestory, while the transepts, and possibly the nave aisles as well, were revaulted.

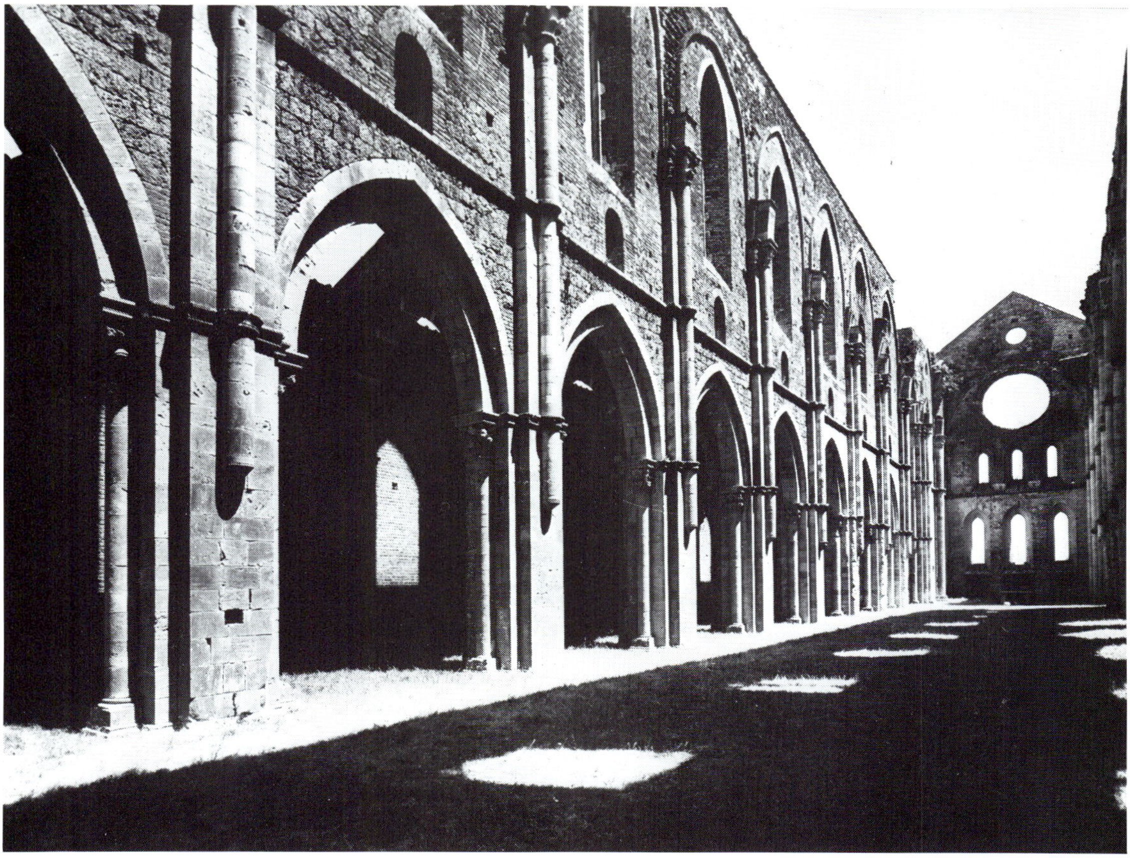

2 San Galgano, the former Cistercian abbey church, looking east. The choir of Siena cathedral probably had a similar rear wall before it was enlarged in the fourteenth century.

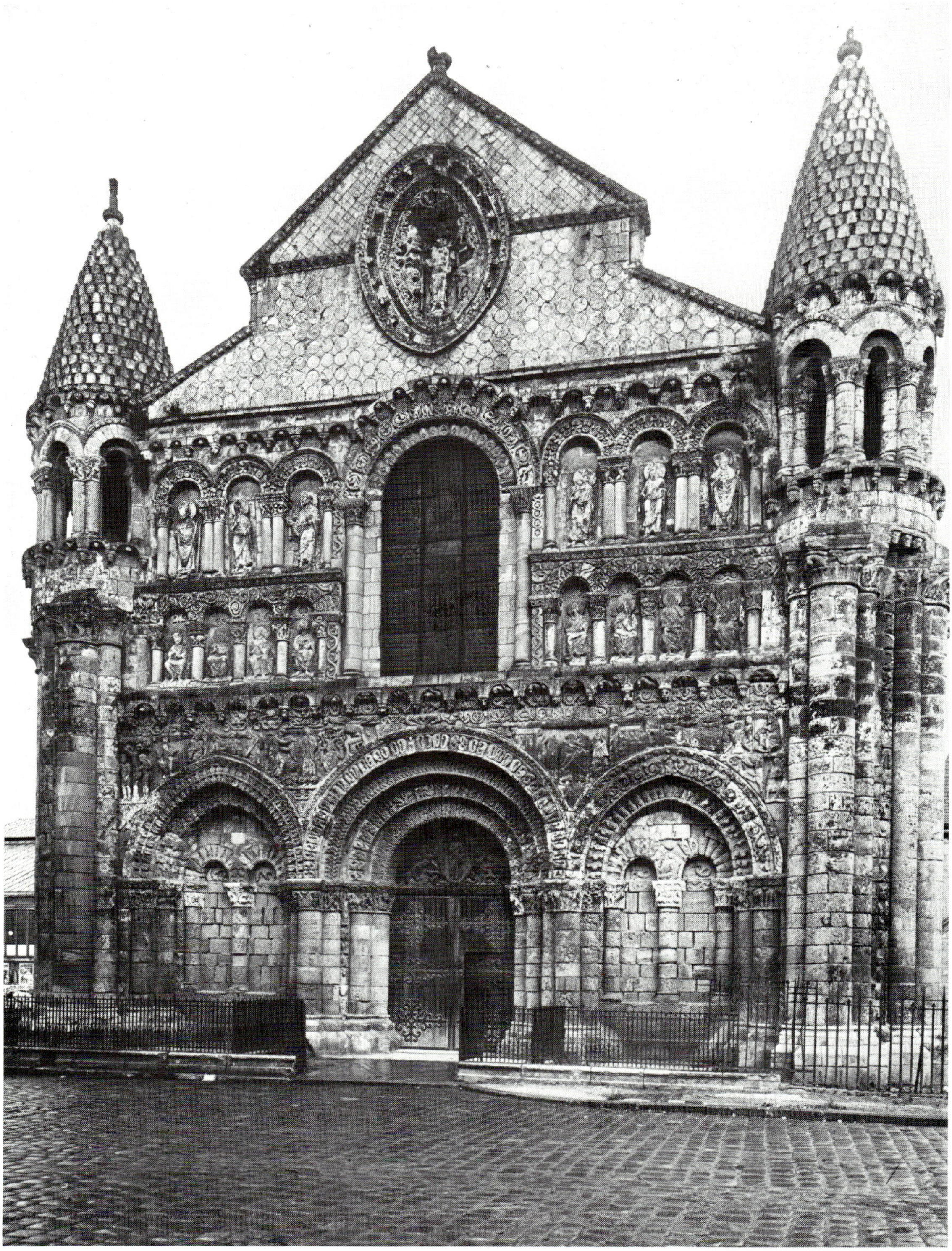

3 Poitiers, Notre-Dame-la-Grande, west front. The large corner towers and the rich ornamentation may have served as a model for Siena cathedral.

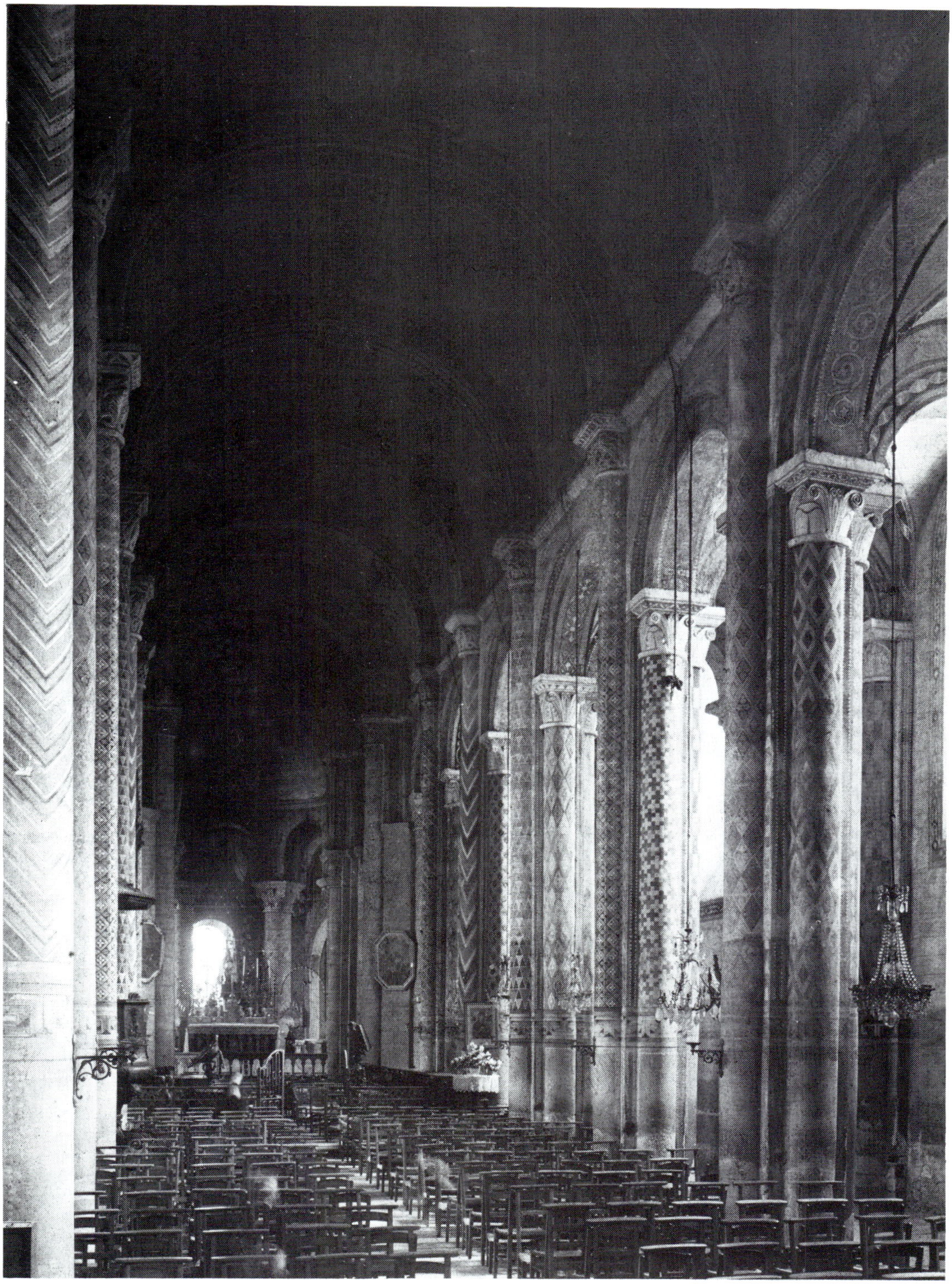

4 Poitiers, Notre-Dame-la-Grande, looking towards the choir. The original thirteenth-century nave of Siena cathedral, with its barrel vault, must have looked very similar.

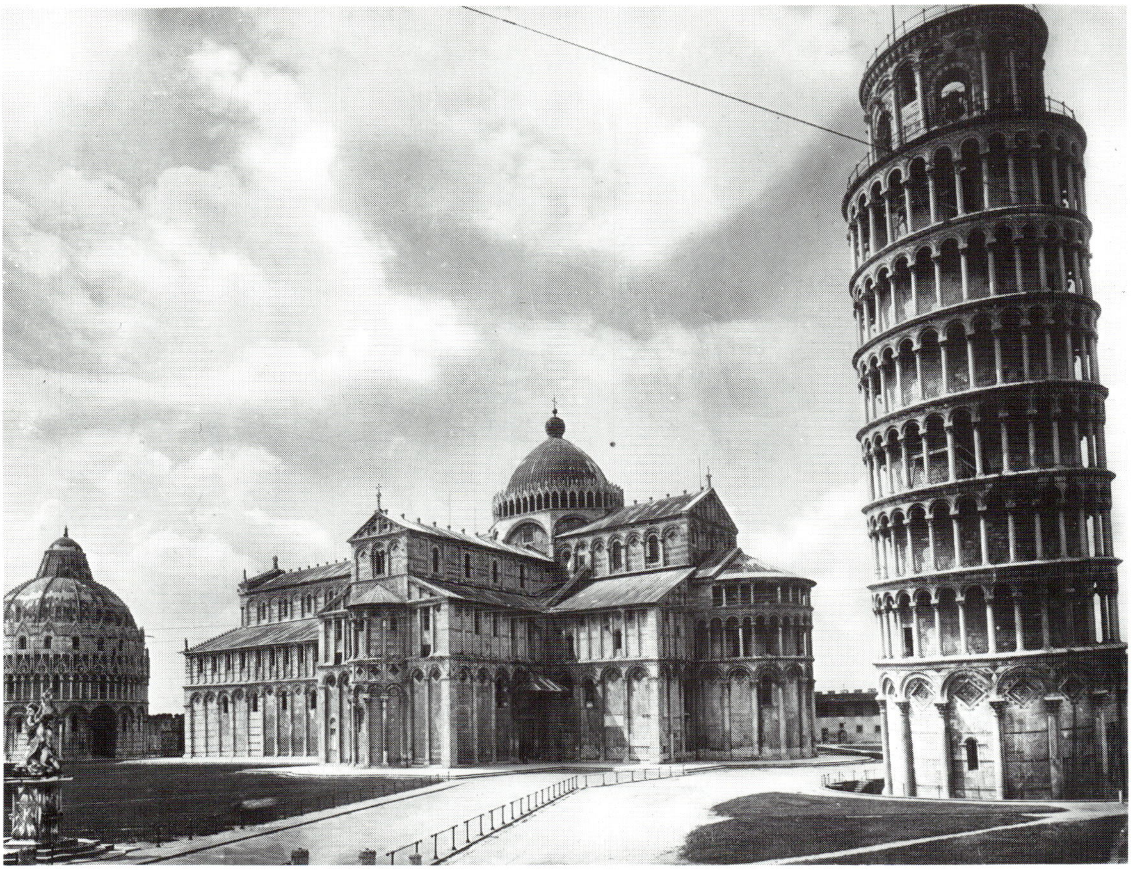

5 Pisa, Baptistery, Cathedral and Campanile. The elliptical dome is one of the earliest examples of dome construction in Tuscany.

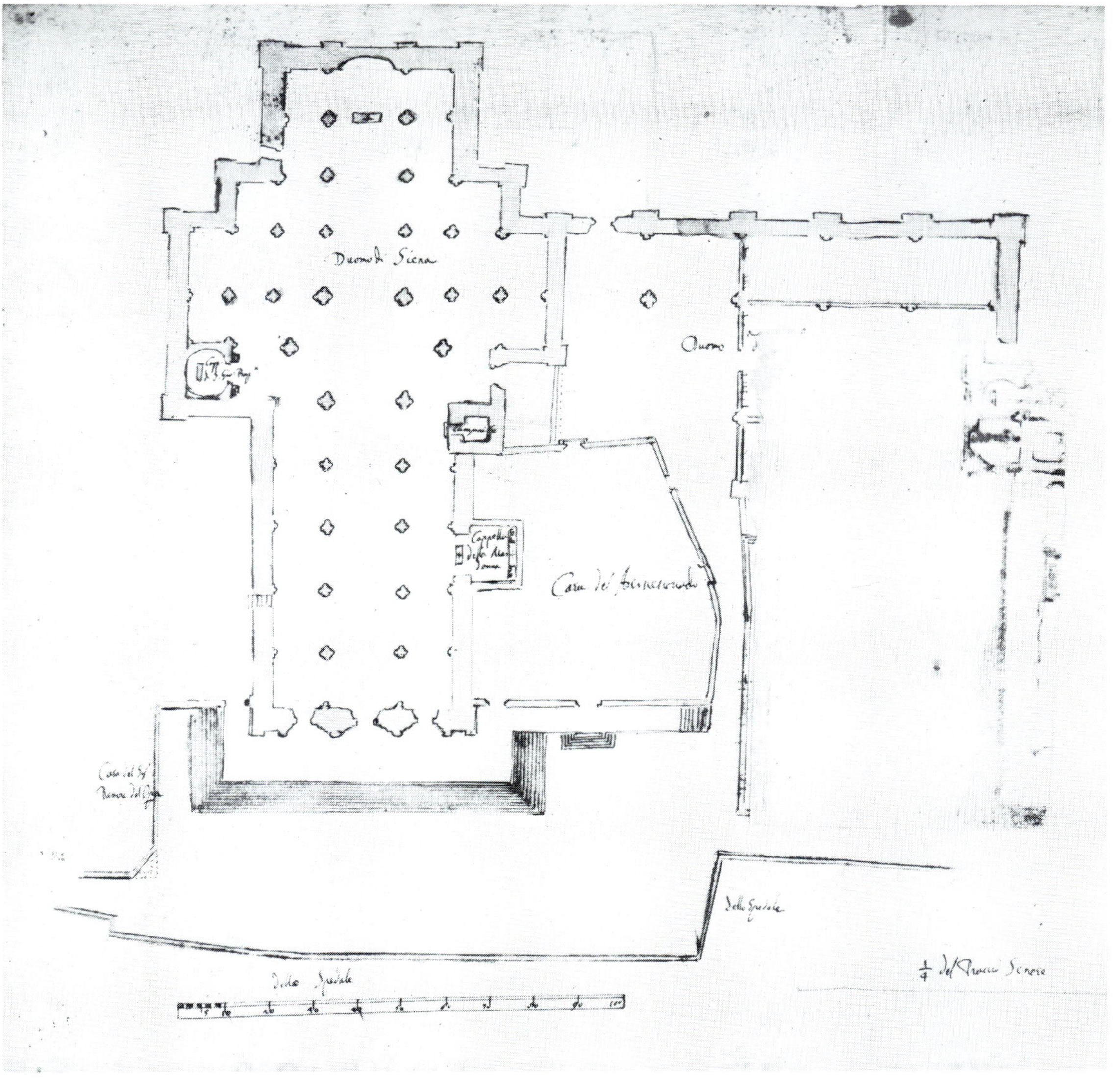

6 Siena, Cathedral and Archiepiscopal Palace, ca. 1658. The former Porta del Perdono is beside the campanile. Rome, Biblioteca Apostolica Vaticana, Archivio Chigi, cod. Chig. P.VII.11., fols. 38v-39r.

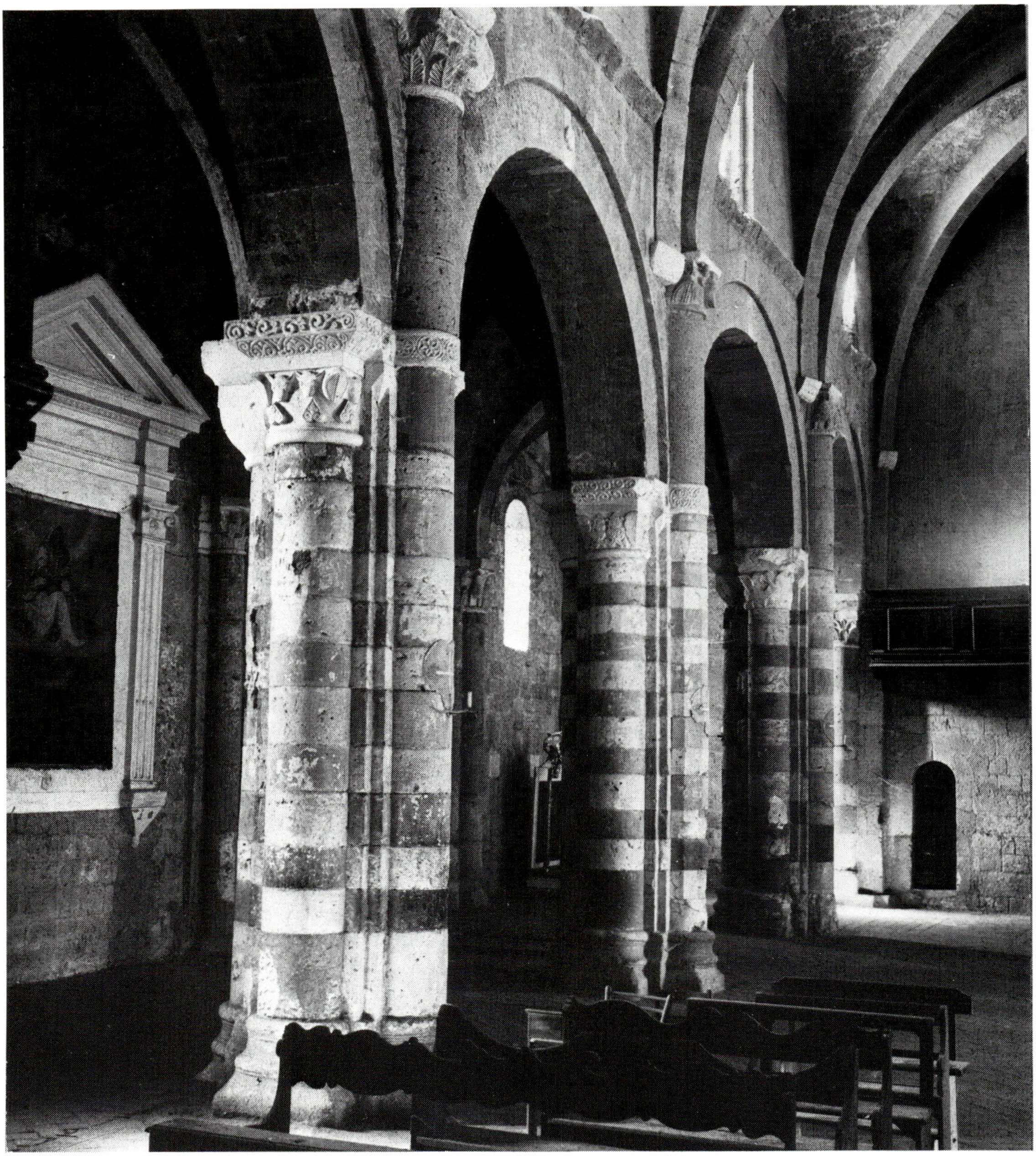

7 Sovana (Sorano), Cathedral, west end. The wall construction is very similar to that of Siena cathedral in the thirteenth century.

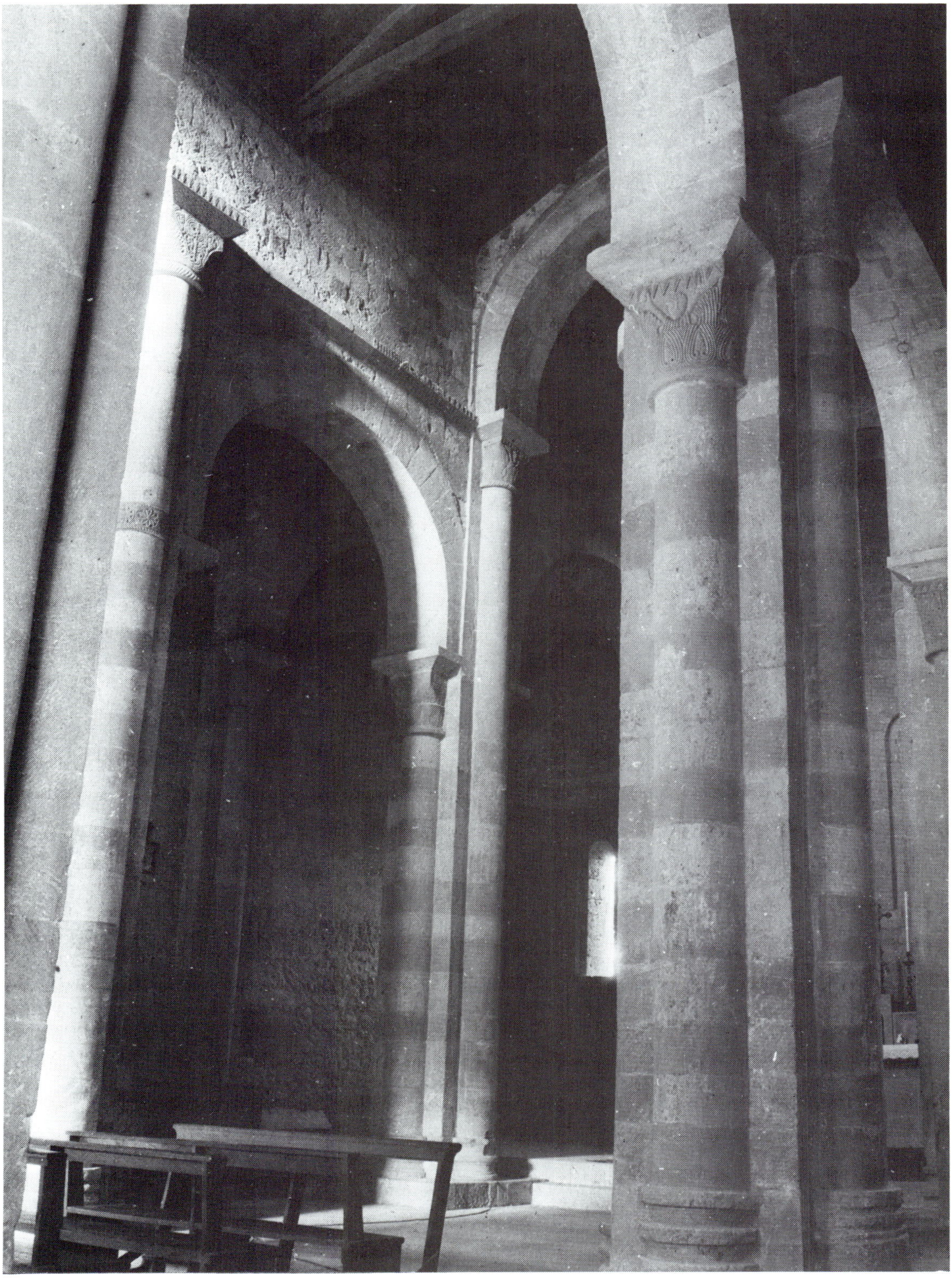

8 Ponte allo Spino (Sovicille), San Giovanni Battista. The nave arcades are closely related to the thirteenth-century arcades of Siena cathedral.

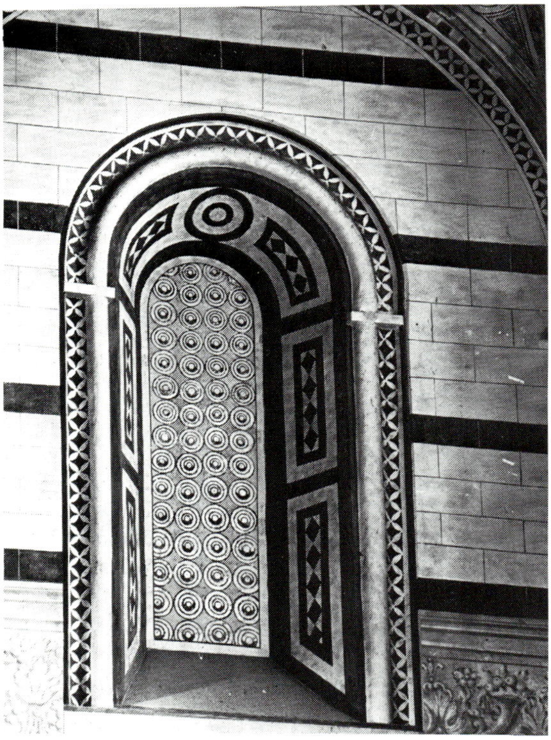

9 Siena, Cathedral. The only surviving Romanesque window is in the side wall of the transept near the chapel of St John the Baptist.

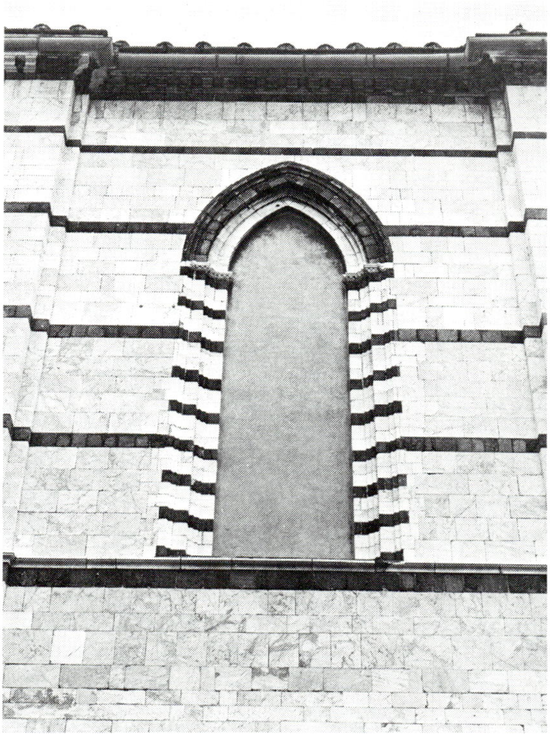

10 Siena, Cathedral. The early fourteenth-century window in the side wall opposite the archiepiscopal palace.

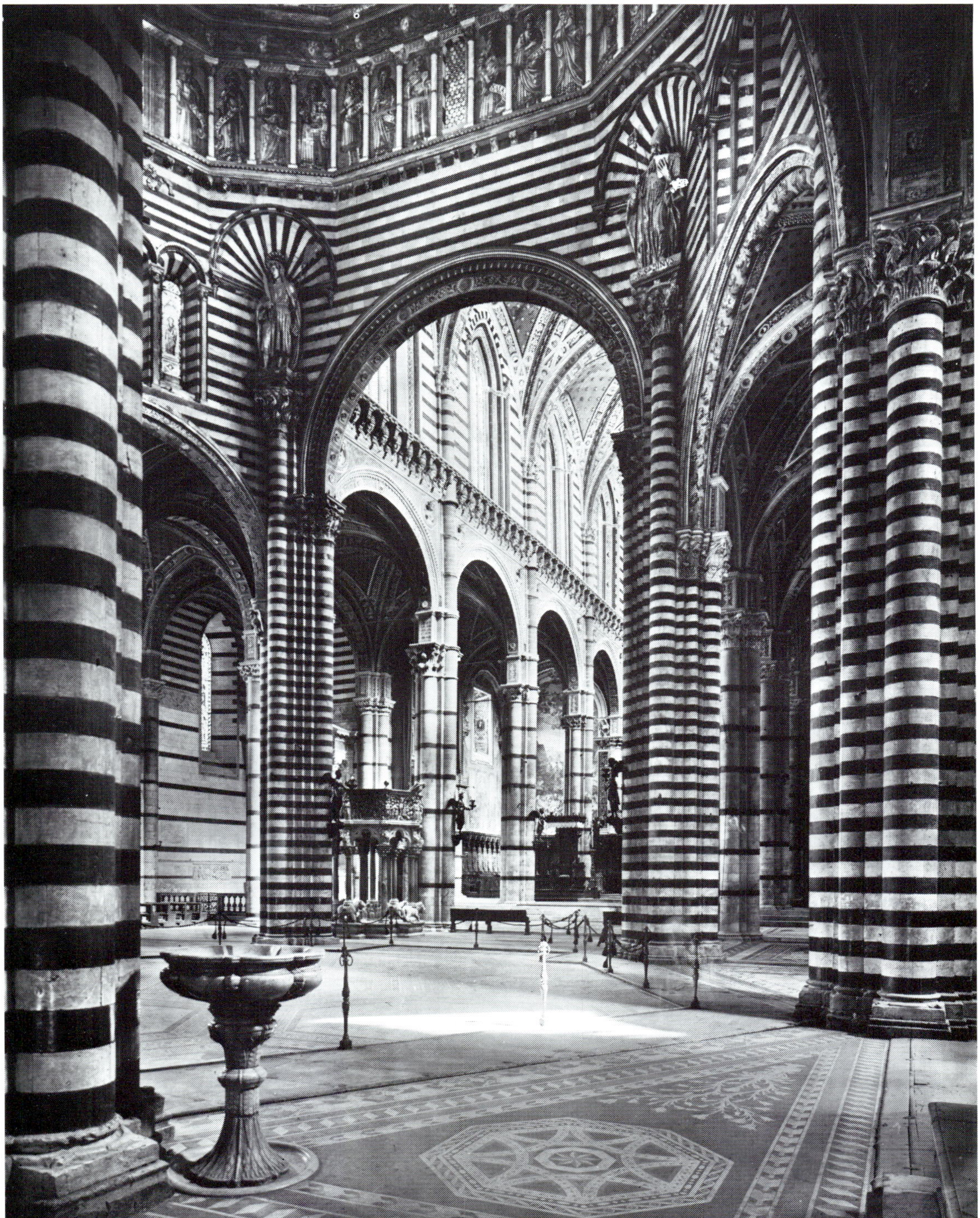

11 Siena, Cathedral, the choir seen through the crossing from the south aisle. The arcade capitals in the first choir bay clearly differ from the others in the choir. The pulpit originally stood on the other side of the choir.

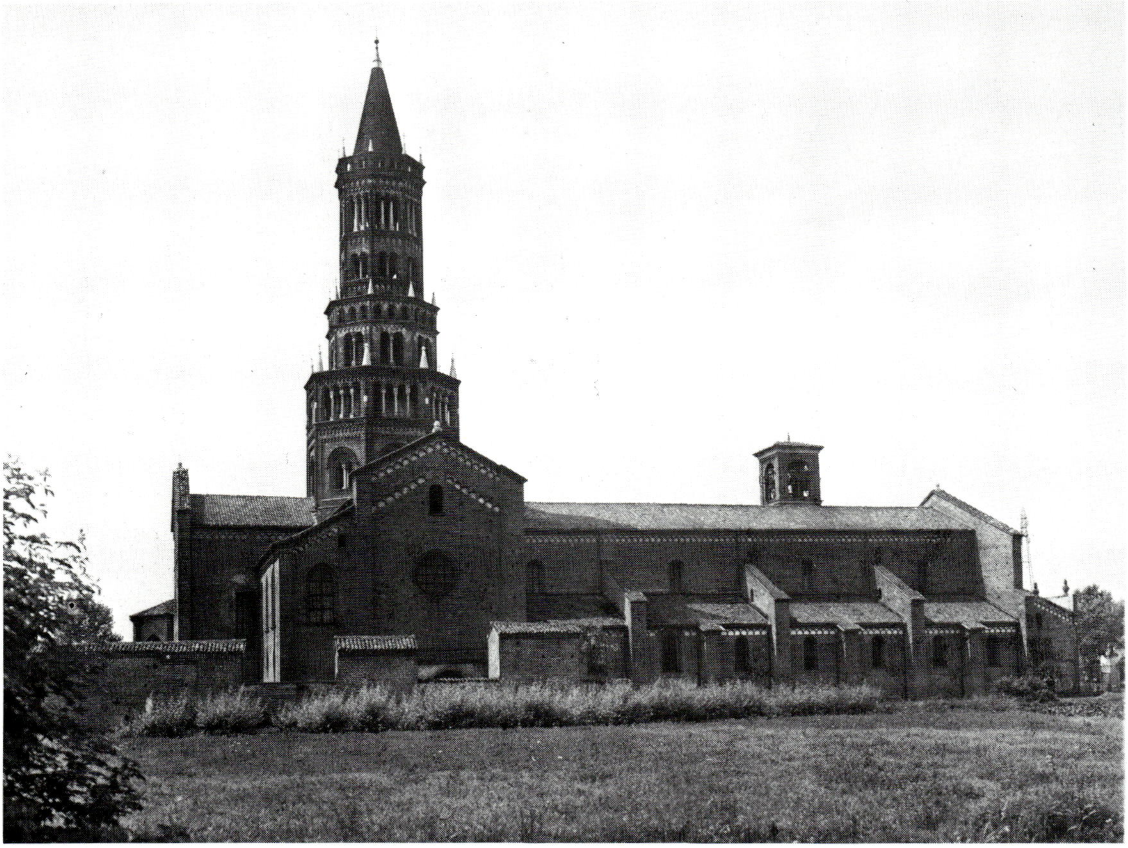

12 Chiaravalle Milanese, abbey church. The church was built in the thirteenth century, but the greater part of the tower is early fourteenth-century.

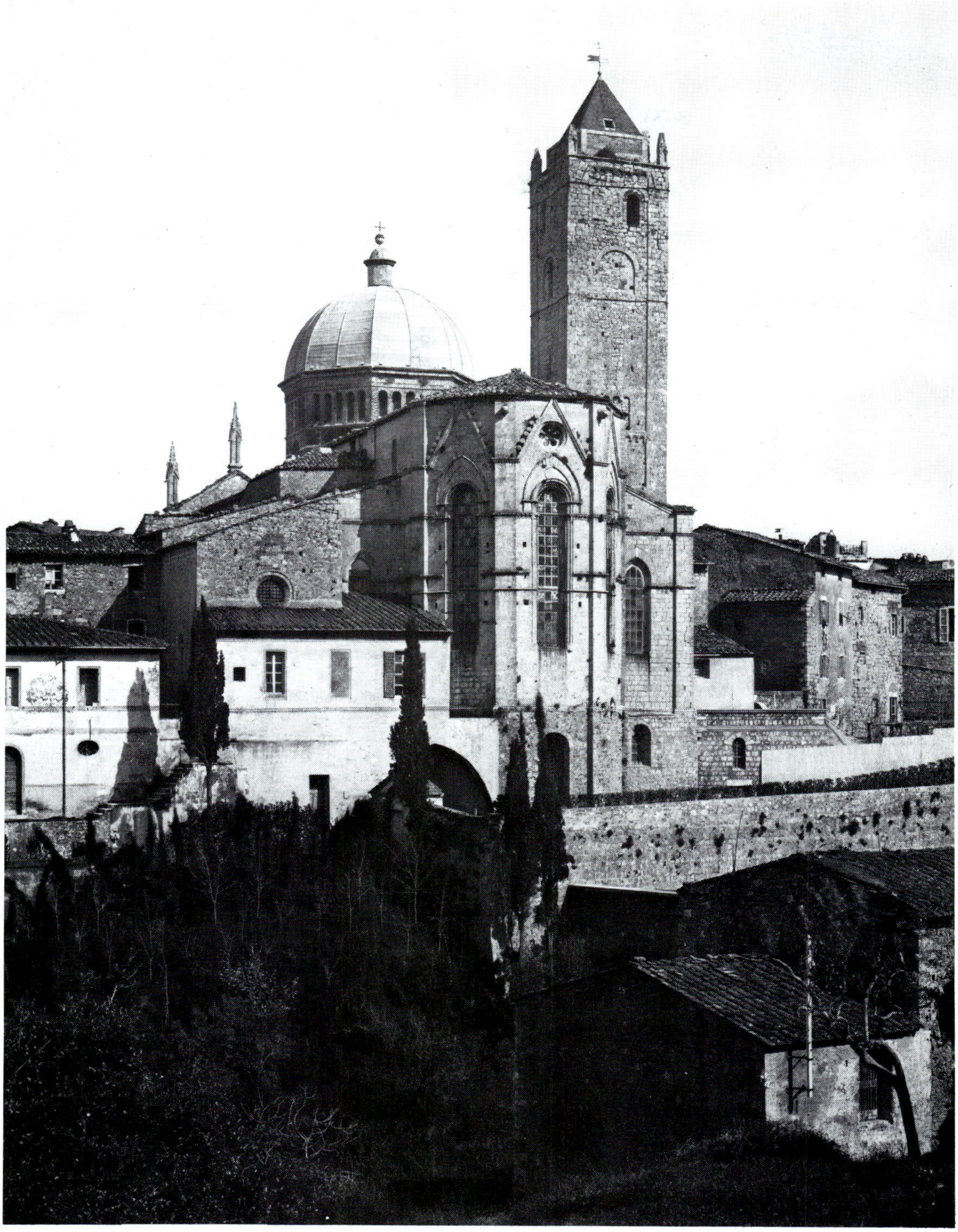

13 Massa Marittima, Cathedral. View of the choir, crossing dome and campanile before the restoration.

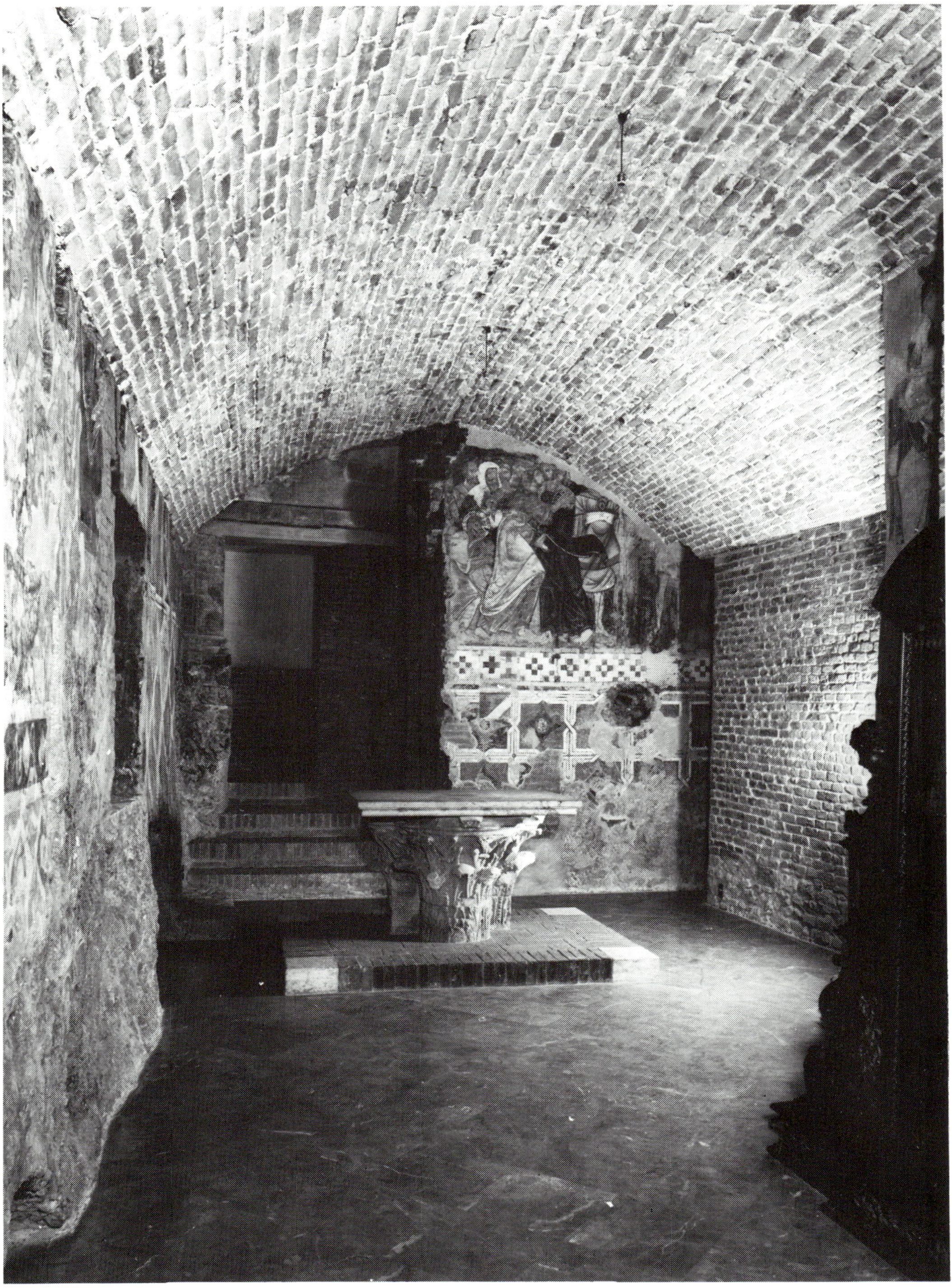

14 Siena, Cathedral. The 'Cripta degli affreschi' is all that remains of the twelfth-century crypt beneath the choir. The crypt was originally reached from the church by a staircase which emerged at the point now occupied by the four steps. The base of the pillar running up through the centre of the staircase can still be seen.

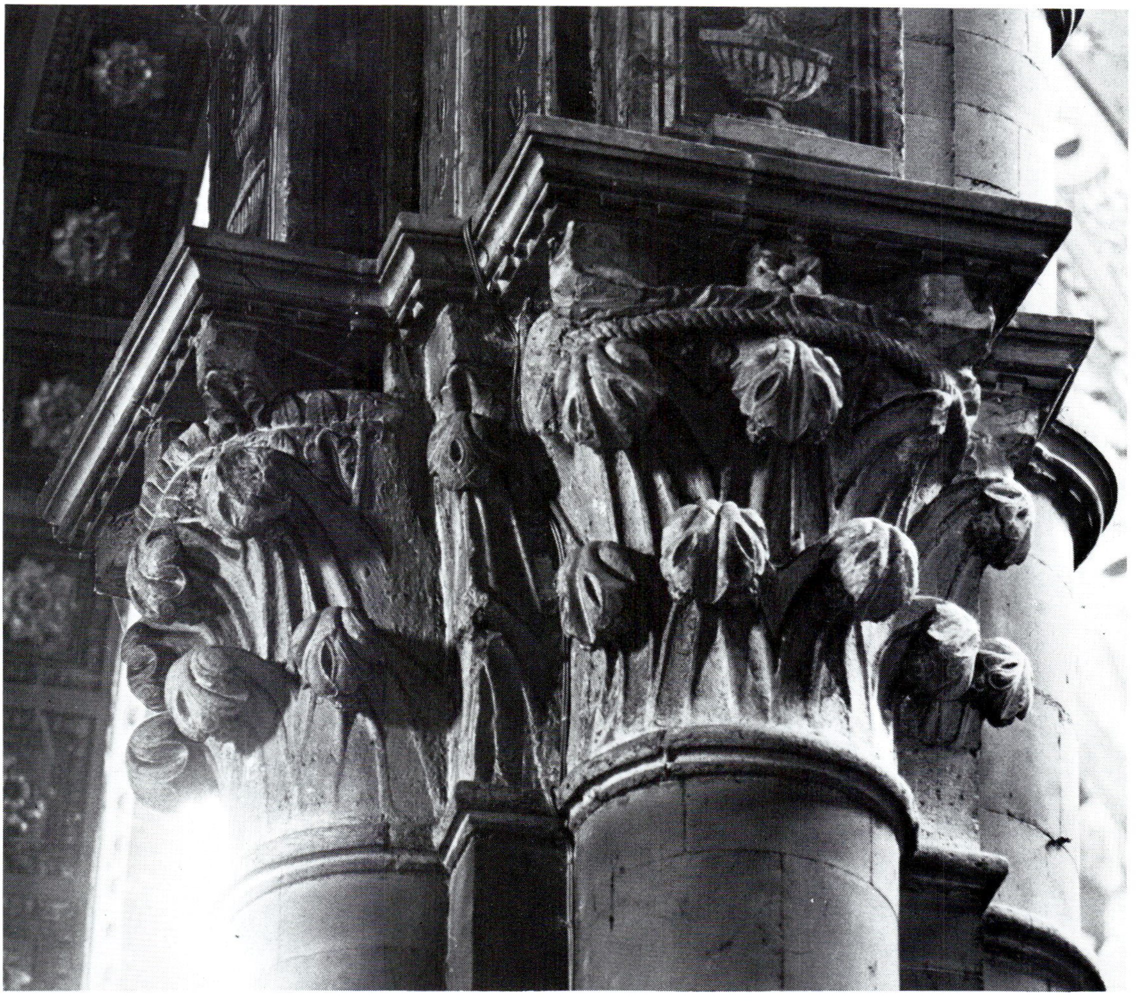

15 Siena, Cathedral. Thirteenth-century capital on the north side of the first choir bay.

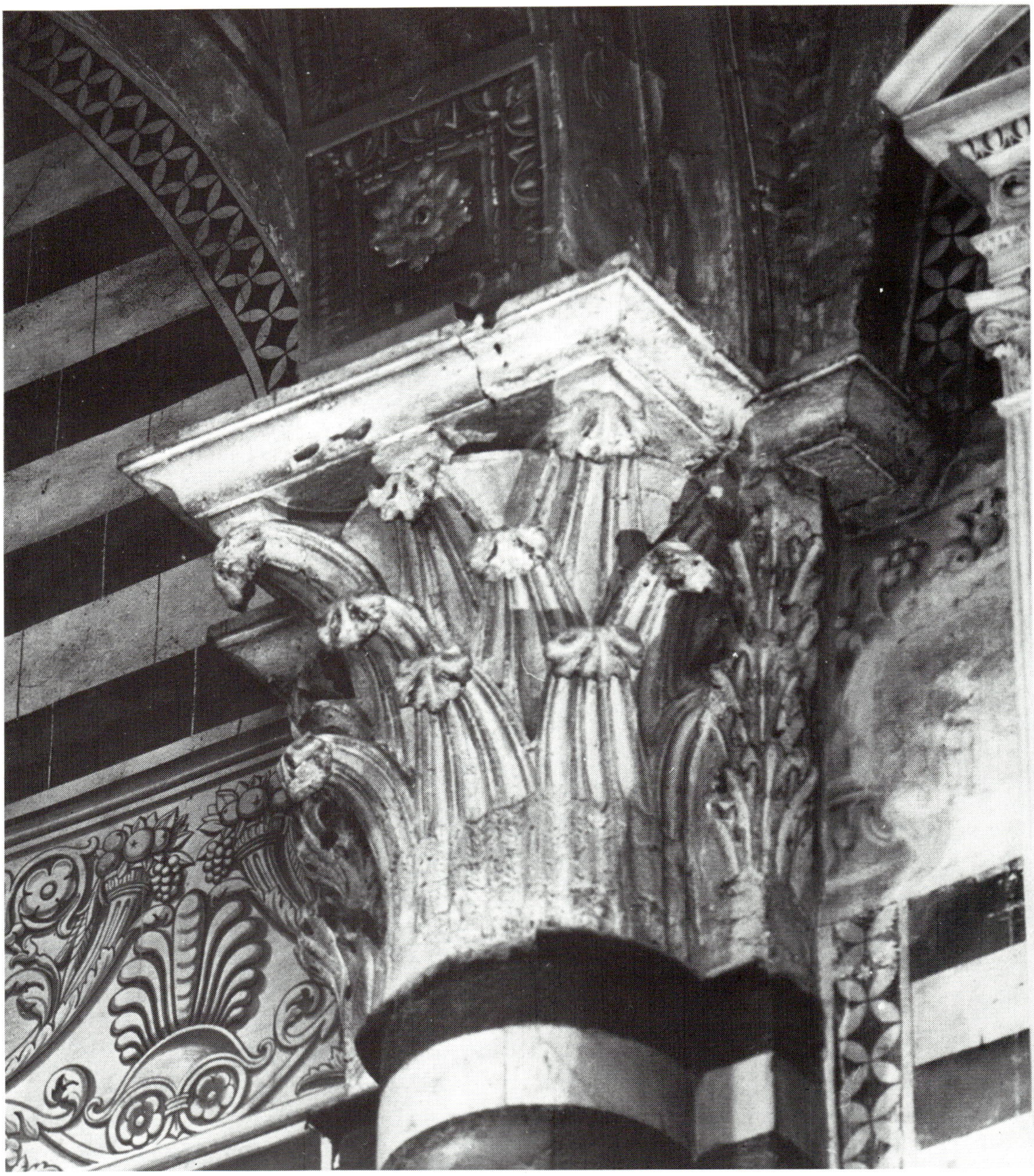

16 Siena, Cathedral. Thirteenth-century capital in the north aisle, near the Piccolomini altar.

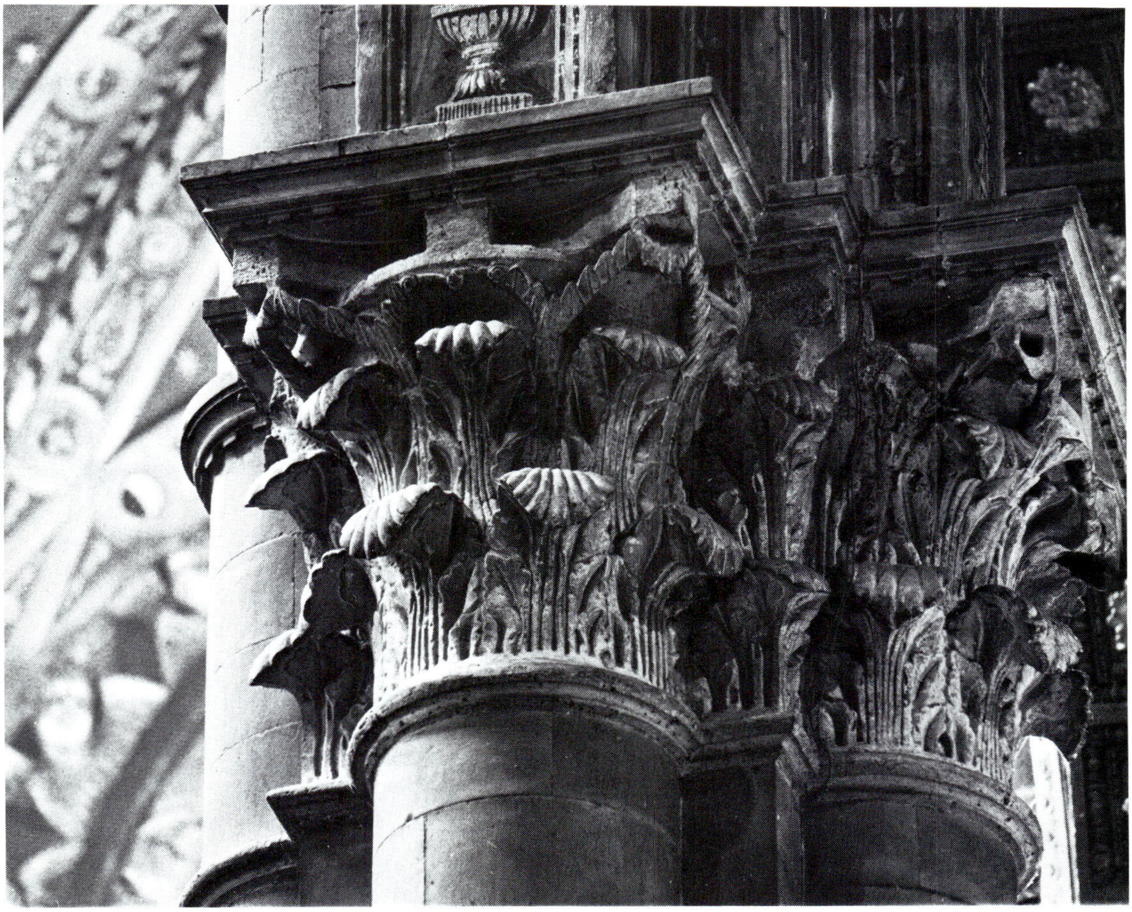

17 Siena, Cathedral. Thirteenth-century capital on the south side of the first choir bay.

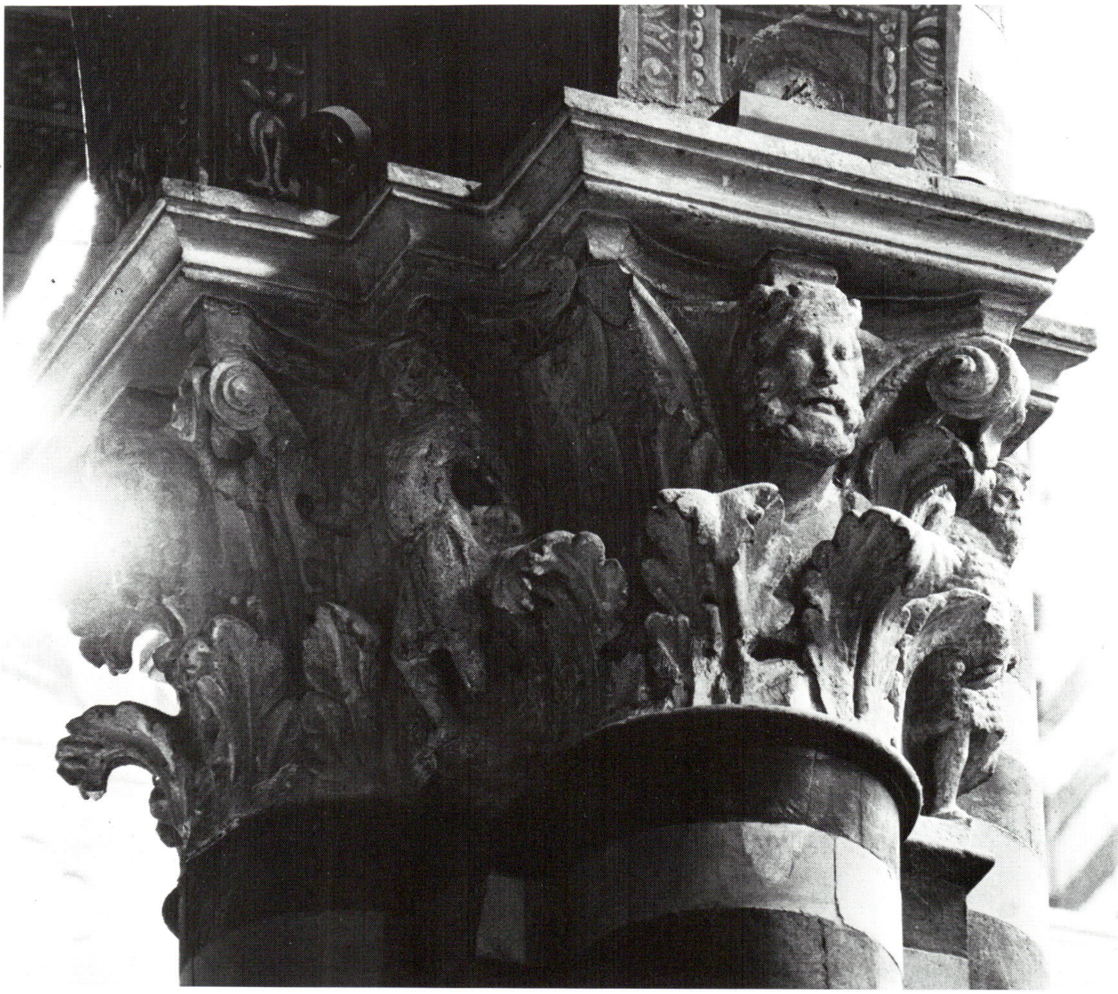

18 Siena, Cathedral. Thirteenth-century capital of one of the arcades on the south side of the nave.

2
THE ARRANGEMENT OF THE CHOIR BEFORE 1215

The most valuable source for the reconstruction of the layout and liturgical function of the choir of Siena cathedral is an extensive collection of procedural directives which was compiled at the beginning of the thirteenth century.* This *Ordo officiorum ecclesiae Senensis* (referred to below as the *Ordo*) contains precise and detailed guidelines for the performance of divine office, the celebration of the mass, the procedures to be followed on feast days, the order of precedence for processions, and so on. A detailed ordinal of this kind clearly did not originate overnight, but was probably a compilation of earlier, uncodified rules. Many of those procedures would therefore have been used in the twelfth century, and it is this which makes the *Ordo* such a valuable source of information on the history of the cathedral which preceded the present Duomo. Strangely enough, though, previous researchers have paid very little attention to this *Ordo*.[73]

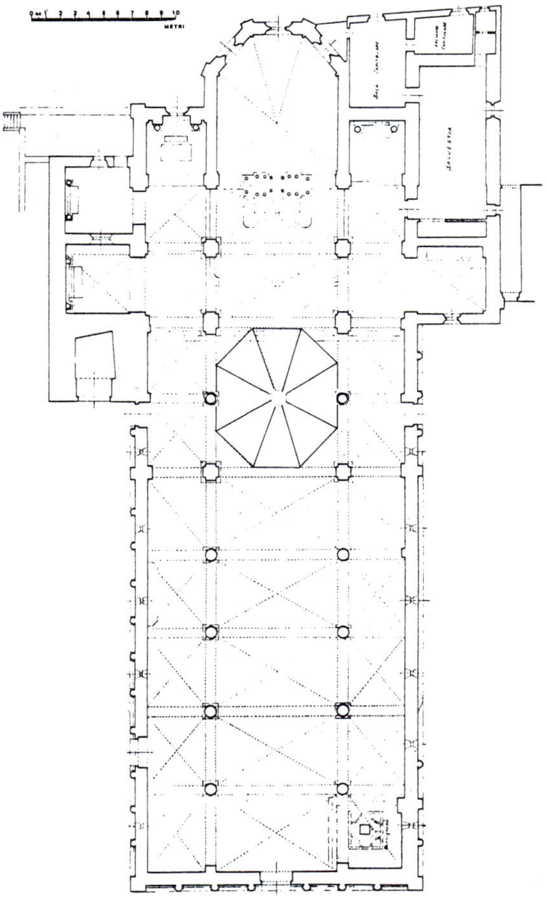

Diag. 9 Massa Marittima, Cathedral. Plan.

What does the *Ordo* tell us about the crypt, which was also to play such an important role in the thirteenth-century cathedral (diag. 11)? Odericus speaks of it in a chapter devoted to the preparation of the altars early on Easter morning. It is entitled: 'On the blessing of the new fire, the procession with the fire, and the blessing of the Paschal candle.'

'Around the third hour the altars are dressed and adorned with the ceremonial cloths. At the ninth hour the sacristan descends to the altar of St Crescentius in the crypt and ignites the fire, which has been newly struck from crystal or flint and kindled with dry wood to prevent it smoking. Then, when all the clergy of the city have arrived, the bishop and the clergy proceed to the crypt.'[74] The word used for the crypt is 'confessio', but this is identified almost immediately as the 'Altare Beati Crescentii', so in other words a 'confessio' was the tomb of a saint with an altar.[75] In the chapter on burials the word 'exedrae' is used to refer to the crypt: 'Bishops are by custom buried in the church, while priests are buried in the church or in the elevated choir of the church.'[76] Middeldorf-Kosegarten gave the church an apse on the basis of this reference to 'exedrae',[77] but as I have already argued it is unlikely that the church ever had one. 'Exedra' can also mean 'elevated choir', and that is undoubtedly what is meant here.[78] The terms 'intra Ecclesiam' and 'in Ecclesia' are explained in a passage on the feast of the Assumption: '...the lord bishop and the canons, singing the responsory polyphonically with the other clergy, proceed to the tomb of bishops through the centre of the church. Upon their arrival they form a choir, and after the Responsory the bishop or the arch-priest censes the tomb...'.[79] It can be deduced from this that the bishops were buried in the middle of the church, probably near the crossing. Priests, on the other hand, could also be buried in the 'elevated choir'. In other words, they were buried beneath the elevation of the choir, and in this context this can only refer to the crypt.

We know from various other passages that the choir above the crypt was four steps higher than the floor of the nave. In the description of the liturgy for Christmas night we find the sentence: 'The cantor, with three brothers, then commence the Invitatory with the greatest solemnity, standing at the top of the four steps...'[80] There is a similar direction for the Easter service: '...the cantor with three brothers,

*This manuscript, written in 1215 by canon Odericus, will be discussed at length in my dissertation *Architecture and liturgy: the development of Siena cathedral during the middle ages.*

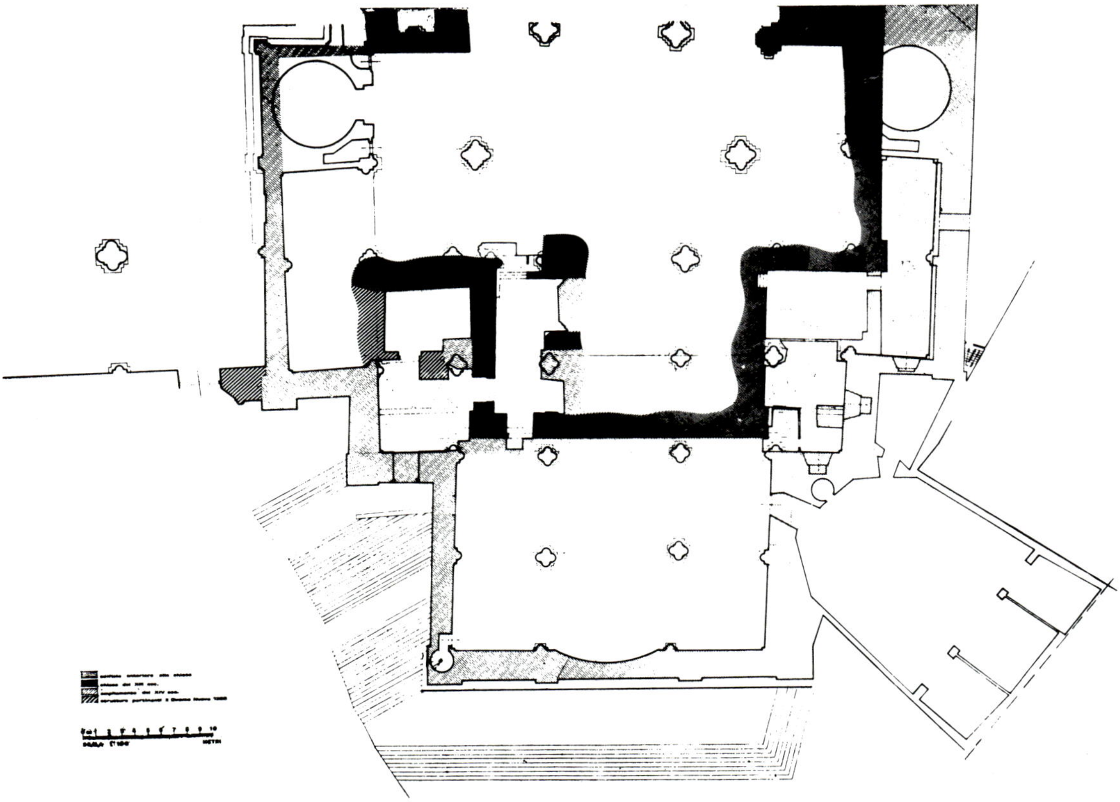

Diag. 10 Siena, Cathedral. Plan of the surviving area of the crypt.

wearing copes, then immediately mount the fourth step before the altar of the Virgin...' (diag. 12).[81] This also pinpoints the position of the high altar, which had long been dedicated to the Virgin Assumptive.[82] Carli follows Lusini in regarding this difference in height as the reason why Odericus uses the words 'superius' and 'inferius' when referring to the altars. Carli interprets 'altaria superius' as altars in the choir, and 'altaria inferius' as altars in the nave.[83] Pietromellara's explanation, however, is more persuasive. She regards these terms as distinguishing between the altars in the choir and those in the crypt.[84]

At the beginning of the *Ordo* we find the following sentence: 'The priest shall sprinkle the altars above and below with holy water, whereupon he is to return to the choir.'[85] This is explained a little further on in the chapter on the removal of the altar-cloths. 'When the day finally draws to a close and night falls it is our custom to strip the altars in our church... . Two brothers first go below to the altar of St Bartholomew... and one of the brothers has a vessel with burning incense... and after they have censed throughout they immediately remove the cloths from the altar... . They then proceed to the other altar.'[86] 'They follow the same procedure with the other altars, until all the altars above and below have been stripped, and they are left bare until Holy Saturday.'[87] Here we find the church structure ('superius') clearly distinguished from the crypt ('inferius'), which contained the altars of Sts Bartholomew, Crescentius, Fabian and Sebastian. However, the sequence of altars above and below could also be reversed. Under the heading 'The manner in which services are to commence on feast days, and the time when this is customarily done in our church', Odericus writes: 'But when the lord bishop commences the service he customarily censes the upper altars at Vespers and Matins, while the priest, who is vested in a cope and assists the bishop, censes the other altars, which are down below... . But at high mass, once the priest has ignited the incense, the thurible is passed to a deacon, who censes the altar up above before giving the thurible to the subdeacon, who goes down below and censes the altars and the clergy in the choir.[88] The sequence to be followed clearly depended on the liturgical occasion.

In the passage just quoted 'altare superius' was undoubtedly the high altar, while the preceding 'altaria superioria' could refer to yet another altar in the chancel. We find the same distinction a little further on, when the learned canon writes in an addendum entitled: 'On the reverences to be made by the bishop when he begins the services on feast days: '...but then the arch-priest or the priest reads a chapter, and the bishop censes the upper altars, and the priest censes the others, which are below...'[89]

As we have seen, the high altar stood on a raised platform which was four steps above the vaulting of the crypt, and this was also the location of the bishop's throne: '...proceeding in pairs they return with the lord bishop to the choir and they go with him as far as the bishop's chair set up above, and there, before the altar of the Blessed Virgin Mary...'.[90] The throne evidently stood beside the altar, whose position can be pinpointed more precisely from other passages in the *Ordo*. In the chapter entitled 'On the office of the Holy Cross, which takes place after prayers on Friday' we read: '...two brothers, standing in the middle of the choir, sing the Hagios and the Sanctus..., but the others, who are in the choir-stalls above, kneel... . Finally, those who bear the Cross in front of the altar, are to move forward...'.[91] The canons sat in the choir-stalls ('sunt ad sedes') and were at a higher level ('et superius'), in other words they were in the raised choir above the crypt. The two cantors stood at the bottom of the steps, but they were still 'in medio Chori', which means that they were still beyond the arch of triumph. In view of the fact that a clear distinction is made between them and the canons in the choir-stalls the word 'chorus' cannot possibly refer to the stalls. Odericus must have been treating the choir area as a spatial unit. All this points to the steps being in the first choir bay. Above them, as we have seen, stood the high altar, with the bishop's throne close by. The altar must have been set back at least halfway into the first bay if there was to be enough room to move around it.

Odericus has the following to say about preparations for high mass: '...they [the priests] don the sacred vestments in the sacristy, namely behind the altar of the Blessed Virgin, and while they are vesting they say Terce. Similarly, Terce is then sung solemnly in the choir'.[92] This makes it clear that the space behind the altar must have been enclosed, and this is confirmed in a subsequent passage on the high mass: '...they [the canons] enter the church and proceed to their seats in the choir'.[93] This is an explicit reference to the choir-stalls. A further indication that the choir was enclosed is found at the end of the order of service for Easter, after the clergy have walked in procession through the church at Vespers and have returned to the choir: 'When the brothers arrive at the cancello at the entrance to the choir the antiphon is to be recited there, outside the choir...'.[94] We also

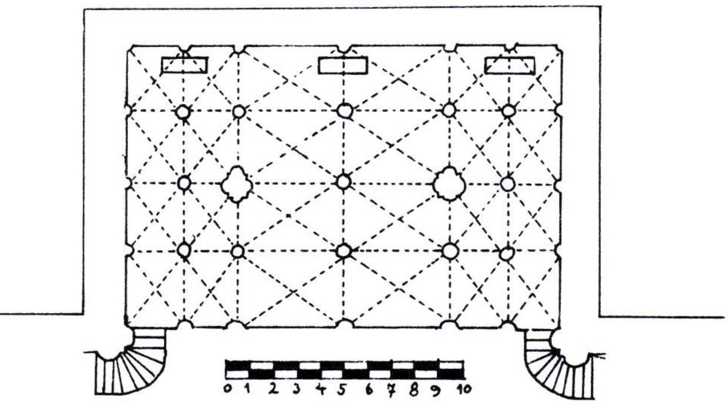

Diag. 11 Reconstruction of the crypt. Plan.

find the space behind the altar being used as a sacristy in the description of the great Easter procession. 'The arch-priest, the deacon and the subdeacon don the sacred vestments behind the altar of the Blessed Virgin Mary, namely in the sacristy, and then leave the choir singing with the clergy, who are gathered there as described earlier.'[95] It can be deduced from this that the celebrants vested within the confines of the choir-stalls, behind the altar of the Virgin. This tells us that the church was divided clearly into two parts. The choir area was reserved for the clergy, while the nave and the transept were for the laity. The high altar of the Virgin stood on the border between the two.[96]

We learn a little more about the arrangement of the choir-stalls behind the altar from the addendum quoted above: 'On the reverences to be made by the bishop'. In a passage dealing with the kiss of peace Odericus writes: 'Similarly, after the Agnus Dei, they [the celebrants] give the kiss of peace to the bishop one by one... and then the subdeacon enters the choir and gives the kiss of peace to the chief person on the one side, namely the provost, and likewise to the chief person on the other side, namely the archdeacon... and it should be stated that he [the subdeacon] receives the kiss of peace each Sunday after the Agnus Dei from the priest who sings the mass and, bringing it to the choir, gives it first to the provost or to the arch-priest, and on the other side to the archdeacon. He then brings the kiss of peace outside, to the congregation, giving it first on the one side to the chief magistrate or to one of the dignitaries, and likewise on the other side, but on all other days he gives the kiss of peace only to the clergy in the choir, as described'.[97] The kiss of peace was thus given first to the bishop, after which the subdeacon went to the choir, or rather to the choir-stalls (which confirms that there was a special place for the bishop's throne by the altar), in order to give the kiss to the most senior members of the clergy sitting on either side of the altar. He then brought the kiss of peace 'extra

Populo', in other words he left the choir and approached the congregation in the nave, who were represented by the civic dignitaries.

A close comparison of the above passages (which enabled us to deduce the position of the high altar) with a number of other sentences leads one to believe that there was a second altar in the choir and that it was situated behind the area occupied by the canons. We find the following words in the description of the morning office for Ascension Day: '...they are to begin the hymn at the same place in the choir, before the altar.'[98] Since the complete passage deals solely with prayers in the choir, which were recited by the clergy alone, Odericus would have been using 'choro' in the sense of the space used by the canons, i.e. where their stalls stood. The point is that those choir-stalls were *behind* the high altar. We find a comparable quotation in a section dealing with the duties of the cantor: '...the officiating cantor... proceeding to the centre of the choir in front of the altar... . Similarly, at mass he begins the service in the choir'.[99] A remark at the beginning of Odericus's massive work, on the subject of the ordering of the morning office, appears at first sight to contradict the above two quotations: '...that the cantor and two brothers customarily commence the first Responsory in unison behind the altar of the Blessed Virgin Mary'.[100] Here, in other words, the cantor is placed behind the high altar, where the choir-stalls stood. Later on there is an almost identical passage in the section dealing with Lauds on Friday: 'The cantor goes with the brothers behind the altar of the Blessed Virgin... they commence the Kyrie, singing in polyphony'.[101] The only way to explain all these confusing references to 'in front of' and 'behind' is to assume the presence of a second altar at the other end of the choir-stalls, i.e. behind the high altar and in front of the second altar. That second altar was very probably used for the canons' conventual masses, but it may also have been the cathedral's altar of the Blessed Sacrament. The doctrine of transubstantiation received official approval at the fourth Lateran Council in 1215, which legitimated the notion that the host was not just the symbol of Christ crucified but that in some mysterious way it was turned into his true body by the ritual of consecration.[102] The host therefore had to be kept in a setting which matched its importance, and this was provided by the altar of the Blessed Sacrament.[103] This also makes it clear why Odericus constantly refers to the high altar as 'Altare Beatae Virginis Mariae', and why, when he speaks of what I believe was this second altar, he simply used the word 'altare'. Originally an altar of the sacrament had no title in the usual sense of the word. One apparent problem is raised by a passage in the directions on the singing during the office for Christmas night: '...thus one part [of divine office] must be said behind the altar, and the other part in the choir'.[104] If 'altare' is being used here for the high altar the passage becomes, tautological. Presumably, then, on this

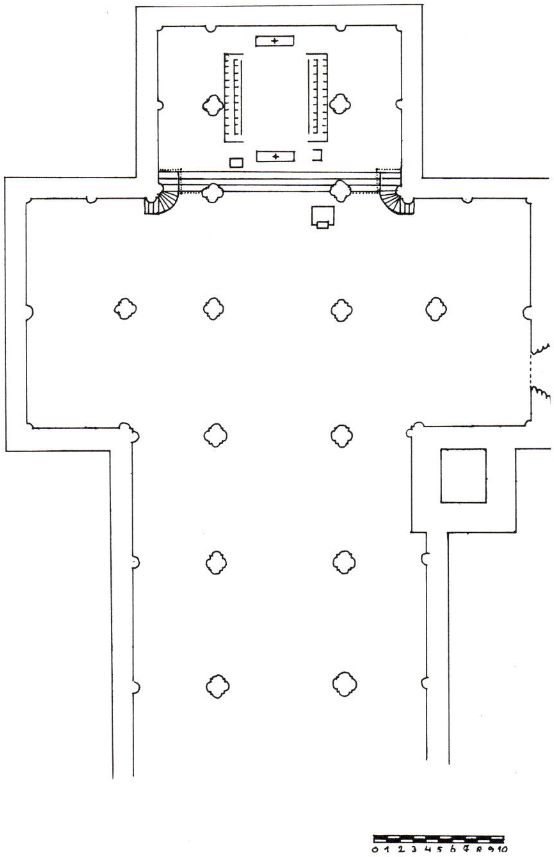

Diag. 12 Reconstruction of the twelfth-century choir and its furnishings.

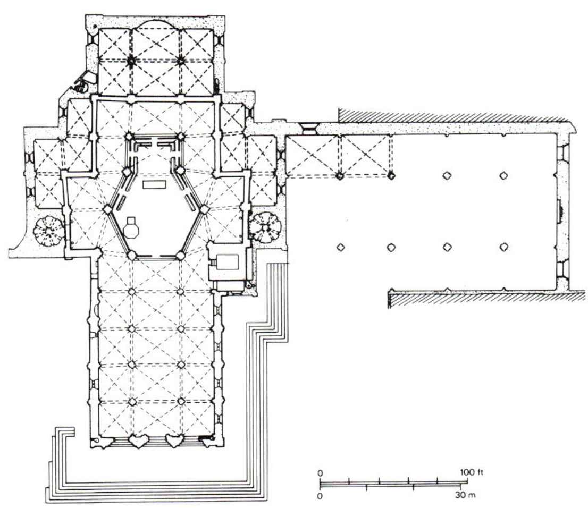

Diag. 13 White's reconstruction of the thirteenth-century choir and its furnishings.

very special occasion in the church year, part of the liturgy was recited right at the very back of the church, behind the altar in the canons' part of the choir, in other words behind the altar at the rear of the choir which was used for the canons' conventual mass.

It can also be deduced from the *Ordo* that there were two pulpits at the front of the choir. Odericus makes a distinction between the 'great pulpit' ('majus pulpitum') and the 'wooden pulpit' ('ligneum pulpitum'), which suggests that the great pulpit was made of stone.[105] 'During this most solemn ceremony all readings are given from the great pulpit', as we read in the description of the third office of the night ('De Mysterio Tertii Nocturni').[106] In a section dealing with the procession through the church in the early morning we read '...and standing there before the altar he [the deacon] has the book in front of him on the wooden pulpit, where the gospel is usually read'.[107] The following phrase is found in the directions for the service on Easter night: '...and the readings take place at the great pulpit'.[108] The phrase 'at the great pulpit' is also found in connection with morning prayers on Ascension Day.[109] There are also two passages which tell us something about the position of these pulpits. The first comes in the chapter 'Qualiter in Senensi Ecclesia Scrutinia fiant', referring to the examination of the faith of a candidate for holy office.[110] The sentence reads: 'After the prayer two priests ascend the pulpits, one on the right and the other on the left'.[111] We must imagine these pulpits as forms of ambo at the front of the choir, one on the left side and the other on the right, as was customary.[112] We must also assume that the large stone pulpit was further forward than its wooden counterpart, for we read the following in the directions for the Sundays between Septuagesima and Easter. 'On Sundays they [the priests] do not ascend the ceremonial pulpit [i.e. the stone pulpit] but read from beside the altar, and the wooden pulpit there is always covered with a white cloth for the reading of the gospel.'[113] The wooden pulpit therefore stood at the top of the steps leading to the altar, while the monumental pulpit probably stood below the steps but was raised on pillars, as we can still see from Nicola Pisano's pulpit. It appears from this passage and from the section on the morning procession that the wooden lectern stood on the gospel side, on the left of the altar as seen from the nave. This was unusual in that the gospel pulpit was generally the more monumental of a pair of ambones.[114] Nevertheless, it is clear from the above excerpts that the different uses of the two pulpits were not determined by the kind of reading (gospel or epistle) but by the degree of solemnity of the day in question. The marble pulpit was not even used on Sundays, but only on major festivals.

The above information gives us the following picture. The high altar stood at the entrance to the choir at the top of the four steps leading down to the nave. Behind the high altar, and on either side of it, were two rows of choir-stalls facing each other in the central aisle of the choir. At the far end of the choir-stalls stood the altar of the Blessed Sacrament, and there was a certain amount of room between that altar and the rear wall of the choir. At some distance from the high altar were, on the left (seen from the nave) a simple wooden pulpit for the reading of the gospel, and on the right a more monumental stone pulpit for the epistle. The bishop's throne was also on the right, approximately opposite the high altar.

3
THE ARRANGEMENT OF THE THIRTEENTH-CENTURY CATHEDRAL

It was towards the end of the 1250s, when work on the new church was nearing completion, that new choir-stalls were ordered. The earliest receipt dates from 29th September 1259.[115] The order could only have been placed shortly before, for on 16th November of that year the Gran Consiglio passed a resolution on the arrangement of the choir-stalls.[116] The furnishing of the new choir evidently caused a number of difficulties, for twelve days later the question was again the subject of a lengthy discussion, this time at a meeting of the Nine. The minutes of that meeting tell us 'that the altar of the Blessed Virgin and the choir of this cathedral must be built beneath the great dome with steps on all sides so that the people can ascend to the choir and altar of the said church'.[117] Middeldorf-Kosegarten used this passage as a basis for reconstructing the dome space as part of the priests' choir, which extended into the first bay of the choir.[118] White recently came to the same conclusion (diag. 13). He believes that the floor of the hexagon and of the first bay of the central choir aisle were raised and surrounded by a balustrade. He places Nicola Pisano's pulpit on the north side, and locates the altar just in front of the triumphal arch between dome and choir. He arranges the canons' stalls in such a way that some are behind the altar, while others extend forwards in two wings along two sides of the hexagon.[119] He also proposes a processional route past the altar, despite the fact that it would have been obstructed by the stalls which he

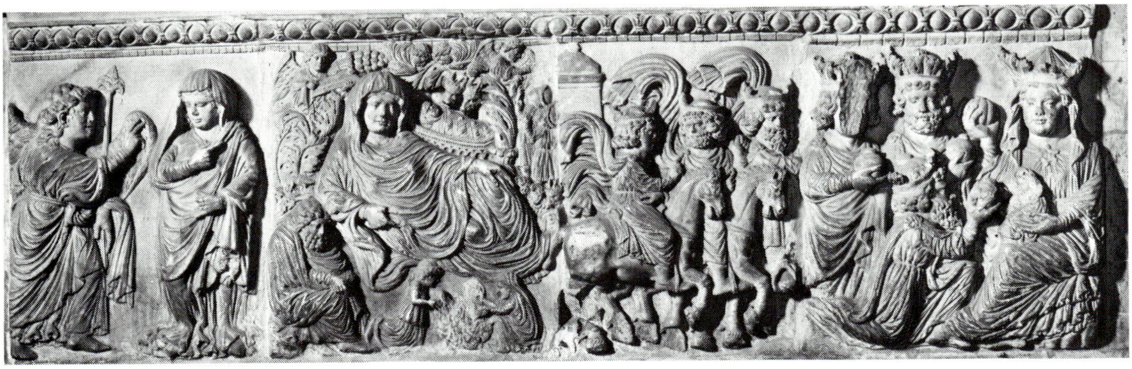

19 Four reliefs. From left to right: the *Annunciation*, the *Nativity*, the *Magi travelling to Bethlehem*, and the *Adoration of the Magi*. Probably from the pulpit in Ponte allo Spino (Sovicille). Siena, Museo dell'Opera del Duomo. (The photograph was taken before the reliefs were transferred from the cathedral to the museum.)

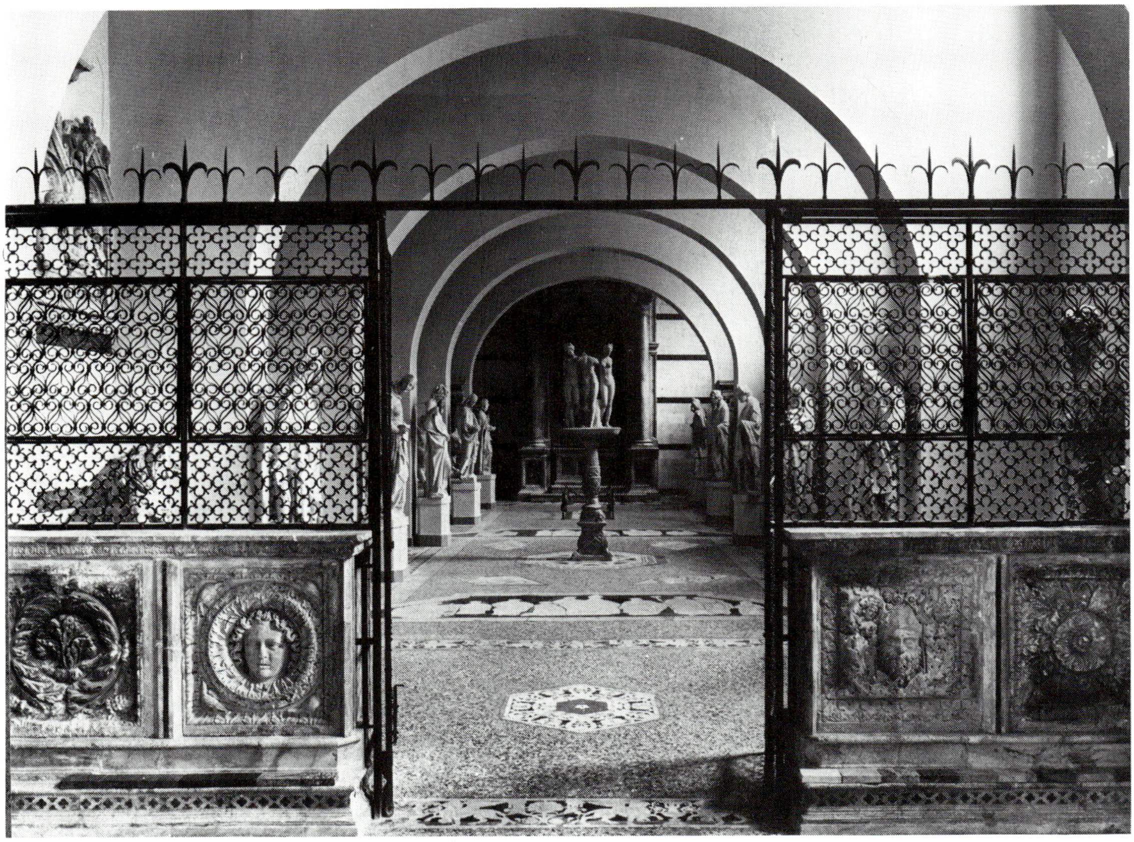

20 Remains of the thirteenth-century choir cancello. The fifteenth-century wrought-iron screen came from the Ospedale di Santa Maria della Scala. Siena, Museo dell'Opera del Duomo.

has allowed to extend a long way in front of the altar.[120] He explains the iconographic difference between the front and rear faces of Duccio's altarpiece in terms of their function. The Virgin, as the patroness of the city, faced the nave and the laity, while the canons in their stalls saw the Passion scenes on the reverse.[121] The trouble is that White's own reconstruction nullifies this explanation, since he places the clergy partly in front of and partly behind the altar. Moreover, how would the canons have been able to perform divine office properly if they were split into two separate groups by such a high altarpiece as the *Maestà*? Anyway, divine office generally took place around a single, large choir lectern.

A close reading of the minutes of the meeting of the Nine on 28th November 1259 shows that both authors have failed to appreciate the nature of this document. It is not a resolution but a record of two points of view within the city government. As far as we know no document recording a final resolution has been preserved in the Siena archives, but even without it we believe that the centralising reconstruction which White and Middeldorf-Kosegarten have derived from the minutes of the meeting is quite untenable.

The major rebuilding programme of the thirteenth century had little effect on the spatial organisation of the church (diag. 14). It is true that the choir bays were enlarged, but otherwise the presbytery remained as it had been: a tripartite space two bays deep. The difference in floor levels between choir and nave remained the same because the crypt was retained. The most obvious assumption, then, is that there was equally little change in the layout of the choir, and that the liturgy in the new cathedral continued in accordance with the *Ordo officiorum*, which was barely fifty years old when the new building was completed.

The Gran Consiglio's resolution of 16th November 1259 directed that two entrances were to be preserved when the choir was laid out: '...provided the entrances on the side of Guido Trajani's house and on the side of the "ponte" are not closed'.[122] The latter would have been the rear door to the crypt which gave onto the steep slope behind the choir. 'Ponte' therefore means a sort of staircase to compensate for the difference in levels.[123] This tells us that the council was anxious about the accessibility of the choir area. As already noted, the subject of the choir-stalls came up again during a meeting of the Nine, shortly after it had been discussed in the Gran Consiglio. Opinions were clearly divided. One group felt 'that the altar of the Blessed Virgin and the choir of the aforesaid cathedral and all pertaining to the choir must be built and completed as planned by the

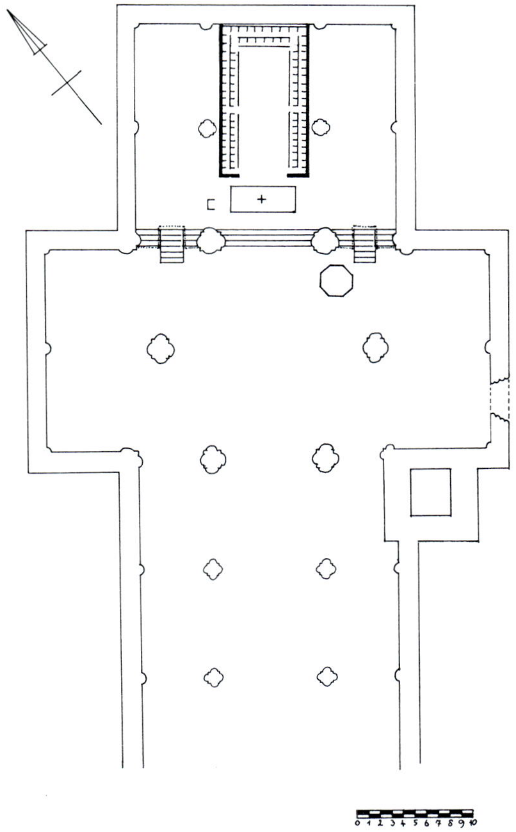

Diag. 14 Reconstruction of the thirteenth-century choir and its furnishings.

lords canons of this cathedral and by the directors of the Opera del Duomo, but with the proviso that a certain door at the rear of the said cathedral, namely the one that is now open, must remain open, and that a wall must be built in the church beside this entrance to protect it and to safeguard ingress and egress to and from the said cathedral through that entrance, and also in order to hold the ground leading to the choir of the said cathedral, so that it [the soil] should not slip away or obstruct access to the said entrance'. However, there were other council members who believed '...that the entire church should be lowered and that the earth should be excavated down to the level of the cathedral square; also that the main entrance to the cathedral, which is at the rear and is presently closed, should be opened and made more serviceable, so that people may enter and leave the aforesaid cathedral easily'.[124] This is followed by the passage quoted above on the altar of the Blessed Virgin, which was to be built beneath the dome.

The first part of this document is a lengthy recapitulation of the resolution of 16th November 1259.

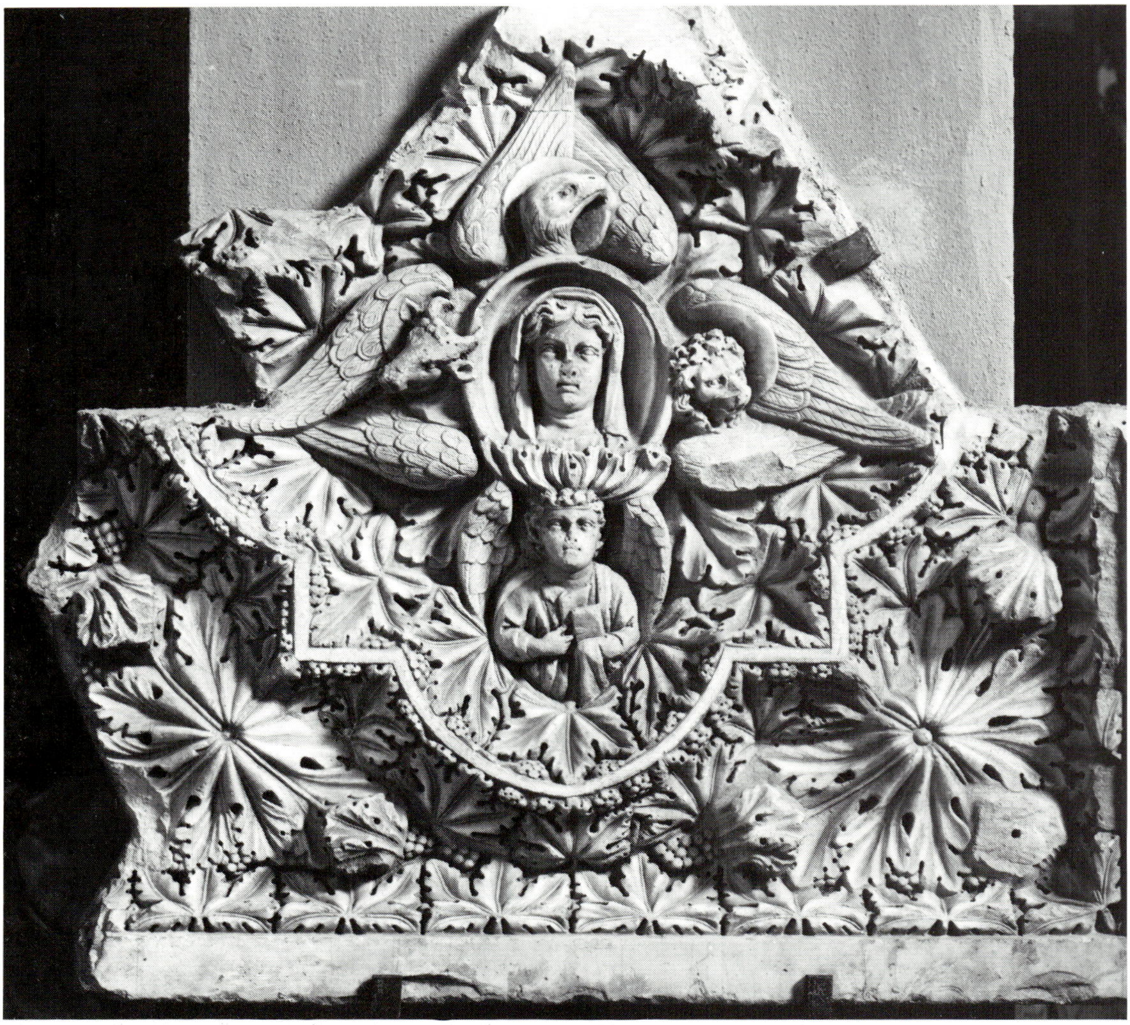

21 Fragment of the thirteenth-century high altar with the personification of Ecclesia surrounded by the symbols of the four evangelists. Siena, Museo dell'Opera del Duomo.

The point at issue was the retention of the rear entrance to the crypt. Now that there was a new, more spacious choir, it was necessary to take special measures to keep the entrance open, particularly in view of the steep escarpment falling away at the back of the site. This is why 'a wall' had to be built 'beside this entrance'. The object, evidently, was not just to protect the entrance, but also to prevent a landslip beneath the choir. The 'murus', then, would not have been a straightforward wall, but a more extensive structure in the form of a retaining wall to hold the soil in position.[125]

The second part of this document of 28th November 1259 opens with a discussion of an entrance which was also at the back of the church. However, it cannot possibly be the same entrance as that referred to in the first extract, for it is specifically stated that it 'is presently closed'. However, we can deduce from what follows that this entrance must have provided access to the main body of the church (ill. 6). There was indeed a door in the south front, the Porta del Perdono, which was enlarged in 1260.[126] This is probably the entrance which the Nine were referring to, for as the document suggests, there was a busy route to and from the church on the Campo side, which is where the Porta del Perdono lay.[127] The key statement as far as Middeldorf-Kosegarten and White are concerned comes at the end of the minutes, when a minority of the Nine recommend erecting the altar and choir-stalls 'beneath the great dome'.[128] The question, though, is whether the authors are right to take this at face value. Given the other remarks in the document on the movement of people through the church it would have been highly impractical to clutter up the space beneath the dome. It is true that many people entered the church from the side, but that does not change the fact that the main axis of the church, both physically and liturgically, runs from the nave to the choir. Seen from the nave the altar would certainly appear to be 'suptus metam', even if it stood halfway back in the first bay of the choir. Behind it, to the left and right, were the choir-stalls.[129] The stipulation about the steps on all sides ('quod fiant gradi ad ipsum corum ex omnibus partibus') is not necessarily contradictory, for it is perfectly conceivable that the choir-stalls were elevated slightly above the floor of the choir, as they still are in Siena cathedral and in many other churches. It seems from the subsequent building history of the cathedral that the idea of erecting the choir-stalls and the altar beneath the dome was dropped. It would certainly have had major repercussions for the building for, so the proposal ran, the entire church was to be lowered, with the ground being excavated down to the level of the cathedral square ('quod tota ecclesia debassaretur et fodere debeat ad modum platee episcopatus'). That, in turn, would inevitably have led to the demolition of the crypt, but as we have seen that did not happen until the fourteenth century.[130] A centralising canons' choir clustered around an altar beneath the dome would have been a most unusual development. The choir-stalls had always been in the customary position behind the altar, and that is where they remained in future, in two groups facing each other.[131] Moreover, we have a document of 2nd July 1368 which deals with the construction of new choir-stalls. It contains the following reference to the previous seating arrangement: '...that the stalls are to be built in a straight line, as in the former choir'.[132] This virtually rules out everything but the original rectangular layout.

The choir-stalls of 1260 were very probably surrounded by a stone cancello (ill. 20). In the nineteenth century a series of reliefs were discovered which are now in the cathedral museum.[133] Their design suggests that they came from the circle of Nicola Pisano. There are two similar reliefs in the Victoria and Albert Museum in London. Although there is no supporting documentary evidence there is every reason to accept Carli's hypothesis that these reliefs are the remnants of the surrounds of the choir-stalls. The dating to the third quarter of the thirteenth century, with the documents of 1259-60 as the *terminus post quem*, also accords with this theory.[134]

How did the altar itself appear in this period? Another fragment of sculpture in the cathedral museum was found beneath the choir floor in 1870 (ill. 21). In the centre of a quatrefoil, surrounded by the symbols of the four evangelists, is the bust of a woman with her head covered. The style and treatment point clearly to the influence of classical sculpture, and this fragment can also be attributed to the circle of Nicola Pisano. Carli assumes that the female figure symbolises the church, and Pope-Hennessy agrees. Carli believes that it could be a fragment of the high altar, and given the symbolism employed there can be little argument with this theory.[135] We can deduce the approximate width of the altar from that of Duccio's *Maestà*, which measures 420 centimetres without the supporting structures on either side.[136] Duccio's painting was placed on the high altar in 1311, before the major building programme which started in 1317. This means that it was placed on the altar of 1260. The documents dealing with the altarpiece contain not a word which would suggest that there was any intention of building a new altar.[137] It was not until 1375, when the extended choir was furnished, that a new altar was erected.[138]

Nor is there any indication around 1260 that there was still a second altar in the choir, whose presence in the church of Odericus's day we had deduced from his *Ordo*. On those grounds alone there is every reason to assume that the stone high altar was so deep that it could be used from both the front and the back.[139] Moreover, we know that in the thirteenth century there was a permanent place on the high altar for a pyx containing the host, which strengthens our belief that the high altar now became the sacrament altar as well.[140] This would mean that the two altars which we believe to have existed in the early years of the century had been combined into a single, large high altar by 1260. The old ambones also disappeared in the internal reorganisation. The large stone pulpit on the epistle side mentioned by Odericus was replaced by Nicola Pisano's richly ornamented marble pulpit.[141] We can assume that the sermon was given from a simple wooden pulpit, as had been the case in the early thirteenth-century church.

If we use the above facts and hypotheses to reconstruct a picture of the church we find that, after 1260, there was a completely renewed choir which nevertheless followed the broad lines of the previous layout. A large, stone high altar stood at the top of the steps to the choir. Behind it, to the left and right, were the choir-stalls within stone cancelli. In all probability the second altar, which we have cast as the altar of the Blessed Sacrament, was moved to the back of the high altar of the Virgin, which thus became double-sided. The new choir differed from its predecessor in being more spacious and in having ornate sculpture on the altar and the cancelli. It must have been extremely imposing, particularly after Nicola Pisano's marble pulpit had been erected on the south side of the dome in 1268. This magnificence

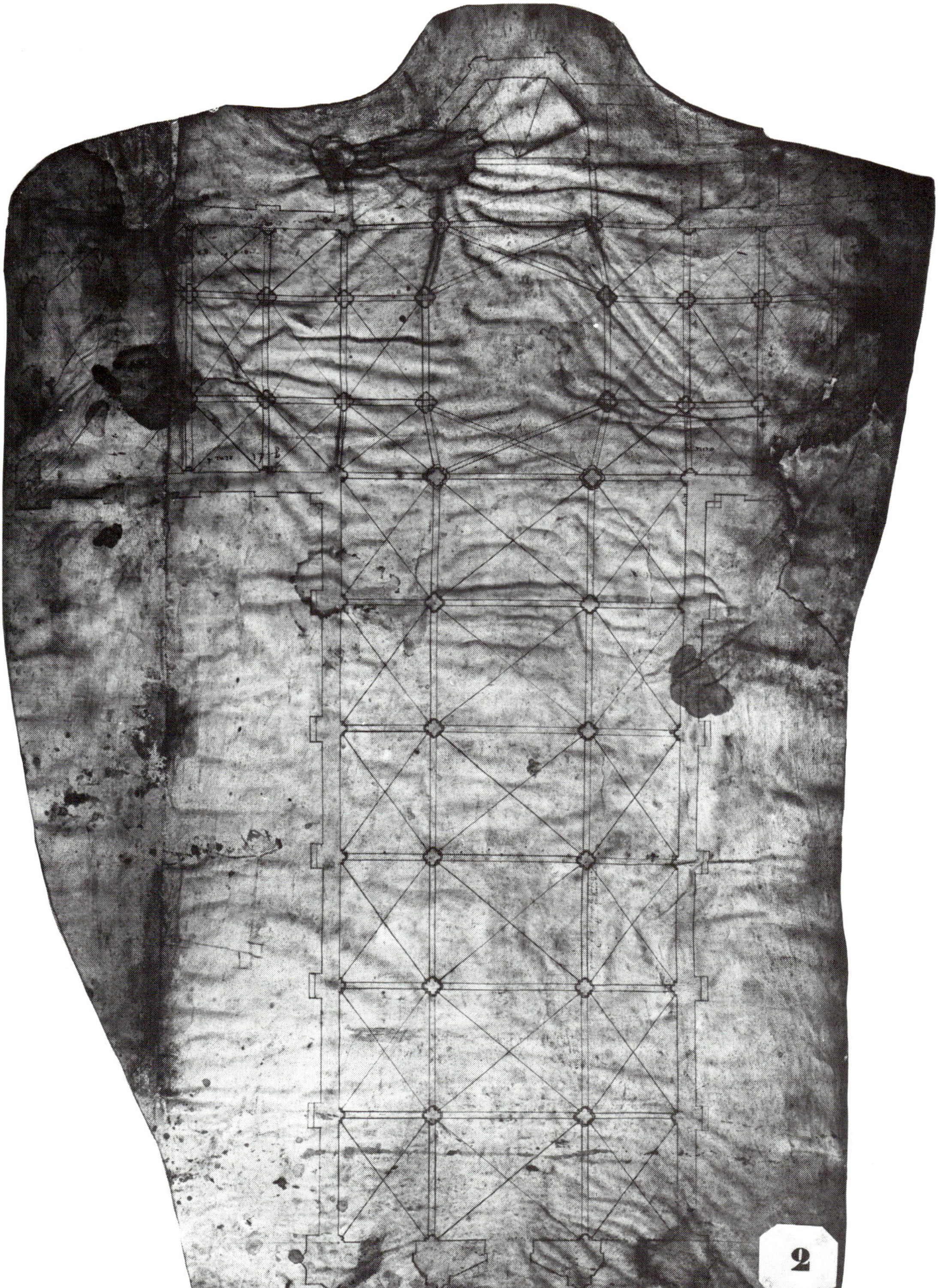

22 Ground plan of the Duomo Nuovo with three-sided apse, 1322(?), 93 x 67 cm. Siena, Museo dell'Opera del Duomo.

was further enhanced in 1311, when the high altar was adorned with that other masterpiece, Duccio's *Maestà*. The 'Domus Dei' had acquired a 'Domus Virginis'.

4
FOURTEENTH-CENTURY PLANS FOR THE CHOIR

Siena's great victory over Florence at Montaperti in 1260 ushered in a period of unprecedented prosperity for the city. Trade and industry flourished, and farmers, safe at last from the depredations of marauding armies, could get on with their task of growing food for the thriving city. Law and order prevailed under the rule of the Nine, who now had an even firmer grasp of the reins of government. This nine-member governing council emerged from the prosperous middle classes who finally eclipsed the feudal nobility in 1287. The Nine commissioned Ambrogio Lorenzetti to illustrate their ideals of good government in frescoes which covered the walls of the council chamber of the Palazzo Pubblico.[142]

This city hall was built around 1300 in a remarkably short space of time as a sign of the new self-assurance which had infused the city.[143] The building work was entrusted to the Opera del Duomo. In Tuscany the masons' yard often acted as a sort of 'Public Works Department', being a secular rather than an ecclesiastical organisation.[144] There is no mention of any building activity in the cathedral in this period, so evidently all the architects' energies were concentrated on the new city hall. But no sooner had the Palazzo Pubblico been finished than new plans were once again being made to enlarge the church. The relevant decision was taken in 1316, and one year later work started on the two-bay extension of the choir.[145] The steepness of the escarpment falling away behind the choir meant that enormous substructures had to be built. They were so large that they could easily accomodate the baptistery, which had originally stood to the south-west of the church near the Ospedale di Santa Maria della Scala.[146]

However, it was not long before the builders began running into difficulties. According to a group of experts headed by Lorenzo Maitani, the chief architect of Orvieto cathedral, the existing vaults and the dome of the old building would be endangered, and there were also grave doubts about the foundations, as we learn from a document of 1322.[147] Nevertheless, it was decided to press ahead with work on the choir, but then another plan was put forward of truly megalomaniac proportions. Its effect would have been to reduce the existing church to the transept of a vast new cathedral. Work began on this mammoth undertaking in 1339.[148] Our knowledge of this plan does not rest solely on the written documents and the actual remains of the structure, for by a fortunate accident two ground plans for the new cathedral have survived (ills. 22, 23).[149] They must be dated between 1316 and 1339, for in 1316 the only plan was for the enlargement of the choir, and work did not start on this Duomo Nuovo until 1339. The ground plans show two variants of the church. The nave is the same in both cases: tripartite and six bays long. The bays themselves were to be large, as was customary in Italy. The rib vaults were to be supported by clustered columns, as in the existing church.

The proposed choir, for which there were two designs, is of particular interest to us here. Once again the nature of the terrain demanded extensive supports. In one ground plan there is a shallow bay between the hexagon and a three-sided apse. The transition to the transept takes the form of square side chapels. There is a similar type of choir from the end of the thirteenth century in the cathedral of Massa Marittima, which Paatz attributes reasonably convincingly to Giovanni Pisano.[150] The reason why it was stated so emphatically in 1339 that further work would have to be carried out on the choir extension which had been begun in 1317 is that in both ground plans the former choir, now the right transept, has been extended by two bays.

The dome posed an almost insuperable problem. If the building was rotated through 90° two of the supporting piers would come to lie on the main axis of the church. Those two piers are simply omitted in the design with the three-sided apse, with a remarkably audacious arrangement of intersecting arches taking their place. It is extremely doubtful whether such a structure could ever have been built with the dome in position. Only the pier in the proposed choir is shown on the second ground plan. Its counterpart at the front of the nave has been replaced by two massive intersecting arches.

In both plans the right transept is shorter than the left, and this recalls a remark in the 1322 report in which the Maitani commission stated that: '...this work [the enlargement of the choir] should not proceed because the cupola would no longer stand at the cross's centre [i.e. the centre of the cruciform plan of the church], as it should if it is to conform to the proper proportions'.[151] Strange as it may sound, this indicates that the expert commission was already turning its thoughts to a Duomo Nuovo a mere five years after work had started on the enlargement of

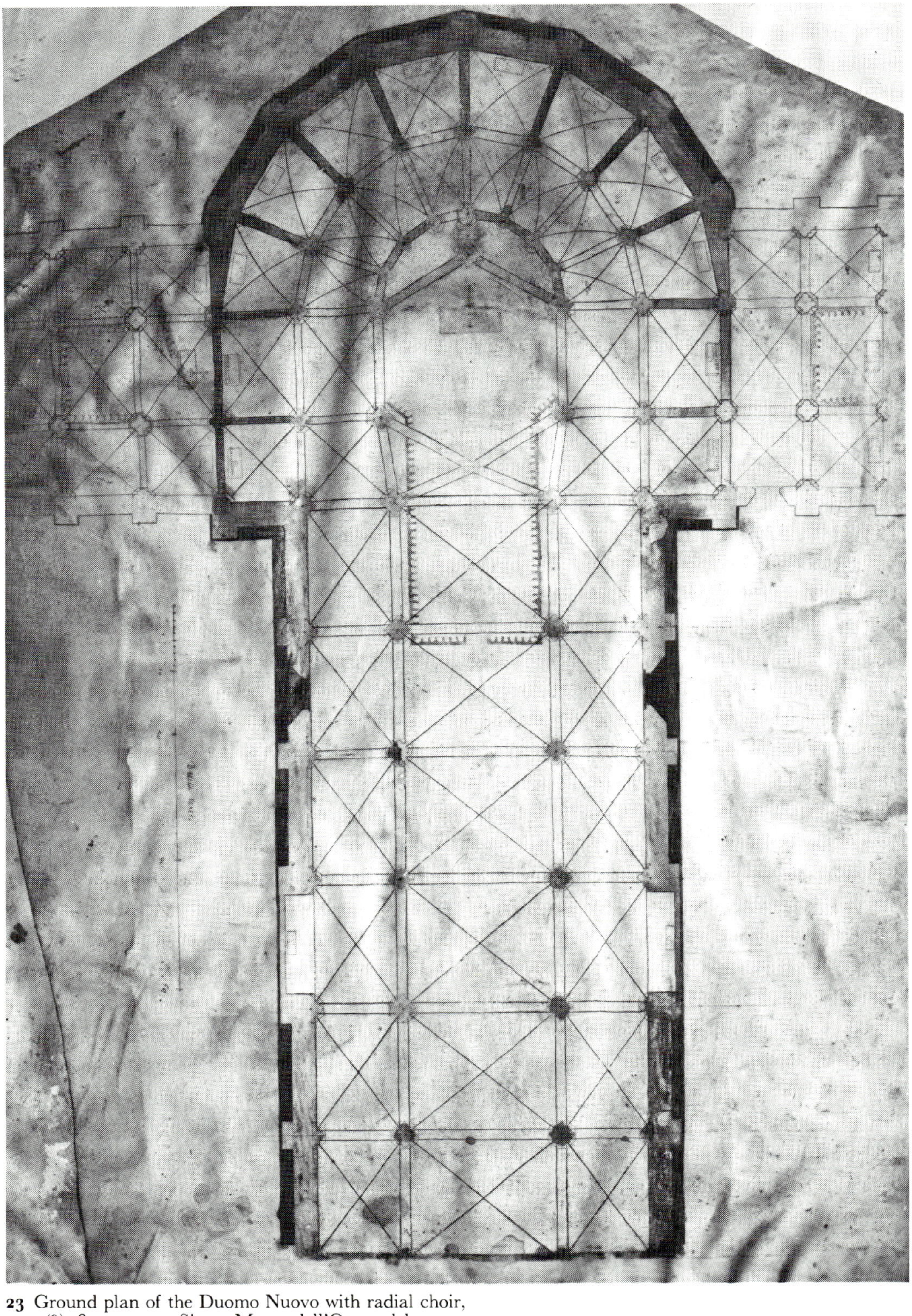

23 Ground plan of the Duomo Nuovo with radial choir, 1322(?), 80 x 54 cm. Siena, Museo dell'Opera del Duomo.

the choir. This observation has absolutely no relevance to the choir extension as such, for a choir is rarely as long as a nave. The asymmetry could only be caused by unequal transept arms, and yet the first time they appear as such is in the plans for the Duomo Nuovo. This enables us to arrive at a more precise dating for the two ground plans. The year 1316 is the *terminus post quem* for the design of the Duomo Nuovo, for it was only then that the decision was made to enlarge the choir. The document of 1322, however, definitely refers to the Duomo Nuovo, so the two ground plans must have originated at some time between those two dates. This also serves to close the interval between the choir of Massa Marittima, a town which had come under Sienese suzerainty shortly before, and the plan for the three-sided end to the choir at Siena. It is not possible to rule out the influence of Giovanni Pisano, who died in 1320, but an attribution of the design to him or even to his workshop would have to be supported by more information than is currently available. This type of choir is too widespread in this period to warrant such an identification.[152] However, it is worth remembering that Pisano had old ties with Siena, for some thirty years previously he had designed the facade of the cathedral.[153]

The second drawing shows a radial choir with self-contained radiating capels which are trapeziform in shape. This design is very similar to that of the choir of the abbey church of Clairvaux, which was dedicated in 1174, and of the choir of the abbey church in Pontigny, which dates from around 1200.[154] Both belonged to important Cistercian monasteries. It is certainly a rather unusual ground plan for central Italy, and it differs from the other design in that it appears to be based on idealistic considerations. The main body of the church has been made symmetrical (possibly as a concession to the objections of Maitani and his fellow experts) by erecting walls to close off the extremities of the choir and nave of the existing church. The former choir wing appears to have been converted into a chapel with its own entrance, which would have been cut into the side wall. There are three altars up against the end wall, with the choir-stalls grouped around the central altar. A similar arrangement of altars and choir-stalls was envisaged for the former nave. There is also a pulpit against the north wall, but as far as one can tell it does not appear to be Nicola Pisano's pulpit of 1264. The new section of the church contains many more altars than there were titles at the time. Two of these altars are set in niches in the central bay of each aisle. All the choir chapels have an altar, and the high altar is set beneath the dome in the position suggested back in 1260. A large range of choir-stalls extends from the crossing to the front of the second nave bay. This kind of arrangement of radiating chapels around the high altar, with the canons' stalls extending deep into the nave, is more typical of northern fourteenth-century churches, and is particularly common in France.[155] However, this is undoubtedly Siena cathedral, for the four altars flanking the high altar are actually labelled with the names of the city's four patron saints: Ansanus, Savinus, Crescentius and Victor of Siena.

Having arrived at this point it is necessary to recall the actual arrangement of the church which resulted from the decision of 1316. It has already been demonstrated in Section II that the floor of the choir was lowered to the level of the nave by the demolition of the crypt. This, of course, meant that there was no longer any place for the relics of the patron saints. They therefore had to be transferred to the body of the church where, not surprisingly, they were placed in four patronal altars. The cathedral inventories, which are complete from 1388, tell us that these altars were in the church itself.[156] This marks a sudden intensification of Siena's veneration of its patrons, which until then had taken place underground in the dark and enclosed space of the crypt, where there was only room for a limited number of worshippers. From now on the 'Quattro Santi Avvocati' would each have his own relic altar in the church, visible to all.

From the thirteenth century Siena had begun to attach increasing importance to its patron saints. They had first been depicted flanking the Madonna in the choir window of 1288 (van Os, fig. 65). Then, in 1311, they had occupied the same honoured position in Duccio's *Maestà*, with the difference that the widely venerated Bartholomew had had to surrender his place to the strictly local St Victor of Siena, whose tradition is distinctly hazy (although that is equally true of his three compatriots).[157] The translation of their relics from the crypt underscored their actual, physical presence in the church.

This led logically to the erection of altarpieces on the four patronal altars. The first commission, for the altar of St Ansanus, was given to Simone Martini in 1329, and it was followed by three others.[158] This altarpiece programme and the ground plan of the Duomo Nuovo with the four identified altars must therefore be seen as the logical outcome of the process whereby the city's patron saints were displaced by the closure of the crypt. As already noted, the preparations for the Duomo Nuovo were probably set in train as early as the 1320s, but it is not entirely clear why work did not start on the plan until 1339. It would not be far wide of the mark to assume that it took a considerable time to overcome doubts about the feasibility of this ambitious proposal. The objections expressed by Maitani and his colleagues in 1322

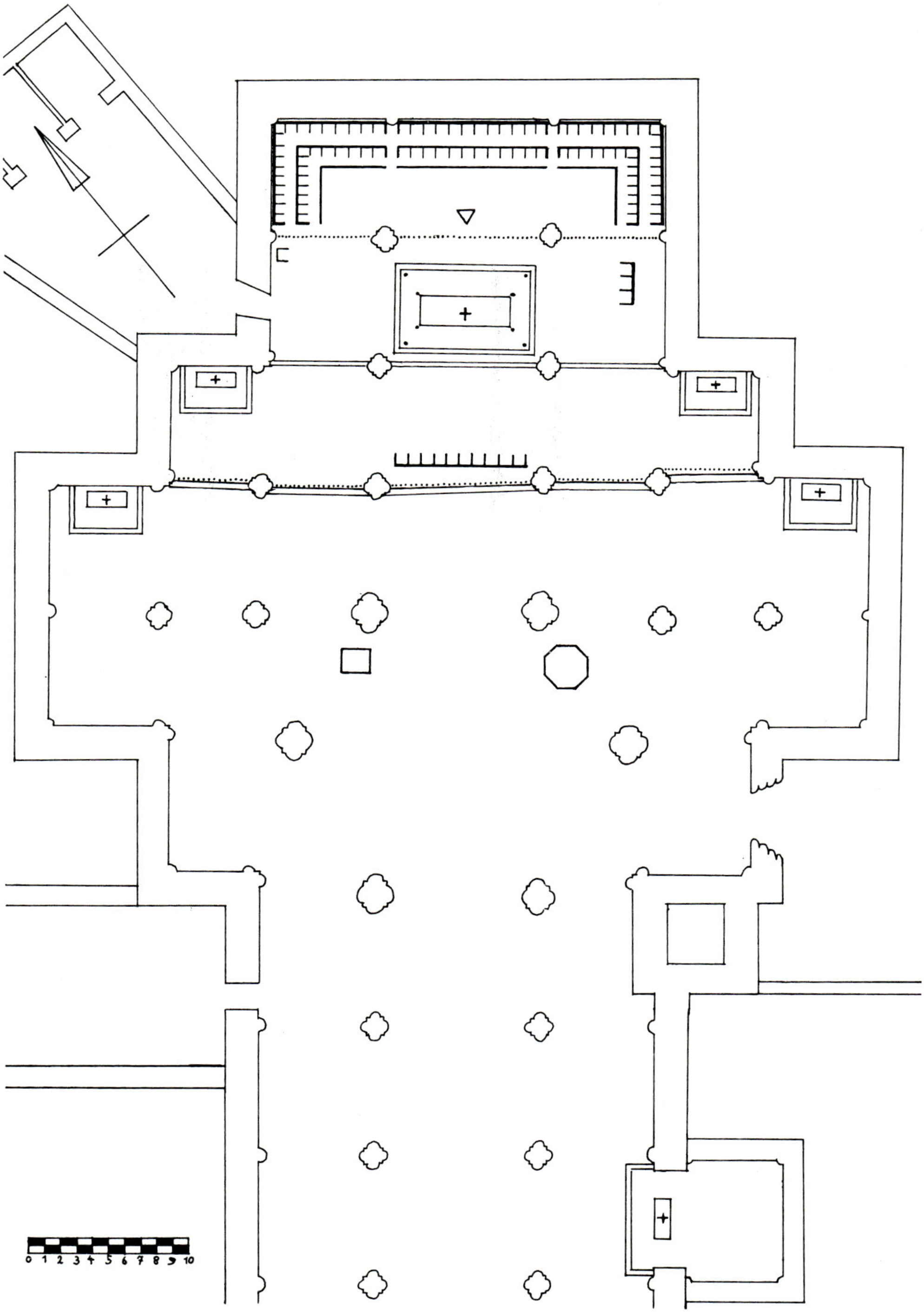

Diag. 16 Reconstruction of the fourteenth-century choir and its furnishings. To the left of the high altar are the altars of Sts Savinus and Ansanus, to the right the altars of Sts Victor of Siena and Crescentius. The plan also shows the new sacristy off the choir and the 'Cappella del Voto' in the south aisle, both of which were added in the fifteenth century.

would certainly have focussed attention on purely structural questions.

A little earlier we touched on the subject of the *Maestà*. It was intended that this huge and costly altarpiece, which had been installed on the high altar with great pomp and ceremony in 1311, only a few years before, should also adorn the high altar in the Duomo Nuovo. This is apparent from a document (which also dates from 1339, interestingly enough) concerning the manufacture of a new angel to add greater glory to the *Maestà* on the high altar.[159] In 1375, when the church was almost completed, Duccio's altarpiece was indeed placed on the new high altar.[160]

What is more important, though, is that the *Maestà* dates from the period just prior to the major rebuilding projects. It was commissioned in 1308, and in 1311 it was installed on the high altar. In other words it must be viewed in the spatial and liturgical context of the thirteenth-century cathedral, as reconstructed in Section IV. At the front of the choir, which was still raised above the nave, stood a large altar which combined two functions, that of high altar and altar of the Blessed Sacrament. The *Maestà* met that dual requirement in full. On the front, and visible down the full length of the nave, was the enthroned Madonna, the supreme protectress of the city, surrounded by a multitude of saints and angels. At the bottom are Siena's patron saints, prominently displayed. It was against this background, with its specific allusion to Siena, that the sacrifice of the mass took place. The Blessed Sacrament was kept on the back of the altar, and it is there that we find the eminently functional narrative of Christ's Passion. The individual scenes are on a far smaller, more intimate scale than the scene on the front. The Passion narrative faced the choir-stalls, and was for the eyes of the canons alone. The altarpiece thus served as a sort of screen, closing off the area where the clergy performed their divine office.

A detailed analysis of the radial ground plan for the Duomo Nuovo shows that the *Maestà* would no longer have served the same function in its new location. The choir-stalls are now in front of the altar, while the ambulatory, which would have given a view of the rear of the altarpiece, was accessible to the general public. It is possible that the altarpiece might have been erected so as to leave sufficient space at the rear of the altar table for an altar of the Blessed Sacrament. There is certainly no special altar in the radiating chapels on the ground plan which would have served the same purpose. The front of the altarpiece would have acquired an added emphasis in this new arrangement in the Duomo Nuovo. Not only does it show the Virgin enthroned as the protectress of the city, flanked in the fore-

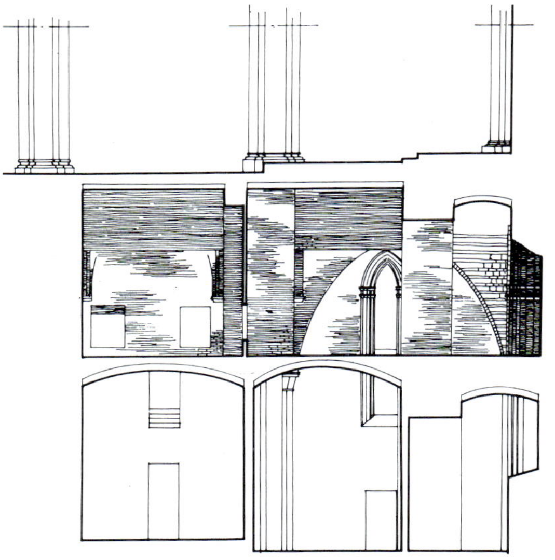

Fig. 15 Transverse section of the fourteenth-century structures supporting the choir.

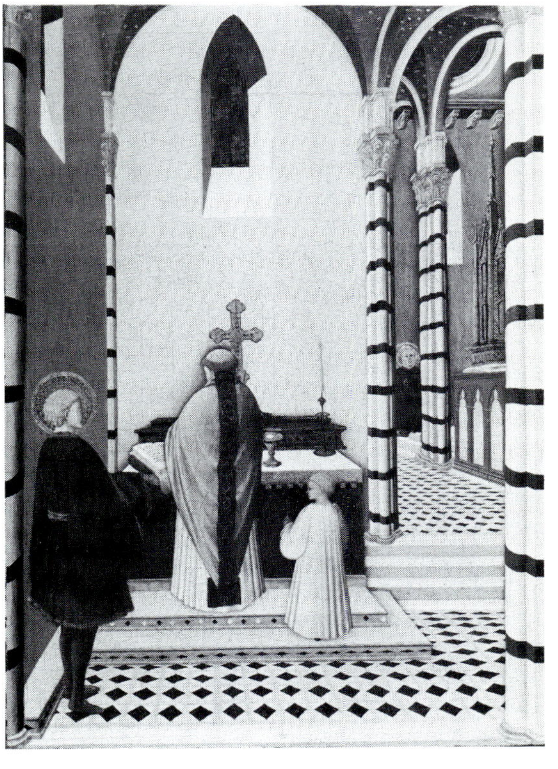

24 Sassetta, *St Antony attending mass*, ca. 1440, 46.8 x 33.4 cm. View from the north aisle of the choir, past the side of the high altar, towards the rear wall of the choir with the round window. One of the side pinnacles of the *Maestà* is visible. Berlin-Dahlem, Gemäldegalerie.

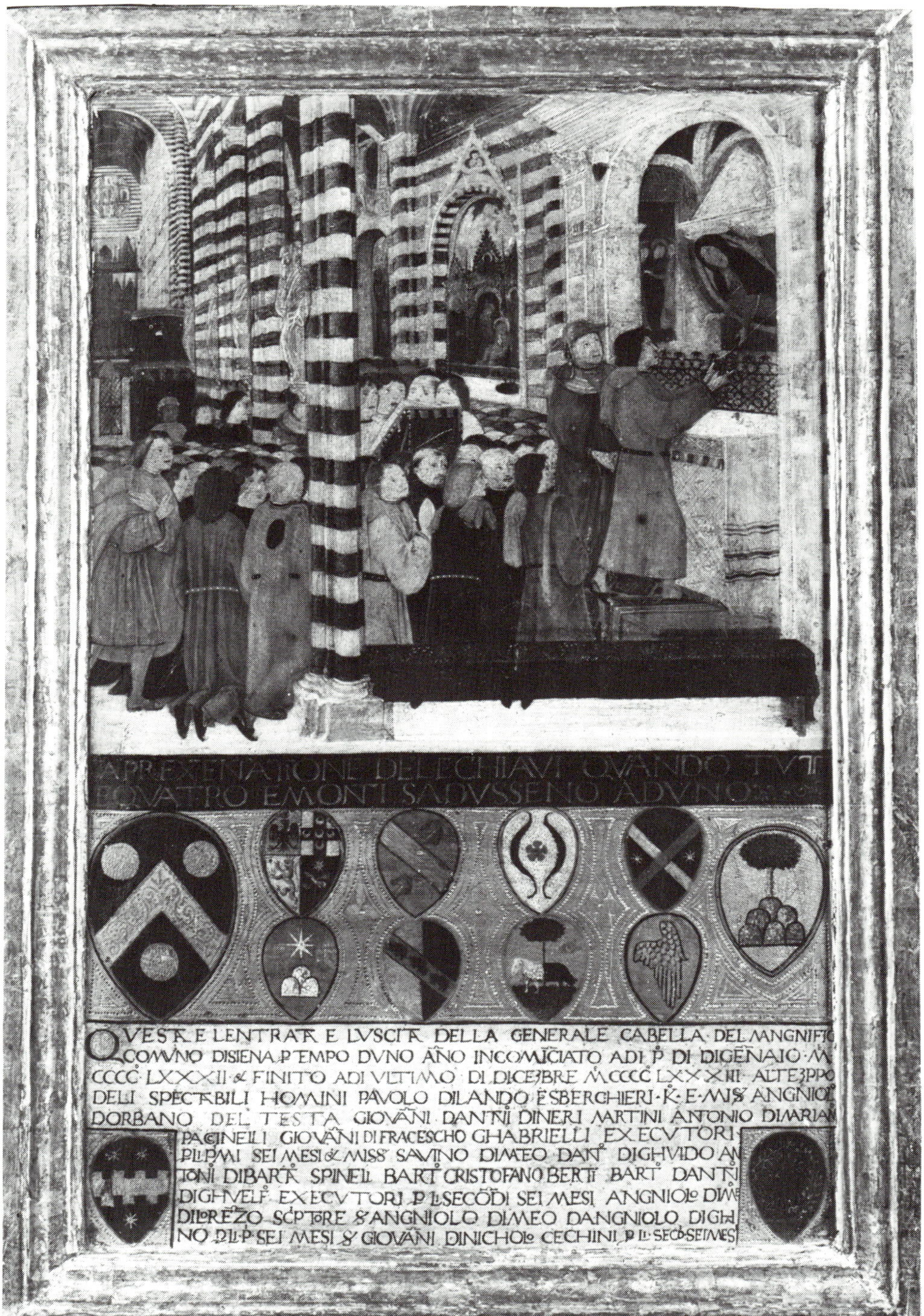

25 Sienese school, Biccherna panel, 1482, 59 x 40 cm. In the distance the pulpit can be seen in its original position. Behind it is the *Maestà* beneath a canopy. High up in the rear wall of the choir is the thirteenth-century stained glass window. On the right the fifteenth-century 'Cappella del Voto'. Siena, Archivio di Stato.

ground by the city's saints, but the visitor would also have found those four intercessors at their own individual altars, which were planned in pairs close to the high altar. If the plan had gone through the demolition of the crypt would at last have led to a brilliant synthesis.

However, this all belongs in the realm of hypothesis and speculation, for the Duomo Nuovo was never completed. Within ten years the work had been halted by a combination of circumstances. In 1348 Siena was ravaged by the Black Death, and this was one reason for the city's economic decline, coupled with internal and external political problems, the latter again involving that arch-rival, Florence.[161] Given all these difficulties it is not unlikely that the plan for the Duomo Nuovo ran into insurmountable problems while it was being carried out.

The Duomo Nuovo was doomed to remain a magnificent but unfulfilled dream. When work resumed in 1356 Siena had to be content with the completion of the enlarged choir, the heightening of the clerestory in the nave, the revaulting of the aisles and the completion of the facade, which was enough to provide work for many years.[162] In 1375 a new high altar was erected further back in the almost completed choir, and as we have seen it was crowned with Duccio's *Maestà* (diag. 16). New choir-stalls were built in the two new bays behind the altar,[163] so ultimately the *Maestà* retained the liturgical function which it had had in 1311. We are given a glimpse of the post-1375 cathedral on a panel which was probably painted by Sassetta and is now in Berlin (ill. 24).[164] The scene is clearly set in Siena cathedral, for it is only there that we find the combination of the great round window in the rear wall of the choir, the massive cornice, and the black-and-white banded piers with their imposts above the classicist capitals. On the right, in the central aisle of the choir, we can see an arcaded altar and on it the pinnacle of an altarpiece. Behind the altar a young man kneels in worship. There could hardly be a clearer indication of the double-sided nature of the invisible altarpiece, which can be none other than the *Maestà*. The space in which the priest is saying mass is one of the square chapels which form the transition from the transept to the choir. And it is in those chapels, however much they have changed in the intervening centuries, that we still find the altars of the four patron saints of Siena.[165]

NOTES

1 H. Hager, *Die Anfänge des italienischen Altarbildes: Untersuchungen zur Entstehungsgeschichte des toskanischen Hochaltarretabels*, Munich 1962, was one of the first to consider the more material aspects of altarpieces. Research into the function of works of art was mainly initiated by art historians with an interest in iconology (see H.W. van Os, *Marias Demut und Verherrlichung in der sienesischen Malerei*, The Hague 1969), but there were a few pioneers to be found among liturgical specialists (see J. Braun, *Der christliche Altar in seiner geschichtlichen Entwicklung*, 2 vols., Munich 1924).

2 C.J. Herington, *Athena Parthenos and Athena Polias: a study in the religion of Periclean Athens*, Manchester 1955, p. 38.

3 V. Lusini, *Il Duomo di Siena*, 2 vols., Siena 1911 and 1939.

4 E. Carli, *Vetrata duccesca*, Milan 1956; R. Wagner-Rieger, *Die italienische Baukunst zu Beginn der Gotik*, 2 vols., Graz & Cologne 1956.

5 W. Braunfels, *Mittelalterliche Stadtbaukunst in der Toskana*, Berlin 1953.

6 A. Middeldorf-Kosegarten, 'Zur Bedeutung der sieneser Domkuppel', *Münchner Jahrbuch der bildenden Kunst*, third series 21 (1970), pp. 73-97.

7 Although the cathedral could hardly be described as being oriented (the main axis from facade to apse runs south-south-west to north-north-east) I have used the cardinal points of the compass throughout for the sake of simplicity, pretending that the choir faced due east. East, in other words, refers to the choir, west to the facade, and so on for the other parts of the church. This departure from the general practice of orientation would have been due to the difficulties presented by the site. See Lusini, op. cit. (note 3), vol. 1, pp. 11-12. On the orientation of churches in general see J. Sauer, *Symbolik des Kirchengebäudes und seiner Ausstattung in der Auffassung des Mittelalters*, Freiburg-im-Breisgau 1902, pp. 88 ff.

8 H. Brauer and R. Wittkower, *Die Zeichnungen des Gianlorenzo Bernini (Römische Forschungen der Bibliotheca Hertziana 9)*, vol. 1 Berlin 1931, pp. 59-61. *V. Golzio, Documenti artistici sul Seicento nell'archivio Chigi*, Rome 1939, pp. 79-106. The same happened with the Palazzo Pubblico, which was enlarged in 1680 entirely in the Gothic style of the original facade. See A. Cairolo and E. Carli, *Il palazzo pubblico di Siena*, Rome 1963, p. 35.

9 For the earliest data see Lusini, op. cit. (note 3), vol. 1, ch. 1. A good summary of the architectural history of the cathedral will be found in Z. Pepi, *Il Duomo di Siena*, Siena 1964. The cathedral was dedicated in 1186 (Lusini, op. cit. (note 3), vol. 1, p. 18), but that could hardly apply to the present structure. The earliest mention of the 'Opera di S. Maria', which was responsible for the construction and maintenance of the cathedral, is found in a will of 1196 (Lusini, op. cit. (note 3), vol. 1, p. 12). The accounts for 1226 show that large amounts of money were spent on black and white marble (Lusini, op. cit. (note 3), vol. 1, p. 16). These documents are summarised in C. Pietromellara, *Il Duomo di Siena: evoluzione della forma dalle origini alla fine del Trecento*, Florence 1980, p. 63. By that date the Opera had apparently grown into a full-fledged administrative body (Lusini, op. cit. (note 3), vol. 1, pp. 12-15). The *Ordo officiorum ecclesiae Senensis* of 1215 (see Section 2) says nothing at all about a church being built at the time, so the start of construction work can probably be dated between 1215 and 1226. Stylistic considerations also argue against an earlier dating.

10 Lusini, op. cit. (note 3), vol. 1, pp. 39 ff.

11 Carli, op. cit. (note 4), pp. 55-56, note 30; *idem*, 'Affreschi senesi del Duecento', *Scritti di storia dell'arte in onore di Ugo Procacci*, vol. 1, Milan 1977, pp. 82-92.

12 Carli, op. cit. (note 4), pp. 12-13. We can pass over the question of whether the present window is of thirteenth-century workmanship, as Carli believes. See G. Milanesi, *Documenti per la storia dell'arte senese*, vol. 1, Siena 1854, p. 311, note; J.H. Stubblebine, *Duccio di Buoninsegna and his school*, vol. 1, Princeton 1979, pp. 13-14; J. White, *Duccio: Tuscan art and the medieval workshop*, London 1979, pp. 137-40. The design, however, can quite clearly be traced back to the thirteenth century. J. White, *Art and architecture in Italy 1250-1400* (The Pelican History of Art), Harmondsworth 1966, p. 128, points to the 'possibly fortuitous' parallel with the early thirteenth-century circular window in the cathedral at Poitiers. A more obvious parallel, however, is with the large west window of Notre Dame la Grande in Poitiers. Admittedly this large round-headed window is not an oculus, but neither, like the version in Siena, does it have any tracery; it is just a large expanse of glass (illustrated in *Dictionnaire des églises de France*, vol. 3C, n.p. 1967, p. 135). It is closest, though, to the rose window without tracery in the choir front of the abbey church of S. Galgano, see R. Fraccaro de Longhi, *L'architettura delle chiese cistercensi italiane*, Milan 1958, pp. 248-56.

13 In 1264 payment was made for the bronze ball on top of the dome, see Milanesi, op. cit. (note 12), vol. 1, p. 145, note. This indicates that the church was already finished, or was completed shortly afterwards. See note

19 below for other documents bearing on the final stages of construction, and also Lusini, op. cit. (note 3), vol. 1, p. 61. Nicola Pisano received the commission for the pulpit in 1265; see M. Seidel, 'Die Verkündigungsgruppe der sieneser Domkanzel', *Münchner Jahrbuch der bildenden Kunst*, third series 21 (1970), pp. 18-72, esp. p. 23 and p. 63, note 37. The relevant documents are in E. Carli, *Il pulpito di Siena*, Bergamo, Milan & Rome 1943, pp. 41-49.

The Sienese year began on 25th March, but in order to avoid unnecessary complications I have followed the modern calendar throughout, unless otherwise specified.

14 Wagner-Rieger, op. cit. (note 4), vol. 1, p. 207, is wrong when she states that Carli's reconstruction finally cleared up the difficulties in interpreting the report submitted by Lorenzo Maitani and his colleagues in 1322 (1321 Sienese style), see Milanesi, op. cit. (note 12), vol. 1, pp. 186-87, nr. 34. The argument that the crossing would no longer be at the centre of the new cathedral (a reference to the fact that the transept arms would be of unequal length) applies *a fortiori* to the situation with a choir, as suggested by Lusini. In fact, Maitani's report concerned the Duomo Nuovo, in which the existing choir was to be deepened by two bays to turn it into a transept arm. This extension of the choir was actually added after 1316; see Section 4 of this Appendix, and Lusini, op. cit. (note 3), vol. 1, pp. 115 ff. and 154 ff.

15 Braunfels, op. cit. (note 5), pp. 152-53. It appears from Lusini's list of *operai* (op. cit. (note 1), pp. 353-55) that the occasional layman acted as *operaio* during this period, and that a monk was again appointed in 1313-14.

Until 1218 the *operai* were always provided by the cathedral chapter. The archives then fall silent until 1226, when we find the appointment of the first *operaio* who was not a canon. From then until 1258 the office was filled by laymen. It was the general practice to recruit public officials from the clergy, who not only knew how to read and write but could be expected to be honest. It was only later that a secular administrative apparatus came into being. It seems that Siena decided to try laymen after the last canon had filled the post, and when that did not work it turned to the monks of San Galgano. See L. Douglas, *A history of Siena*, London 1912, pp. 112-13, and W.M. Bowsky, *The finance of the Commune of Siena 1287-1355*, Oxford 1970, pp. 7, 15. The development of the civil service in Siena is described in L. Zdekauer (ed.), *Il costituto del Comune di Siena dell'anno 1262*, Milan 1897, pp. xiv-cvii.

Wagner-Rieger, op. cit. (note 4), vol. 1, p. 211, rejects any Cistercian influence on the choir although without giving any clear grounds for doing so. On the other hand she does not rule out that influence on the far less characteristic arcade around the drum. As noted by Braunfels, op. cit. (note 5), p. 221, it was the *capomaestro* who was in charge of the actual construction work, and not the *operaio*, although that would not necessarily preclude the inclusion of Cistercian ideas in the structure.

16 Wagner-Rieger, op. cit. (note 4), vol. 1, pp. 198 ff.

17 R. Crozet, *L'art roman en Poitou*, Paris 1948, p. 108.

18 Wagner-Rieger, op. cit. (note 4), vol. 1, p. 205. The iconographic parallels which she sees between the two facades (p. 205, note 12) are not at all convincing. In Poitiers the central motif is Christ's redemption and glory, while in Siena the entire sculptural programme is devoted to the Virgin. Siena had established close trading links with France at an early date, notably at the annual markets of Champagne, so this French influence is hardly surprising. See Douglas, op. cit. (note 15), esp. pp. 343 ff., and L. Zdekauer, *Il mercante senese nel Dugento*, Siena 1925, pp. 14 ff.

19 R. Wagner-Rieger, 'Siena und Ruvo', *Festschrift Prof. Dr. Anselm Weissenhofer*, Vienna 1954, pp. 97-111. She also points out (pp. 103-04) that a cornice immediately below the vault springing is more in the French idiom than the Italian. In Italian basilicas, which were often unvaulted, the cornice runs directly above the nave arcades; see W. Krönig, 'Toskana und Apulien: Beiträge zum Problemkreis der Herkunft des Nicola Pisano', *Zeitschrift für Kunstgeschichte* 16 (1953), p. 127. Krönig gives Pisano most of the credit for the distinctive features of Siena cathedral, although his argument is not entirely convincing. Wagner-Rieger, in *Festschrift*, cit., p. 108, regards Poitiers as the model for both Ruvo and Siena, while Krönig, p. 131, traces the cornice with consoles from Siena to Ruvo and thence to France.

20 Krönig, op. cit. (note 19), pp. 102, 139, note 7. See further note 9 above.

21 See note 27 below for the relevant passage and its interpretation.

22 Krönig, op. cit. (note 19), p. 101.

23 P. Sanpaolesi, *Il Duomo di Pisa e l'architettura romanica toscana delle origini*, Pisa 1975, pp. 208 ff., and 224, fig. 31.

24 Lusini, op. cit. (note 3), vol. 1, pp. 207-08. The present ribbed vaulting of the aisles and transept is of the same design as that in the clerestory, and would have been installed at the same time.

25 Lusini, ibid. The relevant documents are Milanesi, op. cit. (note 12), pp. 276-77, nr. 76, and pp. 278-79, nr. 78.

26 Pisa cathedral, for example, and S. Paolo a ripa d'Arno in the same city.

27 Wagner-Rieger, op. cit. (note 4), vol. 1, p. 207. There is a reference to this in the document of 20th February 1260 (1259 Sienese style, see Milanesi, op. cit. (note 12), pp. 142-43, nr. 5): '...that a vault should be erected between the last two marble pillars, namely those which are closest to the wall of the section of the church of the Blessed Virgin, mentioned below, and that this vault must extend to that wall' ('...quod fieri faciat unam voltam inter ultimas duas columnas marmoreas, que quidem columne site et posite sunt proprinquiores muro ex parte retrodicte ecclesie sancte Marie et usque ad illum murum dicta volta perveniat'). 'Retrodicte' should probably be read as 'retrodicta', which makes the passage far more logical. Since it is clear from the form of words used that it was intended to be a separate vault it was very probably divided into bays, which would indicate a cross vault rather than a barrel vault. The next document tells us that the choir was also being vaulted in this period. It is dated 13th May 1260 (Milanesi, op. cit. (note 12), pp. 143-44, nr. 6), and gives the location as the altar of St Bartholomew ('ex parte altaris sancti Bartholomei'), who was one of Siena's patron saints until displaced by Victor of Siena (Carli, op. cit. (note 4), pp. 45, 47-48). St Bartholomew's altar was in the crypt, and it is rather strange that it should be used to describe the position of work being carried out in the choir, but it seems that there were not many altars in the choir (see Section 2 below). Another passage in the document of 20th February 1260 must refer to the entrance in the south transept: 'Likewise that the entrance on the side near the church of St Desiderius be made wider and higher than it is [at present]' ('Item quod fieri faciat portam ex parte ecclesie sancti Desi-

derii ampliorem et altiorem quam sit'). This was originally the position of the Porta del Perdono, see Lusini, op. cit. (note 3), vol. 1, pp. 46-47. For a more precise description of its position see M. Butzek, 'Die Papstmonumente im Dom von Siena', *Mitteilungen des Kunsthistorischen Institutes in Florenz* 24 (1980), vol. 1, pp. 20-22, figs. 4, 5. Pietromellara, op. cit. (note 9), pp. 37-38, tav. XIX, also believes that there was cross vaulting, although without ribs, which would have been almost as old-fashioned as a barrel vault.

28 An accurate picture of the internal architecture of the fourteenth-century choir will be found on a panel attributed to Sassetta (ill. 24) which is now in the Gemäldegalerie in Berlin-Dahlem (Staatliche Museen preussischer Kulturbesitz). That panel also shows that the lancet window below the round window was originally glazed. See J. Pope-Hennessy, *Sassetta*, London 1939, pp. 69 ff., plate XI; G. Kaftal, *Iconography of the saints in Tuscan painting*, Florence 1952, p. 63; *Gemäldegalerie Berlin. Katalog der ausgestellten Gemälde des 13.-18. Jahrhunderts*, Berlin-Dahlem 1975, p. 389.

29 M. Moretti, *L'architettura romanica religiosa nel territorio dell'antica reppublica senese*, Parma 1962, pp. 101-08, esp. p. 103.

30 Moretti, op. cit. (note 29), pp. 115-30, esp. p. 126.

31 Moretti, op. cit. (note 29), p. 103.

32 M. Salmi, *Chiese romaniche della campagna toscana*, Milan 1958, p. 24; Moretti, op. cit. (note 29), p. 117.

33 See Wagner-Rieger, op. cit. (note 4), vol. 1, pp. 200-01, 206-07; *idem*, op. cit. (note 19), *passim*; Krönig, op. cit. (note 19), pp. 103-05, 131-33.

34 Krönig, op. cit. (note 19), pp. 102-03. It is certainly not impossible that the unusual nature of this cornice could be attributed to the influence of Nicola Pisano, as Paatz had earlier pointed out, see W. Paatz, *Werden und Wesen der Trecento-Architektur in Toskana*, Burg 1937, p. 204.

35 Illustrated in M. Salmi, *L'architettura romanica in Toscana*, Milan & Rome 1927, tav. 189; Lusini, op. cit. (note 3), vol. 1, p. 45, and Pietromellara, op. cit. (note 9), tav. XXII.

36 This can also be deduced from the only surviving Romanesque window in the wall of the transept between the chapel of St John the Baptist and the nave (ill. 9). All the other windows date from the fourteenth century or later (ill. 10). The oldest Gothic window (now bricked up) in the wall of the aisle opposite the present archiepiscopal palace, is entirely in the style of the Trecento, so it evidently took some time to put all the finishing touches to the thirteenth-century church. It can be seen from a seventeenth-century painting in the Palazzo Pubblico (reproduced in Lusini, op. cit. (note 3), vol. 1, p. 253) that the canon's house, which had not yet been demolished, left this window completely free. It was therefore definitely made in the fourteenth century and is not a seventeenth-century imitation, as on the other side. For the canons' house see Lusini, op. cit. (note 3), vol. 1, pp. 17-18, 251. For the more ornate windows on the opposite side of the nave see note 8.

37 In S. Trinità in Florence, for instance. Paatz, op. cit. (note 34), p. 24, draws attention to the Burgundo-Cistercian origins of this feature. There is a similar arrangement in the Cistercian abbey church of S. Galgano, which was begun in 1224, at approximately the same time as Siena cathedral (see note 9 above); Fraccaro de Longhi, op. cit. (note 13), p. 248.

38 Wagner-Rieger, op. cit. (note 4), vol. 1, pp. 202-04.

39 This is also borne out by the documents cited in note 27. Vaults, of course, are always the last elements to be added to a church.

40 Lusini, op. cit. (note 3), vol. 1, p. 25, note 45.

41 See *Dictionnaire*, cit. (note 12), for examples of churches with crossing towers.

42 Fraccaro de Longhi, op. cit. (note 13), pp. 37 ff.

43 In the cathedral and in S. Paolo a ripa d'Arno in Pisa, for instance, and in Sovana and Sovicille. See Sanpaolesi, op. cit. (note 23), pp. 220, 223-29, figs. 28-32, tav. LXXV b, who dates the initial design of the cupola of Pisa cathedral no later than the dedication of the church in 1118, while the cupola of S. Paolo, which is modelled on that of the cathedral, must have been built before the church was consecrated (1148). See notes 30 and 31 above for Sovana and Sovicille.

44 E. Carli, *L'arte a Massa Marittima*, Siena 1976, pp. 22, 25.

45 D. Negri, *Chiese romaniche in Toscana*, Pistoia 1978, pp. 408 ff.

46 See Fraccaro de Longhi, op. cit. (note 13), pp. 37-82.

47 The cathedral was shown with a large dome as early as 1224 in a depiction of the city in the *Liber census communis Senensis et liber memorialis offensarum*; see Middeldorf-Kosegarten, op. cit. (note 6), p. 79, the literature listed in note 55 on p. 79, and p. 73, fig. 1. See Braunfels, op. cit. (note 5), *passim*, for architecture as propaganda in medieval Tuscany.

48 Middeldorf-Kosegarten, op. cit. (note 6), pp. 84 ff. Braunfels, op. cit. (note 5), p. 161, also gives a rather symbolic interpretation of the passage about the dome in the advisory report of 1322 (see note 14 above), although it in no way suggests such an interpretation. 'We also believe that this work should not proceed because the cupola of the abovementioned church would no longer stand at the cross's centre [i.e. at the centre of the cruciform plan of the church], as it should if it is to conform to the proper proportions' ('Item nobis videtur quod in dicto opere non amplius procedatur, quia metis predicte ecclesie, finito novo opere, non remaneret in mediis crucis, ut rationabiliter remanere deberet'). It is also worth noting Sauer's comment: 'In sehr vielen Fällen... hat die Symbolik einfach post factum von der gegebenen Tatsache ihre Gedanken abstrahiert' (Sauer, op. cit. (note 7), p. 2, quoted in G. Bandmann, *Mittelalterliche Architektur als Bedeutungsträger*, Berlin 1951, p. 61). For the cult of the Virgin in Siena see note 82, Middeldorf-Kosegarten, op. cit. (note 6), pp. 80 ff., and the literature given in her note 64.

49 Lusini, op. cit. (note 3), vol. 1, p. 262. There is good documentary evidence on the new choir-stalls, the first of which were commissioned as early as 1362, followed by a second and much larger order in 1377, see Milanesi, op. cit. (note 12), pp. 328-83, nrs. 109-34. See also Lusini, loc. cit., and E. Carli, 'Le sculture del coro del Duomo di Siena', *Antichità viva* 17 (1978), nr. 1, pp. 25-39, gives a resumé of the detailed history of these choir-stalls. Various other documents on the choir-stalls are in P. Bacci, 'Una tavola inedita e sconosciuta di Luca di Tommè con alcuni documenti ignorati della sua vita', *Rassegna d'arte senese e del costume*, new series 1 (1927), pp. 58-61.

50 Lusini, op. cit. (note 3), vol. 1, p. 63; Carli, op cit. (note 4), pp. 55-56, note 30; *idem, Scritti*, cit. (note 11), pp. 82-92.

51 Carli, *Scritti*, cit. (note 11), p. 88.

52 See Section 2, pp. 131-33.

53 Carli, op. cit. (note 4), *passim*. See also White, *Art and architecture*, cit. (note 12), pp. 126-29, and *idem, Duccio*, cit. (note 12), pp. 137-40.

54 See note 65 below.

55 Compare these with the supports in Sovana and Sovicille.

56 Middeldorf-Kosegarten, op. cit. (note 6), p. 76, rightly observes that 'diese Kryptenreste... wohl nicht identisch sind mit dem zurückliegenden Teil der vom südöstlichen Querhaus aus zugänglichen, heute sog. "Cripta delle statue" '. She has not a word to say about the adjoining 'Cripta degli affreschi', and yet that is the last remaining section of the old crypt.

57 See Pietromellara, op. cit. (note 9), p. 11, tav. XVIII.

58 Carli, *Scritti*, cit. (note 11), pp. 84-85.

59 I agree with Carli, *Scritti*, cit. (note 11), p. 82, that this barrel vault and that of the later, adjoining space were built when the choir floor was lowered (see below). Pietromellara, op. cit. (note 9), p. 10, is incorrect when she says that these vaults were added in the sixteenth century 'insieme al pavimento marmoreo soprastante', for the simple reason that the floor above was laid in the fifteenth century; see R.H. Hobart Cust, *The pavement masters of Siena*, London 1901. Nor is there any reason to follow Pietromellara, loc. cit. (whose argument is anyway rather unclear on this point), in dating the vaults after the departure of the 'Compagnia di S. Giovanni Battista dell Morte' around 1450 (see note 69 below).

60 See Section 2, where this is discussed in connection with the *Ordo officiorum*.

61 *Domini Bartolomei Benevolenti ecclesie Senensis prepositi philosophiae quondam professoris insignis de urbis Senae origine et incremento opusculum*, Siena 1506, p. 122 (Biblioteca Communale degli Intronati, Siena, Ms o.VI.90): '...submixam columnis quindecim con camerationibus tribus'.

62 Other examples include the earlier crypt of S. Minato al Monte in Florence; see W. and E. Paatz, *Die Kirchen von Florenz*, vol. 4, Frankfurt 1952, pp. 226-28. The same arrangement is found in the large crypts of the Rhineland. Carli, *Scritti*, cit. (note 11), p. 84, does not consider Benvoglenti's description to be entirely reliable, for the crypt had been closed long before he wrote. However, it appears from what remains of the crypt that Benvoglenti was absolutely scrupulous in his account. Moreover, since he was a member of the cathedral chapter he could well have had sources at his disposal which have since disappeared. The fact that Carli could find none of the original pillars and vaults proves little or nothing, since the remains of the crypt have been severely mutilated. As we have seen, though, there are a few remains, and scanty as they are it is interesting to note that Carli actually discusses them himself.

63 Carli, *Scritti*, cit. (note 11), p. 84.

64 We know that there was a processional route through the church from the description of a number of ceremonies in the *Ordo officiorum* for the cathedral. See K. von Fischer, 'Die Rolle der Mehrstimmigkeit am Dome von Siena zu Beginn des 13. Jahrhunderts', *Archiv für Musikwissenschaft* 18 (1961), nr. 3/4, pp. 167-82.

65 Carli, *Scritti*, cit. (note 11), p. 83, also traces the closure of the crypt to this enlargement. Lusini, op. cit. (note 3), vol. 1, p. 63, note 16, had formed the same opinion, although without giving any reasons. Evidence supporting this hypothesis is provided by the pillars in the first bay of the choir (ill. 11). Their regular subdivision into four white bands and one black band indicates that the present height of the basement dates from that period. Moreover, these two rebuilt pillars have capitals whose thirteenth-century formal vocabulary sets them apart from the others in the choir (ills. 15, 16, 17, 18). They were evidently taken from elsewhere and reused. The crocket capital of one of these pillars is virtually identical to the one at the top of the engaged column to the left of the Piccolomini altar in the nave. The other capital matches the classicist capitals in the nave. The far smaller capitals of the internal and external thirteenth-century dome arcades are of a similar early Gothic type as the two crocket capitals in the choir. The other choir capitals, however, are closely related to those of the Duomo Nuovo, which was begun in 1339. For the fourteenth-century nature of these choir pillars see P. Toesca, *Storia dell'arte italiana*, vol. 1, Turin 1927, p. 692.

66 Middeldorf-Kosegarten, op. cit. (note 6), pp. 76-77, believes that the relics were only transferred after completion of the enlargement programme in 1375, when the high altar was moved to the choir. We know from the *Ordo officiorum* that the relics of St Crescentius were certainly in the crypt (see note 74 below, *Ordo*, ed. Trombelli, p. 147). For further information on the relics in the crypt see Gigli, op. cit. (note 8), vol. 1, p. 435; G.A. Pecci, *Storia del Vescovado della città di Siena*, Lucca 1748, p. 129, and Section III below.

67 See Braun, op. cit. (note 1), vol. 1, pp. 568-86.

68 See O. von Simson, *The Gothic cathedral: origins of Gothic architecture and the medieval concept of order*, Princeton 1974 (second edn.), pp. 186 ff., and esp. pp. 201 ff., where the author discusses the problems facing the architect of Chartres cathedral, who had to build a Gothic cathedral while retaining a Romanesque crypt. See also E. Panofsky, *Gothic architecture and scholasticism*, New York 1957, esp. pp. 44-45, where the author gives a lucid account of Gothic space, although the essay as a whole is disappointing.

69 Carli, *Scritti*, cit. (note 11), p. 85.

70 Ibid.

71 Milanesi, op. cit. (note 12), vol. 2, Siena 1854, pp. 267-69, nr. 188.

72 Compare the window in the first bay of the north aisle (see note 36).

73 Von Fischer, the musicologist, has clarified a number of difficult points, including the repeated use of the word 'organum' in Odericus's text, which frequently appears in the plural ('cum organis', 'in duobus organis', etc.), where it refers not to organs but to choral singing; see von Fischer, op. cit. (note 64), pp. 167-82. See also *Handwörterbuch der musikalischen Terminologie*, Wiesbaden 1979, s.v.

Middeldorf-Kosegarten was the first to combine the *Ordo officiorum* with art-historical research, but was unfortunately far from thorough in her approach; see Middeldorf-Kosegarten, op. cit. (note 6), *passim*.

74 All quotations from the *Ordo* are taken from the eighteenth-century edition: G.C. Trombelli (ed.), *Ordo officiorum ecclesiae Senensis*, Bologna 1766. This particular passage is on p. 147: 'De Benedictione novi Ignis, et ejus Processione et Cerei Consecratione. Circa horam tertiam vestiantur Altaria, et solemnibus paramentis adornantur: hora autem Nona Sacrista in Confessione ante Altare Beati Crescentii ignem de Cristallo, vel lapide noviter excussum accendit de lignis siccis, ne fumigent, et eo accenso, com totus Clerus Civitatis convenerit in Ecclesia, Episcopus et totus Clerus vadunt in Confessionem'.

75 See Braun, op. cit. (note 1), vol. 1, pp. 549 ff. for the various kinds of 'confessio' and their occurrence at different times and places. According to Braun (p. 553)

'confessio' acquired the meaning of 'crypt' in the late middle ages, and that is the sense in which we must interpret Odericus's use of the word. Moreover, as we shall see, there was an altar (and possibly even two) above the crypt in Siena, which agrees with Braun's definition of a 'confessio' (p. 551).

76 Trombelli, op. cit. (note 74), p. 505: 'Episcopi intra Ecclesiam, Sacerdotes vel in Ecclesia, vel in exedris Ecclesiae sepeliri convenerunt.'

77 Middeldorf-Kosegarten, op. cit. (note 6), p. 79.

78 J.F. Niermeyer, *Mediae Latinitatis lexicon minus*, Leiden 1976, s.v.

79 Trombelli, op. cit. (note 74), p. 352: 'Dominicus Episcopus, et Canonici cum aliis Clericis cantantes dicunt Responsorium cum Organo, vadunt ad Sepulcrum Episcoporum per medium Ecclesiae, et cum illuc pervenerint, faciunt Chorum, et cantanto Responsorio, Episcopus, vel Archypresbyter thurificat Sepulchrum...'.

80 Trombelli, op. cit. (note 74), p. 34: 'Mox Cantor cum tribus Fratribus super quatuor gradus cum summa reverentia incipiat Invitatorium...'.

81 Trombelli, op. cit. (note 74), p. 173: '...et statim Cantor cum tribus Fratribus indutis Pluvialibus ascendat super quartum gradum ante Altare Virginis...'.

82 Lusini, op. cit. (note 3), vol. 1, p. 1, gives 913 as the earliest known date of this patrociny. Odericus's introduction to his description of the feast of the Assumption alludes to this tradition of the Virgin Assumptive: '...for it was an ancient custom that the entire clergy of the city attended Vespers in the main church on this evening' (Trombelli, op. cit. (note 74), p. 352: '...ex antiqua enim consuetudine, Clerus Civitatis in Majori Ecclesia tali sero Vesperis interesse consuevit').

83 Lusini, op. cit. (note 3), vol. 1, p. 19; Carli, *Scritti*, cit. (note 11), p. 83.

84 Pietromellara, op. cit. (note 9), p. 21. If we are correct in assuming (see below) that there was a second altar in the choir, so that strictly speaking the plural 'altaria superius' would refer to the choir alone, rather than to the choir and nave together, then Odericus's description leaves much to be desired and is in marked contrast to his otherwise scrupulous choice of words.

85 Trombelli, op. cit. (note 74), p. 12: 'Sacerdos aspergat aquam benedictam Altaribus superius et inferius et revertatur in Chorum.'

86 This must be a reference to the altar of St Crescentius; see Trombelli, op. cit. (note 74), pp. 147, 372, and the quotation given in note 74 above.

The altar of St Bartholomew had already acquired the subsidiary title of Sts Fabian and Sebastian, witness Trombelli, op. cit. (note 74), p. 288: '...their altar, that is to say the altar of St Bartholomew' ('...Altare ipsorum, scilicet Sancti Bartholomaei'). Pursuing our reconstruction of the crypt this leaves room for a third altar. Odericus himself is silent on this point, although it is reasonable to assume that this would have been the resting-place of the relics of Sts Ansanus and Savinus, which Odericus refers to specifically (ibid., pp. 273, 376). We do know that St Victor's head was kept in or on the altar of St Savinus (ibid., p. 325), and that Victor supplanted St Bartholomew as one of the city patrons at the end of the thirteenth century (see Carli, op. cit. (note 4), pp. 45, 47-48). It seems not unlikely that this would have been reflected in the range of altars in the sense that, in addition to the old altar of St Crescentius, there was then a combined altar for Sts Victor and Savinus, while Ansanus may well have been venerated at a third crypt altar.

Odericus goes into great detail on the cermonies in honour of Sts Fabian and Sebastian; see Trombelli, pp. 288 ff.

87 Trombelli, op. cit. (note 74), p. 132: 'Jam die ad occasum tendente, et nocte incipiente, Altaria nostrae Ecclesiae consuevimus dicooperire... . Duo Fratres vadunt primo loco inferius ad Altare Beati Bartholomaei..., et unus Fratrum habeat thuribulum cum incenso..., et statim tollunt pannos de Altari, eo tamen prius undique incensato... . Deinde accedunt ad aliud Altare... . Similiter facientes per singula Altaria, donec subtus, et desuper omnia discooperiantur, et usque in Sabbatum Sanctum sic dicooperta reliquuntur'.

88 Trombelli, op. cit. (note 74), p. 391: 'Qualiter in festis incipiantur Officia, et quando in Ecclesia nostra fieri consuevit. ... . Sed quando Dominus Episcopus incipit Officium, tunc idem Episcopus incensare Altaria superiora consuevit in Vesperis, et Matutinis, et Sacerdos qui adsistit Episcopo cum Pluviali, thurificat alia Altaria, quae sunt inferius... . Sed ad Missam Majorem, Diaconus accepto thuribulo, post factum incensum a Sacerdote, thurificat Altare superius, et postea dat thuribulum Subdiacono, qui vadit inferius, et dat incensum Altaribus, et Clero in Choro'.

89 Trombelli, op. cit. (note 74), p. 410: 'De reverentia Episcopali, cum Episcopus incipit Officia in festis diebus. ...sed postea Archypresbyter, vel Sacerdos dicit Capitulum, et Episcopus incensat Altaria superiora, et Sacerdos alia inferiora... .

90 Trombelli, op. cit. (note 74), p. 34: '...et bini redeunt in Chorum cum Domino Episcopo, et vadunt cum eo usque ad superius sedile Episcopi, et sic ibi ante Altare Beatae Virginis Mariae...'.

91 Trombelli, op. cit. (note 74), p. 139: 'De Officio Crucis, quod sit post Orationes in Parasceve. ...duo fratres stantes in medio Chori cantant Agios et Sanctus..., alii vero qui sunt ad sedes, et superius..., flectuant genua... . Demum qui bajulant Crucem ante Altare, procedant... .' It is remarkable that the Hagios was still in use at this period of the Greek liturgy; see L. Brou, 'Les chants en langue grecque dans les liturgies latines', *Sacris Erudiri: Jaarboek voor Godsdienstwetenschappen* 1 (1948), pp. 165-80, and 4 (1952), pp. 226-38; and Th. Klauser, 'Der Übergang der römischen Kirche von der griechischen zur lateinischen Liturgiesprache,' *Miscellanea Giovanni Mercati*, vol. 1 (Studi e Testi 121), Vatican City 1946, pp. 467-82.

92 Trombelli, op. cit. (note 74), p. 45: '...praeparant se solemnibus indumentis in Sacristia, vel post Altare Beatae Virginis, et interim dum parantur, dicunt Tertiam. Similiter in Choro solemniter tunc cantatur Tertia.'

93 Trombelli, op. cit. (note 74), p. 98: '...vadunt in Ecclesiam intra Chorum ad sedes...'.

94 Trombelli, op. cit. (note 74), p. 186: 'Cum autem Fratres venerint ad cancellos in ingressu Chori, ibi extra Chorum finita Antiphona dicatur....' 'Chorus' can refer both to the singers at mass and divine office and to the choir as an architectonic unit; see du Cange, *Glossarium mediae et infimae Latinitatis*, 10 vols., n.p. 1883-87, s.v. In this particular instance, where a cancello is mentioned, it appears that Odericus is referring to the choir as an area, as in the passage quoted in note 91 about the bishop's throne. In other quotations dealing with the singing of divine office, such as the passage in note 92 about the priests' vestments, 'Chorus' should probably be interpreted not as the space around the altar but in the narrower sense of the actual choir-stalls. The word is used in the same sense in the document of 28th November 1259 (see also note 90).

95 Trombelli, op. cit. (note 74), p. 178: 'Arcipresbyter cum Diacono et Subdiacono post Altare Beatae Virginis Mariae vel in Sacrario sacris vestibus induuntur, et de Choro cum Clero ibi Collecto, ordinato, ut dictum est, exeunt cantando...'.

96 On the general question of choir-stalls see W. Loose, *Die Chorgestühle des Mittelalters*, Leipzig 1931.

97 Trombelli, op. cit. (note 74), p. 410: 'Similiter post Agnus Dei singuli dant pacem Episcopo... et postea Subdiaconus vadit in Chorum et dat pacem majori ex una parte, scilicet Praepositio, ex altera parte similiter alteri, scilicet Archidiacono... et est notandum quod omnibus diebus Dominicis... post Agnus Dei accipiens pacem a Sacerdote, qui canit Missam, portat eam in Chorum dans primo Praepositio, vel Archipresbytero, ex altere parte Archidiacono, et postea portat extra Populo, dans primo ex una parte Consuli, vel uni ex majoribus, et post altera parte similiter, aliis autem diebus cotidie dat pacem tantum in Choro Clericis, ut dictum est.'

98 Trombelli, op. cit. (note 74), p. 220: '...ibidem ante Altare in Choro incipiant Hymnum...'.

99 Trombelli, op. cit. (note 74), p. 418: '...Cantor qui officiare debet... vadens in medium Chori ante Altare.... Item ad Missam ,ipse incipit Officium in Choro'.

100 Trombelli, op. cit. (note 74), p. 9: '...quod Cantor cum duobus Fratribus post Altare Beatae Virginis Mariae aequali voci incipere consuevit primum Responsorium'.

101 Trombelli, op. cit. (note 74), p. 122: 'Cantor cum duobus fratribus vadit post Altare Beatae Virginis Mariae... incipiunt cantores cum organo Kyrie...'.

102 The Lateran Council's decision in H. Denziger (ed.), *Enchiridion symbolorum, definitionum et declarationum quae de rebus fidei et morum a conciliis et summis pontificibus emanerunt*, Freiburg-im-Breisgau 1955 (thirtieth edn.), p. 430. See further G. Barbara, *La dottrina eucaristica negli scritti di papa Innocenzo III*, Rome 1953.

103 See Braun, op. cit. (note 1), vol. 2, pp. 574 ff., esp. pp. 582-90. In the middle ages many large churches had two altars on the east side, arranged more or less as a pair; see G. Bandmann, 'Zur Bedeutung der romanischen Apsis', *Wallraf-Richartz Jahrbuch* 15 (1953), p. 39. Previously the consecrated host had generally been kept in a pyx, often in the shape of a dove; see O. Nussbaum, *Die Aufbewahrung der Eucharistie* (Theophaneia 29), Bonn 1979, pp. 351 ff. The growing veneration of the host did not immediately lead to the widespread introduction of altars of the Blessed Sacrament (ibid., pp. 430 ff.). The feast of Corpus Christi, which could be regarded as the ritualisation of the doctrine of transubstantiation, was only made a holy day of obligation in 1264, by Pope Urban IV. The preceding period was marked by a number of miracles involving the host, the best-known being that of Bolsena in 1263. As early as 1230, however, a similar miracle took place in Florence; see R. Davidsohn, *Firenze ai tempi di Dante*, Florence 1929, p. 147. Theologians had been emphasising the mystery of the Eucharist throughout the twelfth century; see J. de Ghellinck, 'Eucharistie au XIIe siècle en Occident', *Dictionnaire de Théologie Catholique*, vol. 5, Paris 1913, cols. 1285-1302. This appears to be reflected in Odericus's discussion of the non-consecration of the host on Good Friday (Trombelli, op. cit. (note 74), p. 142) and, later on, in his allegorical treatment of the mystery of the bread and wine (ibid., pp. 460-61). Attention should also be drawn to the antipendium of 1215 in the Pinacoteca in Siena. The lateral scenes of the legend of the Cross are also an expression of the veneration of the Lord's body (van Os discusses this in detail on p. 12 above).

104 Trombelli, op. cit. (note 74), p. 37: '...et sic una pars post Altare, altera in Choro dicatur.'

105 The four reliefs of the *Annunciation*, the *Nativity*, the *Magi travelling to Bethlehem*, and the *Adoration of the Magi*, which are now in the cathedral museum in Siena (ill. 19), are regarded by L. Venturi, *Storia dell'arte italiana*, vol. 3, Milan 1904, p. 1007, as the work of an untalented follower of Nicola Pisano. Even if one wished to date the reliefs prior to Pisano's activity in Tuscany, stylistic arguments would preclude a dating any earlier than ca. 1240, so there is no possibility of an identification (however enticing it might be) with the pulpit mentioned by Odericus in 1215. According to Lusini, op. cit. (note 3), vol. 1, pp. 70-73, and 144, note 33, the panels can only be traced back with certainty to 1671, when they were in the church of Ponte allo Spino. As Moretti points out (op. cit. (note 29), p. 131) there was originally a small monastic community attached to Ponte allo Spino, making it more than a mere parish church. This suggests that the reliefs were made specifically for the church, possibly to adorn the pulpit.

106 Trombelli, op. cit. (note 74), p. 38: 'In hac tanta solemnitate omnes Lectiones leguntur in majori pulpito'.

107 Trombelli, op. cit. (note 74), p. 148: '...et stans ibidem ante Altare habens ante se librum super ligneum Pulpitum in loco, ubi legi consuevit Evangelium...'.

108 Trombelli, op. cit. (note 74), p. 74: '...et leguntur Lectiones in majori pulpito'.

109 Trombelli, op. cit. (note 74), p. 280: '...super maius Pulpitum.'

110 See *Liturgisch Woordenboek*, vol. 2, Roermond & Maaseik 1965, col. 2534.

111 Trombelli, op. cit. (note 74), p. 106: 'Dicta oratione, duo sacerdotes ascendunt Pulpita, unus ad dextrum, alius ad sinistrum'.

112 For the ambo and its doubling since the ninth century see *Dictionnaire d'archéologie chrétienne et de liturgie*, vol. 1, Paris 1907, cols. 1330-47; and *Liturgisch Woordenboek*, vol. 1, Roermond & Maaseik 1958, cols. 127-28.

113 Trombelli, op. cit. (note 74), p. 293: 'In Dominicis diebus... non ascendunt solemne Pulpitum, sed iuxta Altare legunt, et ibi in ligneo Pulpito semper ad legendum Evangelium superponitur albus pannus'.

114 See *Liturgisch Woordenboek*, cit. (note 112), cols. 127-28. Carli, op. cit. (note 12), p. 48, comes to a different conclusion. He mentions two passages in the *Ordo* (without identifying where they come) in which Odericus gives locations as 'in the gospel corner' ('in cornu Evangelii') and 'in the epistle corner' ('in cornu Epistoli'). Carli's subsequent interpretation places the marble pulpit on the gospel side and the wooden lectern on the epistle side. He also states that Nicola Pisano's thirteenth-century pulpit stood 'da lato del Vangelo', but fails to give his source for this piece of information (ibid., p. 43). However, the Biccherna panel of 1482 shows the pulpit on the south side, which was the usual side for reading the epistle (see note 141 below). Moreover, it does not have the Paschal candle, which was generally placed by the gospel ambo; see *Liturgisch Woordenboek*, cit., (note 110), col. 2103; and G. Malherbe, 'Le chandelier pascal', *Bulletin paroissal et liturgique* 12 (1930), pp. 108-16, 134-40, 155-62, 167-77. A possible reason for this confusion is that in the early days of Christianity the sanctuary in many churches on the Italian peninsula faced west. The epistle and gospel sides were therefore transposed when churches were oriented; see Sauer, op. cit. (note 7), pp. 88 ff. The

terminological confusion was made complete when the mass 'facie ad populum' made way for the mass in which the priest faced east. See *Liturgisch Woordenboek*, cit. (note 112), col. 728. For the mass 'facie ad populum' see O. Nussbaum, *Der Standort des Liturgen am christlichen Altar vor dem Jahre 1000*, 2 vols. (Theophaneia 18), Bonn 1965. Of particular interest in this context is the fact that the ambones in S. Clemente in Rome are the exact reverse of those in S. Maria in Cosmedin, also in Rome; see R. Krautheimer, *Corpus basilicarum christianarum Romae*, vol. 1, Vatican City 1937, p. 130; vol. 2, Vatican City 1959, p. 285. In view of the above we believe that Carli's hypothesis must be rejected, and that there was a monumental pulpit on the south side, which was in fact the epistle side, and that there was a simpler lectern on the gospel side. For a discussion of the epistle and gospel sides of an altar see J.A. Jungmann, *Missarum sollemnia*, vol. 1, Vienna 1952, pp. 528-35.

115 Milanesi, op. cit. (note 12), pp. 139-40, nr. 1.

116 Milanesi, op. cit. (note 12), p. 140, nr. 2.

117 Milanesi, op. cit. (note 12), pp. 140-41, nr. 3: '...quod altare sancte Marie, et corum ipsius episcopatus fiant et construantur suptus metam majorem dicti episcopatus; et quod fiant gradi ad ipsum corum ex omnibus partibus per quos gentes ascendant et accedant ad Corum et Altare ejusdem episcopatus'.

118 Middeldorf-Kosegarten, op. cit. (note 6), pp. 74-76.

119 White, *Duccio*, cit. (note 12), pp. 99-100, fig. 61. Stubblebine, op. cit. (note 12), p. 34, simply assumes, without giving any reasons, that the high altar stood beneath the dome in the fourteenth century, and even in the fifteenth century as well. For the location of the pulpit see Carli, op. cit. (note 13), pp. 48-49.

120 White, *Duccio*, cit. (note 12), p. 99. See also Middeldorf-Kosegarten, op. cit. (note 6), p. 80.

121 White, *Duccio*, cit. (note 12), p. 99.

122 Milanesi, op. cit. (note 12), p. 140, nr. 2: 'Dum modo non claudantur porte, que sunt versus domum Guidi Trojani, et versus pontem'.

123 Lusini, op. cit. (note 3), vol. 1, pp. 46-47, places these entrances elsewhere. Unfortunately, though, his solution runs counter to the clear indications given in the documents to be mentioned below. The staircase may have been similar to that in front of the Palazzo del Capitano at Todi. For the military meaning of 'pons' which is the closest to this particular use of the word, see du Cange, op. cit. (note 94), s.v.; and A. Forcellini, *Lexicon totius Latinitatis*, 6 vols., n.p. 1864-1926, s.v.

124 Milanesi, op. cit. (note 12), pp. 140-41, nr. 3: '...quod altare sancte Marie et chorus prefati episcopatus et que pertinent ad ipsum corum construantur et compleantur sicut ordinatum est per dominos Canonicos dicti episcopatus et operarios hoperis sancte Marie, salvo quod quedam janua ex parte retro dicti episcopatus videlicet illa que nunc est aperta, sit et remaneat aperta, et fiat in ecclesia, iusta [iuxta] ipsam portam quoddam murum pro conservando ipsam portam, et ingressum et egressum dicti episcopatus per ipsam portam et pro retinendo terram qui mittit in quoro [coro] dicti episcopatus ut non cadat, nec impediat dictam portam et viam ipsius porte... ...quod tota ecclesia debassaretur et fodere debeat ad modum platee episcopatus et quod major janua episcopatus, que est ex parte retro dicti episcopatus que nunc est clausa aperiatur et actetur ut melius potest actari: ita quod homines et gentes possint commode ire et intrare episcopatum predictum'.

125 See Lusini, op. cit. (note 3), vol. 1, p. 31

126 See note 27 above. The expression 'que nunc est clausa' (note 124 above) probably indicates that there was an entrance to the former church at this point and that it was to be incorporated in the new building. The remark in the document of 16th November 1259: 'provided the entrances on the side of Guido Trajani's house and on the side of the "ponte" are not closed', must therefore be regarded as slightly elliptical. What was meant was that the rear door of the crypt was to remain open and that the former south door of the choir was to be reopened.

127 It was only after 1284, when Giovanni Pisano started work on it, that more attention was devoted to the facade opposite the hospital. See H. Keller, 'Die Bauplastik des Sieneser Doms: Studien zu Giovanni Pisano und seiner künstlerischen Nachfolge', *Kunstgeschichtliches Jahrbuch der Bibliotheca Hertziana* 1 (1937), pp. 141-47; and P. Bacci, *Documenti e commenti per la storia dell'arte*, Florence 1944, p. 29.

128 The document quoted in note 125 above (Milanesi, op. cit. (note 12), pp. 140-41, nr. 3), continues: '...that the altar of the Blessed Virgin and the choir of this cathedral must be built beneath the great dome, with steps on all sides so that the people can ascend to the choir and altar of the said church' ('...quod altare sancte Marie, et corum ipsius episcopatus fiant et construantur suptus metam majorem dicti episcopatus, et quod fiant gradi ad ipsum corum ex omnibus partibus per quos gentes ascendant et accedant ad corum et ad altare ejusdem episcopatus').

We find the same word for the dome ('meta', 'metis') in Lorenzo Maitani's report of 1322 (see note 151 below). See also Milanesi, op. cit. (note 12), pp. 186-87, nr. 34.

129 The church was viewed in the same 'optical' way in other documents. The committee of experts under Lorenzo Maitani express their reservations about the fact that, if the new building programme were implemented, the dome would no longer be at the centre ('non remaneret in medio crucis', Milanesi, op. cit. (note 12), pp. 186-87, nr. 34; see also Braunfels, op. cit. (note 5), p. 161). The reason for this is that the nave and the choir of the existing church, which were to be transformed into the transept of the Duomo Nuovo, did not have the same number of bays, as viewed along the main axis from the nave to the choir (see note 14 above).

The same sight-line is used in documents dealing with the round window in the choir. A directive of September 1287 states: '...that the great round window behind the altar of the Blessed Virgin Mary in the principal church is to be glazed...' ('...quod fenestra rotunda magna que est post altare beate Marie Virginis Maioris ecclesie debeat vitrari...'). In two receipts of 1288 we read: '...concerning the glass to be fitted above the altar of the Blessed Virgin' ('...de vitro que fieri debet supra altare Sancte Marie'), and '...for the window glass to be fitted above the altar of the Blessed Virgin' ('...pro vitro fenestre fiende supra altare sancte Marie'). In Bacci, op. cit. (note 128), p. 22, and in Carli, op. cit. (note 4), pp. 12, 14.

130 See p. 114 above.

131 See Section 2 above, and, for the fourteenth-century choir, Carli, op. cit. (note 49), pp. 25-39.

132 Milanesi, op. cit. (note 12), p. 331, nr. 111: '...che 'l coro murasse, secondo che va el vecchio a retta linea.'

133 The reliefs have been in the museum since 1930; see Bacci, op. cit. (note 128), p. 21.

134 Carli, op. cit. (note 105), p. 12; *idem*, 'Lapo Donato e Goro', *La critica d'arte* 8 (1949/50), nr. 3, pp. 177-91; J.

Pope-Hennessy, *Catalogue of Italian sculpture in the Victoria and Albert Museum*, vol. 1, London 1964, pp. 18-20, vol. 3, London 1964, fig. 34. Pope-Hennessy attributes the reliefs to the workshop of Nicola Pisano, but Carli is more cautious.

The earliest form of partition between choir and nave consisted of a low cancello, examples of which will be found in S. Clemente (514-31), S. Sabina (ninth century) and S. Maria in Cosmedin (twelfth century), all in Rome; see Krautheimer, op. cit. (note 114), vol. 1, p. 133, vol. 4, Vatican City 1970, p. 96, and vol. 2, pp. 302-03. It is not until the Gothic period, in the later middle ages, that we find the tall screens in front of the choir which gradually established a more formal segregation of clergy and laity, culminating in the fifteenth-century rood screens in many Flemish churches and the virtually self-contained choir in Albi cathedral. See J. Steppe, *Het koordoksaal in de Nederlanden*, Brussels 1952; *Dictionnaire*, cit. (note 12), vol. 3, A3. See also *Liturgisch Woordenboek*, cit. (note 110), col. 1370; and Braun, op. cit. (note 1), vol. 2, pp. 649 ff.

135 Carli, op. cit. (note 105), p. 12; *idem*, op. cit. (note 134), p. 181; Pope-Hennessy, op. cit. (note 134), p. 19.

136 C. Gardner-von Teuffel, 'The buttressed altarpiece', *Jahrbuch der Berliner Museen* 21 (1979), pp. 36-38, believes that the panel was supported by two massive pinnacles. In this she differs from the reconstruction proposed by J. White, 'Measurement, design and carpentry in Duccio's *Maestà*', *The Art Bulletin* 55 (1973), p. 562. Her theory is borne out by the depiction in a painting now in Berlin (see note 139 below).

137 All the documents on the *Maestà* will be found, with translations, in White, *Duccio*, cit. (note 12), pp. 192-97. The relevant passages from the chronicles are in E.B. Garrison, 'Sienese historical writings and the dates 1260, 1221, 1262 applied to Sienese paintings', *Studies in the history of medieval Italian painting* 4/1, Florence 1960-62, pp. 23-58.

138 See note 49 above and note 160 below.

139 The altar was more than four metres wide, and would have been correspondingly deep. Part of the high altar can be seen on a panel in Berlin which is attributed to Sassetta (see note 28 above; ill. 24). However, that arcaded altar must have been the new structure of 1375 which was demolished in 1506. As we have seen, though, it was just as large as the altar of 1260; cf. Pepi, op. cit. (note 9), p. 174. The soldier kneeling in worship is a further indication of the dual use of the altar. Altarpieces generally stood at the rear edge of an altar, or even hung behind it; see Hager, op. cit. (note 1), pp. 155-58.

140 B. Steuart, *Lineamenti di storia della liturgia cristiana*, Brescia 1957, p. 300.

141 See note 13 above for publications on this pulpit. In 1543 it was moved to its present position on the north side of the hexagon; see Pepi, op. cit. (note 9), p. 97. On the Biccherna panel of 1482 it is shown in its original position on the south side (ill. 25).

Seidel, op. cit. (note 13), pp. 53 ff., deals at length with the original position of the pulpit, the former flight of steps and the placement of the reliefs and the figures at the angles of the casket. See also E. Carli, *Il Duomo di Siena*, Genoa 1979, pp. 34-35. A second marble pulpit, probably square in shape, was ordered in 1423; Lusini, op. cit. (note 3), vol. 1, pp. 277, 331, note 146. Given the descriptions in the cathedral inventories of 1429 and 1435 it seems that this second pulpit was used solely for preaching sermons; see Seidel, op. cit. (note 13), p. 60. Pisano's pulpit was then being used for the reading of both the epistle and the gospel, but that in no way implies that there were two lecterns, as Seidel assumes (ibid., p. 71, note 137). The use of the great pulpit for both readings matches the earlier custom described by Odericus (see p. 135 above). The 1429 inventory also mentions a wooden pulpit which stood in the St Nicholas chapel (Seidel, op. cit. (note 12), p. 60). It is possible that this wooden pulpit was moved to make way for the second marble pulpit.

142 See W.M. Bowsky, *A medieval Italian Commune: Siena under the Nine 1287-1355*, Berkeley, Los Angeles & London 1981.

For Ambrogio Lorenzetti's frescoes see N. Rubinstein, 'Political ideas in Sienese art: the frescoes of Ambrogio Lorenzetti and Taddeo di Bartolo in the Palazzo Pubblico', *Journal of the Warburg and Courtauld Institutes* 21 (1958), pp. 179-207.

143 A. Cairola and E. Carli, op. cit. (note 8). A wealth of historical data will be found in F. Donati, 'Il palazzo del comune di Siena', *Arte antica senese* (corresponding to *Bullettino senese di storia patria* 11), vol. 1, Siena 1904, pp. 311-54.

144 J. Larner, *Culture and society in Italy 1290-1420*, London 1971, pp. 65-67.

145 Lusini, op. cit. (note 3), vol. 1, pp. 115 ff., 154 ff.

146 Braunfels, op. cit. (note 5), p. 157; ibid., pp. 257-58 for the documents of 1297 on the dilapidated state of the baptistery.

147 Milanesi, op. cit. (note 12), pp. 186-87, nr. 34.

148 Milanesi, op. cit. (note 12), pp. 228-30, nr. 50; Lusini, op. cit. (note 3), vol. 1, pp. 161 ff.

149 Siena, Museo dell'Opera del Duomo, inv. nr. 61 (radial choir with chapels: 80 x 54 cm, pen and wash on parchment), and inv. nr. 2 (three-sided apse: 93 x 67 cm, pen on parchment, with a later (nineteenth-century?) addition in pencil of a tower with angle buttresses. These plans are reproduced and discussed in B. Degenhart and A. Schmitt, *Corpus der italienischen Zeichnungen*, vol. 1-1, Berlin 1968, pp. 94-95, 96, note 14.

150 Paatz, op. cit. (note 34), pp. 37-43.

151 Milanesi, op. cit. (note 12), pp. 186-87, nr. 34: 'Item nobis videtur, quod in dicto opere non amplius procedatur, quia metis predicte ecclesie, finito novo opere, non remaneret in medio crucis, ut rationabiliter remanere deberet'.

152 It was particularly common in Lombardy; see A.M. Romanini, *L'architettura gotica in Lombardia*, 2 vols., Milan 1964.

153 Keller, op. cit. (note 128), pp. 141 ff.; Lusini, op. cit. (note 3), vol. 1, pp. 96 ff. Giovanni is first mentioned as *capomaestro* of the cathedral in 1290 (Milanesi, op. cit. (note 12), pp. 161-62, nr. 18), but both Keller and Lusini have good grounds for believing that he designed the facade which was begun in 1284.

154 R. Branner, *Burgundian Gothic architecture*, London 1960, pp. 127-28, 163.

155 In France we find choir-stalls which had been erected in front of the altar gradually evolving into self-contained structures within the church. One of the most ornate examples is in Albi cathedral; see: E. Mâle, *La cathédrale d'Albi*, Paris 1950, pp. 22 ff., figs. 46, 84-85. Italy, on the other hand, only had rood screens in the form of a row of arches separating the choir from the area for the laity; see M.B. Hall, *Renovation and Counter-Reformation*, Oxford 1979.

156 Siena, Archivio dell'Opera del Duomo, inv. nrs. 864 ff.

157 See *Bibliotheca sanctorum*, 12 vols., Vatican City 1961-69; Ansanus: vol. 1, cols. 1324-35; Savinus: vol. 11, cols. 705-16; Crescentius: vol. 4, col. 292; Victor of Siena: vol. 12 (as 'Victor'), cols. 1276-78. It is clear that even

the editors of this reference work had problems with Victor of Siena. In vol. 1 they identify the saint in a miniature by Sano di Pietro in a gradual from the cathedral's Libreria Piccolomini as St Ansanus, and then change the identification to St Victor of Siena in vol. 12. See Carli, op. cit. (note 4), pp. 44-49, for the relationship between the four saints and Siena, and also for the replacement of St Bartholomew by St Victor between 1288 (payments for the choir window) and 1311 (installation of the *Maestà*).

158 Simone Martini painted an *Annunciation* for the altar of St Ansanus (the documents in Bacci, op. cit. (note 128), pp. 163 ff.) The inscriptions on the other two altarpieces tell us that Pietro Lorenzetti completed his *Birth of the Virgin* for the altar of St Savinus in 1342 (documents in P. Bacci, *Dipinti inediti e sconosciuti di Pietro Lorenzetti, Bernardo Daddi ecc. in Siena e nel contado*, Siena 1930, pp. 75 ff.), and that his brother Ambrogio painted a *Presentation in the temple* for the altar of St Crescentius in the same year (documents in P. Bacci, 'Il pittore Mattia Preti a Siena', *Bullettino senese di storia patria*, new series 2 (1931), pp. 2 ff.). For St Victor's altarpiece see van Os, Chapter V of the present work.

159 See Stubblebine, op. cit. (note 12), p. 34. The original text is in A. Lisini, 'Notizie di Duccio pittore e della sua celebre ancona' *Bullettino senese di storia patria* 5 (1898), p. 23, nr. 1. C. Brandi *Duccio*, Florence 1951, pp. 145-46, rightly deduces the existence of a canopy from the cathedral inventories of 1423 and 1435. Hager, op. cit. (note 1), p. 147, believes that the canopy dates back to 1339, on the evidence of a document of that year. It is worth pointing out that Simone Martini painted a canopy over his *Maestà* of 1315 in the Palazzo Pubblico; see van Os, his fig. 71 of the present work; and E.C. Southard, *The frescoes in Siena's Palazzo Pubblico, 1289-1359*, New York 1979, pp. 216-28, figs. 39-44.

160 Lusini, op. cit. (note 3), vol. 1, pp. 261 ff. The decision to move the high altar had been taken some years before, in 1362; the documents are in Bacci, op. cit. (note 49), pp. 58-61. The artists Lorenzo di Vanni and Nuccio di Nerucio were commissioned to decorate the new sanctuary in 1375 (Milanesi, op. cit. (note 12), p. 274, nr. 73).

161 W.M. Bowsky, 'The impact of the Black Death upon Sienese government and society', *Speculum* 34 (1964), pp. 1-34.

162 On the resumption of building work see Milanesi, op. cit. (note 12), p. 252, nr. 57.

163 For the documents on the choir-stalls see note 49 above.

164 See notes 28 and 140 above.

165 The entire furnishing of the choir, which we have extended to cover the pulpits for the sake of convenience, was not completed until the early fifteenth century (diag. 16). There are numerous references to this work in the documentary sources, most of which are accounts, and they give the following picture. The reader is warned to be on his guard here, for the note numbers in Lusini's text do not always correspond to the notes belonging to a particular passage. In the following summary I have given the numbers of the correct notes following the appropriate chapter in Lusini.

As we have seen (note 159 above), there was a canopy over the high altar shortly after the *Maestà* had been installed in 1311. Further work was done on this covering in 1362, and it acquired its final form in 1376 (Lusini, op. cit. (note 3), vol. 1, pp. 262-65, notes 81, 83). The *Maestà* was removed from the altar in 1362 to enable the choir to be expanded, and it was replaced on the new altar in 1382 (ibid., pp. 261-62, note 82, and p. 265, note 84). In 1367 we come across the first mention of a screen on a marble base which was to enclose the choir-stalls behind the altar (ibid., p. 265, notes 85, 88). Screens are mentioned repeatedly in the 1380s, but it is here that Lusini's text and notes become hopelessly muddled. After discussing the screen to be placed behind the altar he starts describing another partition, without making any distinction between them. The documents in Milanesi enable us to deduce that this second screen must have been placed in the first bay of the choir to partition off the sanctuary from the nave, which was at a slightly lower level, as was the floor of the hexagon and the adjoining transepts (Milanesi, op. cit. (note 12), p. 309, nr. 97; p. 316, nr. 101; pp. 316-17, nr. 102; pp. 322-23, nr. 105; cf. Lusini, op. cit. (note 3), vol. 1, p. 265, note 87).

It was in this period that screens were placed in front of the chapels of Sts Ansanus and Victor (Milanesi, op. cit. (note 12), p. 310, note; p. 317, nr. 103). The two pulpits were enclosed at the beginning of the fifteenth century (Lusini, op. cit. (note 3), vol. 1, p. 277, note 145, and vol. 2, p. 25; for the pulpits themselves see note 141 above). The Opera del Duomo commissioned a bishop's throne in 1356 (ibid., p. 276, note 137). A large lectern for the choir, decorated with intarsia and small figures, was ordered in 1362 (Milanesi, op. cit. (note 12), p. 329, nr. 110; cf. Lusini, op. cit. (note 3), vol. 1, p. 276, notes 133-35). In 1399 there is mention of stalls for the use of the celebrant, deacon and subdeacon during the mass (ibid., note 136), and in 1426 the cathedral paid for stalls for the civic dignitaries (ibid.), which were probably erected in the choir, in other words inside the screen closing off the choir. Finally, there are records of payments in 1382 and 1426 for four angels holding candles, two in front of the altar and two behind (ibid., notes 139-40). The 1426 invoice was probably for repair and maintenance work on the angels, which by then were over forty years old. There were also candlesticks in the form of angels on the altar itself, as we learn from an early document of 1355 and a receipt of 1382 (ibid., note 140).

It is clear from this that neither expense nor effort were spared to provide the most ornate furnishing for the choir, with Duccio's *Maestà* as the shining jewel at its centre.

BIBLIOGRAPHY

1 Bacci, P., 'Una tavola inedita e sconosciuta di Luca di Tommè con alcuni documenti ignorati della sua vita', *Rassegna d'arte senese e del costume*, new series 1 (1927), pp. 31-62.
2 Bacci, P., *Dipinti inediti e sconosciuti di Pietro Lorenzetti, Bernardo Daddi ecc. in Siena e nel contado*, Siena 1930.
3 Bacci, P., 'Il pittore Mattia Preti a Siena', *Bullettino senese di storia patria*, new series 2 (1931), pp. 1-16.
4 Bacci, P., *Documenti e commenti per la storia dell'arte*, Florence 1944.
5 Bandmann, G., *Mittelalterliche Architektur als Bedeutungsträger*, Berlin 1951.
6 Bandmann, G., 'Zur Bedeutung der romanischen Apsis', *Wallraf-Richartz Jahrbuch* 15 (1953), pp. 28-46.
7 Banner, R., *Burgundian Gothic architecture*, London 1960.
8 Barbara, G., *La dottrina eucaristica negli scritti di papa Innocenzo III*, Rome 1953.
9 Bargellini, P., 'Abbadia a Monastero d'Ombrone Castelnuovo Berardenga', *Bullettino senese di storia patria*, new series 3 (1932), pp. 284-99.
10 Baxandall, M., *Painting and experience in fifteenth century Italy*, Oxford 1972.
11 Belting, H., *Das Bild und sein Publikum in Mittelalter: Form und Funktion früher Bildtafeln der Passion*, Berlin 1981.
12 Belting, H., 'The "Byzantine" Madonna's: new facts about their Italian origin and some observations on Duccio', *Studies in the History of Art. National Gallery of Art Washington (D.C.)* 12 (1982), pp. 7-21.
13 Benedictis, C. de, *La pittura senese 1330-1370*, Florence 1979.
14 [Benvoglienti, B.], *Domini Bartolomei Benevolenti ecclesie Senensis prepositi philosophiae quondam professoris insignis de urbis Senae origine et incremento opusculum*, Siena 1506.
15 (Berlin) *Gemäldegalerie Berlin. Katalog der ausgestellten Gemälde des 13.-18. Jahrhunderts*, Berlin-Dahlem 1975.
16 *Bibliotheca sanctorum*, 12 vols., Vatican City 1961-1969.
17 Borsook, E., *The mural painters of Tuscany*, ed. Oxford 1980.
18 Boskovits, M., *Pittura fiorentina alla vigilia del Rinascimento 1370-1400*, Florence 1975.
19 [Bossio, F.], *Visita apostolica di monsignor Bossio 1575*, Archivio arcivescovile di Siena, Ms 21.
20 Bowsky, W.M., 'The impact of the Black Death upon Sienese government and society', *Speculum* 34 (1964), pp 1-34.
21 Bowsky, W.M., *The finance of the Commune of Siena 1287-1355*, Oxford 1970.
22 Bowsky, W.M., *A medieval Italian Commune: Siena under the Nine 1287-1355*, Berkeley, Los Angeles & London 1981.
23 Brandi, C., *Il restauro della Maestà di Duccio*, Rome 1959.
24 Brauer, H. and R. Wittkower, *Die Zeichnungen des Gianlorenzo Bernini* (Römische Forschungen der Bibliotheca Hertziana 9-10), 2 vols, Berlin 1931.
25 Braun, J., *Der christliche Altar in seiner geschichtlichen Entwicklung*, 2 vols. Munich 1962.
26 Braunfels, W., *Mittelalterliche Stadtbaukunst in der Toskana*, Berlin 1953.
27 Brou, L., 'Les chants en langue grecque dans les liturgies latines', *Sacris Erudiri: Jaarboek voor Godsdienstwetenschappen* 1 (1948), pp 165-80, and 4 (1952), pp. 226-38.
28 Butzek, M., 'Die Papstmonumente im Dom von Siena', *Mitteilungen des Kunsthistorischen Institutes in Florenz* 24 (1980), pp. 15-78.
29 Cairola, A. and E. Carli, *Il Palazzo Pubblico di Siena*, Rome 1963.
30 Caleca, A. 'Tre polittici di Lippo Memmi, un ipotesi sul Barna e la bottega di Simone e Lippo', *Critica d'Arte* 41 (1976), nr. 150, pp. 49-59, and *idem, Critica d'Arte* 42 (1977), nrs. 151-53, pp. 55-80.
31 Cämmerer-George, M., *Die Rahmung der toskanischen Altarbilder im Trecento*, Strasbourg 1966.
32 Cannon, J., *Dominican patronage of the arts in Central Italy: the Provincia Romana, c. 1220-c. 1320*, typescript Ph.D.thesis, University of London 1980.
33 Carli, E., *Il pulpito di Siena, Bergamo*, Milan & Rome 1943.
34 Carli, E., *Vetrata duccesca*, Milan 1956.
35 Carli, E., 'Lapo Donato e Goro', *La critica d'arte* 8 (1949/50), nr. 3, pp. 177-91.
36 Carli, E., *L'arte a Massa Marittima*, Siena 1976.
37 Carli, E. 'Affreschi senesi del Duecento', *Scritti di storia dell'arte in onore di Ugo Procacci*, vol. 1, Milan 1977, pp. 82-92.
38 Carli, E., 'Le sculture del coro del Duomo di Siena', *Antichità viva* 17 (1978), nr. 1, pp. 25-39.
39 Carli, E., *Il Duomo di Siena*, Genoa 1979.
40 Cole, B., 'Old and new in the early Trecento', *Mitteilungen des Kunsthistorischen Institutes in Florenz* 17 (1973), pp. 229-48.
41 Contini, G. and M.C. Gozzoli, *L'opera completa di Simone Martini*, Milan 1970.
42 Coor-Achenbach, G., 'A visual basis for the documents relating to Coppo di Marcovaldo and his son Salerno', *The Art Bulletin* 28 (1946), pp. 233-247.
43 Crozet, R., *L'art roman en Poitou*, Paris 1948.

44 Davidsohn, R., *Firenze ai tempi di Dante*, Florence 1929.
45 Davies, M., cat. *National Gallery: the earlier Italian schools*, London 1961.
46 Degenhart, B. and A. Schmitt, *Corpus der italienischen Zeichnungen*, vol. I.1., Berlin 1968.
47 Denziger, H. (ed), *Enchiridion symbolorum, definitionum et declarationum quae de rebus fidei et morum a conciliis et summis pontificibus emanerunt*, Freiburg i. Br. 1955.
48 Deuchler, F., 'Duccio doctus: new readings for the Maestà', *The Art Bulletin* 61 (1979), pp. 541-50.
49 Deuchler, F., 'Siena und Jerusalem: Imagination und Realitat in Duccios neuem Stadtbild', *Sitzungsberichte der österreichischen Akademie der Wissenschaften, Philosophisch-historische Klasse*, Vienna 1980, nr. 374, pp. 13-20.
50 Deuchler, F., 'Duccio et son cercle', *Revue de l'Art* (1981), nr. 51, pp. 17-22.
51 *Dictionnaire d'archéologie chrétienne et de liturgie*, 15 vols., Paris 1907-53.
52 *Dictionnaire des églises de France*, 5 vols., s.l., 1967-71.
53 *Dictionnaire de Théologie Catholique*, 15 vols., Paris 1900-50.
54 Djurič, V.J., 'La peinture murale byzantine: douzième et treizième siècles', *Rapports et co-rapports du XVe congrès international d'études byzantines*, Athens 1976, pp. 1-46.
55 Donati, F., 'Il palazzo del comune di Siena', *Arte antica senese*, (corresponding to *Bullettino senese di storia patria* 11), vol. 1, Siena 1904, pp. 311-54.
56 Douglas, L., *A history of Siena*, London 1912.
57 Du Cange, C. Dufresne, *Glossorium mediae et infimae Latinitatis*, 10 vols., s.l., 1883-87 (ed. princeps 3 vols., Paris 1678).
58 Eisenberg, M., 'The first altarpiece for the "Cappella de' Signori" of the Palazzo Pubblico in Siena... tales figure sunt adeo pulcre...', *The Burlington Magazine* 123 (1981), pp. 134-48.
59 *Élie le prophète* (Études carmélitaines 35), 2 vols., Paris-Bruges 1956.
60 Finet, N., *L'organisation et la fabrication des retables siennois pendant la première moitié du XIVe siècle*, Mémoire de Maîtrise, Paris I 1974.
61 Fischer, K. von, 'Die Rolle der Mehrstimmigkeit am Dome von Siena zu Beginn des 13. Jahrhunderts', *Archiv für Musikwissenschaft* 18 (1961), nr. 3/4, pp. 167-82.
62 Forcellini, A., *Lexicon totius Latinitatis*, 6 vols., s.1. 1864-1926.
63 Forsyth, I.H., *The throne of wisdom: wood sculptures of the Madonna in romanesque France*, Princeton 1972.
64 Fraccoro de Longhi, R., *L'architettura delle chiese cistercensi italiane*, Milan 1958.
65 Franken, M., H.W. van Os, J.R.J. van Asperen de Boer and C. Wiethoff, *Sienese paintings in Holland (1250-1500)*, Florence 1983.
66 Frinta, M.S. 'Raised gilded adornment of the Cypriot icons, and the occurrence of the technique in the West', *Gesta* 20 (1981), pp. 333-47.
67 Gardner, J., 'The Stefaneschi altarpieve: a reconsideration', *Journal of the Warburg and Courtauld Institutes* 37 (1974), pp. 57-103.
68 Gardner, J., 'Guido da Siena, 1221, and Tommaso da Modena', *The Burlington Magazine* 121 (1979), pp. 107-08.
69 Gardner, J., 'Fronts and backs: setting and structure', *La pittura nel* XIV *e* XV *secolo: il contributo dell'analisi tecnica alla storia dell'arte*, ed. H.W. van Os and J.R.J. van Asperen de Boer, Atti del XXIV Congresso del Comitato Internazionale di Storia dell'Arte, Bologna 1979, vol. 3, pp. 297-322.
70 Gardner-von Teuffel, C., 'Masaccio and the Pisa altarpiece: a new approach', *Jahrbuch der Berliner Museen* 19 (1977), pp. 23-68.
71 Gardner-von Teuffel, C., 'Ikonographie und Archäologie: das Pfingsttriptychon in der Florentiner Akademie an seinem ursprünglichen Aufstellungsort', *Zeitschrift für Kunstgeschichte* 41 (1978), pp. 16-40.
72 Gardner-von Teuffel, C., 'The buttressed altarpiece: a forgotten aspect of Tuscan fourteenth century altarpiece design', *Jahrbuch der Berliner Museen* 21 (1979), pp. 21-65.
73 Garrison, E.B., *Italian romanesque panel painting: an illustrated index*, Florence 1949.
74 Garrison, E.B., 'Sienese historical writings and the dates 1260, 1221, 1262 applied to Sienese paintings', *Studies in the history of medieval Italian painting* 4/1, Florence 1960-62, pp. 23-58.
75 Garrison, E.B., 'Toward a new history of the Siena Cathedral Madonna's', *Studies in the history of medieval Italian painting* 4/1, Florence 1960-62, pp. 5-22.
76 Gauthier, M.-M., 'Du tabernacle au retable: une innovation limousine vers 1230', *Revue de l'Art* (1978), nrs. 40-41, pp. 23-42.
77 Gigli, G., *Diario senese*, 2 vols., Siena 1854 (ed. princeps Lucca 1723).
78 Gilbert, C., 'Peintres et menusiers au début de la Renaissance en Italie', *Revue de l'Art* (1977), nr. 37, pp. 9-28.
79 Golzio, V., *Documenti artistici sul Seicento nell'archivio Chigi*, Rome 1939.
80 Gomez-Moreno, C., E.H. Jones, A.K. Wheelock and M. Meiss, 'A Sienese St. Dominic modernized twice in the thirteenth century', *The Art Bulletin* 51 (1969), pp. 363-66.
81 Gordon, D., 'A Perugian provenance for the Franciscan double-sided altarpiece by the Maestro di S. Francesco', *The Burlington Magazine* 124 (1982), pp. 70-77.
82 Gössmann, M.E., *Die Verkündigung an Maria im dogmatischen Verständnis des Mittelalters*, Munich 1957.
83 Hager, H., *Die Anfänge des italienischen Altarbildes: Untersuchungen zur Entstehungsgeschichte des toskanischen Hochaltarretabels*, Munich 1962.
84 Hall, M.B., 'The Ponte in S. Maria Novella: the problem of the rood-screen in Italy', *Journal of the Warburg and Courtauld Institutes* 37 (1874), pp. 157-73.
85 Hall, M.B., *Renovation and Counter-Reformation: Vasari and Duke Cosimo in Sta Maria Novella and Sta Croce*, Oxford 1979.
86 *Handwörterbuch der musikalischen Terminologie*, 2 vols., Wiesbaden 1979.
87 Herington, C.J., *Athena Parthenos and Athena Polias: a study in the religion of Periclean Athens*, Manchester 1955.
88 Hobart Cust, R.H., *The pavement masters of Siena*, London 1901.
89 Ingendaay, M., *Sienesische Altarbilder des sechzehnten Jahrhunderts*, 2 vols., Bonn 1976.
90 Jungmann, J.A., *Missarum sollemnia*, 2 vols., Vienna 1952.
91 Kaftal, G., *Iconography of the saints in Tuscan painting*, Florence 1952.
92 Keller, H., 'Die Bauplastik des Sieneser Doms: Studien zu Giovanni Pisano und seiner künstlerischen Nachfolge', *Kunstgeschichtliches Jahrbuch der Bibliotheca Hertziana* 1 (1937), pp. 138-220.
93 Klauser, Th., 'Der Ubergang der römischen Kirche von der griechischen zur lateinischen Liturgiesprache', *Miscellanea Giovanni Mercati*, vol. 1 (Studi e Testi 121), Vatican City 1946, pp. 467-82.

94 Kleineidam, E., 'Die Nachfolge Christi nach Bernhard von Clairvaux', *Amt und Sendung*, Freiburg i. Br. 1950.
95 Krautheimer, R., *Corpus basilicarum christianarum Romae*, 5 vols. Vatican City 1973-1977.
96 Krinsky, C.H., 'Representations of the Temple of Jerusalem before 1500', *Journal of the Warburg and Courtauld Intitutes* 33 (1970), pp. 1-19.
97 Krönig, W., 'Toskana und Apulien: Beiträge zum Problemkreis der Herkunft des Nicolo Pisano', *Zeitschrift für Kunstgeschichte* 16 (1953), pp. 101-144.
98 Kurth, B., 'Florentiner Trecento-Stickereien', *Pantheon* 8 (1931), pp. 455-62.
99 Larner, J., *Culture and society in Italy 1290-1420*, London 1971.
100 Leroy, F., *Les retables siennois du 14e siècle: les modèles, les styles, l'organisation des formes*, Mémoire de Maîtrise, Paris I 1974.
101 Lisini, A. 'Notizie di Duccio pittore e della sua celebre ancona', *Bullettino senese di storia patria* 5 (1898), pp. 20-51.
102 Little, L.K., *Religious poverty and the profit economy in medieval Europe*, Ithaca 1978.
103 *Liturgisch Woordenboek*, 2 vols., Roermond & Maaseik 1958-65.
104 Loose, W., *Die Chorgestühle des Mittelalters*, Leipzig 1931.
105 Lusini, V., *Il Duomo di Siena*, 2 vols., Siena 1911-39.
106 Maginnis, H.B.J., 'Pietro Lorenzetti's Carmelite Madonna: a reconstruction', *Pantheon* 33 (1975), pp. 10-16.
107 Maginnis, H.B.J., *Pietro Lorenzetti and Assisi: the study of a problem*, master thesis, Princeton 1976.
108 Mâle, E., *La cathédrale d'Albi*, Paris 1950.
109 Malherbe, G., 'Le chandelier pascal', *Bulletin paroissal et liturgique* 12 (1930), pp. 108-16, 134-40, 155-62, 167-77.
110 Marcucci, L., cat *Gallerie Nazionali di Firenze: i dipinti toscani del secolo* XIV, Rome 1965.
111 *Meditations on the life of Christ*, ed. I Ragusa and R.B. Green, Princeton 1977.
112 Middeldorf-Kosegarten, A., 'Zur Bedeutung der sieneser Domkuppel', *Münchner Jahrbuch der bildenden Kunst*, third series 21 (1970), pp. 73-97.
113 Milanesi, G., *Documenti per la storia dell'arte senese*, 3 vols., Siena 1854-56.
114 Morandi, U. and A. Cairola, *Lo Spedale di Santa Maria della Scala*, Siena 1975.
115 Moretti, M., *L'architettura romanica religiosa nel territorio dell'antica reppublica senese*, Parma 1962.
116 Negri, D., *Chiese romaniche in Toscana*, Pistoia 1978.
117 Niermeyer, J.F., *Mediae Latinitatis lexicon minus*, Leiden 1976.
118 Nussbaum, O., *Der Standort des Liturgen am christlichen Altar vor dem Jahre 1000* (Theophaneia 18), 2 vols., Bonn 1965.
119 Nussbaum, O., *Die Aufbewahrung der Eucharistie* (Theophaneia 29), Bonn 1979.
120 Oertel, R., *Frühe italienische Malerei in Altenburg*, Berlin 1961.
121 Olsen, H., *Italian paintings and sculpture in Denmark*, Copenhagen 1961.
122 Ormond, L. and R., *Lord Leighton*, New Haven & London 1975.
123 Os, H.W. van, *Marias Demut und Verherrlichung in der sienesischen Malerei 1300-1450*, The Hague 1969.
124 Os, H.W. van, *Vecchietta and the sacristy of the Siena hospital church: a study in Renaissance religious symbolism*, The Hague 1974.
125 Os. H.W. van, 'The discovery of an early Man of Sorrows on a Dominican triptych', *Journal of the Warburg and Courtauld Institutes* 11 (1978), pp. 65-76.
126 Os. H.W. van, 'The literature of art: Duccio', *The Burlington Magazine* 123 (1981), pp. 165-7.
127 Paatz, W., *Werden und Wesen der Trecento-Architektur in Toskana*, Burg 1937.
128 Paatz, W. and E., *Die Kirchen von Florenz*, 6 vols., Frankfurt 1952-55.
129 Panofsky, E., *Gothic architecture and scholasticism*, New York 1957.
130 Pecci, G.A., *Storia del Vescovado della città di Siena*, Lucca 1748.
131 Pepi, Z., *Il Duomo di Siena*, Siena 1964.
132 Perrig, A., 'Formen der politischen Propaganda der Kommune von Siena in der ersten Trecento-Hälfte', *Bauwerk und Bildwerk im Hochmittelalter, Anschauliche Beiträge zur Kultur- und Sozialgeschichte*, Giessen 1981, pp. 232-34.
133 Pietromellora, C., *Il Duomo di Siena: evoluzione della forma dalle origini alla fine del Trecento*, Florence 1980.
134 Pope-Hennessy, J., *Sassetta*, London 1939.
135 Pope-Hennessy, J., cat. *Italian sculpture in the Victoria and Albert Museum*, 3 vols., London 1964.
136 Preiser, A., *Das Entstehen und die Entwicklung der Predella in der italienischen Malerei*, Hildesheim & New York 1973.
137 Ragusa, I., 'The egg re-opened', *The Art Bulletin* 53 (1971), pp. 435-43.
138 [Ressort, C.], exhib. cat. *Retables italiens du XIIIe au XVe siècle*, Paris (Musée du Louvre) 1978.
139 Romanini, A.M., *L'architettura gotica in Lombardia*, 2 vols., Milan 1964.
140 Rondoni, G., *Tradizioni popolari e leggende di un commune medioevale e del suo contado*, Florence 1886.
141 Rubinstein, N., 'Political ideas in Sienese art: the frescoes of Ambrogio Lorenzetti and Taddeo di Bartolo in the Palazzo Pubblico', *Journal of the Warburg and Courtauld Insitutes* 21 (1958), pp. 179-207.
142 Salmi, M., *L'architettura romanica in Toscana*, Milan & Rome 1927.
143 Salmi, M., *Chiese romaniche della campagna toscana*, Milan 1958.
144 Sanpaolesi, P., *Il Duomo di Pisa e l'architettura romanica toscana delle origini*, Pisa 1975.
145 Sauer, J., *Symbolik des Kirchengebäudes und seiner Ausstattung in der Auffassung des Mittelalters*, Freiburg i. Br. 1902.
146 Schüssler, G.A., 'Zum Thomasfresko des Andrea Bonaiuti in der spanischen Kapelle am Kreuzgang von Santa Maria Novella', *Mitteilungen des Kunsthistorischen Institutes in Florenz* 24 (1980), pp. 251-74.
147 Seidel, M., 'Die Verkündigingsgruppe der sieneser Domkanzel', *Münchner Jahrbuch der bildenden Kunst*, third series 21 (1970), pp. 18-72.
148 Seidel, M., 'Die Fresken des Ambrogio Lorenzetti in S. Agostino', *Mitteilungen des Kunsthistorischen Institutes in Florenz* 22 (1978), pp. 188-252.
149 [Siena], exhib. cat. *Opere d'arte restaurate nelle provincie di Siena e Grosseto*, Siena 1979.
150 Simson, O. von, *The Gothic cathedral: origins of Gothic architecture and the medieval concept of order*, Princeton 1974.
151 Stubblebine, J.H., *Guido da Siena*, Princeton 1964.
152 Stubblebine, J.H., 'Duccio's Maestà of 1302 for the Chapel of the Nove', *The Art Quaterly* 35 (1972), pp. 239-68.
153 Stubblebine, J.H., *Duccio di Buoninsegna and his school*, 2 vols., Princeton 1979.
154 Southard, E.C., *The frescoes in Siena's Palazzo Pubblico, 1289-1359*, New York 1979.

155 Steppe, J., *Het koordoksaal in de Nederlanden*, Brussels 1952.
156 Steuart, B., *Lineamenti di storia della liturgia cristiana*, Brescia 1957.
157 Toesca, P., *Storia dell'arte italiana*, 2 vols., Turin 1927-51.
158 Thode, H., *Franz von Assisi und die Anfänge der Kunst der Renaissance in Italien*, Berlin 1885.
159 Torriti, P., cat. *La Pinacoteca Nazionale di Siena: i dipinti dal* XII *al* XV *secolo*, Genoa 1977.
160 Trombelli, G.C., (ed.), *Ordo officiorum ecclesiae Senensis*, Bologna 1766.
161 Veen, H.T. van, 'Erasmus on the "Carmelite taboo" ', *Bibliothèque d'Humanisme et Renaissance* 43 (1981), pp. 335-39.
162 Venturi, L., *Storia dell'arte italiana*, 11 vols., Milan 1901-40.
163 Vroom, W.H., *De financiering van de kathedraalbouw in de middeleeuwen*, Maarssen 1981.
164 Wagner-Rieger, R., 'Siena und Ruvo', *Festschrift Prof.Dr. Anselm Weissenhofer*, Vienna 1954, pp. 97-111.
165 Wagner-Rieger, R., *Die italienische Baukunst zu Beginn der Gotik*, 2 vols., Graz & Cologne 1956.
166 Warnke, M., 'Italienische Bildtabernakel bis zum Frühbarock', *Münchner Jahrbuch der bildenden Kunst* 19 (1968), pp. 61-102.
167 Weigelt, C., *Die sienesische Malerei des vierzehnten Jahrhunderts*, Leipzig 1930.
168 White, J., *Art and architecture in Italy 1250-1400* (The Pelican History of Art), Harmondsworth 1966.
169 White, J., *The birth and rebirth of pictorial space*, London 1968.
170 White, J., *Duccio: Tuscan art and the medieval workshop*, London 1979.
171 Zdekauer, L., (ed.), *Il costituto del Comune di Siena dell'anno 1262*, Milan 1897.
172 Zdekauer, L., *Il mercante senese nel Dugento*, Siena 1925.
173 Zimmerman, B., *Monumenta historica carmelitana*, Lèrins 1907.

PHOTO CREDITS

Alinari, Florence: 5, 11, 12, 14, 19, 21, 22, 23.
Archives Photographiques, Paris: 3, 4.
Luigi Artini, Florence: 9, 10, 15, 16, 17, 18.
Bibliotheca Apostolica Vaticana, Rome: 6.
Foto Grassi, Siena: 1, 2, 8, 13, 20, 25.
Soprintendenza per i beni ambientali e architettonici delle Provincie di Siena e Grosseto, Siena: 7.
Staatliche Museen preussischer Kulturbesitz, Gemäldegalerie, Berlin-Dahlem: 24.

DIAGRAM CREDITS

diag. 1: E. Guidoni, *Il Campo di Siena*, Rome 1971, p. 31, fig. 23.
diag. 2: G. Dehio and G. van Bezold, *Die kirchliche Baukunst des Abendlandes*, 10 vols., Stuttgart 1887-1901, Atlas vol. 5, Taf. 535, nr. 3.
diag. 3: E. Carli, *Il Duomo di Siena*, Genoa 1979, p. 12.
diag. 4: E. Carli, *Vetrata duccesca*, Milan 1956, p. 56, fig. 1.
diag. 5: Ibid., p. 56, fig. 2.
diag. 6: Dehio and von Bezold, Atlas vol. 2, Taf. 126, nr. 1.
diag. 7: Ibid., Taf. 124, nr. 2.
diag. 8: Dehio and von Bezold, Atlas vol. 5, Taf. 535, nr. 2.
diag. 9: D. Negri, *Chiese romaniche in Toscana*, Pistoia 1978, p. 410.
diag. 10: C. Pietromellara, *Il Duomo di Siena*, Florence 1980, fig. VIII.
diag. 13: J. White, *Duccio*, London 1979, p. 90, fig. 61.
diag. 15: Pietromellara, fig. XI.

GENERAL INDEX